DISCARD

THE MORAL DEMANDS OF MEMORY

Despite an explosion of studies on memory in historical and cultural studies, there is relatively little in moral philosophy on this subject. In this book, Jeffrey Blustein provides a systematic and philosophically rigorous account of a morality of memory. Drawing on a broad range of philosophical and humanistic literatures, he offers a novel examination of memory and our relations to people and events from our past, the ways in which memory is preserved and transmitted, and the moral responsibilities associated with it. Blustein treats topics of responsibility for one's own past; historical injustice and the role of memory in doing justice to the past; the relationship of collective memory to history and identity; collective and individual obligations to remember those who have died, including those who are dear to us; and the moral significance of bearing witness. Relationships between the operations of personal and collective memory, and between the moral responsibilities attached to each, are highlighted and this discussion ties together the various strands of argument in a unified framework.

Jeffrey Blustein is Professor of Bioethics at Albert Einstein College of Medicine and Adjunct Associate Professor at Barnard College. He is the author of *Parents and Children: The Ethics of the Family; Care and Commitment: Taking the Personal Point of View,* and most recently, *Ethics for Health Care Organizations* and *Handbook for Health Care Ethics Committees* (both with Linda Farber Post and Nancy Dubler). He has published numerous articles in journals such as the *Journal of Applied Philosophy, Metaphilosophy, Journal of Social Philosophy, Journal of Value Inquiry,* and *Bioethics.*

THE MORAL DEMANDS OF MEMORY

Jeffrey Blustein

Albert Einstein College of Medicine

CAMBRIDGE
UNIVERSITY PRESS

CAMBRIDGE UNIVERSITY PRESS
Cambridge, New York, Melbourne, Madrid, Cape Town, Singapore, São Paulo, Delhi

Cambridge University Press
32 Avenue of the Americas, New York, NY 10013-2473, USA

www.cambridge.org
Information on this title: www.cambridge.org/9780521883306

First published 2008

Printed in the United States of America

A catalog record for this publication is available from the British Library.

Library of Congress Cataloging in Publication Data

Blustein, Jeffrey.
The Moral demands of memory / Jeffrey Blustein.
p.   cm.
Includes bibliographical references and index.
ISBN 978-0-521-88330-6 (hardback)
1. Memory (Philosophy)   2. Ethics.   3. Conduct of life.   I. Title.
BD181.7.B58   2007
170–dc22   2007017358

ISBN   978-0-521-88330-6 hardback
ISBN   978-0-521-70972-9 paperback

To Joseph and Eva, whom I have forgotten

To speak the name of the dead
Is to make them live again.

Ancient Egyptian Belief

CONTENTS

ACKNOWLEDGMENTS

A number of philosophers read and commented on portions of this manuscript while it was going through various stages of development or shared their thoughts with me on topics I discuss here. These include: Jonathan Adler, Sue Campbell, Maudemarie Clark, Chris Gowans, David Heyd, Tziporah Kasachkoff, Eva Feder Kittay, John Kleinig, Lukas Meyer, Hilde Lindemann Nelson, James Nelson, Ross Poole, Joseph Raz, William Ruddick, Michael Stocker, and Margaret Walker. I thank all of them for their help and, perhaps most of all, for their encouragement and support of this project.

An early version of Chapter 4 was read as part of an Invited Symposium on Memory and Morality, Pacific Division Meeting of the American Philosophical Association, March 26, 2004. Chapter 2 draws on material that first appeared in my article, "On Taking Responsibility for One's Past," in the *Journal of Applied Philosophy*, *17*, 1, 2000, 1–19 (used by permission of Blackwell Publishing, Ltd.).

PREFACE

Two personal experiences led me to think more deeply about issues that are taken up in this book. The first concerns my father, who died in 1982. Although we were never particularly close, especially in the last decade of his life, I never doubted that the way I saw the world and my place in it owed much to his influence. My weekly calls, brief and perfunctory though they might be, and my occasional trips back home, underscored for me how much I resembled him, for better or for worse. But in the years after his death, I thought less and less about him. Except in rare moments, he quite literally vanished from my conscious life. I had, for several years, lit the yearly Yahrzeit candle in his memory but even that small gesture lapsed. Perhaps my failure to hold on to his memory, and therefore hold on to him, said something about our lack of intimacy while he was alive. Perhaps it was just the more or less inevitable erosion of memory by the passage of time and the accretions of a life lived forward. Whatever the explanation, I was troubled not so much by his death as by my failure to keep him in mind after he was gone. Vaguely, I felt that perhaps I had done something wrong, that I ought to have done more to preserve my father's memory, and that I had somehow been disloyal to him and what he meant to me by the apparent ease with which I forgot him. I wondered if others had similar experiences of forgetting and, if so, whether they had similar feelings. These thoughts were as yet inchoate, and I was unsure if they were even coherent. But believing that the thoughts and feelings relating to my deceased father were probably not idiosyncratic, I wanted to find out – to think philosophically about – whether and to what extent they were warranted.

The second concerns a trip to Eastern Europe that my wife and I and another couple took in the fall of 2004. We visited Prague, Budapest, and Krakov, and, understandably, given the history of these places, memory was much on my mind. One afternoon in the Jewish quarter of Prague, where we were visiting several of the synagogues that had been spared Nazi destruction, my friend complained about what he characterized as the "wallowing" of some Jews (I was clearly included in his indictment) in the horrors of the Nazi past. "What good does all this remembering do, anyway?" he protested. "Shouldn't we stop dwelling on the past? What's done is done, what's past is past. Why keep exposing oneself, in this masochistic fashion, to what can only be intensely painful memories? To what end?" I did not necessarily disagree with him that Holocaust remembrance was an inordinate preoccupation of some contemporary Jews. I knew, too, that in saying what he said, he had no intention of denying or downplaying the significance of the Nazi atrocities. But I could not agree with the sentiment he expressed, and I felt strongly that he had not properly appreciated the value and significance of memory or correctly understood what limits there might be to how much and how long we should remember. I had already started to think about these matters, but the episode in Prague, echoing views I had heard from many quarters before, brought home to me why this inquiry was of more than just theoretical interest.

These two experiences stand out in my mind as I try to account for my personal interest in the subject of this book. I am sure there have been others as well that have played a role. But memory, as I shall have more than one occasion to point out in what follows, is highly selective, and I am willing to concede that 10 years from now, if I think back to the circumstances surrounding the writing of this book, I might tell a different story.

Jeffrey Blustein
February 22, 2007

1

MEMORY AS A SUBJECT OF EVALUATIVE INQUIRY

When we study, discuss, analyze a reality, we analyze it as it appears in our mind, in our memory. We know reality only in the past tense. We do not know it as it is in the present, in the moment when it's happening, when it *is*. The present moment is unlike the memory of it. Remembering is not the negative of forgetting. Remembering is a form of forgetting.

– Milan Kundera, *Testaments Betrayed*[1]

1. ELEMENTS OF A MORALITY OR ETHICS OF MEMORY

This is a book about memory and our relations to the past – our individual pasts and our collective pasts – written from the standpoints of the moral, social, and political branches of philosophy. The subject of memory has a long history within certain branches of philosophy, of course. In epistemology and metaphysics, philosophers going back to Plato have been intrigued by a phenomenon at once so familiar and yet mysterious.[2] They have addressed such questions as: is memory a form or source of knowledge? What sort of link with the past does memory establish? Can skepticism about memory be avoided? Is our concept of the past derived from memory, or does memory presuppose a concept of the past?

Since Locke, memory has also played a central role in philosophical discussions of the unity and continuity of the self. However, evaluative inquiry about memory has been curiously neglected by philosophers, at least those working within the analytic, or the Anglo-American, tradition. By and large, those who have engaged in this sort of inquiry have not been philosophers. For example, historians, political scientists, and legal scholars have written about how societies can and should confront large scale wrongdoing in their pasts, and about memory in relation to this task, but the philosophical literature on the relationship between doing justice to the past and memory is still relatively small. Moreover, few analytic philosophers have contributed to the vast scholarly literature on memory in relation to the Holocaust or reflected on the critically important moral role that memory has come to play in its aftermath.

This book, a work of philosophy, examines a number of interrelated aspects of this neglected dimension of memory. It concerns itself with how and why memory should be preserved and transmitted, with the reciprocal relationship between memory and identity and the moral significance of this relationship, and with the moral responsibilities associated with memory. An account of these matters constitutes a good part of what I call a morality or an ethics of memory.[3] To begin this inquiry and set the stage for the chapters that follow, I will take up three sets of issues in this opening chapter. They are, roughly speaking, issues of *value*, of *responsibility*, and of *identity*. Each of these elements of a normative account of memory is addressed in later chapters to one degree or another.

The overarching theme of the book is what and why individuals and groups have responsibilities to remember. Identity, which shapes, and is shaped by, memory, is a source of these and other responsibilities, so identity will be part of my discussion of the main theme. But what I propose to begin with is the value of memory and the good of remembrance,[4] as judged from the individual as well as the collective standpoints. It makes sense to begin here, because doing so will help us to understand the grounds of our responsibilities to remember and the nature of the demands they place on us. I do not claim, and indeed it would be foolish to claim, that remembrance is a good at all times and in every circumstance. My contention is rather that, within limits and with respect to especially significant events, experiences, or people from the past, remembrance is an indispensable ingredient of a good life and a necessary condition of civic health. The question of what these limits should be is partly answered by considering when it is well, or good, or all-things-considered best, to forget. As we will see, reflection on the value of remembering is intimately wrapped up with reflection on the value of forgetting.

The topic of memory and value occupies Sections 2–4 of this chapter. Few philosophers have understood so well the interplay between remembering and forgetting and the potential cost, in human terms, of memory and the value of forgetting, as Friedrich Nietzsche did. It is with his rich and rewarding early work, "On the Uses and Disadvantages of History for Life," that I begin Section 2. For Nietzsche, the question is not *whether* we should remember – for we would not be human at all if we did not – but *how* we should do so, that is, how memory should be integrated into and function within the lives of individuals and groups. He inveighs against different sorts of misuse of memory, and we should be able to appreciate the concerns that led him to defend the value of forgetting, whether or not we fully accept his positive account of the proper operation of memory.

I continue in Section 3 with the theme of the misuse of memory by introducing the notion of a "surfeit of memory." This notion has both personal and political relevance, and I give some examples of situations in which it might be said to apply. The so-called *Historikerstreit* [the quarrel among historians] of the 1980s in West Germany, for instance, was in part a debate about the appropriate limits of reflection on and remembrance of the Nazi past.

This is followed in Section 4 by a discussion of the criteria for judging whether we, individually and collectively, have achieved an acceptable balance of remembering and forgetting. The balance is dynamic in the sense that what is an appropriate balance under some historical or psychological conditions might not be appropriate under others. This section affirms, with Nietzsche, that memory is not an unqualified good and provides a way of thinking about its value. The section is also relevant to the sections on memory and responsibility because it suggests that the duties associated with memory are not independent of their social and historical settings. For this reason too, they are not duties to engage in acts or practices of remembrance no matter what other values we have and what other commitments we have reason to consider.

The next element of a morality or ethics of memory – the responsibilities that attach to it – is the subject of Sections 5 and 6. In this book, I alternately speak about the "responsibility," "obligation," "duty," and "imperative" to remember. These terms may be given different meanings: for example, "responsibility" may be thought to involve a discretionary element lacking in duty, or to apply in the first instance to interpersonal relationships, whereas "duty" is more impersonal. Although distinctions can be made between them, and may be useful in some contexts, I will use them more or less interchangeably. In my usage, these terms have the following features in common: they refer to acts that (a) one "ought" to perform; (b) are not fully morally elective and so not merely one among many morally good acts that one might choose; and (c) it is wrong not to perform. As to (c), there are various reasons why this might be so. For example, it may be wrong both to forget the victims of injustice as well as to forget one's deceased loved ones, but the reasons will have to be at least somewhat different in the two cases.

As I suggest in Section 5, talk about an "imperative" to remember seems particularly appropriate in the wake of large scale wrongdoing and crimes against humanity: these are events that, intuitively, it seems we ought to remember and do wrong not to remember. No doubt the currency of the language of obligation in this connection can be traced in large measure to the inescapable fact that we live today in the shadow of the Holocaust. But responsibilities of memory are not confined to such extreme situations. It is a central contention of this book that remembrance is not only a good when properly constrained, but also in various circumstances morally imperative for us. Yet this is problematic because memory, as I note, is notoriously fragile and manipulable. To fulfill the requirements of a morality of memory, therefore, individuals and groups have to engage in an ongoing struggle against the natural and social processes of forgetfulness.

I suppose that this struggle against the erosion of memory is one that morality can at least sometimes win, and that the various impediments to taking responsibility for the past can be overcome, even if only unsteadily. On this basis, I go on, in Section 6, to briefly discuss the meaning of taking responsibility for the past and the moral significance of doing so. I also introduce a distinction that plays a central role in subsequent chapters: between different modes of justifying the responsibilities of remembrance and, in particular, the responsibilities that we commit ourselves to follow through on when we take responsibility for the past. I call these the consequentialist and the expressivist modes. "Past" refers to both an individual's past and a group's past.

In Section 7, I explain why identity should be included as an element of a morality or ethics of memory by linking memory with identity and identity with obligation. Identity is a source of obligations in the sense that there are normative considerations of this sort that someone with a particular identity must take into account by virtue of having this identity. When identity is implicated in remembrance, identity can supply powerful ethical reasons for regarding remembrance as an obligation. "Identity," in this context, refers to what is sometimes called *biographical identity* and to its group analogue.

2. NIETZSCHE ON THE MISUSES OF MEMORY

The morally significant questions about remembering do not simply have to do with whether we should remember or not. The questions are considerably more nuanced and complex than this. Remembering is not an activity that we can think about normatively in isolation from other important elements of personal and social life, because it is intertwined with these elements. So we also need to ask about the role that remembering should play in the lives of individuals and societies and the extent to which they should concern themselves with the past. One way of making the point is that the value of remembering must be understood in relation to the value of forgetting. More specifically, we can plausibly say that the responsibility to remember must be regulated and tempered by an appreciation of the need to forget, to shift whatever portion of the past is at issue away from the center and toward the periphery of our constellation of concerns. (The needs are of various sorts and include psychological as well as political ones, as I will discuss in Section 4.) But in our contemporary post-Holocaust world, where memory, however painful its contents, is prized, socially sanctioned, and even sanctified, there is understandable reluctance in many quarters to seriously take up the matter of forgetting and to consider what value it may have. In view of this, we would do well to turn to a philosopher who argued against a bias in favor of memory, Friedrich Nietzsche. The work I will focus on is the second of his early *Untimely Meditations*, "On the Uses and Disadvantages of History for Life."[5] This essay, although targeting a certain kind of "historicism" popular in nineteenth-century German philosophy of history, also sheds light on aspects of our complex relationship to memory and, for this reason, deserves a close look.

To understand Nietzsche's basic stance toward memory, be it individual or collective memory, we should initially distinguish between two examples of what is meant by *not remembering*. Dumb animals, such as cattle, live without boredom or pain because they do not remember: they have neither the capacity to remember, nor, strictly speaking, the capacity to forget. Because cattle "do not know what is meant by yesterday or today" (60), they have a kind of happiness that men, in their weaker moments, cannot help envying, but which, they realize on reflection, could not satisfy them. Much the same is true, Nietzsche says, of the very young child who "plays in blissful blindness between the hedges of past and future" (61). Neither the animal nor the very young child is capable of willed abandonment of the past (i.e., forgetting) and of selective remembering, and it is this capacity that is the key to the sort of happiness appropriate to man:

> In the case of the smallest or the greatest happiness, however, it is always the same thing that makes happiness happiness: the ability to forget or, expressed in more scholarly fashion, the capacity to feel *unhistorically* during its duration.... A man who wanted to feel historically through and through, would be like one forcibly deprived of sleep, or an animal that had to live only by rumination and ever repeated rumination. (62)

One can exist happily without memory, in the manner of animals, but "it is altogether impossible to *live* [the italics are Nietzsche's own] at all without forgetting" (62). Nietzsche makes it clear, moreover, that his remarks about the value of living unhistorically, "within which alone life can germinate" (63), are intended to be quite general in the sense that they apply not only to individual persons, but to peoples and their shared way of life as well:

> *The unhistorical and the historical are necessary in equal measure for the health of an individual, of a people, and of a culture*... The question of the degree to which life requires the service of history at all... is one of the supreme questions and concerns in regard to the health of a man, a people or a culture. (63, 67)

Happiness for an individual or a people, that is, the sort of happiness that is suited to their nature, depends on the capacity to forget, more precisely, on the capacity to forget when it is appropriate to do so:

> on one's being just as able to forget at the right time as to remember at the right time; on the possession of a powerful instinct for sensing when it is necessary to feel historically and when unhistorically. (63)

The capacity to forget as well as to remember "at the right time" is an intelligent habit, and how much we can do this in the right measure not only determines our happiness but also bears on how admirable we are as individuals as well as peoples and nations.[6]

It is critically important that human happiness requires both the capacity to forget and the capacity to remember, because human beings cannot live without forgetting any more than they can live without remembering. Or rather it requires, in Nietzsche's view, the intricate *balancing* of living unhistorically (i.e., forgetting one's history) and remembering. We can clarify what Nietzsche has in mind here by considering different sorts of orientation toward the past that fail this balancing test and, therefore, are not conducive to the health and happiness of individuals and peoples. I will draw on Nietzsche's discussion of *monumental, antiquarian,* and *critical history* for this purpose, more specifically, on his discussion of the "disadvantages" of these sometimes useful forms of historical consciousness.[7] (As I discuss them in this chapter, they refer not only to different approaches to the *study* of the past, that is, to history as a branch of human inquiry, but, more broadly, to different ways of conceiving of and engaging with the past.) Although there are "services [each] is capable of performing for life" (77), and although each has an important and valuable role to play in the formation of an individual's and a society's character, Nietzsche warns that "sufficient dangers remain should [they] grow too mighty and overpower the other modes of regarding the past" (75), should one "mode of regarding history *rule[s]* over the others" (70). These are dangers that threaten individuals, groups of people, and their cultures, and the warnings are at least as pertinent today as they were in Nietzsche's time.

(a) *Monumental history and the influence of the past*

Monumental history, or "the monumentalistic conception of the past" (69), involves belief in former greatness as "worthy of imitation, [and] as imitable and possible for a second time" (70). Past events are depicted as epic and worthy and, viewed in this way, inspire the present generation to acts of heroism and self-sacrifice to redeem and pay homage to the past. On the macroscopic level, nations and social groups renew their strength and their sense of their identity not by delving deeper into the details of what actually happened in the past – monumental history has "no use for that absolute veracity" – but by celebrating a fictional past that "come[s] close to free poetic invention." Indeed, the "same stimuli can be derived" from "a monumentalized past and a mythical fiction" (70). Similarly, in the life of an individual, forebears can provide inspiring examples of courage, dignity, and wisdom when hope dims or energies flag; encouragement might even come from returning in memory to one's own former accomplishments or promise of extraordinary achievement. In summary, by looking to the past in this way and for this purpose, man (i.e., individuals and peoples) can "gain, from great examples of what man can do, courage for his present activity, elevation of his nature, and consolation in despair."[8]

But the dangers of this way of regarding the past are not difficult to discern. Monumental history "inspires the courageous to foolhardiness and the inspired to fanaticism" (71). We can see ample evidence of this in our contemporary world where ethnic conflicts between groups seeking to avenge some past injustice and restore their former standing are fueled by this sort of history. When history is supplanted by political myth and memory is absorbed in work of preserving exemplars of greatness for our emulation, we become locked into a stultifying and potentially destructive relationship with the past. For the individual, there is the danger that the example of his forebears, or his own former self, will dispirit rather than inspire, will fill him with despair rather than console him, will mislead rather than direct him in constructive ways. He may know what greatness is but trying to emulate it may deform his character and cripple his potential for self-realization.

(b) *Antiquarian history and nostalgia*

The second mode of historical consciousness is antiquarian in the sense that an individual or nation looks to the past – and it must be to his or its *own* past – with "love and loyalty" (72). The value of the antiquarian sense lies in the fact that it gives individuals and peoples a sense of rootedness and historical continuity and in this way comforts them with a sort of existential reassurance. That is, although an individual's life or a people's way of life may seem contingent when viewed from a standpoint detached from those who life it is, the antiquarian sense saves them from indifference, despair, and anomie. It does this by showing those whose life it is that their life or way of life is linked to a past that gives it a meaning and a purpose:

> the feeling antithetical to this [i.e. to a restless, cosmopolitan hunting after new and ever newer things], the contentment of the tree in its roots, the happiness of knowing that one is not wholly accidental and arbitrary but grown out of a past as its heir, flower and fruit, and that one's existence is thus excused and, indeed, justified. (74)

This is the feeling that the antiquarian sense imparts and the valuable, indeed essential, contribution that it makes to life.

The antiquarian sense goes wrong, however, for individuals as well as groups of people, when it reveres things of the past merely because they are past and does not distinguish among them as worthy, less worthy, or unworthy. In other words, the antiquarian sense errs when it treats the past as if it were worthy of veneration simply because the passage of time has given it some special authoritative status. When not carried to extremes, or when confined to matters that are of trivial importance, this sort of veneration is no doubt innocent enough, perhaps even commendable. Otherwise, there are clear dangers when critical reflection on the past and its lessons for the present is discouraged or, in more extreme cases, dismissed as failing to show proper respect for tradition:

> The antiquarian sense of a man, a community, a whole people always possesses an extremely restricted field of vision; most of what exists it does not perceive at all, and the little it does see it sees much too close up and isolated; it cannot relate what it sees to anything else and therefore accords everything it sees equal importance and therefore to each individual thing too great importance. There is a lack of that discrimination of value and that sense of proportion which would distinguish between the things of the past in a way that would do true justice to them. (74)

It is when "the antiquarian sense" becomes a more-or-less general orientation to the past, or when having a sense of proportion in relation to the past matters, that this indiscriminateness "hinders any firm resolve to attempt something new" (75) and causes paralysis in the man of action through too much emphasis on a certain kind of memory or conception of the past. When this happens, the past, we might say, has no present; it is wrapped in a kind of aura that effectively insulates it from the present.

As a consequence, our veneration renders us powerless to move beyond the past.

One manifestation of an antiquarian orientation to the past is *nostalgia,* and Nietzsche's critique can be taken as a warning about its dangers.[9] Avishai Margalit expresses the common understanding of nostalgia as something negative:

> An essential element of nostalgia is sentimentality. And the trouble with sentimentality in certain situations is that it distorts reality in a particular way that has moral consequences. Nostalgia distorts the past by idealizing it.[10]

On this view, nostalgia is a defect of memory or of memory accuracy: nostalgic memory is not faithful to the past because it distorts it. Another author goes farther and claims, in very Nietzschean spirit, that "nostalgia and remembering are in some sense antithetical, since nostalgia is a forgetting, merely regressive, whereas memory may look back in order to move forward and transform disabling fictions to enabling fictions, altering our relation to the present and future."[11] Nostalgia is a kind of escapism, typically escape from the complications and disappointments of the present into an imagined golden past of unalloyed happiness. The past is frozen in time and the nostalgic person either seeks to restore that ideal, usually with disastrous consequences, or broods over the impossibility of doing so. Thus understood, nostalgia is characterized by just those qualities that Nietzsche condemns in the antiquarian attitude toward the past.

We do well to take Nietzsche's warnings about the antiquarian sense to heart. Nostalgia, a manifestation of that sense, saturates our popular culture,[12] but it is a highly selective form of remembering and forgetting and we should be alert to how it may distort political and personal, public and private life. Nietzsche, however, also sees value in the antiquarian regard for the past and, like him, we should consider whether nostalgia can function positively in laying the foundation for innovation and growth. There are in fact other understandings of nostalgia – chiefly discussed in the psychology and sociology literature[13] – according to which nostalgia is not merely regressive and a longing for an idealized and unrealistic past. To be sure, nostalgia always involves (explicitly or implicitly) drawing a contrast between the present and the past, a contrast that is emotionally charged and that has existential import. There is a strong affective attachment to past episodes, persons, places, or eras – typically out of proportion to what was actually felt at the time – that commonly signals the experience of some sort of disruption of continuity in people's personal or collective lives. Indeed, according to one suggestion, nostalgia just is a bittersweet emotional reaction to the experience of this discontinuity.[14] Alternatively, nostalgia has been characterized as "an interpretive stance in which a person is aware of the element of discordance in her life."[15] But this contrast or discordance between present and past is conceptual of nostalgia, not a moral or psychological criticism of it.

Two types of psychological benefit or positive uses of nostalgia are noteworthy here, and because these benefits explain how nostalgia figures in people's shaping and evaluation of their own lives, nostalgia can be said to have not only psychological but ethical value as well. One relates to identity. Nostalgia and "homesickness" are often used interchangeably, and sometimes homesickness refers quite literally to a kind of yearning for one's home or homeland. But whether it is intended this way or not, the connection to home is telling and provides a clue to nostalgia's larger existential significance. When the characteristics that contribute to making up one's identity are in flux or are being challenged, one is left unsure of which characteristics are central to who one is and which characteristics truly belong to one's identity. It is useful, at this time, to have an evaluative standpoint from which one can make sense of one's experience and identity, that is, a point of reference from which one can assess the changes one is undergoing.[16] This is the function of "home," as it is figuratively understood, and of the nostalgia that is drawn to it. It can serve to protect identity, not by preventing change of self-defining traits but by helping to make that change intelligible to oneself. By shaping our perception of the present on the basis of our past and making sense of the former by reference to the latter, nostalgia facilitates identity continuity.

Another positive function of nostalgia is to regenerate and sustain a sense of the meaningfulness of one's life. Nostalgia has a social dimension: it typically connects us to cultural traditions and rituals that are larger and more enduring than ourselves and, thereby, helps alleviate feelings of isolation and alienation. This connection may also ground a sense of our lives as having an importance that is not purely self-ascribed, which in turn can enhance self-esteem and confidence in our ability to face up to life's challenges.

Nietzsche warns that the antiquarian attitude toward the past "knows only how to preserve *life*, not how to engender it" (75), and in a similar vein we can say that nostalgia knows only how to preserve an idealized past and that it can be faulted for closing one to new opportunities, experiences, and relationships. But it is not an antiquarian attitude or nostalgia per se that is objectionable. They are so only when they are uncontrolled and excessive, which is to say, only when they are our dominant way of relating to the past, as something that is fixed, over and done with, suitable for preservation only, rather than taken up by and integrated with the present.

(c) *The moderating role of critical history*

Discussion of this third type of history will have to be brief, because it involves ideas that were to occupy Nietzsche for the rest of his philosophical life and were to receive much more extensive treatment in a number of his more mature works. Given the limited purposes for which I am using Nietzsche in this chapter, it would take me too far afield to go into these ideas in any detail. But something has to be said about critical history in order to complete Nietzsche's account of memory.

For Nietzsche, both monumental and antiquarian history have their uses but also their significant limitations. In the monumental conception of the past, historical accuracy does not matter. Rather, past events are transformed into inspiring moments of mythic import. Inspiration of this sort is sometimes needed for the achievement of worthwhile goals and, to this extent at least, useful "to the man of the present" (69). But there is a danger in this mode of regarding the past, namely, that the line between history and myth will be blurred, or that myth will take the place of history, and this has potentially disastrous consequences for individuals as well as peoples.[17] As for the antiquarian orientation to the past, it has value insofar as it connects individuals and peoples to something larger and more enduring than themselves. Both extreme individualism and "transitory existence" (75) are transcended in a relationship of loving piety. But there are dangers here as well: if left unchecked, antiquarianism loses itself in the past. It takes the form of an indiscriminate love of the old, a regressive attachment to a past that is as much fiction as the monumental past.

To counteract the dangers of both kinds of relationship to the past, it is necessary for individuals as well as peoples to develop habits of critical reflection on and distance from their own history. Critical history, as Nietzsche calls it, cannot stand alone, in his view. Man needs critical history for many reasons, but there are many needs that it cannot satisfy. It cannot, by itself, inspire courageous deeds in the present, for example, and it cannot instill a sense of the meaningfulness of life. Yet, critical history can help contain the excesses of both monumental and antiquarian history:

> If he is to live, man must possess and from time to time employ the strength to break up and dissolve a part of the past: he does this by bringing it before the tribunal [of criticism], scrupulously examining it and finally condemning it. (75–76)

By critically examining the past in the light of current needs, interests, beliefs, and values (and from what other standpoint could one conduct the examination?), the past can become a force for personal growth and political and social betterment. Moreover, *no* group or individual, according to Nietzsche, can survive such critical scrutiny unscathed: "every past, however, is worthy to be condemned – for that is the nature of human things: human violence and weakness have always played a mighty role in them" (76). If one's past is confronted honestly and dealt with scrupulously, one cannot fail to find in it much to justify guilt or shame.

If monumental and antiquarian history need to be restrained by critical history and their excesses contained by it, the converse is true as well. At the extreme, Nietzsche warns, adopting a stance of critical detachment from our past becomes a kind of alienation from it:

> It [i.e. critical history] is always a dangerous process, especially so for life itself. . . . For since we are the outcome of earlier generations, we are also the outcome of their aberrations, passions, and errors, and indeed of their crimes; it is not possible wholly to free oneself from this chain. If we condemn these aberrations and regard ourselves as free of them, this does not alter the fact that we originate in them. (76)

To avoid the dangers of monumental and antiquarian history, we need to some extent to "forget" the past, as Nietzsche puts it; or in less dramatic language, to put it behind us or get beyond it. Critical history can help us to do this, and can help to free us from the tyranny of the past, he claims, through a kind of retrospective historical reconstruction: "It [critical history] is an attempt to give oneself, as it were *a posteriori*, a past in which one would like to originate in opposition to that in which one did originate" (76). But critical history can go too far in this direction, toward too much forgetting both in the sense of alienation from the particular personal and social attachments that give life substance and meaning and in the sense of a failure or refusal to own up to (aspects of) one's past as truly one's own: "sometimes...this same life that requires forgetting demands a temporary suspension of this forgetfulness" (76). It demands a moderation of the monumental and antiquarian stances and of the critical historical impulse as well.

Nietzsche is concerned with how to live an *admirable* life (which he distinguishes from what we usually mean by a moral life[18]) and to achieve an admirable character. In evaluating individuals and peoples along these dimensions it is essential, in his view, that we look to the sort of balance they have achieved or are striving to achieve between remembering and forgetting. Whether or not individuals or peoples should be praised on account of the lives they lead, or on account of the individual or collective character they possess, crucially depends on how they relate to time, and in particular, to time past. How they relate to the past, moreover, is a function of what Nietzsche calls "the *plastic power* of a man, a people, a culture," that is, "the capacity to develop out of oneself in one's own way, to transform and incorporate into oneself what is past and foreign." It is a type of personal or cultural resilience that some may not have enough of – "they can perish from a single experience, from a single painful event" – and others may have too much of – "they are little affected by the worst and most dreadful disaster, and even by their own wicked acts" (62). But those who are neither too resilient nor insufficiently resilient are able to free themselves from bondage to the past without losing their (historically constrained or shaped, not determined) identity.

Nietzsche does not say very much about this condition in *On the Uses and Disadvantages*, but I will not try to trace the development of this idea in his later work. After all, providing an interpretation of Nietzsche's thought has not been my chief concern, so I have not made a serious attempt to do so or raised objections to his account of the uses and misuses of memory. (No doubt there is much more to be said about our various sorts of relationship to the past than can be captured in terms of monumental, antiquarian, or critical stances or some combination of them.) Rather, my motive in discussing Nietzsche has been to suggest something of the problematic nature of our relationship to the past and of memory in mediating our relationship to it. What also emerges from this brief look at Nietzsche is the suggestion that, whatever we may think about the existence of *obligations* of remembrance, there is something we can call a *virtue* of remembrance. It consists, in part, in knowing when, what, how, and how much to remember, and also in properly integrating this understanding into our lives, whether the lives of individuals, of individuals as members of a group, or of groups of individuals. In Nietzsche's terms, to possess this virtue is to have a certain "plastic power," an ability to acknowledge and take up the past without becoming enslaved to it. I will continue to explore this Nietzschean challenge in the next two sections.

3. A SURFEIT OF MEMORY

Individuals and groups of individuals might fail to make sufficient effort to remember or to resist the erosion of memory, and this failure may warrant moral criticism of various sorts. (I will say more about this in Section 5.) This is one way in which they can fail to remember something that they should remember. They might also fail to remember enough of the things they should remember, or they might leave out significant details from what they remember, such as their role in bringing about some past event, and so forth. In various senses and for various reasons, we can sometimes say of individuals or groups of individuals that they remember *too little*. There is also another possibility, that of remembering *too much*. This characterization can express criticism of different sorts, including, but not limited to, moral and political criticism. Like other faculties, memory is a faculty that must be exercised or activated wisely and in moderation. For this to happen, both individuals and groups of individuals need to forget a great deal of what took place in their past and, as we will see, for somewhat similar reasons in the two cases. To continue with the theme of the last section, what I have called the Nietzschean challenge, they need to achieve the right balance between remembering and forgetting or, if there is more than one right way of doing this, a balance that falls within the range of acceptable alternatives.

Jorge Luis Borges's short story, *Funes, the Memorious*, powerfully illustrates in an extreme way the phenomenon of too much memory.[19] Its subject is Ireneo Funes, a man who acquires a new and quite extraordinary facility as a result of being thrown by a wild horse: infallible memory. Borges describes it this way: "He remembered the shapes of the clouds in the south at dawn on the 30th of April of 1882, and he could compare them in his recollection with the marbled grain in the design of a leather-bound book which he had seen only once.... In effect, Funes not only remembered every leaf on every tree of every wood, but even every one of the times he had perceived or imagined it." And, yet, Borges has Funes himself say of his prodigious memory that it is a "garbage disposal," and its effects are devastating. He is rendered immobile, "monumental as bronze"; he loses the capacity for thought, hence problem-solving and decision-making, because "to think is to forget a difference, to generalize, to abstract" but his mind is overwhelmed by particulars; and he is cut off from conversation and interaction with others, because his interlocutors realize that each one of their words and gestures will be preserved in his "implacable memory," and they are "benumbed by the fear of multiplying superfluous gestures." Although an affliction like Funes's is quite unusual to say the least, his story is clearly intended to speak to how we should think about memory in more ordinary circumstances. Specifically, we assess the operation of memory over time by considering its impact on other important dimensions of a person's life and functioning, on the ability to meaningfully recall the past, and on the possibility of forming and maintaining personal relationships and engaging in social intercourse more broadly.[20]

There are also phenomena and pathologies in the social and political domains that are instances of what, following historian Charles S. Maier and others, we can refer to as a "surfeit of memory."[21] In one sense, we may speak of *too much* memory when a community, say, is obsessively preoccupied with wrongs committed against itself in the past and constructs its collective identity predominantly around the notion of victimization. It may also as a result fail to properly acknowledge the seriousness of wrongs committed against others: these are either downplayed or disregarded.[22]

Similarly, an individual may be consumed by anger over the wrongs he or she suffered in the past and, as a consequence, overlook the suffering of others. In another sense, there is too much memory when preoccupation with the past hinders the collective action that is required for desirable social and political transformations. Thus, Maier expresses uneasiness about the current popularity of memory when he claims that "the surfeit of memory [at the end of the twentieth century in Western societies] is a sign not of historical confidence but of a retreat from transformative politics."[23] This claim can be defended in a way that raises important normative questions about features of our memorial practices.

Maier's contention gets support from the following considerations. According to F. R. Ankersmit, "testimony and commemoration have become the much preferred matrices for our relationship to the past,"[24] and neither is conducive to creative politics that require identification with a nation and a robust sense of a shared, national past. Testimony personalizes or privatizes the past, embodying a privileged and intimate connection between the witness and an historical reality, whereas commemoration transforms memory into empty rituals or objects devoid of historical significance and incapable of galvanizing collective action. Lacking larger historical connections, decontextualized, commemorations – for example, Fourth of July or Bastille Day celebrations – have become little more than excuses for private entertainment. In David Lowenthal's words, "[commemorative] memory converts public events into idiosyncratic personal experiences."[25] From this standpoint, the problem is not simply that there is too much memory, but that there is too much memory of the wrong sort. Memorial activities of testimony and commemoration, which are our predominant modes of relating to the past, are the wrong sort to motivate projects of collective political change.

The notion of a surfeit of memory can encompass other social phenomena and pathologies as well. We might count it as a surfeit if there is a kind of collective paralysis induced by shame and guilt over past wrongdoing that prevents progressive political change. Or there might be a surfeit of memory insofar as dwelling on the past prevents the realization of various social and political goods, including the goods of peace, stability, democracy, and economic recovery, or the fulfillment of obligations to citizens, such as housing and medical services for the displaced and injured. The latter may require that attention not be drawn, at least for a time, to past injustices, in order not to perpetuate or create social and political divisions. Another possible explanation is that the shame or guilt that accounts for collective memorial activities is excessive relative to the wrongdoing that was committed. Here, what is essential is that the shame or guilt over what is remembered does not only produce undesirable social or political consequences, which it is likely to do, but that it is out of proportion to the original offense.

The question of when we cross over from *enough* memory to a *surfeit* of memory was at the center of the recent historians' debate in West Germany over the degree to which contemporary Germans should be held responsible – that is,, the degree to which attention should be drawn to their responsibility – for the crimes of the Nazi past. As Maier notes, "there may indeed be a difference between maintaining a decent quotient of collective memory and being obsessed by it,"[26] but in the view of some historians (as well as some West German political figures and many ordinary Germans), the calls to acknowledge responsibility for these crimes had crossed the line. Thus, Ernst Nolte, one of the protagonists in the historians' debate, spoke for a number of commentators when he lamented the fact that the Nazi past "seems to become more alive and powerful, not as model but as specter, as a past that is establishing itself as a present, or as a sword of judgment hung over the present."[27] It is possible, Nolte argued, both to accept responsibility for these crimes *and* to resist the demand constantly to dwell on the past and on the current generation's responsibility to make reparation for those crimes. Understandably, in a country as sensitive about its past as post–World War II Germany, many there found these arguments highly suspect, a suspicion that was reinforced by the claims of Nolte and others that their objective was the "historicization" of National Socialism.[28] To their opponents, historicization came perilously close, and in some cases actually led to, an apology for its crimes, and while there were perhaps consequentialist considerations that spoke in favor of this agenda – for example, it might facilitate postwar Germany's re-entry into the community of nations as an equal partner – in the critics' view this could not justify what amounted to an evasion of historical responsibility.[29] Other efforts by some West German historians to rewrite the history of the Third Reich, to portray the vast majority of Germans under Nazism not as guilty collaborators but as victims of a repressive regime, sought to alleviate contemporary Germans' sense of responsibility for Nazi crimes and, with that, to undercut the need for the constant renewal of memory.

The above are some examples, as controversial though the last one may be, that illustrate what I have in mind by the phenomenon of remembering *too much*. Let me now look more closely at the nature of this problem – in both the political and personal domains – and at why and how it should be contained.

4. THE DYNAMIC OF REMEMBERING AND FORGETTING

(a) *Collective memory*

*One explanation of the phenomenon of a "surfeit of memory" is the fail-*ure to understand that (as Maier puts it) "responsibility for a burdened past can justifiably become less preoccupying as other experiences are added to the national legacy."[30] Change, however, can also justifiably go in the other direction, toward more as well as less preoccupation with responsibility, so I propose a more general thesis of which Maier's remark is an instance: not only *how* the past is collectively remembered, but (in a sense different from this) *the extent to which* past wrongdoing is at the fore-front of public consciousness and attention, may properly shift over time, depending on the historical situation in which the issue of responsibility for the past may be raised. In other words, what, under one set of circum-stances, counts as a "decent quotient of collective memory," may, under a different set be either excessive (a surfeit) or deficient. Public memorial activity, whose purpose is to express a community's sense of responsibility for past wrongdoing and to create and preserve a record of it,[31] properly plays a variable role in the life of that community, depending on a range of other (as yet unspecified) social and political factors. Memory of past wrongdoing – by those responsible for it as well as by those who suffered from it – is appropriately sometimes more, sometimes less, central in a community's array of needs, projects, and responsibilities to its members and others.

One way of understanding these claims is that they represent an appro-priately modest and realistic view of what we can expect of collective mem-ory, in the following sense: there is inevitable tension and conflict between the demands of memory and the multiplicity of other projects that communities undertake; and memorial activities must compete with and to some extent give way to these. Put in these terms, however, the argument is plainly incomplete because it does not tell us why activities of remembrance should be limited by these other projects, what there is about them that explains why these activities should, and not just as a matter of fact do, give way to them. Memory, that is to say, truthful memory, may be in competition with social and political interests and projects of various sorts that consume social resources, and sometimes it is these that should give way to memory, not the other way around.

We can make some headway on this, and better explain why the attention devoted to past wrongdoing not only does but should vary, if we focus instead on *goods and obligations*, that is, on what is valuable about remembrance and on other social goods and obligations with which it might come into conflict and whose achievement or fulfillment it might hinder. Consider some of what we can say about the former. Memorial activities embody and express our values. In cases that involve collective efforts to repair the harm done to the victims of past injustice, as well as others in which the memories do not have this reparative function, participants may be expressing attitudes that they take to be owing or appropriate and acting out of moral conviction. Such activities are not just subjectively valuable for those engaged in them, however: they are often objectively valuable as well, intrinsically as well as instrumentally. Acts of remembrance are sometimes morally imperative, a claim that I will defend at some length in the following chapters. Even when they are not obligatory, they may be valuable because the attitudes and emotions they express are actually warranted or fitting, as I assume they sometimes are. In addition, those who seek to preserve the memory of wrongdoing are commonly moved to action by an intrinsically valuable impulse, what might be called a *passion for righting wrongs*. Marc Gallanter describes it this way:

> To devote ourselves to these claims [of history] represents an impulse to confront and undo the injustice of history, to retrospectively and retroactively move the line separating misfortune and injustice so that all human depredations are seen as remedial injustice. It attempts to make history yield up a morally satisfying result that it did not the first time around.[32]

Remembrance itself, as I will argue in Chapter 3, can to some extent repair past wrongs and express respect for the victims. It is also a precondition for anything else that is to count as a collective remedy for old wrongs, whether the remedy be material or symbolic. And finally, uncovering hidden crimes and holding them in collective memory may promote reconciliation between victims, perpetrators, and their successors and be an important part of political reconstruction.

It is not just the value of remembrance, but its value all things considered, that should be our concern, and to assess this we have to look at its impact on other social goods and obligations. Acts and practices of remembrance may have consequences that compete with and hinder the realization of these other important goods or the fulfillment of these obligations, a possibility I alluded to earlier in discussing the notion of a surfeit of memory. How conflicts between remembrance and these various goods and obligations are to be adjudicated, and what means are best employed to achieve them, are matters of practical and political judgment. For example, certain ways of memorializing the victims of past injustice may be extremely costly, materially speaking, and this may siphon off public monies from other socially worthwhile projects. There is a conflict here between competing social projects. The chief objection to the proposed memorial project being its expense, we have a rough idea how the conflict might be resolved. Perhaps some other, less costly, form of memorial observance would suffice (although the victims and their descendants might not regard it as an adequate substitute). However, when the chief objection is different, other remedial actions will be necessary.

Some conflicts might only be resolvable with difficulty, and might even involve agonizing trade-offs, because memory might be perilous. One such conflict is faced by "transitional justice" mechanisms, such as truth commissions, that have met with considerable resistance from powerful institutions in their societies to full disclosure about the crimes of the past. Although the South African Truth and Reconciliation Commission has achieved high marks for being able to carry out this task without risking serious social disruption, elsewhere groups such as the military, whose support is a condition of a successful transition from dictatorship to democracy, have refused to cooperate with the new regime and have threatened retaliation if investigations go too far.[33]

Nancy Rosenblum states the general problem this way: "when is remembrance fatal – an obstacle to reconciliation and repair?" And she offers
this suggestion: "We may want to temper memory enough to permit reconciliation between warring groups who must emerge from violence to
share a society and a government."[34] How we assess and respond to this
conflict between memory and reconciliation depends on what reconciliation involves in this context, on whether reconciliation really requires
restraint of memory and if so what sort, and on the relative value we assign
to memory and reconciliation in the case at hand. It should also be noted
that the circumstances justifying restraint of memory may change once
reconciliation is achieved and that over time the society may become
stable and peaceful enough to permit a less fettered examination of the
past. As the earlier conflict moderates, the balance among the various
goods and obligations may shift in memory's favor.

The reverse can also happen and is not uncommon, namely, past wrongdoing, to which so much public attention is directed at an earlier stage of
collective accounting, becomes *less* preoccupying over time, and this shift
can sometimes be justified in part in terms of memory's relationship to
other social goods and obligations. Some of these, like peace and stability,
may not be achievable without proper acknowledgment of past wrongdoing, even if dwelling on the past can be dangerous and threaten their
achievement. But once they have been realized, some moderation in the
extent to which society focuses on the past may be appropriate, perhaps
even obligatory. This is a claim, it may be said, about the need to forget
and the value of willed forgetting, but perhaps it would be clearer to say
that it is a point about avoiding excessive preoccupation with the past.[35]
That is, it does not have to do with whether the past should be collectively
remembered at all: elimination of all traces of the past is not usually a
wise or ultimately successful strategy. Rather, it has to do with managing
the influence of the past so that it does not become an exaggerated focus
of social and political concern.

I have argued that whether or not attention to past wrongdoing constitutes objectionable preoccupation with the past, as opposed to a "decent
quotient" of collective memory, partly depends on its consequences
for other social goods and obligations. If these consequences are dire
enough, the former criticism may be warranted. But it isn't just consequences that determine this. Collective memory may also be deemed

excessive insofar as a group dwells on its past out of proportion to the severity of the wrongdoing for which it is responsible or which it suffered, or out of proportion to its degree of responsibility for it. And there is still more to be said about how to achieve a proper balance between remembrance and important social requirements.

In some cases of conflict between remembrance and other goods, the problem might be thought to be simply one of the *quantity* of collective memory that is devoted to past wrongdoing. However, this explanation leaves a great deal unsaid, because the notion can encompass a variety of factors and there may be no clear test of when some quantitative threshold has been passed. More important, framing the problem solely in these terms misses a critical factor in the assessment of memorial activities and projects. Whether a group or community is properly concerned about past wrongdoing cannot be determined solely by taking account of the frequency with which memorial activities are engaged in, their duration, the amount of capital resources invested in them, or how many members of society take part in them. It also has to do with the *form* that collective memory takes, and various forms are possible. Thus, one of the grounds of criticism of collective memory is that, given the competing values and goods at stake, some other form would have been preferable.

Martha Minow distinguishes between various modalities of collective memory and social response to past wrongdoing:

> Collective efforts, notably growing in legal idioms during the past fifty years, include criminal prosecutions, reparations, and truth commissions.... Of course, there are other paths: the creation of artistic memorials; stripping former officials of their pensions and offices; developing educational programs for children and for the entire society; declaring days of commemoration.[36]

No single form of collective memory is best, all relevant goods considered, in every social and historical situation. Although "tribunals and their work offer rituals of accountability... defying forced forgetting,"[37] in some circumstances, insisting on criminal prosecutions may merely perpetuate violence and delay the restoration of peace and stability in societies trying to recover from a period of social upheaval.[38] Truth commissions may be better suited than prosecutions to achieve certain valuable goals, namely, public acknowledgment for past wrongs and the forging of a coherent, socially shared account of what happened; but by emphasizing truth-telling and reconciliation, critics argue, they may fail to deter future abuses and properly do justice to the past and its victims.[39] How we assess these commissions depends, in part, on whether future acts of injustice are considered likely in the particular society in question. Memorials, educational programs and scholarship funds, days of commemoration, and the like can have significant symbolic value for the descendants of the perpetrators and their victims. Even after prosecutions and truth commissions have finished their work, these acknowledgments of the past can serve a useful social function, and if there are no witnesses left who can testify to the injustice that was committed, these symbolic measures may be all that is left under the circumstances. The basic point is this: whether or not the past is being remembered in the right way depends, in part, on a comparative assessment of the social consequences (as well as of the feasibility) of these different modes of collective remembrance. The notion of a surfeit of memory is probably not the best way to describe what can go wrong here, but whether the past is being remembered in the right way is a function of many factors, including the social impact of different transitional justice mechanisms and policies.

I have been focusing on past wrongdoing in this discussion of balancing remembering and forgetting, and my conclusion is simply this: to assert that past wrongdoing should be collectively remembered leaves much to explain about how this is to be done, and prudence, restraint, and flexibility – that is, the ability to adjust to changing social and historical circumstances, to take account of greater and lesser degrees of receptivity to dealing with the past in designing the form and content of memorial activities – are all required in order to realize a "decent quotient" of collective memory. It is reasonable to suppose that similar points can be made about collective remembrance in other situations as well, when what is remembered is not past wrongdoing but, say, some positive achievement in the group's past. However, I will not try to work out the details here.

(b) *Personal memory*

Personal remembrance can also be excessive, and the analysis of what makes it so is formally similar to the analysis given for collective memory.

The Borges story is an extreme but instructive foil in this context, because it describes so vividly the pathology of one who is unable to achieve a proper balance between remembering and forgetting. If anyone can be said to have a surfeit of memory, it is Funes. No experience is too trivial to escape the net of his memory; no differentiation is made between those experiences and events that are worth remembering and those that are not (his memory is a "garbage disposal"); and in this state, he does not and cannot live a recognizably human life at all. In most dramatic fashion, he cannot get on with his life because he is unable to exert control over and to modulate his memories – in Nietzsche's words, he is not "just as able to forget at the right time as to remember at the right time" – and something like this, although not as totally debilitating, happens in other cases where, for one reason or other, an individual cannot let go of or move beyond the past.

This state is inevitably characterized by some degree of distress or suffering. It can be episodic or relatively long-term, and its causes are varied. In one type of case, some real or imagined wrongdoing for which a person holds himself responsible dominates his thoughts. It gnaws at his self-esteem and colors the way in which he interprets other episodes and experiences in his life. On the one hand, he may think that he should not forget that past episode, and his recurrent self-reproach reminds him of what he does not want to forget. On the other hand, he may realize that his self-reproach has become disabling and that it is important for him to try to put this part of his past behind him. The shame or guilt he experiences may also seem to others out of proportion to the seriousness of the wrong that was done, his suffering a ploy to gain sympathy or a wallowing in self-pity, and in time he may come to regard it this way himself.

In another sort of case, it is the feeling of loss with the death of a loved one that a person cannot overcome. Here too the effort to move beyond the past may be beset with ambivalence. C. S. Lewis, in his moving reflection on the death of his wife, *A Grief Observed*, describes the sense of betrayal that commonly hampers this effort:

> Still, there's no denying that in some sense I 'feel better' [after some time has passed since my wife's death], and with that comes at once a sort of shame, and a feeling that one is under a sort of obligation to cherish and foment and prolong one's unhappiness.[40]

The deceased loved one may become such an overwhelming presence in the survivor's life that it undermines his capacity to move forward in and with it. As with the person who is racked by guilt or shame over real or imagined wrongdoing, the survivor experiences the mental suffering that marks what Norman Care calls "tyrannization by one's past."[41] The challenge he or she faces is how to free himself or herself from this tyranny without denying either responsibility for a burdened past or love for the one who has died. Care calls it "the going-on problem."[42]

Joan Didion's powerful account of her husband John's death and the year that followed, *The Year of Magical Thinking*,[43] meticulously and honestly documents the effects of grief on the survivor and the long and tortuous process of partial recovery that permits her to go on with her life. Her grief, she says, was "obliterative, dislocating to both body and mind" (188); she was unprepared for "the unending absence that follows [the death of a loved one], the void, the very opposite of meaning, the relentless succession of moments during which we will confront the experience of meaninglessness itself" (189). Frequently "sideswiped by memories" (197) of her husband and their lives together, she found she had little control over how or when the past came back to her, and this made her diffident and anxious in her dealings with others. After a year passed, Didion did "not yet actually feel this faith in the future" (212), but she knew "that if we are to live ourselves there comes a point at which we must relinquish the dead, let them go, keep them dead" (225–226), and with sadness she anticipated how this would go:

> I did not want to finish the year because I know that as the days pass, as January becomes February and February becomes summer, certain things will happen. My image of John at the instant of his death will become less immediate, less raw. It will become something that happened in another year. My sense of John himself, John alive, will become more remote, even "mudgy," softened, transmuted into whatever best serves my life without him. (225)

Would it be correct to say of Didion that she suffered from a surfeit of memory during her year of magical thinking? The answer may depend on what we take to be the norm for such experiences. To be sure, the onslaught of memories was disabling and disorienting. But if hers was normal, not pathological grief, and appropriate to the magnitude of her loss, then "surfeit" may not be the right term to use. Interestingly, Didion considers how to categorize her grief during this period and leaves the issue unresolved.

The going-on problem in its various manifestations is not merely of a psychological order. It is also a moral problem, or a problem with moral implications, and it is not difficult to understand why. An inability to get beyond the past and move forward with one's life may indicate a degree of self-reproach that is unwarranted because excessive, given what was done and/or one's responsibility for it. In some cases, one might reproach oneself for something about one's past that clearly doesn't involve one's agency at all. Even when the self-reproach is (initially) a fitting response to one's past involvement, there may be grounds for criticism. What makes self-reproach excessive is in part its relationship to effective agency, which includes self-confidence and a sense of self-worth, a capacity to conceive and pursue plans, projects, and values, and to actively choose those one wishes to pursue. Dwelling on the past becomes problematic when it diminishes effective agency thus understood, when it undermines the capacity for self-determination, disrupts peace of mind, and weakens self-confidence.[44] We may say, therefore, that managing the influence of the past on one's life is sometimes an exercise in the recovery of effective agency, including the recovery of personal autonomy, and that there are better and worse ways of managing this. As in the collective case, properly managing the influence of the past involves moderating the extent and intensity of the attention one devotes to it in response to other important goods, values and obligations. Whether or not preoccupation with a shameful or guilt-inducing episode in one's past is excessive depends in part on its in relation to other goods in life, in particular those that it precludes or impedes, and this might only become evident over an extended period of time.

Emotionally difficult as it may be to get on with one's life after suffering a loss or doing wrong, there is much at stake morally in being able to do so, in being able to rekindle sufficient interest in and enthusiasm for life to give meaning to one's activities. There are different ways of going-on, of course. One can go one with one's life by ignoring the past altogether or by deceiving oneself about its significance or the extent of one's blameworthiness. Alternatively, one can face the past honestly and without evasion and still be able to go one with life, as long as one is not crippled by feelings of loss, shame, or guilt. In this condition, life is able to go forward, even if somewhat encumbered by the emotional burdens of the past, and it is only this sort of clear-sighted going-on that evinces the recovery of effective agency.

Finally, getting on with one's life, in the way I have been characterizing it, is crucially a matter of getting on with one's life *with others*, that is, establishing a new basis of how one will live with and relate to others. Others can facilitate this reintegration into the community, but the task for them is a delicate one, requiring tact, sensitivity, and patience. As we know, people are often counseled by concerned friends after some period of mourning the loss of a loved one, or some major life disappointment, that it is time to stop grieving and get on with life. The advice, well-meaning though it may be, is often aligned more with the needs of the advice giver than the advice receiver, which is not surprising, given that our culture provides few scripts for how to relate to and assist those who are grieving. Getting on with one's life, then, is a challenge not just for those who suffer but also for those who care about him or her, and it can only be met by both working together.

To sum up the last two sections, remembrance has its social and personal uses. Nietzsche told us what some of them are, and the discussion of collective memory, in particular, memory of past wrongdoing, revealed more. I have also claimed that how we remember something or someone can be intrinsically valuable because it expresses valuable attitudes and emotions. These are broad and fairly abstract generalizations about the values of memory. But as we have seen, to say this much about memory is not to say nearly enough because memory, although sometimes a good or an instrument of good, might also come into conflict with other goods and obligations of a personal or social and political nature. Even if it is conceded that memory must be preserved and that something important is lost if it is not, the hard question for individuals and groups is how this is to be done so that not too much of these other goods is thereby sacrificed or these obligations do not remain unfulfilled. This is another way of expressing what I have called the Nietzschean challenge: a challenge that Nietzsche believed required critical detachment from the attractions and demands of memory.

5. MEMORY AS OBLIGATION

I propose now to move to the second topic under the rubric of a morality or ethics of memory, that of responsibility or obligation, and I start by saying something about the historical context in which such notions have come to be attached to memory. I preface this with the following bridging comment: an account of the obligations of memory should be informed, in theory as well as in practice, by an account of its value, in itself and in relation to other things of value. Simply to assert that "S has an obligation to remember y" provides little in the way of concrete guidance, and it remains seriously incomplete without an explanation of the good, intrinsic and instrumental, of memory and an appreciation of the constraints that other goods and obligations place on its activities and practices.

Now for some brief remarks about the historical setting of these reflections. Few would disagree that for us in the United States, memory, individual as well as collective, has acquired heightened importance and visibility in the wake of the terrorist attacks of September 11th, 2001. On the individual level, survivors, loved ones, and eyewitnesses struggle with and suffer from traumatic memories of the events of that day. On the collective level, calls to remember and tokens of the resolve to remember surrounded us and served for a time to bind us together by invoking the experience of a shared national catastrophe. Signs proclaiming "We will never forget," "We will always remember our fallen comrades. . . . ," and the like adorned homes, government buildings, and places of business; yearly memorial services continue at Ground Zero; and architectural firms and different political constituencies publicly competed for how best to memorialize the dead on hallowed ground.[45] This is but one example – and the number could be multiplied many fold – of how memory is called on to perform a function that Avishai Margalit and Gabriel Motzkin have identified as "a distinctive feature of postwar conceptions of what memory is," namely, a "focus on the process of how people are made to vanish."[46]

It should not be surprising to find that works about the moral and political significance of memory, written at this time in history, have been colored and shaped by personal and public responses to the Holocaust.[47] Indeed, for Margalit and Motzkin, it is the Holocaust that provides the context for the "postwar conceptions" of memory and that explains their particular orientation: "The Holocaust has become the focal point for the current discussion of memory; how the past should be remembered, how the past should be commemorated, and what should be the relations between memory and history."[48] The subject of the Holocaust has inspired a range of reflections on memory, trauma, and history, and it is no exaggeration to say that the current preoccupation with memory in departments of history and literary studies and elsewhere in the academy (in the United States, at any rate) is in large measure an outgrowth of work in this area. "Discourse on the Holocaust," notes Gabrielle M. Spiegel, "with its tendency to privilege questions of memory and, not least, trauma, has been the seedbed of the growing industry devoted to these topics, which have now generalized themselves to virtually every field in the profession."[49] Pierre Nora seems to suggest something similar when he notes, cryptically, "Whoever says memory, says Shoah."[50]

To be sure, it would be much too simplistic to assert that the contemporary interest in memory, in the public or the academic arena, can be traced to this source alone. As Jay Winter observes, the "obsession with memory arise[s] out of a multiplicity of social, cultural, medical, and economic trends and developments of an eclectic but intersecting nature."[51] But if Margalit and Motzkin are right about the influence of the Holocaust on our moral and political thinking about memory, this would help to explain why there is a tendency in much of that thinking to deal with memory chiefly from the point of view of traumatic, not normal, memory. It would also help to explain why memory has come to be talked about not just as a psychological phenomenon or as something that may be harmful or beneficial to the health of individuals and societies but, as I do here, as the subject of a *moral imperative.*[52]

To hold that remembrance is not just a morally optional good but sometimes a moral imperative is to make a particularly strong claim. "There are some actions," Joel Feinberg asserts, "which it would be desirable for a person to do and which, indeed, he *ought* to do, even though they are actions he is under no *obligation* and has no *duty* to do." The sense of "ought" that seems to be operative in some of the cases under consideration here, by contrast, is the "ought" of obligation, and all obligations or duties, Feinberg goes on, "share the common character of being *required.*"[53] Of course, we forget a great many things in daily life without incurring (serious) moral censure for doing so. Morality is selective with respect to what it requires us to remember and much of what we forget just does not have the sort of importance that brings it within the scope of moral obligation. However, with respect to some trauma-inducing events in particular, most people's moral intuitions are very different. The thought is that, because of the gravity of what was done, and perhaps also because of our relationship to it, there are occasions when we ought to remember and do wrong not to remember or at least not to make an effort to do so. One of the main tasks of this book is to examine the sorts of arguments that can be given in support of intuitions about a moral imperative to remember, in these and other nontraumatic cases.

The claim that there can be a moral imperative or responsibility to remember, in this or any other situation, may seem puzzling because in the view of most philosophers, choice or voluntary control is a precondition of moral responsibility, whereas memory is not in any straightforward way under our control. Margalit raises this worry when he notes: "We cannot be morally or ethically praised for remembering, or blamed for failing to remember, if memory is not under our control.... Remembering and forgetting may, after all, not be proper subjects for moral or ethical decrees and evaluations."[54] And yet we certainly do sometimes praise people for remembering and blame them for forgetting. If someone promises you that he will do something important for you and fails to do so, and tells you afterward that he just forgot, it is unlikely that you will forgive him on the ground that he had no control over whether he remembered his promise or not. He ought to have remembered and could have done so, you will probably think, and you will blame him for forgetting unless he gives you a satisfactory excuse. Alternatively, you might praise someone for remembering her promise if, despite many competing pressures and perhaps a rather poor memory on top of everything else, she carried it out. As these examples suggest, a moral imperative to remember makes sense if for no other reason than that our moral responsibilities endure over time and have implications for future conduct, and in order to fulfill them we have to remember them. If control is a precondition of legitimately holding someone morally responsible, there are ways of having control over one's memory that are well within the capacities of most people.

It is perhaps even more obvious that memory is susceptible to voluntary control when we turn from individual to collective memory. Societies have various means at their disposal to ensure that their members do not forget important historical events and to shape how those events will be remembered. Erecting monuments, constructing museums, and holding regular commemorative ceremonies are ways of managing collective memory, although their efficacy usually diminishes over time.

So far, we have not found a reason why, in principle, we should disallow talk of a moral imperative to remember. Supporting this conclusion is the fact that remembrance, in the cases Margalit and Motzkin have in mind and probably others as well, has a certain phenomenology: it is generally felt to be nonoptional in a way that we believe has implications for moral assessment, and we are often moved by this to commit ourselves to remember. Sometimes this commitment is open-ended in that we do not set a time limit to how long we will remember. Indeed, there are cases in which to do so might seem to cast doubt on the sincerity of that resolve. Sometimes, as in the immediate aftermath of a disaster or serious injustice, the survivors may even declare their intention to *remember it forever.*

It doesn't take much acquaintance with history and human psychology, however, to appreciate the fragility and transience of memory and its vulnerability to social, cultural, and political forces. History is replete with examples of deliberate efforts by those in power to control memory by suppressing the truth about the past. But memory also fades without the use of direct manipulation, especially in non-traditional and highly individualistic societies like our own that lack a strong sense of inter-generational continuity and do not provide social structures to support individual memory. Future generations forget what the present generation vowed to remember because of the social and other changes that the passage of time brings with it, and memory is evanescent even within the lifetime of a single individual. Writing about the forgotten monuments of New York City, for example, Michael Miscione remarks that "New Yorkers have a shamefully short collective memory.... not a single memorial has successfully held the attention and affection of New Yorkers for more than a generation or two."[55] Although the social forces that contribute to the erosion of collective memory may operate at a particularly rapid pace in major urban centers, the phenomenon is obviously considerably more widespread than this.

To say that there are imperatives of memory is to imply that persons, operating individually or collectively, must make an effort to guard the past, to hold on to it or retrieve it from the traces it leaves behind. They must take measures to resist the natural erosion of memory caused by the passage of time and the artificial erosion caused by the work of human agents and their institutions. Memory, viewed in this way as the subject of an imperative or obligation, is to be distinguished from what W. James Booth variously calls "habit," "thick" or "autonomous" memory. This sort of memory

> is not the fight to hold on to the often fleeting traces of the absent, but rather a rich deposit of habit, of body memory and habits of the heart, of institutions, and so on. Here there is a solidity and a stability, a memory beyond active or conscious remembrance, and therefore often only barely visible to us in the present. Far from standing in need of constant efforts to preserve the past against erosion, this form of memory, it seems, does it work almost automatically.[56]

Habit memory, in its collective form, is sedimented in a society's institutions, conventions, and laws and in the civic habits of its people, and although it does preserve the past, it typically does so in an unself-conscious way that does not make explicit reference to the past. (The inculcation of habit memory can of course be the aim of deliberate memory work, but the distinction between these types of memory remains.) Collective memory encompasses these embodiments of habit memory as well as practices and activities that are explicitly memorial in intent, and there are analogues to both in the case of personal memory. However, insofar as I speak about memory as an imperative or obligation, I refer to an intentional calling to mind, publicly or privately, of the past, a calling to mind that is required, and not to habit memory, except indirectly.

Moral theorizing about memory, in particular about the responsibilities associated with it, should take the well-known susceptibilities of memory into account and should have something to say about how to constructively respond to them. Not to do so, to neglect these facts, is to engage in a kind of idealization that invites the charge of naivete or irrelevance, a charge whose point is that memory, ironically, has not been taken seriously as a personal or social imperative after all. An account that fails to confront the problem of memory manipulation might even be accused of abetting the forces of social control. For these and other reasons, a morality of memory must be realistic, in the sense that it acknowledges memory's transience and vulnerability, and it should take up, as matters of *moral* import, a number of questions to which these facts give rise. These include the following: How strenuously should we, individually or as a group, resist the erasure of memory? On what factors does this depend? Is resistance, rather than acceptance, always the appropriate attitude to have to the erosion of memory? More generally, by what measure or standard may we determine whether we are adequately discharging the imperatives of remembrance? These are difficult questions and, admittedly, easily misinterpreted as well. To simply ask them, and to point out the obstacles to discharging the imperatives of memory, might be interpreted as an attempt to evade having to take responsibility for the past. Yet if the temptations for evasion are significant, this is all the more reason to take up these questions in a serious way.

6. RESPONSIBILITIES OF REMEMBRANCE AND TAKING RESPONSIBILITY FOR THE PAST

I have claimed, on largely intuitive grounds, that remembrance can be morally imperative in some instances. I have not, however, provided much of an argument for this or for the existence of such imperatives more generally, so I turn to this now. This will also lead me to introduce another notion that figures prominently in this book. Part of the justification of imperatives of remembrance is this: people, individually as well as collectively, should recognize and act on their responsibilities of remembrance, because this is both instrumental to and constitutive of taking responsibility for the past, and this is something that, for various reasons and in certain circumstances, they should do. In this way, the notion of taking responsibility for the past enters the picture as part of the normative underpinning of these imperatives.

Moral imperatives to remember may be explained and justified by prior violations of moral standards of right and wrong, as I have already suggested. But this is not their only setting. For one thing, normally there are obligations to remember friends and loved ones who have died. Memory is pervasive in human life, intertwined in complex ways with human goods as well as evils, and if we are going to allow that there are moral imperatives with this content at all, there seems to be no good reason why they should only arise in connection with wrongdoing on either a small or large scale. But once we enlarge the scope of the imperative to include more than wrongdoing, we appear to have made the task of justifying the imperative more difficult. For the question that is often, perhaps most often, elicited by claims about an imperative to remember is one that invites a reference to outcomes: *what good will come from remembering?* And the common answer to this is something along the following lines: we need to acknowledge what we have done in the past in order to make amends for it; we will be more vigilant in the future to prevent a repetition of what happened in the past; or remembering will promote collective or individual healing. However, if there is nothing to repair or prevent because past wrongdoing is not what we are called on to remember, or if because of the circumstances memory is not likely to promote healing, the assertion that we ought to remember anyway may strike some as evidence either of an excessively sentimental attachment to the past or worse, a masochistic desire to rehash parts of the past that we cannot change and that can only cause pain or social unrest.

I believe it is possible to justify an imperative to remember in such cases, but to do so we need to supply nonconsequentialist reasons. What consequentialist views do not acknowledge are other critical dimensions of moral assessment, including the expressive. On these grounds, there may be good reasons why, depending on the nature of the act itself and its context, we ought to remember, even if no good, and perhaps even some bad, is thereby promoted. For example, from an expressivist standpoint, there may be compelling reasons to remember wrongdoing even if this doesn't make recurrence less likely or bring about social reconciliation. My contention, therefore, is that there are different theories of value and reasons for action as they relate to memory. I label these, following Elizabeth Anderson,[57] *consequentialist* and *expressivist* accounts, and it is the fundamental differences between these general types rather than particular versions of each that I want to note here.

Consequentialism holds that rational principles guide action by giving it an end to pursue and justify action by appeal to the intrinsic goodness or value of the end. We are instructed to adopt whatever intentions will best bring about or promote the existence of intrinsically valuable states of affairs. The value of memory or memorial activities, on such an account, may be extrinsic in the sense that it derives from memory's *causal relations* to valuable states of affairs. Or, because consequentialism can allow that a state can be intrinsically good in virtue of the relation it bears to a past state, memorial activities might be *constitutive ingredients* of

intrinsically valuable states of affairs. When this is the case, consequentialism might direct us to adopt means to promote the state of affairs that
consists in the preservation and dissemination of memory.

Arguments purporting to show that there are moral obligations of collective remembrance are commonly consequentialist in form. In these
arguments, obligations of collective memory are justified by the role
memory plays within a instrumental structure of values. For example,
preserving the memory of past injustices may be claimed to be imperative on the ground that, as the saying goes, "those who forget the past are
condemned to repeat it"; or it may be proposed that collective memory
is an important social good that we should seek to protect and promote.

However, when we turn to friends and loved ones who have died, to
those whom I call, somewhat quaintly, the dear departed, consequentialism about reasons to remember and the value of remembering pretty
obviously cannot be the entire story. To be sure, even with regard to the
dear departed, memory may have instrumental importance. But to think
about memory entirely from a consequentialist standpoint is to fail to
appreciate the full evaluative significance of the attitudes and emotions
of those who are engaged in acts of remembering. Instead, we need to
view remembering the dear departed in a different light, as an *expression*
of love, honor or admiration for these persons, of emotions and attitudes
that are not directed solely toward the living but naturally and appropriately persist long after their deaths. An expressivist theory, as applied to
memory, holds that the expression of such emotions and attitudes in the
memory of the dear departed can have intrinsic value,[58] and it seeks to
justify responsibilities of remembrance on this basis, without appealing to
the intrinsic values of states of affairs. This sort of theory is required for a
complete account of the moral foundations of responsibilities of remembrance. A consequentialist understanding of these responsibilities will
not suffice.

Stuart Hampshire makes a similar point in his discussion of obligations
of memory:

> Betrayal and ingratitude are indelible offenses against the past, render-
> ing it empty and useless. . . . Within many conceptions of the good, there
> is a loss and an evil which are independent of any bad consequences in

the future. It is a fundamental objection to any utilitarian morality that it looks only to future improvements to explain the duties and obligations of a person.[59]

I would only add to this that we have obligations of memory both with respect to what was good in the past and what was bad, and that a consequentialist analysis of these obligations is perhaps more likely to be given in the latter case. The passage also suggests that on some views, remembering itself can be the primary locus of responsibility and that obligations of remembrance can be justified on grounds that are independent of whatever role it may play in bringing about good consequences and preventing bad ones. I count my own view among these.

Even if an expressivist theory captures central features of our relation to the dear departed that a consequentialist theory cannot, it may be claimed that what the former does not do is deliver *obligations* of remembrance. We naturally mourn the passing of our loved ones and friends in quite personal ways, and we experience their deaths with a sense of deep personal loss. In light of this, the argument goes, it is not only unnecessary but inappropriate to talk about having a responsibility or an obligation to remember these individuals, even setting aside questions about what exactly this involves. For are not these the very persons whom we do not have to be told to remember because they mean so much to us and we cherish them? This will often be true. However, the critical issue is not whether a sense of obligation enters into our motivation, but whether remembering deceased friends and loved ones can properly be characterized as something that we are obligated to do.

Misgivings about the appropriateness of this characterization may be rooted in the timeworn dichotomies of duty and affection, responsibility and desire. It is not difficult to show, however, that these are not mutually exclusive concepts and that one can fulfill obligations of remembrance even though the notion of obligation is not part of the description under which one acts. Friends have duties of special care and attention that are constitutive of and grounded by the friendship; parents are normally moved by their love for their children to fulfill their parental obligations. But there may also be circumstances in which we *do* need to be reminded of our obligations of remembrance. For even with respect to our close friends and those we love dearly, what is initially experienced as a loss when they die may, in time, become what is past and gone, then become an object of indifference, and finally be forgotten altogether. The language of obligation is important and necessary here insofar as one should resist the erosion of memory by the passage of time.[60]

Let me now turn from the responsibilities of remembrance to the idea of taking responsibility for the past and the connections between them. The pasts that I am interested in are either personal or collective. The term "personal" as used here is intended to cut across the distinction between the private self and the public self, because actions performed in one's public role are as much part of one's personal past as actions performed in the so-called private domain. The "personal past" also includes contributions that one has made to group efforts and one's entanglements in the personal lives of others, as well as traits that would be contained in a description of the sort of person one was in the past. As for a group's collective past, it is not just the personal pasts of its members summed up. Rather, it is the past that individuals who belong to a group *share* (as distinguished from have in common with each other) because of their membership in that group. So when I talk about taking responsibility for *the* past, I mean either an individual taking responsibility for *his or her personal* past or the members of a group taking responsibility for *their collective* past.

Memory plays an extremely important role here because memory links us to the past. Indeed, it is hard to see how persons individually or collectively could take responsibility for their past if remembrance were not an aspect of their endeavor. Consider the collective case. Taking responsibility for the past might involve acknowledging past wrongdoing, atoning for it, and offering reparations (economic and other sorts) to the victims and their descendants. Or it might involve keeping the agreements that were made by one's predecessors. These tasks give memory moral significance: because there is no taking responsibility for the past if the past is not remembered, it follows that those who are responsible for past wrongdoing have a moral obligation to remember it, and those who are bound by prior agreements have an obligation to remember them. Individuals might also have wronged others in the past and made agreements with others, and remembering those aspects of their past is morally important and imperative for similar reasons. That is, they have to remember the wrongdoing for which they are responsible if they are to make reparations for it, and they have to remember the agreements they have made if they are to keep them.

In these ways, memory is morally significant for individuals for reasons analogous to those for groups of individuals. However, there are two caveats. First, the process of group members taking responsibility for their collective past is not to be understood simply as a case of taking responsibility for one's personal past writ large. For it is common in political communities for there to be competing interpretations of the past vying for acceptance as *the* authoritative account of what happened and who was responsible for it, and it is not helpful to think of this competition as just the collective version of whatever indecision or ambivalence an individual might have about his own past. How much agreement is attainable in a particular society concerning what happened and how it should be judged is largely a political question, and disagreements may persist within and among different groups to a greater or lesser degree. This is not surprising, given how much is riding on the interpretation of the historical record. But fortunately the end of all controversy about this is not a necessary condition of the collective assumption of responsibility for past acts and practices.

Second, the reasons why it is imperative for an individual to take responsibility for his or her past do not all have straightforward or simple analogues in the collective case. Taking responsibility for one's personal past consists partly in taking responsibility for what *one has done* in the past, and if this involved wrongdoing, it consists of a number of tasks, including the ones just noted. But it also involves taking responsibility for *oneself* and one's contributions to becoming who one is. This includes, among other things, owning up to parts of one's personality even if they are unflattering and one would prefer to disavow them; reproaching oneself for past flaws and shortcomings when and as appropriate; being clear about one's share in the formation of one's character and patterns of one's conduct and eschewing excuses for being the kind of person one is; appreciating that one has the capacity to control the direction of one's life and acknowledging the past influences and acquired limitations that constrain its exercise. There may be group analogues of a sort to these various conditions, but it is a complicated question what evidence would show that a group possesses these attributes.

It follows from this characterization that taking responsibility for one's past is morally important and desirable for the individual to do, whether or not there is wrongdoing in the past for which he ought to take responsibility. For it is also a way of taking oneself seriously and is necessary if one is to have a realistic, responsible conception of oneself. Its importance is to be explained, therefore, partly in terms of what is essential to leading a good human life, because these are plausibly regarded as constitutive ingredients of it. A person who does not come to terms with and take responsibility for important aspects of his past, or who selectively and defensively takes responsibility for only certain portions of it, will likely have only a superficial understanding of his abilities, inclinations, and attitudes. The past will continue to influence how he represents the present and future, whether or not he is reflective about the manner in which it does so. But it is a mark of a kind of shallowness of character to lack self-knowledge and self-awareness of this fundamental sort, either to fail or refuse to see oneself as having a history or to see oneself merely as a bystander to it.[61]

Arguably, taking responsibility for one's personal past is not only good to do, but something one *ought* to do, in a strong sense of the word. Here I think the notion of duties to oneself is apt: one cannot take responsibility for oneself if one does not take responsibility for one's past, and taking responsibility for oneself is among the duties one has to oneself. We might defend this in Kantian terms as required by the categorical imperative: act so as to treat humanity, whether in *your own person* or that of another, always as an end. That is, a person who does not take responsibility for his past – or more specifically, for those ingredients of his personal past that have shaped his identity and self-conception – fails to exercise self-determination in that he is not as concerned with his own responsibility for what he is like as he ought to be.

We might fill out the Kantian argument in the following way. To take responsibility for one's past is in part to be willing to learn from it in a moral sense and to interpret it in ways that may be very different from how one interpreted it at the time one acted. What may have seemed to me at the time of action to be morally innocent or a matter of no moral significance may be reunderstood and re-experienced by me later as cruel or insensitive, and openness to this kind of reflection on the moral meaning of one's actions is essential to the development of responsible moral agency. Memory, as we might put it, is the medium through which a certain kind of moral progress is possible, and how one remembers and one's memories are shaped reveals a great deal about what sort of moral agent one is.[62]

The failure to exercise autonomy is not the only defect in the person who does not take responsibility for his past, so an argument focused only on that would not provide the entire justification for the imperative. This much, at any rate, is clear: if there is a duty to take responsibility for one's past, perhaps conceived as a duty to oneself, then there must also be an imperative to remember it, because, to a significant degree, it is through memory that our past is accessible to us.

7. MEMORY, IDENTITY, AND RESPONSIBILITY

I argued in Section 5 that remembrance is in some circumstances an obligation of individuals as well as groups of individuals. However, even with respect to the specific normative notion of obligation, this only partly explains the moral and ethical significance of memory. There is also a connection between memory and obligation that is mediated by identity, individual as well as collective. In this connection, memory (not all memories, of course) constructs and reflects identity, and identity is partly constituted and defined by obligations, among which are obligations of remembrance. I will try to defend both parts of this claim in what follows. But first I need to draw a distinction between different senses of personal identity to clarify my interest in identity's relationship to memory.

The basic distinction in this area is between *numerical identity over time* and what we might call *biographical identity*. Diachronic personal identity is a temporal relationship in which a person at time t_1 is the same person as a person at time t_2, even though that person might have undergone qualitative change; personal identity in the second sense refers to the characteristics, actions, and experiences that make someone the person she is, and are or contribute to what she considers to be most important to who she is. An analogous distinction can be drawn between different senses of group identity. Thus, we can focus on the conditions that must be satisfied for a group to continue to exist through time; alternatively, we might be interested in the norms, basic institutions, traditions, and civic habits that give a group its particular defining character.

Psychological continuation is widely if not universally regarded as a crucial element of diachronic personal identity, and Locke's psychological continuity theory is perhaps the most famous in the philosophical literature. Locke's theory, roughly speaking, is a memory theory and, as usually interpreted, it states that the fact of my being able to recollect a past experience, or to appropriate it to myself in self-consciousness, is what constitutes my identity with the subject of that experience. Other psychological continuity theorists expand the list of psychological connections to include more than memory connections.[63] Nevertheless, there is a strand of ordinary thought about diachronic personal identity in which memory has special importance among the various kinds of direct psychological connection. In Marya Schechtman's words, "personal continuation, on this view, depends crucially on *having access* to one's history and recognizing the connections between one's present and one's past."[64] Amnesia, in this way of thinking, threatens loss of identity.

Most philosophers have argued that in order to consider an individual or group a responsible agent, accountable for past deeds and able to assume commitments to the future, we have to have an account that answers the question, What makes this person or group at one time the same person or group at another time?[65] Be this as it may, this is not the only, or always the most important, question to ask about personal and collective identity. Very often, we are most interested in the things that contribute importantly to and help define one's life, as these are viewed or would be viewed from one's own perspective: in the significant things one has done and experienced; the roles and relationships in which one is invested; the values, goals, and features of character that guide and explain one's conduct, and the ways in which one is seen by others, where this enters into how one regards oneself. We are most interested, in other words, in biographical identity (and its group analogue), which Joseph Raz distinguishes from numerical identity over time as follows:

> ...when talking of 'identity' I do not mean the term in the sense in which it fixes the limits to the continuity of an object, or an object of a kind: is this pile of timber which made up Thesesus' boat Theseus' boat still? We mean the identity revealed in answers to the question who am I? I am a man, an academic, a father, etc. These make me who I am.[66]

This is the sense of identity that I am centrally concerned with in this book, and it is revealed not only in answers to the question "Who am *I*?" (asked by an individual about himself or herself[67]), but also "Who are *we*?" (asked by individuals about themselves as a group).

Memory is critically important for personal identity thus understood: it preserves and makes available for us the past experiences, actions, relationships, and so forth that furnish our sense of self.[68] Psychologists Jefferson Singer and Peter Salovey call the specific memories that do this *self-defining*: they are the ones "that give shape to and are shaped by our lives, memories of our proudest success and humiliating defeats, memories of loves won and lost – memories that repetitively influence our manner of intimacy or our pursuit of power – the memories that answer the question of who we are."[69] The relationship between these memories and our sense of who we are is reciprocal and evolving. Our current experiences condition how we remember and what we remember of the past, and the meanings that past experiences have for us at one age will probably be very different from those they have many years later. But at any given time, these self-defining memories reflect aspects of our identity and shape (usually without conscious awareness or deliberate effort on our part) the way we understand our lives and our interactions with others. Loss of memory as it occurs in cases of extensive amnesia would therefore not only completely sever a link to the past that many regard as necessary if one is to be the same person as some earlier person. It would also confound our sense of who we are and, insofar as our identities are constituted by our self-conceptions, would involve a loss of identity in the biographical sense.

Analogous points can be made about the importance of collective memory for group identity. In this context, group identity does not refer to the part of individual identity that is constituted by membership in a particular group, such as a nation or an ethnic or religious group. Granted, there is a sense of "belonging" to a particular nation or community according to which it is an identity-forming attachment. But what I have in mind here is a genuinely collective identity, an identity that belongs to *us*, not to *me* and *you* and *you*, and so forth, in virtue of our all belonging to the same group.[70] Historian Charles Maier notes that memory is important for the collective identity of national groups as well as the personal identity of individuals and that it is important for similar reasons in the two cases:

> Memory certainly is a prerequisite of identity. . . . The hunger for memory has been a remarkable cultural feature of the last decade. It underlies the interest in *Alltagsgeschichte*, the compulsion to think through the painful episodes of the past, the media presentations, and the museums. . . . The concept of personal identity presupposes an individual consciousness which is psychologically integrated in some way and which will cease with death. At best national identity remains an analogue. . . . In both cases memory (or a history) seems to constitute much of identity, such that individual or collective personality need not be created anew every instant. In that sense we are what we have become.[71]

Of course, as Maier himself emphasizes, to say that memory "constitute[s] much of [personal as well as national] identity" is not to imply that individuals and nations are *only* what the past has made them or that "identity is like some sediment deposited by history."[72] This fatalistic explanation betrays a fundamental misunderstanding of the complex and dynamic relationship between memory and identity.

I have said enough to establish the first part of my original claim about memory and obligation, that memory conditions and shapes biographical (individual or collective) identity and is reciprocally shaped by it. The point is a familiar one and has been made by social scientists from various disciplines, by psychologists (the concept of identity owes much to models from psychology, after all), and sometimes by sociologists and historians. I now want to consider identity from a different angle and to ask about its moral or ethical significance. This is a question about the normativity of identity, one aspect of which is the connection between identity and obligation. I begin, as before, with personal identity.

Identity is not only a descriptive category but a normative one as well, and part of its normative significance consists in its being a source of *values*. It is a source in this sense: one's having a particular identity makes it valuable for one to do certain things that might not be valuable or valuable in the same way for someone with a different identity. Or there are values that someone with a particular identity has and must take into account precisely because he has that identity, and that someone with a different identity does not have to take into account or take into account in the same way. Consider, for example, a person whose identity as a union organizer makes it valuable for him to risk his personal well-being in the struggle to improve the working conditions of the rank and file. Someone else who did not have this sort of stake in the union struggle might still think it a good thing, impersonally considered, if the working conditions were to improve. But there is a dimension of value, that is, agent-relative value, in the former case that would be missing here. In another example, it is part of my having an identity as an orthodox Jew that I eat only kosher food and observe the Sabbath as a day of rest. These are values for me, and their being so is naturally explained by pointing to my particular identity. Someone with a different religious or nonreligious identity might not have these among his values. What's more, my having the particular religious identity that I do does not necessarily commit me to wanting it to be the case that someone else is influenced by the same values that I am. Yet another: because being an American is part of my identity, certain of my country's achievements have a special value for me over and above whatever value they may have for people in general, a (relative) value that I would not expect those achievements to have for someone who did not identify himself as such. In these and many other similar examples, there are values that are internal to the possession of a particular identity, that flow from and are explained by it, and that would not exist without it.[73]

Identities also have normative authority because of their internal connection to *obligations*. Arguably, there would be no genuinely normative identities at all (where having an identity involves living one's life in accordance with a certain self-conception) without obligations, because such identities are partly constituted by them. Or if there could be normative identities without obligations, they would be relatively superficial. Raz explains the crucial role that duties play in the constitution of identity by contrasting them with rights:

> Our duties rule out many options – exclude them from our mental horizon. This is a way of guiding our life, perhaps the deepest and most profound way. Rights too can have such an aspect. Some rights determine status: establish that one is a citizen, or just a member of society, and so on. Consciousness of them may be important to our sense of who we are. Yet, unless the status brings with it duties, and therefore responsibilities, rights are less intimately engaged with our life. Our duties define

our identities more profoundly than do our rights. They are among the primary constituents of our attachments, among the fundamental contributors to meaning in life.[74]

Part of what I take Raz to be arguing here is that our identities are more profoundly determined by our duties than our rights because duties establish the boundaries of what it is possible for us to be and to do in a way that rights alone cannot. It is duties, more so than rights that give our lives their particular normative contours. Furthermore, Raz suggests, we cannot make sense of having a worthwhile "attachment," whether to a person or cause or whatever, without invoking notions of commitment and duty; and insofar as our identities are constituted by such attachments, duties will be central to those identities.

For similar reasons, Christine Korsgaard holds that there is an intimate connection between obligation and what she calls "practical identity." A practical identity, she writes, is a conception of oneself "under which you value yourself, a description under which you find your life to be worth living and your actions to be worth undertaking."[75] Not all of our identities are practical in this stipulated sense, because there may be some that do not contribute to making our life worth living and that are not the source of anything we regard as valuable in our lives. There may be identities that we do not embrace and that we want to be rid of. But presumably if one finds one's life to be worth living at all, then one must have some identities that are practical. Moreover, and this is the main point, identities of this sort, she claims, are normative for us. That is, they give rise to reasons and obligations: "your reasons express your identity, your nature, your obligations spring from what that identity forbids."[76]

Although, like Korsgaard, I want to draw a connection between identity and obligation, more needs to be said about when having a practical identity generates actual as opposed to merely apparent obligations. In order to establish a link between *practical identity* (a conception under which one finds one's life to be worth living) and *obligation*, it is critically important to consider the normative credentials of this conception. For one can find one's life to be worth living for all sorts of reasons, some better than others, some not good at all, and it would seem that if the practical identity in question is irrational or abhorrent[77] or permissible but trivial, it cannot generate genuine obligations, even if we feel compelled to act as this identity directs. In general, it is only insofar as, broadly speaking, a person has *good reasons* for organizing his life along certain lines that the obligations arising from a practical identity can reasonably be regarded as truly normative for him. And, to underscore the point, whether or not one has good reasons to do so is not merely a function of how much one cares about the activities that are constitutive of a particular practical identity.

One can, of course, have genuine obligations arising from a particular practical identity and not recognize that one has them. Genuine obligations can also arise from a practical identity aspects of which – as sanctioned by social custom or local convention – one rejects. The obligations that spring from an identity, moreover, are not necessarily coterminous with that identity: one can find oneself with some of the obligations that arose from one's having a particular identity even when one no longer has it. In all of these cases, identities create obligations, but the identities themselves are to a significant extent beyond our control and our capacity to shape them is limited. Neither the identities, nor the obligations that we have in virtue of them, are entirely matters of our own choosing. This would pose a serious problem for my normative claims if the following were true: the roles and relationships that help determine our identities are morally significant for us only to the extent that we choose them and decide how much significance they will have in our lives. But, as many philosophers have argued, it is a voluntaristic excess, a fantasy of unbridled autonomy, to suppose that this is so.[78]

I have been discussing the links between *personal* identity and obligation, but clearly we can't use the very same arguments to establish links between *collective* identity and obligation. (As before, I am not speaking here about group identity as a part of individual identity.) A collective is not some mysterious entity with a mind of its own that operates independently of the minds of the group's members, such that we can attribute properties to it in the same way that we can attribute them to individual persons. Nevertheless, as with personal identity, it can plausibly be maintained that collective identity would not be normative in a deep sense if there were only group rights and no group duties. Normative identity of this sort, whether personal or collective, entails commitments; identities are constituted by organizing principles in the lives of individuals as well as collectives; and these principles set limits to what is allowed, given that identity, and forbid what is inconsistent with it. We need to have a notion of collective obligation to make sense of these features of normative collective identity.

The claim I have been defending is that obligations are internally related to identities, or more accurately, those identities that give us good reasons to organize our lives by them. But specifically what these obligations might be I have not so far said. There is an obvious reason why I have not done so: the obligations that help to define these identities are enormously varied, depending on the nature of the role or relationship under consideration. The obligations that flow from a parental identity are plainly different from those that spring from a professional identity, the latter from obligations that are constituents of a national identity, and so forth. However, I want, at this point, to return to the theme of this chapter, namely, the elements of a morality or ethics of memory, and ask how identity fits into this larger project.

The moral or ethical significance of memory is related to identity in different ways. First, as noted earlier in this section, memory shapes and is shaped by identity, and identity is internally related to values as well as obligations. How and what we remember partly determine who we are, and who we are is normative for us, that is, a ground of values and obligations of various sorts. Here memory's normative significance consists in its relationship to *whatever* specific values and obligations can plausibly be construed as ingredients of a particular identity. In addition, memory is normatively significant in a negative sense because of its relationship to obligations that it may prevent agents from recognizing, specifically, because it influences their identifications in a way that precludes this recognition. Neither individuals nor collectives are infallible when it comes to determining what their identities are. Indeed, they may be mistaken in various ways, some innocent, some (the more interesting cases) not so innocent, and the mistakes might be explainable at least partly in terms of how they remember their pasts. So there may be circumstances in which we can properly say the following: x's identity as y gives rise to obligations z, but because x does not identify himself as y, x does not recognize the obligations z that flow from y.

Second, remembrance of certain events or episodes or persons is itself among the obligations that are explained as arising from an identity that is antecedently shaped in diverse ways by memory. Consider the following example. The injustices committed against Native American tribes, by settlers and the United States government during the nineteenth century, make up part of the identity of those tribes; the injustices are woven into their account of who they are as distinct peoples. If their identity gives them reasons and obligations, and a history of injustice has played a central role in the formation of that identity, then it would be an offense against that identity, and a violation of identity-based obligation, if they did not (at least) remember those injustices. Generally speaking, obligations deriving from identity include obligations to remember aspects of one's past that are or are internally related to constitutive ingredients of one's identity. A similar argument can be given for the memorial obligations of the perpetrators of these injustices and their successors. Their collective identity, properly understood, also requires them to remember the injustices that were committed. However, in the case of the perpetrators and their successors, there may be strong incentives to remember the past in such a way as to construct a collective identity that does not entail obligations of remembrance.

I want to be clear what I am *not* claiming. I am not asserting that individuals or groups of individuals have obligations with respect to the past only when what occurred in the past informs and gives shape to their identities. Further, I am not asserting that obligations of remembrance only arise in connection with features of identity: if individuals or groups have obligations that do not implicate their identity, they also have obligations to remember that they have these obligations, or the facts about their past that ground them. I am rather suggesting something about the role that identity plays in a general theory of obligation, namely, that when obligations (obligations of remembrance as well as others) are internally related to identity, they acquire a normative weight that obligations not having this feature lack. Even if an obligation does not have its source in an identity, once the obligation becomes entangled with it, it acquires this additional weight. The reason for this seems to have to do with the fact that when obligations implicate our identity they also engage our integrity, so there is much more at stake, morally speaking, in fulfilling them.

8. GOING FORWARD

I began by lamenting the relative lack of philosophical engagement with normative issues in writings on memory. Hopefully this chapter has shown that there is important work to be done in this area and has begun to make a contribution to it by exploring the connections between memory, responsibility, and identity. In the chapters that follow, I will continue my examination of these themes in relation both to personal and collective memory, moving back and forth between them.

Chapters 2 and 3 form a pair. One of them analyzes a phenomenon that I call taking responsibility for one's personal past and shows why this is a topic that warrants the attention of those who are interested in moral psychology. The other deals with taking responsibility for the past as a *collective* phenomenon and addresses a number of issues, conceptual as well as normative, specifically having to do with taking collective responsibility for past wrongdoing. Collective memory continues to be my concern in Chapter 4 where I discuss the relationship between collective memory, history and myth and the different normative bases of collective memorial obligations. Shifting gears, I then return in Chapter 5 to the personal domain and consider whether and why we have responsibilities to remember those dear to us who are dead. And finally, Chapter 6 ties together the different strands of this book, the individual and social aspects of memory, by concentrating on one type of remembrance, that of bearing witness, and reflecting on its moral significance.

NOTES

1. Milan Kundera, *Testaments Betrayed* (London: HarperCollins, 1995), p. 128.
2. See, for example, the essays on memory in *Meaning and Knowledge: Systematic Readings in Epistemology*, Ernest Nagel and Richard Brandt (Eds.). (New York: Harcourt, Brace and World, 1965); D. W. Hamlyn, *The Theory of Knowledge* (Garden City, NY: Anchor Books, 1970); Norman Malcolm, *Knowledge and Certainty* (Ithaca: Cornell University Press, 1963).
3. Philosophers sometimes distinguish between morality and ethics, but it is unnecessary to elaborate on this here. I will have more to say about the distinction in Chapter 4.
4. We may distinguish between these two assertions:

    (a) X (an individual or group) has a memory of Y (a dispositional notion); and

    (b) X (an individual or group) remembers Y (an occurrent notion).

As Iwona Irwin-Zarecka puts it, "when our sense of the past becomes "activated," memory becomes remembrance." See Iwona Irwin-Zarecka, *Frames of Remembrance: The Dynamics of Collective Memory* (New Brunswick, NJ: Transaction Publishers, 1994), p. 14.

5. F. Nietzsche, *Untimely Meditations*, D. Breazeale (Ed.), R. J. Hollingdale (Trans.). (Cambridge, UK: University Press, 1997). Page numbers in parentheses refer to this edition. Originally published in 1874.

6. There is an interesting question here as to whether Nietzsche thought that one has control over what one forgets and remembers and that this powerful instinct can be deliberately cultivated. If we do not have control over it, this raises the problem of whether and how one can hold people (individuals and groups) responsible when they fail to forget or when they fail to remember when they should. In an important passage about forgetting from *On the Genealogy of Morality*, Nietzsche says that among the characteristics of a "noble human being" is his inability.

for any length of time to take his enemies, his accidents, his *misdeeds* themselves seriously – that is the sign of strong, full natures in which there is an excess of formative, reconstructive, healing power that also makes one forget (a good example of this from the modern world is Mirabeau, who had no memory for insults and base deeds committed against him and who was only unable to forgive because he – forgot). Such a human being is simply able to shake off with a single shrug a collection of worms that in others would dig itself in. (Maudemarie Clark and Alan J. Swensen (Trans.). (Indianapolis: Hackett Publishing Company, 1998), p. 21).

Among the nonmoral virtues of ancient nobles is a certain sort of self-sufficiency that enables them to shrug off the "insults and base deeds" that have been directed against them. They simply do not experience the insults and base deeds as injuries. But this is not the same as forgiveness. The noble human being does not forgive and is in fact incapable of true forgiveness, for forgiveness occurs in the face of the judgment that what was done against oneself was wrong or bad, and this is only possible if the misdeed is not forgotten but is remembered as a misdeed. Being self-sufficient and possessing "an excess of healing power," however, the noble person is not injured by what his enemies do to him and so he has no reason to hold on to it in memory. He is, as we might say, beyond forgiving and remembering. It is the weak person, the "slave," who remembers the insults and wrongs committed against him and who proclaims that there is an imperative to remember because he needs to define himself against "an opposite and external world" (p. 19). Nowhere in these remarks, however, does Nietzsche suggest that one has control over what one forgets and remembers. I thank Maude Clark for pointing this out to me.

I note, as well, that Nietzsche's account of "slave" morality and its relationship to memory gives us an explanation of what troubles Nietzsche about memory. The "slave" has an investment in preserving the memory of past injustice and oppression and in seeing himself as the victim of them. By creating an identity for himself as victim, the slave does not free himself from the past but chains himself to it and reproduces and perpetuates it.

7. See Linda Bishai, "Forgetting Ourselves: Nietzsche, Critical History and the Politics of Collective Memory," *Political Studies Association – UK 50th Annual Conference*, 10–13 April 2000, London. Available at http://www.psa.ac.uk/cps/2000/Bishai%20Linda.pdf.

8. Karl Jaspers, *Nietzsche: An Introduction to the Understanding of his Philosophical Activity*, Charles F. Wallraff and Frederick J. Schmitz (Trans.). (Baltimore: Johns Hopkins University Press, 1997), p. 236.

9. The term does not occur in Nietzsche's discussion of antiquarian history.

10. A. Margalit, *The Ethics of Memory* (Cambridge, MA: Harvard University Press, 2002), p. 62.

11. Gayle Greene. "Feminist Fiction and the Uses of Memory." *Signs: Journal of Women in Culture and Society 16*,2 (winter 1991): 290–321, at 297–298.

12. See F. Davis, *Yearning for Yesterday: A Sociology of Nostalgia* (New York: Free Press, 1979).

13. See Andreea Deciu Ritivoi, *Yesterday's Self: Nostalgia and the Immigrant Identity* (Lanham, MD: Rowman and Littlefield, 2002); Constantine Sedikides, Tim Wildschut, and Denise Baden, "Nostalgia: Conceptual Issues and Existential Functions," in Jeff Greenberg (Ed.), *Handbook of Experimental Existential Psychology* (New York: Guilford Publications, 2004), pp. 200–214; Janelle Wilson, "'Remember when. . . .' A Consideration of the Concept of Nostalgia," *ETC: A Review of General Semantics 56*, 3 (September 22, 1999): 296–304.

14. See Sedikides et al., pp. 208ff.

15. Ritivoi, op. cit., p. 165.

16. Sedikides, op. cit., pp. 206–207; Ritivoi, op. cit., especially chapter 1.

17. For more on myth and its relationship to history, see Chapter 4, "Ethics, Truth, and Collective Memory."

18. Maudemarie Clark helpfully distinguishes between a wider and a narrower sense of "morality" in Nietzsche, which corresponds to Bernard Williams' distinction between "ethics" and "morality." I am here using the term "moral" in the narrow sense. See Clark's introduction to *On the Genealogy of Morality*, op. cit., note 6.

19. Available at http://www.bridgewater.edu/~atrupe/GEC101/Funes.html.

20. See Robin Marantz Henig, "The Quest to Forget," *New York Times Magazine*, (April 4, 2004), pp. 32–37. Psychologists and psychiatrists toward the end of the nineteenth century coined the term "hypermnesia" to refer to a mental disorder in which the individual is burdened and confused by too many memories. See, for example, Albert Guillon, *Les maladies de la memoire: Essai sur les hypermnesies* (Paris: Libraire J.-B. Bailliere and Fils, 1897). The diagnosis would certainly apply to Ireneo Funes.

21. C. S. Maier, "A Surfeit of Memory," *History and Memory: Studies in the Representation of the Past 5*, 2 (1993); also Omar Bartov, "Intellectuals on Auschwitz: Memory, History, and Truth," in M. L. Morgan (Ed.), *A Holocaust Reader: Responses to the Nazi Extermination* (New York: Oxford University Press, 2001), pp. 290–321.

22. For more on this, see Eva Hoffman, "The Uses of Hell," *New York Review of Books*, XLVII, 4, (March 9, 2000), 19–23.

23. Maier, op. cit., p. 150.

24. F. R. Ankersmit, *Historical Representation* (Palo Alto, CA: Stanford University Press, 2001), p. 174.

25. D. Lowenthal, *The Past is a Foreign Country* (Cambridge, UK: Cambridge University Press, 1985), p. 195.

26. C. S. Maier, *The Unmasterable Past: History, Holocaust, and German National Identity* (Cambridge, MA: Harvard University Press, 1997), p. 15.

27. Quoted in C. S. Maier, p. 15.

28. Ibid., pp. 91–99.

29. Ibid.

30. Ibid., p. 15.

31. Of course, preserving a sense of responsibility for past wrongdoing is not the only communal function of public memorial activity. It is simply the one I focus on here. For more, see Chapter 4, especially Section 7.

32. M. Gallanter, "Righting Old Wrongs," in M. Minow (Ed.), *Breaking The Cycles of Hatred: Memory, Law, and Repair* (Princeton: University Press, 2002), pp. 107–131, at 122.

33. See Priscilla Hayner, *Unspeakable Truths: Facing the Challenge of Truth Commissions* (New York: Routledge, 2002).

34. N. Rosenblum, "Memory, Law, and Repair," in M. Minow (Ed.), *Breaking the Cycles of Hatred*, p. 5.

35. There is some advantage to putting it the second way. When we say, for example, "It's time for you to forget the past," we frequently mean "You should stop dwelling on the past." Or consider the following expression of outrage: "Have you forgotten where you come from"? The one addressed here is being accused of betraying his values or his upbringing or his class, of not caring any more about these things as he should, not merely of failing to have certain thoughts. Perhaps we can say that there are thicker and thinner (purely cognitive) senses of remembering and forgetting.

36. M. Minow, "Breaking the Cycles of Hatred," in M. Minow (Ed.), *Breaking the Cycles of Hatred*, p. 19. See also M. Minow, *Between Vengeance and Forgiveness* (Boston: Beacon Press, 1998).

37. Ibid., "Breaking the Cycles of Hatred," p. 22.

38. See Gary J. Bass, "Jus Post Bellum," *Philosophy and Public Affairs* 32, 4 (2004):386–412.

39. See David A. Crocker, "Truth Commissions, Transitional Justice, and Civil Society," in R. I. Rotberg and D. Thompson (Eds.), *Truth v. Justice* (Princeton: Princeton University Press, 2000), pp. 99–121.

40. C. S. Lewis, *A Grief Observed* (New York: Harper, 1996), p. 53.

41. N. Care, *Living with One's Past* (Lanham, MD: Rowman and Littlefield, 1996), p. 81.

42. Ibid., p. 127. Care is chiefly interested in the problem of going-on after damaging what he calls "the moral personality" (pp. 10–11) of another. I am construing the problem more broadly than this.

43. Joan Didion, *The Year of Magical Thinking* (New York: Alfred A. Knopf, 2005).

44. Care, op. cit., p. 131; also N. Care, "Forgiveness and Effective Agency," in S. Lamb and J. Murphy (Eds.), *Before Forgiving* (Oxford: University Press, 2002), pp. 215–231.
45. Public commemoration of 9/11 offers an excellent example of the political uses (and misuses) of remembrance. David Simpson, in *9/11: The Culture of Commemoration* (Chicago: University of Chicago Press, 2006) argues that commemoration of 9/11 has been manipulated by government – with the assistance of the media to some extent – to promote a hyper-patriotic and militaristic agenda.
46. A. Margalit and G. Motzkin, "The Uniqueness of the Holocaust," *Philosophy and Public Affairs* 25 (1996): 65–83, at 83.
47. We should add here that the collapse of the Soviet Union was another historical factor that propelled memory into the public arena: it liberated memory and unleashed struggles in Central and Eastern European countries over how to remember the past. See Tony Judt, "From the House of the Dead: On Modern European Memory," *New York Review of Books* 52 (October 6, 2005): 12–16 for an excellent discussion.
48. Op. cit., pp. 81–82.
49. G. M. Spiegel, "Memory and History: Liturgical Time and Historical Time," *History and Theory* 41 (2002): 149–162, at 150.
50. Quoted in Jay Winter, "The Generation of Memory: Reflections on the "Memory Boom" in Contemporary Historical Studies," *German Historical Bulletin* 31 (2002). Available at http://www.ghi-dc.org/bulletin27Foo/b27winterframe.html.
51. Ibid.
52. Again, the distinction between moral and ethical imperatives is not important for my purposes in this chapter, but it plays a role in Chapter 4.
53. Joel Feinberg, "Supererogation and Rules," in Judith J. Thomson and Gerald Dworkin (Eds.), *Ethics* (New York: Harper and Row, 1968), pp. 391–411, at 393, 394.
54. Avishai Margalit, *The Ethics of Memory*, p. 56.
55. M. Miscione, "The Forgotten," *New York Times*, December 23, 2001.
56. W. James Booth, *Communities of Memory: On Witness, Identity, and Justice* (Ithaca: Cornell University Press, 2006), p. x. See also Maurice Halbwachs's discussion of "social frameworks for memory," in *On Collective Memory*, Lewis A. Coser (Ed. and Trans.). (Chicago and London: Chicago University Press, 1992), 38, 52–53, 171–173.
57. Elizabeth Anderson, *Value in Ethics and Economics* (Cambridge, MA: Harvard University Press, 1993).
58. Expressive value is a type of nonteleological value. That is, taking acts of remembrance to be good or have value because of what they express, is not a matter of thinking that acts of remembrance ought to be promoted. On teleological and nonteleological conceptions of value, see T. M. Scanlon, *What We Owe to Each Other* (Cambridge, MA: Harvard University Press, 1998), chapter 2.

59. S. Hampshire, *Innocence and Experience* (Cambridge, MA: Harvard University Press, 1989), p. 147.
60. This last point raises issues that require further discussion. For example, suppose, as seems plausible, that duties to remember deceased friends are grounded in the former friendship. If this is the case, and, moreover, we do not have an obligation to remain friends with someone regardless of changes in our feelings for him, why should we have an obligation to remember him long after his death? I say more about this in Chapter 5, Sections 1 and 8.
61. See Jonathan A. Jacobs, *Virtue and Self-Knowledge* (Englewood Cliffs, NJ: Prentice-Hall, 1989), especially chapter 2, "Unity and Historical Self-Conceptions."
62. See Sue Campbell, *Relational Remembering: Rethinking the Memory Wars* (Lanham, MD: Rowman and Littlefield, 2003), p. 186.
63. Thus, according to Derek Parfit,

    besides direct memories, there are several other kinds of direct psychological connection. One such connection is that which holds between an intention and the later act in which it is carried out. Other such direct connections are those which hold when a belief, or a desire, or any other psychological feature, continues to be had. (*Reasons and Persons* (Oxford: Clarendon Press, 1984), p. 206)

64. Marya Schechtman, "Personality and Persistence: The Many Faces of Personal Survival," *American Philosophical Quarterly 41*, 2 (April 2004): 87–105, at 89.
65. This is the view, for example, of W. James Booth, op. cit., pp. 1–16. Against the mainstream, Marya Schechtman has argued that the question of identity that is relevant to assignments of moral responsibility is not answered by an account of personal identity over time. See *The Constitution of Selves* (Ithaca, NY: Cornell University Press, 1996).
66. Joseph Raz, *Value, Respect and Attachment* (Cambridge, UK: Cambridge University Press, 2001), p. 33.
67. I do not mean that *any* answer to the question "Who am I?" will count as giving part of my identity, only that the problem of defining identity of a certain sort is typically posed in this way.
68. Memory is certainly bound up with a person's or group's persistence, as Schechtman acknowledges in the quote, Note 64. But again my interest in the relationship between memory and identity is memory's relationship to biographical, not diachronic, identity. Booth's discussion of memory straddles both notions of identity. See Booth, Note 56.
69. Jefferson Singer and Peter Salovey, *The Remembered Self* (New York: Free Press, 1993).
70. This distinction is drawn by Nenad Miscevic in "Is National Identity Essential for Personal Identity?" in N. Miscevic (Ed.), *Nationalism and Ethnic Conflict* (Chicago, Open Court, 2000), pp. 239–257, at 242–243.
71. Charles Maier, *The Unmasterable Past*, op. cit., 149–150.
72. Ibid., p. 150.
73. See the discussion in Kwame Anthony Appiah, *The Ethics of Identity* (Princeton: Princeton University Press, 2005), pp. 24–26.

74.   Raz, op. cit., note 58, p. 22.
75.   Christine Korsgaard, *The Sources of Normativity* (Cambridge, UK: University Press, 1996), p. 101.
76.   Ibid.
77.   See the discussion of irrational and abhorrent identities in Appiah, op. cit., pp. 181–192.
78.   See, for example, Samuel Scheffler, "Relationships and Responsibilities," *Philosophy and Public Affairs 26*, 3 (Summer 1997): 189–209; and Ross Poole, *Nation and Identity* (London: Routledge, 1999), pp. 70–73, 138–140.

2

TAKING RESPONSIBILITY FOR ONE'S OWN PAST

In a 1988 interview in The Times, he looked back on some of his early music and offered a simple assessment. "No, I am not like Samuel Beckett, who says, 'Oh my God, I was such an idiot in that period, and I wrote such nonsense at the other time.' I always hear what I have written as a part of myself given sincerely, and it remains a part of me because it is a place where I have lived."

– Obituary for Olivier Messiaen, *New York Times*, April 29, 1992

1. A CASE EXAMPLE

Felicia, the heroine of William Trevor's novel *Felicia's Journey*,[1] is an inexperienced young girl who lives a sheltered life with her family in a small Irish town. There she falls in love with young Johnny Lysaght and becomes pregnant by him. Naively convinced of Johnny's good intentions despite his sudden departure for England, Felicia steals away from home and drifts, penniless, through the industrial English Midlands in search of the boyfriend she hopes to marry. She persists in her search, despite repeated indications of Johnny's faithlessness, indications that she did not but should have taken to heart. Along the way she meets up with the fat, fiftyish, unfailingly reasonable Mr. Hilditch who offers to assist her in her quest for Johnny. He assumes the role of a father figure and even manages to convince Felicia that it would be best for her if she had an abortion. But Hilditch's intentions are far from benevolent. He wants Felicia to be his "friend," as he did five other girls before her, and when, inevitably, she disappoints him, he attempts to kill her. Felicia manages to escape and Hilditch, fearing exposure, commits suicide. Wracked by guilt over her abortion, bereft of any hope of ever finding Johnny, and too ashamed to return to her family and community, she becomes a homeless street person.

So much for the bare outline of the plot. What interests me in Felicia's story is how it ends up, the significance that, in hindsight, she attaches to her past behavior and how she comes to terms with it. Her journey from Ireland to England and from one depressing town in England to another, we are made to understand, is mirrored by a journey of self-transformation. Looking back on all she has lost and been through since leaving Ireland, "she knows she is not as she was; she is not the bridesmaid at the autumn wedding, not the girl who covered herself with a rug in the back of the car." At the same time, the past is very much with her: "The innocence that once was hers is now, with time, a foolishness, yet is not disowned, and that same lost person is valued for leading her to where she is" (p. 207). She does not "disown" her earlier innocence – her own past self – even though she has endured too many misfortunes to consider it now as anything other than folly. She recognizes the continuity between the person she once was and the person she now is, and she values the former, not necessarily in itself, but for having led to her current state, itself valuable because of the greater self-understanding it involves. Despite the shabby circumstances of her street life, Felicia "accepts without bewilderment the serenity that possesses her, and celebrates its fresh new presence" (Ibid.). She manages to triumph over adversity by constructing a narrative of her life in which present is linked to and explained by a past she neither applauds nor denies. She does not deny that she played an active part in bringing herself to this abject condition nor does she make excuses for herself. She takes up this part of her past and acknowledges it as her own, and her acknowledging it as her own uplifts her.

This is a rather remarkable end to a sordid story. How are we to explain the fact that Felicia's acknowledgment both calms and invigorates her? Her psychological state at the end of the novel can plausibly be explained, I propose, in terms of what psychoanalyst Roy Schafer calls "an enhanced sense of responsibility." What she has managed to achieve on her own is what Schafer claims the clinical psychoanalytic process attempts to effect:

> During analysis, one realizes that one has been playing an active role in bringing about apparently passive suffering. One recognizes one's unconscious sabotage of love and work. . . . This increased realization

of having participated decisively in one's fate, even if not from its very influential beginning stages, necessarily brings with it an intensified and genuine sense of choice and responsibility. Contrary to popular distortion, which is a kind of extra-analytic resistance, the deterministic probings of effective analysis ultimately enhance rather than eliminate the analysand's sense of self-rule and the capacity to have a rationale for self-rule.... The analytically enhanced sense of responsibility and choice is an alternative to neurotic guilt, masochism, dread, and compliance.[2]

Similarly, Felicia's not disowning her former innocence may signal her realization of having participated decisively in her fate; a realization that brings with it an intensified sense of responsibility, both for the life of foolish innocence she led and for the life she will lead from this time forward. On this interpretation, Felicia's psychological state is not adequately characterized merely as feeling better about herself or not being angry at herself for contributing to her current predicament. These may be true of her, but they are the consequences of a deeper insight. Terms such as "self-understanding" or "self-awareness" by themselves also fail to satisfactorily explain her condition. Self-acceptance comes closer to describing her state, and perhaps is ingredient in it, but even this is not quite right. For we can also speak of self-acceptance in very different circumstances from the ones in Felicia's case: for example, the person with a major disability or deformity who is able to accept herself as she is, despite the unwelcoming attitudes of others. Felicia does not just accept herself, then. Rather, she understands herself as an active participant in her fate, not as a passive sufferer of it, and this hard-won understanding signifies that she takes or is willing to take responsibility for her fate.

Thus interpreted, the relationship that Felicia forges with her past illustrates what I call "taking responsibility for one's past." It has the sense that one does not hide from one's own agency but acknowledges that one has "participated decisively in one's fate, even if not from its very influential beginning stages," as Schafer puts it; and it conveys further that one makes sense of the past by fitting it into a narrative structure that links it to the present and perhaps the future as well. I certainly don't want to claim that a phenomenon described as "taking responsibility for one's past" couldn't also be illustrated by very different sorts of examples. Indeed, there doesn't seem to be sufficiently widespread agreement on what we mean when we say someone is (or is not) taking responsibility for his past to warrant making this claim. Nevertheless, the account I give characterizes fairly common kinds of cases that are aptly and frequently described in this way. Moreover, there are good reasons for selecting these cases for special attention, as I hope to show later in this chapter. For one thing, a focus on these cases casts light on deeply important aspects of human agency, in particular, on our ability not just to reconcile or resign ourselves to our past but to take ownership of and thereby transform it. For another, it enables us to draw some interesting connections between taking responsibility for one's past and other psychological phenomena explored by moral psychology.

As in Felicia's story, the cases for which my account is designed all involve the *personal past*, that is, the past that consists of elements of one's life history and that one has access to through personal memories. Examples of personal memories include the following: I was very close to my older brother when I was an adolescent; I often behaved in a very immature way when I was around my parents; there was a time when I could have cared less about other people's opinions; I had enormous potential when I was younger; I have been a life-long committed socialist; and for years I loved her without telling her. Because the personal past includes individual acts as well as aspects of personality and character, taking responsibility for one's past, as I conceive it here, encompasses both: taking responsibility for acts and relatively long-term stretches of one's past that are given shape by patterns of choice and action. These patterns can be construed as embodiments of habits and dispositions that generate and are reinforced by individual choices and actions. In this perspective, choices and actions merit attention to the extent that they are more or less characteristic of a period of one's past, or of the sort of person one was in the past, and in what follows, taking responsibility for one's past, insofar as it involves taking responsibility for past acts (or omissions), centrally refers to particular incidents in one's past that fit into these larger patterns.[3] These are also aspects or contents of our personal past that we do or should care about or that figure significantly in our self-descriptions and self-understandings, and I restrict myself to these.

The organization of this chapter is as follows. Section 2 starts off with some preliminary remarks relating taking responsibility for one's past to other familiar senses of taking responsibility. My account of taking responsibility for one's past is presented in Section 3 and involves three interrelated ideas: (1) retrospective construction of meaning, (2) appropriation, and (3) thematization. (These processes are engaged both when an individual takes responsibility for his or her personal past and when a group of people collectively takes responsibility for its past, but I reserve discussion of the latter for Chapter 3.) Appropriation is an active process in which an individual (or group) lays claim to the past, includes it within the ambit of his (or its) agency, and thereby brings about a sort of transformation of the past, a transformation with respect to significance. Section 4 compares psychopharmacologic with psychotherapeutic treatment of psychological problems and disorders in order to further clarify and illustrate the account. Having clarified what I mean by taking responsibility for one's past, I end this part of the chapter (Section 5) by asking why it is that people so often fail to do this, or explicitly disavow such responsibility, even when there are good reasons for them to take responsibility. Social and cultural factors may explain some of this but of more interest to me are the various psychological factors at work here.

In the normative portion of this chapter, I explore the complex relationships between taking responsibility for one's past and the virtues of humility and self-forgiveness. Humility, as I understand it in Section 6, is needed to have an accurate understanding of who one is and why one is who one is, including the role of one's past and the limits of one's agency in determining the content and shaping the contours of one's life. This I connect with taking responsibility for one's past because one cannot do this if one has an exaggerated sense of the potency of one's agency or one's ability to disencumber oneself of the legacy of one's history. Section 7 addresses the connection between taking responsibility for one's past and self-forgiveness. I argue that in order to take responsibility for one's past, one must be able to assimilate it successfully, and that the capacity for self-forgiveness is important in this regard because it permits one to face the past honestly and nonevasively, without being overwhelmed by feelings of self-reproach. Finally, Section 8 makes a few brief remarks about the role of memory in my account.

The concerns of this chapter may not resonate with everyone. For the kind of person that Galen Strawson calls "Episodic," how one is to understand the relationship between one's past and present in narrative terms, or what attention one should pay the past precisely because it is one's past, will *not* be matters of vital personal interest. Strawson describes

the mind-set of the Episodic person (which is how he categorizes himself)
in the following way:

> ...what I care about, in so far as I care about myself and my life, is how
> I am now. The way I am now is profoundly shaped by my past, but it is
> only the present shaping consequences of the past that matter, not the
> past as such.[4]

The sort of person I am interested in, by contrast, is someone for whom
the past matters as past, or who can be persuaded to believe that he or she
should care about this, and who does not only care about how he or she
is now – characteristics of what Strawson calls "the Diachronic person."
Unlike Strawson, I consider myself a Diachronic to this extent and, I
suspect, so do many others.

2. SOME PRELIMINARIES ABOUT TAKING RESPONSIBILITY

If one is to take responsibility for one's past, there are many things that
one must *not* do with respect to it: one must not ignore it, or repress it, or
falsify it, or self-deceptively deny it, or engage in dissociation. However,
for various reasons the past may be distressing to an individual – something about which I will say much more later – and as a result, he may
fail to take responsibility for it. Even if he does not deny outright his responsibility, his failure to take responsibility might be manifested, for
example, in turning his attention away from it and focusing, instead, on
more agreeable portions of his life, or in neurotic acting out of some
repressed past episode. And although the past might not be particularly
painful to contemplate, an individual might simply let it slip away,
preferring instead to concentrate on the present and future. The signs
and modes of failing to take responsibility for one's past are varied and
numerous, as are its possible explanations.

Taking responsibility for one's past, on the other hand, *is* compatible
with repudiating it. That is, there is a sense of "repudiation" according
to which one can repudiate one's past, or some portion of it, and still
take responsibility for it. The case of George Wallace can serve as an
illustration, although admittedly not an uncontroversial one. Wallace, a
staunch proponent of racial segregation through all of his public life as
governor of Alabama and presidential aspirant, professed in the twilight

of his career, after an assassination attempt that left him permanently paralyzed, to a conversion of sorts. Appearing before a conference of three hundred black ministers and lay leaders of Alabama churches in late 1978, he told the gathering:

> I never had hate in my heart for any person. But I regret my support of segregation and the pain it caused the black people of our state and nation... I've learned what pain is and I'm sorry if I've caused anybody else pain. Segregation was wrong – and I am sorry.[5]

On several other occasions in subsequent years, Wallace apologized for his past treatment of blacks and asked for their forgiveness, and he took steps to increase black participation in the political life of his state. One can certainly question the sincerity of Wallace's professed change, and many have done so. But one biographer speculates that, to some extent at least, Wallace's repudiation of his racist past reflected a genuine change of heart, a change of heart that can be explained by or is shown by his taking responsibility for a pattern of conduct as governor that he now recognizes was morally wrong.[6]

One might also have nonmoral reasons for repudiating one's past, that is, reasons having to do with personal defects and inadequacies that don't have much to do with morality narrowly conceived but that bear on how well one has lived. Whatever the grounds, repudiation of the past, as a judgment about the content of the past, is distinct from and possible without repudiation of responsibility for it, which is a judgment about one's relationship to the past. Indeed, repudiation of the past is not only compatible with taking responsibility for it, but may be a constitutive ingredient or a consequence of it in some circumstances.

The focus of this chapter is taking responsibility for one's past: why we don't do it, what it means to do it, and why we should do it. Because the issue of taking responsibility usually arises when the conditions for attributing responsibility have been met, there is considerable overlap between the active *taking* of responsibility and the state of *being* responsible. However, taking responsibility for *x* does not presuppose being responsible for *x*, in the sense of being "open to creditworthiness or blameworthiness for it,"[7] so there is no conceptual bar to taking responsibility for something that one is not responsible for. What's more, we can imagine situations in which, for example, one takes responsibility for something that another person is responsible for in order to prevent a greater wrong, and this may be, if not morally obligatory, at least morally praiseworthy.[8] It is also possible to become responsible as a consequence of taking responsibility. Conversely, one can decline to take responsibility for something that one is or is not responsible for. Normally a person should take, or at least be willing to take, responsibility for what she is responsible for, and should not evade doing so, because taking responsibility is the usual way of showing that one has recognized one's responsibility.

When a person takes responsibility for something in or about his past, it is for actions, episodes, or personal characteristics that somehow implicate his agency, and as one who takes responsibility for his past, he will acknowledge this fact. Personal characteristics include dispositions of character, attitudes, and emotions, and agency's implication in them can be explained in different ways. Prominent among these are what can be called volitional explanations. The characteristics might have developed as a result of a person's prior choices and decisions; or a person might have chosen to endorse or identify with the characteristics, however they came about; or a person might have had the ability to revise or eliminate them through her subsequent choices.[9] In each of these explanations, agency is connected in some way with choice or decision, and, because of this, the person can be said to actively participate in the occurrence of these characteristics. However, as I will discuss in Section 3, these familiar volitional explanations do not exhaust the ways in which one's agency may be implicated when one takes responsibility for something in one's past, so the account of taking responsibility for one's past should not rely on them alone.

There are other characteristics that taking responsibility for one's past has as an instance of taking responsibility more generally. *Taking* responsibility, unlike *accepting* responsibility, connotes an action that is not undertaken grudgingly or merely in response to pressure or threats from others or strictly according to some script that specifies what one is to do in situations like this. Rather, it suggests a willingness to take the initiative in pursuing courses of action that meet current and future needs, and, perhaps, also an openness to experimenting with different ways of meeting one's responsibilities.

Taking responsibility for something also has both forward- and backward-looking dimensions.[10] As a forward-looking task, it involves two stages: a voluntary undertaking and a commitment to follow through, and it entails a readiness to answer for or give an accounting of our failures to do so. Depending on the circumstances, the judgment that someone has taken responsibility for *x* can be withdrawn if she does not follow through on her responsibility. Moreover, one can take responsibility in this forward-looking sense with respect to responsibilities that cannot be assimilated straightforwardly to those that arise from promises and contracts, as is the case with many of our responsibilities. Sometimes we find ourselves with responsibilities to others because of what we did in the past, even though the responsibilities do not precisely align with our conscious or deliberate choices or undertakings, or because we stand in relations to other people whose moral import does not derive solely from our own decisions. We can subsequently choose, however, to accept our responsibilities or not, and can follow through on them or not. Insofar as we do so, we can be said to take responsibility for carrying out these responsibilities.

The forward-looking element of taking responsibility is evident in the case of prior wrongdoing. When someone says that he takes responsibility for having acted wrongly or for not having done something he should have done, we are entitled to take him to mean that he holds himself at fault for having done or not done this or takes the blame for it. We expect that he will not try to manufacture excuses and will not seek to avoid appropriate punishment. If past wrongdoing is attributed to character weaknesses or bad habits, he will take steps to mend his ways and to minimize the likelihood of repetition.[11] Additionally, if he takes responsibility for having done something praiseworthy, that is, takes credit for it, this too will have implications for how he conducts himself with respect to it after the fact.

Taking responsibility for one's past, however, is not merely a matter, even in these cases, of taking responsibility for particular past actions (or omissions). It certainly includes this, but it includes more as well. For in the sense in which I speak of taking responsibility for one's past, the past refers not only to what one has done in the past, but also, as we might put it, to what one has *shown oneself to be like* by what one has done (which I distinguish from the trivial point that one shows oneself to be an agent by acting). A person might accept blame or take credit for her past actions but fail to recognize that they help to define significant portions of her life or form patterns of conduct that point to relatively enduring personal characteristics. Taking responsibility for one's past would, in such a case, involve not only her undertaking to put things right, insofar as this is within her power, but also her making efforts to change herself and how she leads her life, and she will commit herself to following through on this undertaking. Here, incidentally, is another reason why taking responsibility for one's past, as I noted earlier, does not just consist in self-acceptance, that is, the absence of certain negative attitudes toward oneself and the affirmation of one's value as a human being: taking responsibility for one's problematic past has rectificatory and possibly reformative implications, and these are not implications of self-acceptance.

3. THREE ELEMENTS OF TAKING RESPONSIBILITY FOR THE PAST

These preliminary comments have described some general features of taking responsibility for one's past and have given a rough idea of the sort of phenomenon I am concerned with. It is now time to more thoroughly and systematically discuss its defining features.

(a) *Retrospective construction of meaning*

There is a sense in which our past is altered by our taking responsibility for it. I do not mean that it is literally changed, in other words, that once a thing has happened, we can make it not to have happened. This is the notion of backwards causality, and it is something like a logical and not just an empirical truth that any cause later than event E cannot bring E about. As Samuel Gorovitz puts it, to deny this is "to generate absurdities."[12] Unlike the future, which is to some extent fluid and is what it is because of our intentions, the way we understand causality compels us to think of the past as fixed and immune to the causal efficacy of our present intentions.

On the other hand, as Arthur Danto argues,

> there is a sense in which we may speak of the Past as changing; that sense in which an event at t-1 acquires new properties not because we (or anything) causally operate on that event, nor because something goes on happening at t-1 after t-1 ceases, but because the event at t-1 comes to stand in different relationships to events that occur later. But this in effect means that the *description* of E-at-t-1 may become richer over time without the event itself exhibiting any sort of instability.[13]

Historians modify descriptions of earlier events in this way all the time, using what Danto calls "narrative sentences." (Indeed, history cannot be written any other way.) My claim about how taking responsibility for one's past changes it makes essentially the same point and is no more mysterious: what one does *now* can make it the case that the past has a meaning or significance it would not have had if one had now acted differently. This meaning is neither fixed in the past, any more than the significance of historical events is fixed and unaffected by subsequent developments, nor is it necessarily settled once and for all by actions taken at a particular time later in one's life. Indeed, it may be altered and made more or less determinate as one goes along in response to the evolving conditions and circumstances of one's life. This is not backward causality but what I call the *retrospective construction of meaning*, and it is this sort of retroactive alteration of the past, constructing a new meaning for it through one's present choices and actions, that is involved in taking responsibility for one's past.

Altering the meaning of the past works through memory, but not by tacking on, as it were, a new significance to a past event or action that is remembered in more or less the same way as before, similar to how we might put a different caption under the same photo. Indeed, to think this way, as Daniel Schacter writes, is to subscribe to "the longstanding myth" that "memories are passive or literal recordings of reality."[14] In contrast to this naive account, the current scientific consensus claims that memory is, at least to a significant degree, a (re)constructive not a reproductive activity, and that the content of what we remember is inevitably affected by the current state of our knowledge as well as by our present concerns, needs, and goals. Individuals are motivated to prefer certain accounts of their past to others; they interpret past episodes and events in ways that satisfy personal needs and enable them to advance current agendas, and this is how they remember them.[15] They may construct a particular meaning for their past to minimize responsibility for past failures, to project their preferred images of themselves to others, to better understand themselves and anticipate future prospects, and so forth. In this sense, and in these various ways, the past is constituted by the present.[16] The psychologist George Herbert Mead puts the point nicely: "We speak of the past as final and irrevocable. There is nothing that is less so . . . the past (or some meaningful structure of the past) is as hypothetical as the future."[17]

If the content of one's memories is inevitably shaped by a variety of personal factors, this immediately raises questions about what accuracy in memory can mean under these conditions and about the standards by which the accuracy or truthfulness of these memories can be evaluated.[18] On what basis can we distinguish between memories that are distortions or falsifications of one's past and those that are not? This is a general question about truth in memory, but I am considering it now specifically in relation to the retroactive construction of meaning and taking responsibility for one's past. My contention is that although the past can have multiple meanings, depending on the standpoint from which it is remembered, this does not rule out some accounts being true to the past and some not. The naive conception of memory does rule out some influences on memory as incompatible with its accuracy, but it is too restrictive to allow much of what we would count as faithful memory.

An important check on the accuracy of the narratives by which individuals retroactively impart significance to their past is the extent of agreement between how the past is remembered by them and the perceptions and responses of others. This intersubjective check is both relevant and useful because an individual's history does not reside solely in the memory of that person: it also resides in the memories of those with whom he or she has come into contact and is in this sense a public construction. We can test the reliability of our version of our past by trying it out, as it were, on different audiences and comparing their responses to what we are saying about our lives with our own version. This kind of testing goes on in many social situations and in a more deliberate and focused way in some forms of psychotherapy.

As these remarks suggest, taking responsibility for one's past is not something one does or properly does in isolation from others. There are actually a number of reasons why this is so. In addition to the fact that feedback from others is an especially important vehicle for assessing the fidelity to truth of one's retrospective construction of meaning, people are often motivated to take responsibility for their past because others whose opinions matter to them *hold* them responsible. At a deeper level, we are only able to remember our own past, and hence to take responsibility for it, by placing our experience in the framework of collective memory: the collective memory of our family as well as that of larger communities and society. Although responsibility for self is fundamentally first-personal in that no one else is responsible for my life as I am, taking responsibility for one's past is subject to intersubjective criteria of accuracy, responsive to social expectations, and dependent for its very possibility on the existence of what Halbwachs calls "social frameworks for memory."[19]

(b) *Appropriation*

Taking responsibility for one's past confers a certain significance on one's past that it does not have when one does not do so. Retrospective construction of meaning is, therefore, one element in the account of taking responsibility for one's past. However, refusing to accept personal responsibility for some aspect of one's past is no less a way of constructing a particular meaning for it after-the-fact than taking responsibility for it. Obviously, we need more for an adequate account of the phenomenon in question.

Taking responsibility for one's past, I propose, centrally involves this as well: looking back and over how one has lived one's life not merely from a standpoint of disinterested curiosity but with a view to actively taking up the past and annexing it to and integrating it with the present. That is, taking responsibility for one's past is an activity that connects and binds us to ourselves through time. One makes past acts or portions of one's past one's own by *appropriating* them, by enlarging the field of one's agency to include them and laying claim to them.[20]

There may be parts of one's past life or past deeds that are a matter of embarrassment or regret, that one regards as unworthy of the person one now takes oneself to be, or that for other reasons one disapproves of.

Values once held, ideals once aspired to, projects and goals once pursued, relationships once formed and sustained, may now seem to be shallow, demeaning, self-destructive, unreasonable, or unsustainable for some other reason, and one may be right to condemn them in these ways. (Indeed, openness to this sort of self-criticism should be encouraged as essential to moral and personal growth.) But disowning in the sense of *not appropriating* something in one's past is not the same as disowning in the sense of *repudiating*, for as the George Wallace example in the previous section was meant to suggest, one can appropriate a past that one is ashamed of or thinks was misguided or evil and so forth. Rather, the former commonly consists in constructing a narrative of one's life, or just in making sense of it, in such a way that a part of one's past is not taken up within the ambit of one's agency. This happens when one fails to make the past one's own by viewing oneself passively in relation to it, that is, by failing to acknowledge or disclaiming one's authorship of it. Psychoanalytically, according to Roy Schafer, these "disclaimers may be classified in terms of the "mechanisms of defense," such as isolation, splitting, introjection, and projection."[21] One is not willing to acknowledge that one's agency was involved in what occurred in the past, and in this way one dissociates oneself from it. Or one can acknowledge this but dissociate oneself from the past in yet another way, by denying or disregarding its shaping consequences for the present. Here the dissociation signifies something about how one views the limits of one's freedom; specifically, it reflects a belief that one is not morally or otherwise constrained by one's past and that one can make oneself whatever one wants to be by a sheer act of will. I will say more about this in Section 6, when I discuss humility.

To appropriate the past is to extend one's agency to encompass it, by involving one's agency in it and taking it up in the life one is leading. In failing to do this, one dissociates oneself from one's past, and this can happen in different ways. As I have just noted, one might simply *not extend* one's agency to the past. The sense that one is the author of one's life, operative in the present, does not reach back to include the past. If one considers one's past at all, it is from a particular standpoint and with a particular range of attitudes that signify a kind of detachment from it. These are not fundamentally different from the attitudes one might have toward other persons, although the recognition that this past is one's own might give them a special emotional tinge, perhaps through repulsion or anger. Less commonly, perhaps, one might *displace* one's agency from the present to the past, that is, regard oneself as passive in relation to one's present, rather than one's past. Interestingly, in cases like this, because the present, in relation to which one regards oneself as passive, will continually become the past, one will either have to disown more and more of the past as time goes on or to be constantly engaged in reinterpreting the past.

The extension of agency to past stretches of one's life is one dimension along which to judge the unity or coherence of a life over time. The more stretches of one's life one encompasses within the field of one's agency, the more unified or coherent (one makes) one's life. Particularly important in this regard is the appropriation of relatively enduring and stable aims, attitudes, interests, projects, and values that define and structure *phases* or *stages* of one's life. One can refuse to take responsibility for earlier stray desires and preferences, transitory concerns, isolated actions, and the like, by taking the stance that they are not expressive of one's true self. This is troubling enough. But failing or refusing to take responsibility for phases of one's life is a striking way of not seeing one's own agency historically whole and is seriously damaging to the appropriative unity of one's life.

There are different conceptions of appropriation, depending on whether or not we restrict the notion of taking responsibility for something in or about one's past to what one was responsible for in the past. On one view, appropriation involves the recognition that one was responsible, and so the recognition that one's agency was implicated in aspects of one's past, in past dispositions, attitudes, actions, and so on. (Depending on what in the past is to be appropriated, this recognition may be more or less easily arrived at.) There are, in turn, two versions of this.

One is what might be called the *volitional account*, and the kind of agency that is described by this account is *volitional agency*. The volitional account does not restrict appropriation to aspects of one's past that were within one's immediate voluntary control. It requires, however, that these be linked to past, present, or future choices because these are required for responsibility, and responsibility in the past is required for appropriation. Thus, we would be able to speak of taking responsibility for one's past if one made choices in the past that led to the development of certain attitudes or traits or tendencies to perform certain actions; or if one was able to control or modify one's attitudes, traits, or dispositions through one's subsequent choices; or if one chose to endorse or identify with them. Although one need not have seen oneself as choosing to become or to remain a certain sort of person or to engage in objectionable behavior, one might have been responsible for this nevertheless because choice was involved in one of these ways. For example, one can appropriate portions of one's past life when one's capacity to choose was seriously compromised by addiction to alcohol or drugs, on the assumption that this incapacity can be traced causally to one's past choices. However, there are limits to what one can properly appropriate, on this account: one cannot appropriate and so take responsibility for ingredients of one's past unless they were connected to choice in one of these ways.

There is a second account of how agency can be implicated in parts of one's past, and this yields a different understanding of what appropriation involves. Once again, being responsible in the past is required for taking responsibility now, but the view offers an alternative account of responsibility. Call this the *rationalist account* and the notion of agency at work here, *judgmental agency*. Angela M. Smith explains the view and its notion of agency as follows:

> . . . it is in virtue of their rational connection to our evaluative judgments that they [i.e. attitudes] are the kinds of states for which reasons or justifications can appropriately be requested. . . . I am active, and responsible, for anything that falls within the scope of evaluative judgment (i.e. anything that is, or should be, sensitive to my evaluative judgments and commitments). Our deliberate choices certainly fall within this scope, but . . . our desires, emotions, and other attitudes do as well. . . . we express our moral agency and activity not only in our explicit choices and decisions, but also in what we unreflectively think, feel, desire, and notice.[22]

The rationalist account has significant implications for what we can appropriate. If agency does not have to be understood in the terms of the volitional account, if we can be active in the sense that our emotions, desires, and so forth depend on, and are sensitive to our evaluative judgments and commitments, then we don't have to go in search of some connection between a particular aspect of our past and past choice in order to properly engage in the process of appropriation (a connection which we may or may not be able to find). We are still only considering views according to which taking responsibility for one's past entails owning up to and appropriating it, and in which appropriating it presupposes that one was responsible for it. However, the volitional and rationalist accounts understand this in different ways. On the volitional account, questions about how one became a certain sort of person, or how one acquired one's prior attitudes and values, would be relevant to determining whether one could sensibly take responsibility for one's past. On the rationalist account, by contrast, these questions have to do with whether and how one should be criticized for some aspect of one's past, not with whether one is responsible for it.

The volitional and rationalist accounts of appropriation, as I have described them, agree to this extent: they hold that in order to sensibly and appropriately take responsibility for something in one's past, one must have been responsible for it at the time. Arguably, however, this is overly restrictive, because it denies legitimacy to some of our ordinary intuitions about the conditions under which a person may be said to take responsibility for her past. To be sure, I have already said that there may be uses of the expression that my account does not capture. However, there is a sense of taking responsibility for one's past that has much in common with the cases that I have discussed, and it deserves some comment.

On this different understanding of taking responsibility for one's past, one can take responsibility for something that happened to oneself and for which one was not responsible, or at any rate, fully responsible, on either the rationalist or the volitional account. Rather, a person can take responsibility for her past, for example, by refusing to (continue to) be victimized by it, and this does not require that the events in her past be morally attributable to her. In general, taking responsibility in this different sense involves establishing a certain relationship to the past: refusing to accept that one is in bondage to the past; not using the past as an excuse for current inactivity; exerting oneself to see one's past clearly and honestly, without illusion, fantasy, or falsification; and acknowledging the ways in which past experiences and acquired traits have shaped current attitudes, values, and interests. Although one may have been a passive victim in the past, one can become active with respect to it by what one does now, by including it within the ambit of one's agency. In these cases, taking responsibility for one's past consists not in acknowledging that one was responsible for what happened to oneself, for one was not, but in taking control of how the past affects one's life now and going forward. In other words, responsibility attaches to how one leads one's life, and one is taking responsibility for *this* by addressing and taking up some important part of one's past.

Generally speaking, then, there are two sorts of cases: where taking responsibility tracks past responsibility and where it does not. Both have much in common, however. In both, one regards the past as "one's own," not necessarily in the sense that one faults oneself for it (one might not and be right not to), but in the sense that it is within one's power to alter the significance that it has for one's life and one's relations to others. To put this another way, and roughly speaking, it is a defining feature of taking responsibility for one's past in these cases that one does not see it as something that one can do nothing about.

However appropriation is understood, whether it requires prior responsibility or not, it is a complex process that is part cognitive, part volitional, and part affective. It is not just a matter of intellectually understanding that one is or was responsible, that is, of having or acquiring beliefs about one's agency that one has reason to accept as true, and in making correct inferences from these beliefs, where the beliefs and inferences need not engage the will or the emotions. This is clear if we adopt a psychoanalytic interpretation of appropriation,[23] for the analytic process aims at helping the analysand find a new way of being in the world, and this requires more than a change of beliefs about one's past or one's agency. Appropriating the past involves experiencing the past in a certain way, willing to take it up, and feeling the truth of what is experienced, a mode of understanding the past that is partially constituted by emotional engagement. In this case, intellectual understanding alone is defective understanding.

(c) *Thematization*

Appropriation also operates in tandem with another psychological process, "thematization," which is to be distinguished from the mere aggregative inclusion of past episodes or actions. By this I mean that, in reflecting on one's past and present, one identifies themes or motifs and draws connections between them, that is, one organizes significant life events or periods of one's life into meaningful patterns. The themes or motifs might not be evident to the individual until he or she engages in the work of appropriation; or their being evident to the individual might further the process of appropriation.

There are various modes of thematic organization within a person's life, from the rather meager to the quite robust, and taking responsibility for one's past does not necessarily involve seeing one's life as strongly unified. Some persons, in giving a narrative account of their lives, do portray their lives as the linear unfolding of a single persistent and dominant theme, perhaps as the fulfillment of a kind of mission or calling. Their lives possess a strong sort of thematic unity. This, however, seems rather rare. Others see their lives as organized around a plurality of themes that are to varying degrees complementary, compatible, or overlapping, with no overarching theme that gives direction to their lives as a whole. Still others see the various phases of their lives as having their own characteristic themes, with each giving way to its successor in a gradual evolutionary process. The theme of a particular life might even be expressed in terms of having undergone some sort of conversion experience, perhaps religious in nature, with a fairly abrupt and profoundly altering transition from one stage to another. Thematization, as an aspect of taking responsibility for one's past, refers to the discovery or construction of thematic connections of some kind between that in the past for which one takes responsibility and significant features of oneself and one's life in the present.

To take responsibility for one's past is, in part, is to make sense of the present in the light of some aspect of one's past. This can be done by telling a story that reveals developmental coherencies in the diverse elements of one's life. Generally, it involves apprehending one's life, or relatively large-scale parts of one's life, through the medium of some unifying themes or patterns. One common sort of thematic connection between periods of a person's life consists of an *instrumental* relationship between something in one's past and the present, and taking responsibility for one's past might involve finding or constructing such a connection. It might be the case, for example, that had I not taken up that particular career and failed at it, I would not have found my direction; or that had I not been in that disastrous marriage, I would not have gained the psychological insight that enabled me to lead a more fulfilling personal life; or that a period of my life that I have outgrown brought out certain valuable qualities in myself that I now put to better use. In each case, a stage of the past had a formative influence on the present, and one's taking responsibility for one's past would involve, among other things, facing one's past mistakes honestly, owning up to one's earlier life choices, and more than this, seeing oneself as having benefited from them in some way and being able to get beyond them.

A second sort of thematic connection that might obtain between past and present stages of one's life is one in which the past is *constitutive* of the present. In these cases, the past is not just instrumentally important to who I am; rather, it is essential to my self-identity that I am a person with such-and-such a biography. Or as we might put it, modifying a famous line, "The Child is still in the Man." Understanding oneself in terms of this internal relationship between past and present is one way of taking up one's past in a meaningful unity with one's present, and taking responsibility for one's past might partly consist in making or recognizing this connection.

(d) *Interconnections*

Although, for analytic purposes, I have separately discussed retrospective construction of meaning, appropriation, and thematization, in reality, these processes are intertwined in various ways. For one thing, retroactive significance and appropriation do not operate independently of one another. That is, one does not first construct a meaning for part of one's past, then lay claim to it. If this were the case, a person could appropriate parts of his past or not, without this affecting the meaning he constructs for them. In fact, however, events in a person's life borrow significance from succeeding acts of appropriation, so appropriation transforms the meaning of what is appropriated. A part of the past that is appropriated is no longer something with respect to which we are passive bystanders or from which we have dissociated ourselves. In narrative terms, it becomes an episode in a life story that is linked to other episodes by their joint inclusion within the compass of one's agency. This is the significance it acquires by virtue of being appropriated.

Thematization is also linked to both appropriation and retrospective construction of meaning. By appropriating the past and extending one's agency to embrace it, one also connects it in some sort of thematic unity with features of one's present life. Again, this notion is intended to encompass a variety of ways of structuring lives or parts of lives. The unity may often be implicit rather than explicit, but, either way, our relationship to our past is structured by it. Furthermore, retrospectively constructing a meaning for the past and thematizing go hand-in-hand. Constructing a meaning for the past by taking responsibility for it imparts some degree of thematic coherence to one's life because a theme is contained in or suggested by the meaning. And in thematizing, one retrospectively constructs a meaning for the past, a meaning that flows from the particular organizing themes that unify one's life.

4. APPLYING THE ANALYSIS: THE CASE OF PSYCHOPHARMACOLOGY

The increasing reliance in our society on medication to treat a range of psychological problems and disorders raises a number of questions that are relevant to the concerns of this chapter, and I want to use this phenomenon to flesh out a bit more the conceptual analysis I have given of taking responsibility for one's past. At the same time, I want to shed light on some of that phenomenon's problematic features. The questions include these: Can pharmacologic treatment of these conditions be a way of taking responsibility for one's past, or is it, as some have argued, precisely a way of avoiding taking responsibility? Do forms of psychotherapy have features that correspond to elements of my account of taking responsibility for one's past, features that drug treatment lacks? My aim here is to see what the analysis of taking responsibility for one's past implies about certain familiar ways of dealing with emotional problems that are rooted in one's past. It is another matter, which I will not take up, to evaluate the comparative merits of pharmacologic and psychotherapeutic treatment from a therapeutic standpoint. My own view is that sometimes medication is clearly preferable to psychotherapy because of the former's far superior therapeutic benefits and that reliance on medication to achieve psychic health should not be considered a sign of moral weakness if it is unreasonable to expect one to be able to overcome the obstacles to it without this assistance. But that said, it remains an open question whether this should be considered a way of taking responsibility for one's past, on the account of it that I have given. Sometimes, I am willing to concede, when medication alone is used, there may, in fact, be good and sufficient reasons for the individuals concerned *not* to work through the tasks involved in taking responsibility for their past.

Psychotropic medication is generally regarded, among mental health professionals, as an indispensable tool in the treatment of serious mental illnesses, such as schizophrenia and obsessive-compulsive disorder, capable of bringing about positive change in the patient that psychotherapy alone cannot achieve. Medication is used as well in the treatment of less-serious conditions attributable to a mental disorder, and, increasingly, in the management of conditions that are not attributable to a bona fide mental disorder at all (the latter is referred to as "cosmetic psychopharmacology"). As the use of medication expands from seriously disabling and less incapacitating mental disorders to include nonpathological conditions, it is appropriate to step back and reflect on the normative assumptions and implications of its use. Some may allege that the increasing reliance on drugs is symptomatic of a general impatience in our culture with sadness, suffering, and intensive self-examination. Rather than confront and struggle with unpleasant truths about oneself or one's life, many of which can be traced to experiences in our personal past, we tend to opt for the quick chemical fix for deep human problems.[24] In terms of the topic of this chapter, we might say that this tendency points to, or is explained by, an unwillingness to take responsibility for one's past.

Advocates of pharmacologic treatment have at least two rejoinders to these claims. First, if the reference to "quick fix" is meant to be pejorative, they say, we should consider the values underlying this accusation and the grounds for embracing them. Often those who fault the use of medication, the argument continues, embrace a kind of "pharmacologic Calvinism," in Peter Kramer's trenchant expression,[25] the (unwarranted) valorization of suffering and inner struggle as somehow valuable in themselves. The second rejoinder, which I focus on here, is that those who opt for the so-called quick fix do not necessarily fail to take responsibility for their past. For they may acknowledge that their current psychological problems have roots in their past and associate present emotional states with the early experiences that caused them; and they do not just passively wait for change to occur. They are doing something about the conditions that interfere with their ability to function as they want and are taking steps to effect positive personal change.

To evaluate this rejoinder, we should start with the view of "psychic health" that undergirds the pharmacologic approach. Consider the following example. Suppose that, due to traumatic events in her childhood, Jane is prone to painful feelings of rejection that seriously interfere with her ability to form trusting relationships with others. She has been told that people like her have problems with their serotonin levels and that there are drugs that can treat her condition. Convinced by this, and wanting to free herself from the grip of these painful and disabling feelings, she decides against psychotherapy and opts instead for pharmacologic intervention. In this way, Jane treats her emotional problems very much like she might treat a headache: rejection-sensitivity is painful, there are drugs that can alleviate the pain, alleviating the pain enables her to function with greater self-confidence in social settings, she wants to be able to do this, so she takes the drugs. In this way, as we might say, she has been cured of her past or, more accurately, she has been cured of those aspects of her past that explain her current difficulties.

But as Carol Freedman argues, "many emotional problems are precisely not like headaches. They are not *just* painful. And so, even if drugs work, that's not all there is to it."[26] On Freedman's view, with which I agree, emotional problems are constituted in part by particular modes of perception or cognition, by perceptions of loss, rejection, and so forth that give rise to and explain particular painful feelings, and, therefore, they are intrinsically *meaningful* phenomena as mere physical pains are not. On this view, for example, rejection-sensitivity is not essentially a tendency to experience painful feelings of a certain sort in certain sorts of situations, which feelings cause a heightened perception of rejection. Rather, rejection-sensitivity is defined by a heightened perception of rejection, which explains the particular painful feelings that those who are rejection-sensitive are prone to experience. The crucial difference between physical pains like headaches and emotional problems like rejection-sensitivity is that the latter express and are constituted by self-interpretations whereas the former are not. To be sure, pain is typically a symptom and a result of emotional problems and what motivates one to seek help, but for many psychological problems, there are *reasons* why one is prone to suffer painful feelings that are grounded in beliefs about oneself and one's world, beliefs that are in turn traceable to formative early experiences. These reasons may be discoverable through a process of self-examination, and the psychological problems for which they provide an explanation may be resolvable with insight and understanding. This is where psychotherapy makes a distinctive contribution to the treatment of emotional problems and where its particular value lies: it addresses itself to individuals not primarily as patients who experience painful feelings but as agents who are responsive to reasons.[27]

We are now in a position to respond to the claim that those who take medication for their emotional problems are not avoiding taking responsibility for their past but are only going about it in a different and possibly more efficient and effective manner than those who seek help from psychotherapy. To be sure, those who take medication for psychological problems rooted in their past are doing something about them. They are not just passively accepting them as their fate. In the example of rejection-sensitivity, Jane recognizes that she has feelings that seriously interfere with her life, and in taking steps to alleviate her rejection-sensitivity by medication, she deliberately seeks to alter the power of the past to determine her present and future emotional states and the direction of her life. But there are various ways of seeking to alleviate painful feelings that can be traced to early experiences of childhood trauma and the like, and only some of these involve the kind of engagement with the personal past that taking responsibility, on the account of it that I have given, requires.

Taking responsibility for some problematic part of one's past not only weakens its power over us but alters its meaning for us, and a sort of thematic unity is created through appropriation of that past. The role of memory in this process is different from what it typically is when emotional problems are treated with medication. The individual who treats with medication may associate current painful feelings with earlier experiences that caused them, although this association does not seem crucial. But when an individual takes responsibility for the past, his or her memory is engaged to make sense of and come to terms with the past. And because memory narratively connects present and past and is not just interested in the present shaping consequences of the past, taking responsibility for one's past forges and sustains a sense of oneself as an historical self. Contrast this with a model of the self that is suggested by Kramer's remarks about Lucy, an Ivy League undergraduate with a damaged self-image who suffers from rejection-sensitivity:

> Lucy's craving for attention has deep roots. . . . Lucy's neediness, like her sensitivity and her flirtations with violence, is rooted in her history. But her hunger for approval and the disorganizing pain she feels

on rejection will bring to mind, for psychiatrists of a certain ilk, a particular understanding of what ails Lucy, one that all but divorces the present from the past. This other approach entails taking Lucy's hunger for attention and her fear of rejection very much at face value, as discrete symptoms, in the way that insomnia and loss of appetite are symptoms. More broadly, this ahistorical viewpoint sees the combination of applause hunger and rejection-sensitivity as an autonomous syndrome, a category of human behavior that might respond to treatment with medication.... Examination of history, even of so evocative a history as Lucy's will be superfluous, an interesting enterprise in its own right, perhaps, but not crucial to the patient's healing.[28]

To be sure, treating with medication does not necessarily preclude self-examination. In fact, as Kramer argues, many patients may be "better able to explore both their past and their present circumstances" while they are taking medication, and for them, "the drug seems to aid rather than inhibit the struggle to locate the self."[29] But, although pharmacologic intervention may sometimes facilitate self-examination and self-understanding, it is hard to see how these could be the primary goal of psychopharmacology on a view of emotional problems that reduces all of them to the common denominator of painful feelings. As the quote about Lucy suggests, the pharmacologic approach rests on an ahistorical conception of the self that differs from the conception of the self that undergirds psychotherapeutic approaches in which connections are drawn between current psychological problems and past experiences. It also differs from the conception of the self that is embedded in the notion of taking responsibility for one's past.

Finally, we should note the danger that long-term use of medication to treat psychological problems will shape one's self-understandings to conform to this ahistorical conception. Lauren Slater, on antidepressant medication for 10 years, eloquently describes how this happened to her:

What the doctors [I went to] have in common is their reliance on chemicals as an explanatory model for human suffering. The historical aspects of my life mean nothing in these offices.... I myself don't mind sickness.... Sickness can be an escape, a return to childhood, even to Eden.... What I do mind, however, is how I feel I am losing the sense that I posses a historical self. If I buy into the compelling notion that cure defines disease, then it is similarly easy for me, along logical lines, to buy into the notion that neurons cause illness. The only historicity available in the genetic neuron is of the most generic kind.... I have largely ceased to explain myself in terms of my historical connections with others, even while I recognize the stupidity of this. The neurological model is just too tempting.[30]

Although not all long-term users of antidepressants will necessarily experience these effects, the warning implicit in this personal account is a sobering antidote to the optimistic pronouncements of psychopharmacology advocates: treating one's emotional problems with medication can over time alter how one explains and understands oneself in a fundamental (and unintended) way, by gradually eroding one's sense that problems of living are not "autonomous syndromes" but are intimately bound up with historical connections with others and with other parts of one's life.[31]

5. WHY WE DON'T TAKE RESPONSIBILITY FOR OUR PAST

It will hardly come as a surprise that people often do not take responsibility for their past, that more than this, they often actively disavow such responsibility. If what many commentators have argued is correct, there are social, cultural, and even economic factors that can partly explain why this is so prevalent.[32] However, these accounts leave a great deal unexplained about attitudes and responses on the individual level. Individuals do not all react in the same way to large scale social and cultural realities that transcend the particularities of individual lives; nor should these realities always figure as part of the explanation of why particular individuals do not take responsibility for their past. What we have to leave room for and address, in an account of why individuals do not do so, is the quite common psychological reluctance to confront or even acknowledge truths about our past because of the emotional distress this would cause us. There are any number of reasons why reflection on our past might be distressing to us, and in some cases the distress we fear and want to avoid may be of such a degree or nature that it keeps us from taking responsibility for that past.

We can explain why people do not take responsibility for their past in various ways. Sometimes a person does not do so because he regards some past portion of his personal history as just too *insignificant* from the point of view of his life history overall to warrant much concern. These cases may or may not be problematic, depending in part on whether the judgment of insignificance grounds or derives from the decision not to take responsibility. Sometimes the explanation is that it is *difficult* to take responsibility because when he reviews parts of his past and reflects on what they reveal about himself or how he has lived his life, he finds them painful or distressing, or he would find them painful or distressing were he to do so.

The terms "pain" and "distress," as I use them here, cover a range of feelings, including regret, shame, grief, remorse, and guilt, and the degree of this distress may vary depending on several factors. (There is no need to be more specific here about which feelings, or combinations of them, are operative in a particular case.) The cases in which one does not take responsibility for one's past because of the pain it causes one are of interest to me for two reasons. First, I want to understand the relationship between taking responsibility for one's past and exercising effective human agency, and the painfulness of the past has an obvious bearing on the ability to exercise agency effectively. When one does not take responsibility for some problematic part of one's past because it causes one a great deal of mental suffering, that part can become an exaggerated focus of concern and anxiety, and in that respect be debilitating. Second, I want eventually to consider arguments for the proposition that one *ought* to take responsibility for one's past, and commonly attention is not drawn to the fact that one ought to take responsibility for one's past unless one resists doing so because the past is distressing in some way.[33]

The distress that complicates or impedes the process of taking responsibility for one's past springs from different sources. First is *wrongdoing*: one may have committed some wrong in the past and be pained by contemplation of the wrongness of what one has done and one's moral failures on these occasions, and perhaps also by what one believes this wrongdoing reveals about oneself. To be sure, one can be pained, and perhaps should be pained, by contemplation of one's past wrongdoing and can recognize it as something for which one is responsible, even when this does not support a negative evaluation of one's character. But sometimes – the temptation to denial notwithstanding – one regards one's earlier wrongdoing as relevant to an evaluation of oneself or the sort of life one has led, either overall or in some specific area, and contemplating what one has done is painful in part because it occasions such a negative self-evaluation. One does not just feel guilty that one has done wrong but thinks that it reflects unfavorably on one's character or on the way one has conducted one's life.

The past in these cases may come back to haunt us because the fact of our wrongdoing shatters some of the central assumptions that we have about ourselves and our relations to other people. The temptation to deny, forget, or repress the wrongdoing may be strong under these circumstances but, for several reasons, should be resisted. Although the past misdeed cannot be undone, one can still try to atone for it by offering compensation for the harm done or in other ways trying to make amends and put things right. Even when this is not possible, registering the full impact of one's prior wrongdoing may put one on guard against committing similar wrongs now and in the future, or perhaps wrongdoing in general. In addition, acknowledging one's prior wrongdoing may be necessary if one is to rebuild assumptions about oneself and one's relation to the world that are more realistic. At the other extreme, one's reaction to one's past wrongdoing can be excessive in various ways, and these too should be avoided. One might dwell on it out of proportion to the severity of the wrong done. Even if the wrong was serious, one might dwell on it to the extent of allowing it to so dominate one's thoughts that it prevents one from giving reasonable attention to current projects and future plans and from fulfilling one's obligations. What is required is not only that one do something about one's past misdeeds, if at all possible. Important as this is, one should also endeavor to keep them in proper perspective.

Second is the distress may arise from concerns about one's *well-being*. That is, one experiences distress because one's past choices and actions are seen as having adversely affected one's present well-being. One realizes that one's life would have gone much better, or that one would not be as poorly off as one is in important respects, if one had not made the choices and acted as one did in the past, and one reproaches oneself for what one did, and perhaps also for having been the kind of person who could and did make such unwise – as one now sees it – decisions.

These two sources of distress may involve a third: namely, distress relating to one's *self-conception*. Specifically, the pain or distress that one experiences on contemplation of one's past may result from a perceived mismatch between some part of one's past and one's current conception of oneself, where that part need not have involved wrongdoing or been detrimental to one's current well-being (except in the way of causing one distress). It is distressing that something in one's past that it appears one may have to acknowledge as one's own does not agree with one's normative self-conception.

The notion of a normative self-conception used here is not a very demanding one. It is not necessary that one have a clear, well-articulated conception of oneself or that one be particularly self-conscious and reflective about who one is. Indeed, many people, perhaps the majority, could not reasonably be said to have a self-conception at all, if this is what having a self-conception consisted of. I intend this notion to have much wider application, as does Norman Care:

> Insofar as one's life is something one leads, in rather the way in which a story is something one authors ... one leads it according to some sort of conception of oneself that is in part normative in character. This is to say that living a life is something one does to some extent under a view of oneself as being a person of a certain kind or having a certain sort of character, with certain desires, hopes, aspirations, and fears, and possessed of certain principles, policies, and strategies for living.[34]

To be sure, there may be some individuals who do not have a self-conception even in this sense: those who just muddle along from day to day and of whom it cannot properly be said that they "lead" their lives. But most people, it seems, fall somewhere between the extremes of leading one's life according to a clear and sure self-conception and not leading one's life at all.

The lack of agreement between something in or about one's past and one's self-conception may be distressing because one conceives of oneself as a person who is somehow superior to what one's past indicates about oneself. For example, goals and projects one once pursued, and that helped define the sort of person one was at the time, may now seem trivial or foolish, not worth the time and effort expended on them, and one may be embarrassed, perhaps ashamed, for having had them, for having been the sort of person who could have taken such superficial things so seriously. However, if one is honest with oneself, one has to acknowledge that parts of one's past that are problematic in such ways may be essential to who one is, even if they do not fit with how one currently conceives of oneself. Moreover, because this mismatch between one's past and one's self-conception is distressing, it is understandable that one would be tempted to not allow disagreeable or objectionable parts of one's past to challenge this self-conception. This temptation should normally be resisted, even if repairing relations with those we have wronged is not the reason why it should be. There are still normative criticisms of various sorts that can be directed at those who cover over or deny discrepancies between their self-conceptions and their personal histories.

One criticism certainly has to do with the quality of their self-understanding (or self-knowledge). A person who is only able to maintain a high opinion of himself by suppressing unflattering aspects of his history fails to come to terms with incongruities between his self-conception and a portion of his personal history. If this part of the past has an instrumentally important relationship to who he is today or is constitutive of it, then his failure to come to terms with these incongruities is particularly troubling. For then, he fails to understand himself in a deep sense, that is, to understand that his self-identity is partly defined by and in relation to what he did in the past and the choices he made then; that his self-identity bears the traces, if you will, of that past. He also thereby evades warranted self-criticism. Indeed, concerns about the accuracy of one's self-understanding can arise with respect to all three of the cases I have discussed, in which distress is related to past wrongdoing, to imprudent choices, and to discrepancies between history and self-conception. If a person fails to take responsibility for his past for any of these reasons, it will often be appropriate to ask whether and how well he understands his motivations and capacities for judgment and action.

A person who does not take responsibility for his past may say, "That was done, but it was not *me* who did that." I suppose he is not denying, on metaphysical grounds, that that stretch of the past is himself at a different time and that he has persisted as one person over time. The criteria of numerical identity over time tell us how to pick out the individual to whom some life belongs and they are not at issue here. (As I noted in Chapter 1, the sense of identity that principally concerns me is not numerical identity over time.) The issue is rather one of picking out what belongs to that life, and in a sense that I will explain more fully, for the person who fails to take responsibility for some part of his past, that past does not belong to his life. He acknowledges that *he* is the individual to whom that past belongs, not someone else, but he does not make it a part of his life by holding himself accountable for it.

This, as I have said, may demonstrate a lack of self-understanding. But this is not the only evaluative criticism that we may be able to make. The story of Felicia has suggested another: the failure to take responsibility for one's past may indicate a failure to appreciate that one is not merely the product of forces and factors beyond one's control and, as a consequence, a failure to act from a sense of active participation in the shape and direction of one's life. And still other normative criticisms are possible, as we will see in Sections 6 and 7.

6. HUMILITY AND TAKING RESPONSIBILITY FOR ONE'S PAST

What is wrong with failing or refusing to take responsibility for one's past? Does this give us grounds for attributing some moral flaw to the individual? When it is some past wrongdoing for which one is responsible, there is a ready answer to the former question: a person who ignores or suppresses or rationalizes away his past wrongdoing will not acknowledge and seek to make amends for the wrongs he is responsible for having committed, as he should. However, wrongdoing is not all that one might or should take responsibility for in one's past. As the story of Felicia and others like it suggest, we can and perhaps should take responsibility for how we conducted ourselves over some stretch of time in the past, for the values and priorities that motivated and guided us then, and this is not only because we wronged someone, if indeed we did. One reason for this, as I noted in Section 5, has to do with self-understanding or self-knowledge that has intrinsic ethical significance. The person who fails to take responsibility for an important aspect of his past, even when wrongdoing is not at issue, might very well have only a superficial understanding of himself, his abilities, interests, and concerns, and a life led under these conditions is not a life well led. In the terms of the conceptual analysis in Section 3, if he lacks self-understanding, it is because he has not appropriated that part of the past and has not discerned thematic connections between his past and present life – connections that would enable him to make sense of who he is on the basis of important truths about himself in the past.[35]

But it is not only self-understanding of this sort that the person who does not take responsibility for his past may lack. In this section and in Section 7, I want to propose additional related explanations for what may be wrong with not taking responsibility for one's past and to suggest that it may exemplify certain character flaws. The explanation I discuss in this section relates taking responsibility for one's past and *humility*, in the following way. A person who does not take responsibility for his past may for this reason be unable to form an accurate, realistic self-assessment. Not appreciating how he became who he is, the factors that shaped his life and the constraints that limit his options, he may have a distorted, more specifically, an inflated sense of his powers and capacities. This distorted sense of self may have such far-reaching effects in the life of this person that it is integral to our understanding of the kind of person he is. But this is morally problematic because, on one common view of what the trait of humility consists in, this would mean that he lacks humility. The claim, in short, is that an individual's refusal to take responsibility for his past, or his denial of responsibility for it, may engender or indicate a lack of humility. And this raises moral concerns because humility is generally regarded as a valuable trait, although admittedly moral philosophers disagree about the best account to be given of it.

Because there are a number of competing accounts, I need to say more about which one I am adopting here and why, on this account, humility is plausibly regarded as something admirable. The popular conception of humility, according to which, as Henry Sidgwick notes, "humility prescribes a low opinion of our merits,"[36] is deeply problematic because it is difficult to understand why, on this account, humility should be something to aspire to. It would not be problematic in the same way if we could assume that all people are basically without (much) merit, for then having a low opinion of our merits would simply be acknowledging the truth about ourselves. But if we reject this assumption, as I think we should, and allow that some persons may have superior merits, then in some cases humility (thus conceived) will actually be more like stupidity or self-deception than something praiseworthy or admirable. To be sure, people who do not take responsibility for their past often do this in order to be able to maintain a high opinion of themselves, a self-assessment that is not warranted by their actual merits. But the personal failing to which I am drawing attention is not best described as having high self-esteem when what they should really have is low self-esteem. They are not to be faulted for not thinking poorly of themselves so much as for not putting themselves and their accomplishments in proper perspective. Putting these in proper perspective – an idea that I will say more about below – is what the person who appropriately takes responsibility for his past does[37] and what the person who lacks humility does not do.

Most accounts of humility divide into two kinds.[38] *Low-opinion* or *under-estimation* accounts maintain that humility involves having a low estimate of oneself (or one's skills, accomplishments, etc.), not only rating oneself low on some relevant scale but *lower* than one would be ranked by an objective assessment of one's worth or merits. *Accuracy* accounts maintain that humility involves having an accurate and realistic opinion of oneself, one's abilities, and one's accomplishments.[39] Or more precisely, according to Norvin Richards, "having an accurate sense of oneself, sufficiently firm to resist pressures toward incorrect revisions."[40] Pressures can be either of two sorts, to think too little or "too much of oneself."[41] The trait that enables one to resist pressures toward underestimation of oneself, one's abilities, and one's accomplishments is "dignity."[42] By contrast, humility is the trait that enables one to resist pressures toward overestimation. Low-opinion accounts are problematic for the reason already mentioned. Accuracy accounts avoid this difficulty, for on these accounts, the humble person is not required to take no pride at all in herself or her abilities and accomplishments or to think less of herself than she deserves. Rather, there is a close connection between humility thus understood and proper self-esteem. My suggestion about the relationship between failing or refusing to take responsibility for one's past and lacking humility presupposes an accuracy account of humility.[43]

I don't claim that it is only failing to take responsibility for one's past that can be connected to a lack of humility in this accuracy sense: taking responsibility can also be connected to it. Taking responsibility for some aspect of one's past might exhibit a sort of grandiosity or, on the negative side, a tendency to unwarranted self-blame in which the distinction between what has *happened* to oneself and what is the product of or involves one's *agency* is blurred. Here, to be sure, the past is appropriated, but it is appropriated improperly, because one attributes agency and responsibility where they do not belong.[44] I am mainly interested, however, in how *not* taking responsibility for one's past can be bound up in complex ways with a lack of humility on the part of the one who does not take responsibility. And, again, I want to explain this linkage in terms of unrealistic self-assessment, that is, not putting oneself and one's accomplishments in proper perspective.

In what sense might the person who fails to take responsibility for his past not put himself and his accomplishments in proper perspective and lack humility?[45] Here is part of the explanation. To put oneself, one's abilities and accomplishments, in proper perspective is, in part, to examine and take seriously the factors that contribute to one's character, personality, abilities, and accomplishments, including one's prior choices and evaluative judgments. In other words, it includes giving due consideration to how prior experiences, as well as prior exercises of one's volitional or rational agency, have contributed to making one the person one is and help explain one's abilities, successes, and disappointments, and so on. One fails to put oneself in proper perspective, in this view, by giving insufficient attention to or denying the role of these factors. For example, one might acknowledge that certain experiences had a powerful impact in the past but avoid examining how they have affected one's life and self-identity. Or one might improperly deny that one's agency was implicated in these earlier formative conditions and refuse to acknowledge that one played an active part in becoming the sort of person one has become (by which I do not mean that one sees oneself as a passive victim instead). In these ways, one fails to take responsibility for one's past and to put oneself in proper perspective. But this still doesn't fully explain how failing to take responsibility for one's past is connected to a lack of humility.

The connection is this: because one does not take responsibility for one's past, one may be prone to have an exaggerated sense of the role that choice and control play in the construction and direction of one's life. It is exaggerated because it fails to register a deep truth about human agency: though one might have played an active part in one's past, that past becomes an inheritance that conditions and constrains what one is capable of being and doing with one's life now, something that one is "stuck" with, for better or for worse. (This is entirely consistent with my earlier observation that one can retrospectively alter the significance of the past by taking responsibility for it.) To recognize this is to understand that one's agency is impure[46] and that one's control is limited, not only by one's physical characteristics and the things that befall one but also by one's prior exercises of agency. To deny that this is the case or to purposefully overlook it – which is what I am claiming those who do not take responsibility for their past can sometimes be faulted for – flaunts one's potency for choice and control and, if serious enough, justifies a negative judgment about one's character, namely, that one lacks humility. It is also likely to show itself in a variety of attempts to shore up the illusion of undiluted freedom, including a kind of arrogant dismissal of anyone or anything that reminds one of one's past and repeated and desperate attempts to reinvent oneself.

Humility, on the view I have adopted, consists in having an accurate view of one's worth, abilities, and accomplishments, sufficiently firm to resist pressures toward overestimation, and it is a valuable quality to have for this reason. This does not imply, of course, that everyone who acts with humility is equally praiseworthy for doing so. On the contrary, individuals may be more or less praiseworthy, depending on how much effort they must exert to successfully resist those pressures. For some, it might be relatively easy not to have an inflated sense of themselves and their accomplishments, and if our favorable attitude toward a person is partly dependent on how difficult it is for him to act with humility, then they would not be especially admirable on this score. For others, it may be difficult not to overvalue themselves and their accomplishments – perhaps because of their elevated social position or an excessively indulgent upbringing – and if they successfully resist the pressures to do so, they would deserve particular praise for keeping themselves in proper perspective.

These points have implications for how we should judge those who take responsibility for their past, insofar as it is humility that is at issue. The temptation to deny responsibility for problematic parts of one's past may be especially difficult to resist for persons who are disposed to have a high opinion of themselves and their current accomplishments. Their positive self-assessment might also be reinforced by the praise and attention they currently receive from others, making it still more difficult for them to keep themselves in proper perspective. Arguably such a person is especially praiseworthy for resisting the pressures – internal as well as external – toward overestimation and for acknowledging that he cannot entirely escape the influence of parts of his past that he would rather forget. For the same reason, it would be especially admirable if a person who has relatively little to be proud of in his life and who is strongly inclined to deny responsibility for his past as a defense against low self-esteem managed to resist the inclination.

7. SELF-FORGIVENESS AND TAKING RESPONSIBILITY FOR ONE'S PAST

The notion of having an accurate sense of oneself is worth exploring further, and this will lead us to a second explanation of what is wrong with not taking responsibility for one's past and an associated character flaw. Consider some of the ways that one might have a distorted or inaccurate sense of oneself. At one extreme, one takes oneself to be deeply and irremediably flawed, utterly lacking in the capacity for good, and incapable of moral improvement as shown by something in or about one's past. One is filled with such self-loathing and self-contempt that one is effectively incapable of self-forgiveness, although objectively considered one is actually being too hard on oneself. At the other extreme, self-forgiveness does not arise as a concern because one does not see one's problematic past as reflecting negatively on oneself, which it does, or does not regard some past action as wrong or some aspect of one's past self as flawed, which it is. Here one might be said to be too easy on oneself. As described, persons at either extreme – in the former extreme, they believe they are unworthy of self-forgiveness; in the latter extreme, they do not see themselves as having any need for self-forgiveness – do not have an accurate sense of themselves. But the moral problem these cases present does not, or does not only, have to do with a lack of humility. It has to do with what we might call failures of or in regard to self-forgiveness: failure either to appreciate that one is not beyond the reach of proper self-forgiveness or to acknowledge that there is anything in one's past for which one might have to work to forgive oneself.

Although my focus in this section is self-forgiveness and its relationship to taking responsibility for one's past, the discussion of humility in Section 6 is relevant here as well because failures of self-forgiveness can be due to or manifest a lack of humility. Someone who has an exaggerated sense of the role his agency plays in shaping his life might have unrealistically high expectations of himself, and this can have various consequences. For one thing, he might be prone to blame himself for bad outcomes when a more accurate assessment of his situation would reveal the causal contribution of various factors that now determine the context of choice. These are factors whose influence cannot be expunged by an effort of will and that limit the scope for the exercise of his agency. If he is to estimate himself accurately, he has to acknowledge the encumbered nature of his agency. For another, someone with unrealistically high expectations of himself might, for that reason, be more prone to self-deceptively deny that some aspect of his life is problematic than someone with a more realistic self-assessment. Here, humility, in the sense of a trait that enables individuals to resist overestimation of their worth and accomplishments, is properly engaged. It does not demand that we always forgive ourselves, but rather that we leave room for the possibility of self-forgiveness by acknowledging our deficiencies and wrongdoings.

In order to explain how self-forgiveness can illuminate what is wrong with not taking responsibility for one's past, I need to first say something about how I understand what self-forgiveness is and what it involves.[47] The term "self-forgiveness," as I construe it, signifies not only an achievement but a process as well. As an achievement, it consists in overcoming the self-reproach that accompanies a diminished sense of self-worth; as a process, it refers to a number of tasks that have to be performed in order to achieve self-forgiveness (these tasks can be thought of as preliminary to self-forgiveness in the achievement sense or as paving the way for it[48]). Self-reproach – which only makes sense if one can be responsible for the things one reproaches oneself for – covers a range of negative emotions of self-assessment, including guilt, shame, self-loathing, and self-contempt. As for *overcoming* self-reproach, this does not mean that one simply no longer experiences it, in other words, that one is completely at peace with oneself. This is wrong for two reasons. First, there are constraints on what counts as a process of self-forgiveness. One might no longer experience self-reproach because one allows oneself to be distracted by other concerns or because one has forgotten or repressed whatever occasioned the bad feelings, and so on, but none of these ways of going on amounts to a process of self-forgiveness. Second, one can overcome self-reproach without doing away with it completely. One overcomes it when there is a change in the way that one experiences the emotions such that, as Robin Dillon puts it, one is not "in bondage" to self-reproach, and not "controlled or crippled by a negative conception of oneself and the debilitating pain of it."[49] Self-forgiveness, that is, has to do with learning how to live with oneself, despite a problematic past that may very well continue to cause one some measure of distress.

Concerns about self-forgiveness are often occasioned by wrongdoing and the harm one caused others. There is no good reason, however, to restrict the notion of self-forgiveness in this way. We can reproach ourselves not only for the wrongs we have committed, but also for not developing our talents, for personal shortcomings, failures of character, evil thoughts, and malicious desires, as long as they implicate our agency and can be appropriated on this basis. Moreover, even when we do reproach ourselves for our past wrongdoings, it is appropriate to speak about self-forgiveness only because our misdeeds reveal something about an aspect of ourselves or the kind of person we were. The reason for this is that self-forgiveness, as the name suggests, is ultimately concerned not just with what one has done but with one's *self*: it is not just that one has done something wrong, but there is also something wrong with oneself for having done it. Moreover, one's sense of self-worth is normally called into question when one is revealed to oneself in such a negative light. Although it is not the injury to one's sense of worth for which one forgives oneself, self-forgiveness repairs at least some of this damage as it overcomes self-reproach. At the same time, the individual must already have some amount or kind of self-respect, for without this she will not have a secure enough basis from which to undertake the work of self-forgiveness.

Using the terms of this account, we can characterize the failures with respect to self-forgiveness as follows:

(1) one is too easy on oneself, with regard to self-forgiveness, when one does not reproach oneself when one should, or when one overcomes self-reproach without working through the various tasks involved in the process of self-forgiveness;

(2) one is too hard on oneself, with regard to self-forgiveness, when one's self-reproach has a power over oneself that is out of proportion to what is problematic in one's past or warranted by one's situation, and as a result one cannot initiate or work through the process.

Consider the first sort of failure. In cases in which one has wronged another, sought forgiveness from her but not received it, a morally conscientious person will carefully consider whether he has done all he should have to earn it. Although there may be no obligation on the part of the one who has been wronged to forgive, it is possible that she can cease to deserve further efforts by the wrongdoer to make amends. As Claudia Card writes, "just as unscrupulous or abusive benefactors can cease to deserve gratitude, thereby involuntarily releasing beneficiaries from obligation, unscrupulous or abusive victims can cease to deserve apologies or reparations, involuntarily releasing perpetrators from obligation."[50] A morally conscientious person might be warranted in concluding this, in which case he would be entitled to forgive himself despite the refusal of his victim to forgive him. We would not necessarily say, I think, that he is being too easy on himself by forgiving himself. He has, after all, done everything that can reasonably be expected of him. But a morally conscientious person would also consider another possibility – that he has not done as much as he should have, has not been willing to fully admit fault to the one he has wronged, and has granted himself the forgiveness that he has not received from his victim as a kind of end run around her. This is one way to be too easy on oneself: to refrain from taking the difficult steps that show genuine repentance and to improperly attribute the lack of forgiveness to the unreasonableness of the one who has been wronged rather than to one's own inadequacies. Another way to be too easy on oneself is to suppose that there is nothing to ask forgiveness for in the first place.

These examples involving wrongdoing illustrate one sort of case in which a person might be said not to have earned self-forgiveness. In general, self-forgiveness is not warranted unless one has worked through certain tasks that are involved in the process of self-forgiveness, tasks including facing the past honestly, taking reasonable steps to make amends if one has wronged or harmed another, and seeking to change oneself for the better. Individuals who improperly deny that they did anything wrong or that their failings are failings, or who just do not care one way or the other, have not even met the threshold requirement of acknowledging that there is something to reproach themselves for. They are being too easy on themselves, as are those who extend self-forgiveness without properly confronting those they have wronged. And being too easy on oneself is morally objectionable, not only because it shows a failure to respect others, but also because it manifests the lack of a sort of self-respect, which consists in an unwillingness to hold oneself accountable for one's actions and past life.

Now suppose, to change the earlier example, there is nothing the offender feels he is able to do vis-à-vis the one he has wronged to earn his forgiveness. He cannot accept forgiveness, even if offered, because he believes himself unworthy of it. It is not simply that his sense of guilt is profound, for given the seriousness of the wrong he has committed, he may be justified in feeling this way. It is rather that his guilt is beyond the reach of ameliorative measures so that we would say of him that it exceeds what is warranted by the seriousness of what he has done. Here is a case of a person who is too hard on himself: he is not able to overcome the self-reproach that holds him in its grip and cripples him, and his self-reproach is out of proportion to his misdeeds. Perhaps he is so plagued by guilt and shame over something in his past that he cannot even bring himself to examine how it has affected his life or to face the person whom he has wronged. The part of the past in question cannot be completely repressed, however. It repeatedly intrudes itself on his conscious life and becomes a focus of excessive concern and anxiety. In these examples, the individual is too hard on himself because he is gratuitously self-punitive, so incapable of achieving self-forgiveness.

His incapacity is morally objectionable, in part because it is out of touch with moral reality and in part because it saps the energy required for responsible conduct associated with effective human agency. One of the benefits of self-forgiveness is that it contributes toward the regaining of effective agency, including the motivation to fulfill one's moral obligations and to avoid a repetition of wrongdoing. Norman Care clarifies this notion as follows:

> What this recovery is of [viz. "agency"] is then lots of things, including a sense of oneself as intact in a way that allows responsible forward-looking action, plus a measure of self-worth, and perhaps even the capacity to find in oneself interests and enthusiasms with enough strength to give meaningfulness to certain of one's activities.[51]

Among other things, self-reproach, when dominating and unremitting, undermines self-confidence, the sense that one is, within realistic limits, in control of what happens in one's life and has the personal resources to effectively meet challenges and difficulties that life may throw in one's way. Moreover, the psychological capacities required for the possession and exercise of agency are presupposed by moral agency, so when the former suffer the corrosive effects of despair and persistent self-reproach, moral agency is undermined as well.

How are these failures with respect to self-forgiveness related to not taking responsibility for something problematic in or about one's past? First, consider being too easy on oneself. If someone is too easy on himself in the sense that he mistakenly believes that something in his past does not warrant self-reproach, or forgives himself too easily by discounting the significance of his past conduct, then he will not take (full) responsibility for his past. It may be that he cannot bring himself to acknowledge the seriousness of what he has done and honestly face his past, in which case his rejection of responsibility serves as a defense against the loss of self-respect that would come from doing so. Or perhaps we should say that his not taking responsibility for his past shows that he is being too easy on himself. In any case, the two – not taking responsibility and being too easy on oneself with respect to self-forgiveness – are intimately intertwined. Whatever the psychological explanation, he does not appropriate his past as he should because he does not give it the appropriate normative weight.

Next, consider being too hard on oneself. Someone who blames himself excessively for something in his past necessarily takes responsibility for it, but in taking responsibility to this extent he precludes himself from being able to take responsibility for his past in a fuller sense. That is, his self-condemnation is so (unwarrantedly) intense and debilitating that he cannot undertake, or cannot successfully complete, other tasks involved in taking responsibility for one's past, such as putting the past in proper perspective, as well as appropriating the past in a manner that permits one to learn from it and to become, through self-improvement, a different sort of person. In order to forgive oneself, one has to have a certain love or at any rate compassion for oneself of the sort that permits one to believe one is worth the effort that self-forgiveness requires. But this is just what the person who is too hard on himself cannot or does not have, and this prevents him from fully taking responsibility for his past.

Self-forgiveness is not warranted if one is being too easy on oneself (indeed, this is just what being "too easy" on oneself implies); and it may be warranted, even though one is not able to bring oneself to forgive oneself (in which case one is being "too hard" on oneself). These cases are opposite ends of a continuum. In general, self-forgiveness for something problematic in one's past is only warranted – or as some might say, only genuine[52] – if one is willing to take responsibility for it. There may be circumstances in which it can properly be said that one should forgive oneself (in the achievement sense) for something in one's past. But this is only on the condition that one takes responsibility for it, for otherwise the self-forgiveness would be unearned and unwarranted. If there are grounds for saying, in particular cases, that one *should* work to forgive oneself for something in one's past, the way to do this is by taking responsibility for it.

The moral importance of taking responsibility for one's past is thus partly accounted for by its connection with warranted or genuine self-forgiveness. Specifically, not taking responsibility for one's past can be or represent a failure of self-forgiveness, and this helps explain what is wrong with it. In terms of the failures of self-forgiveness that I have discusssed, not taking responsibility for one's past can indicate either that one is being too hard on oneself or that one is not being hard enough.

Taking responsibility for one's past is preliminary to the achievement of genuine self-forgiveness, and the connection to self-forgiveness not only helps explain what is wrong with not taking responsibility but also shows how demanding it can be to take responsibility. The preparatory activity of "responsibility-taking work,"[53] as Dillon calls it, consists of a number of different tasks. To begin with, a person must have the courage to and must engage in an honest appraisal of himself and his past conduct. He must acknowledge to himself that what he did was wrong or that what he did revealed some flaw in himself as a person. Past misdeeds and inadequacies must not be treated with indulgence by manufacturing excuses for them, for to do this is to condone them, and condonation is not self-forgiveness. Furthermore, the acknowledgment must consist in more than the acceptance of the truth of certain propositions about himself. He must acknowledge and allow himself to experience the negative emotions to which his past conduct or shortcomings give rise, for this serves to connect him to the reality of what he has done and been in a way that mere intellectual assent cannot. A further responsibility-taking task for the person engaged in the process of self-forgiveness is to work on problematic attitudes, beliefs, and behavior patterns to make it less likely that he will continue to have these attitudes and beliefs or perform similar acts in the future. And finally, when another has been wronged in some way, the offender must own up to it and seek to make amends. Usually at least an apology will be in order, and commonly more is required to atone for what he has done and to make things right. He must be willing to do what he can to compensate the wronged party for her loss, or if compensation is not possible, to make some other form of reparation, and throughout he must be sensitive to the wronged party's own perception of her needs and to how she will respond to his reparative efforts.[54]

My claim is that one is justified in forgiving oneself for something in one's past only if one takes responsibility for it, not that one will or should forgive oneself if one does so. Indeed, there is no assurance that self-forgiveness will be achieved once one takes responsibility for what one has done or been, and in some extreme situations a measure of one's having truly taken responsibility for one's past may be that one is not able to forgive oneself for it. The relationship between self-forgiveness and taking responsibility is psychologically complex and often opaque. To illustrate the point, consider the case of Traudl Junge, personal secretary to Adolf Hitler from 1942–1945. She was interviewed shortly before her death in the fascinating documentary film, *Blind Spot: Hitler's Secretary*,[55] which appeared in German-speaking countries at the same time as the publication of her wartime memoir (along with her new Foreword).[56] I quote from the film:

> In the early years [after the war], it didn't occur to me to come to terms with my past . . . all that [the murders of millions of people] struck me as very shocking. But I wasn't able at first to see the connection with my own past. I still felt somehow content that I had no personal guilt and had known nothing about it. I had no idea of the extent of what happened. [Later] I sensed that it is no excuse to be young and that it might have been possible to find out what was going on.

It was not until the mid-1960s, she claims, that she began to confront her past, and for a period of 35 years after, that confrontation became what she describes as an "increasingly painful process: an exhausting attempt to understand myself and my motivation at the time."[57] Still, the guilt she experiences over her role as Hitler's secretary continues to oppress her.

As she says in her memoir, "after the revelation of his [Hitler's] crimes, I shall always live with a sense that I must share the guilt."[58] At one point in the film, looking back at her younger self, she reflects:

> It seems to me that I should be angry with the child I was, that juvenile young girl, or that I can't forgive her for failing to recognize in time what horrors that monster caused. The fact that I didn't see what I was getting involved in and above all that I just said yes without thinking at all. . . . I find it hard to forgive myself for everything.

Were Traudl Junge's guilt and self-reproach so crippling that she could not forgive herself for her willful ignorance, her gullibility, and her naivete? Her long periods of depression, hospitalization, unsuccessful psychotherapy, and lack of enthusiasm for her career during this period suggest that this may be so. Does she have difficulty forgiving herself despite having confronted and taken responsibility for her past, or perhaps because of having done so, or is her inability to forgive herself an indication of her failure to fully "come to terms with" her past? Perhaps it was necessary for her not to fully take responsibility because she was not psychologically strong enough to confront her past honestly and constructively.[59] Neither the film nor the memoir provides conclusive answers to these questions, and different interpretations are credible. It is interesting to note in this connection that making the film seems to have had a cathartic effect on her and that her last words to the film's directors before her death were these: "I think now I'm beginning to forgive myself."

Aside from questions about the relationship between taking responsibility for one's past and self-forgiveness, the case of Traudl Junge invites us to consider whether there may be some circumstances in which self-forgiveness is not merely unwarranted but morally objectionable. There are differing views on the question of whether there are some offenses that are so heinous that the person who has committed them should not forgive himself for them. In one view, there are egregious cases in which it is right and proper that the offender should remain alienated from himself and should not be able to achieve peace of mind. In another view, "genuine self-forgiveness is always appropriate and desirable from a moral point of view, regardless of the seriousness and extent of the wrongdoing."[60] The self-forgiveness at issue in the Junge case, however, is not for the heinous deeds of her Nazi employer – after all, she bore no direct and little indirect responsibility for them – but rather for the ignorance and naivete that kept her from recognizing the atrocities her employer was perpetrating. Arguably, under these circumstances, it might well have been excessive of her to withhold self-forgiveness indefinitely.

Humility is generally regarded as an admirable quality. The moral value of self-forgiveness, by contrast, seems less secure. This is partly for a reason similar to the one Kant gives for why one's own happiness cannot be a duty: just as we are naturally disposed to promote our own happiness, so too we are naturally disposed to forgive ourselves, if we are even willing to admit that there is something to forgive ourselves for. But this view does not distinguish between warranted (genuine) and unwarranted (premature, faulty) self-forgiveness, and does not reflect an appreciation of the difficulties the former presents for many people. These difficulties become clearer in the light of what I have said about the connection between warranted self-forgiveness and taking responsibility for one's past.

8. CONCLUDING THOUGHTS ON MEMORY

This chapter is not only about taking responsibility for one's past. It is, obviously, about memory as well because memory is one of our chief avenues of access to the past. I end this chapter by drawing together some of things that I have said or implied about memory, specifically, about how memory interprets the past and how it functions within my account.

First, I want to underscore memory's role in relation to the elements of my account. In order to take responsibility for one's past, one will on occasion have to remember it, but just to remember it is not enough to take responsibility for it. As I have explained, one has to appropriate it, and one can remember one's past without doing this. It is not even enough that one remembers one's past *as* something for which one was responsible, for there is no guarantee that once having done this, one will assimilate and engage with that past. One might instead view one's prior responsibility as an interesting fact about one's past and leave it at that, without considering how that past has influenced the present and one's self-conception. What is particularly significant about memory in my account is that it makes appropriation and a particular retrospective construction of meaning possible.

This leads to a second point. Our reliance on memory to gain access to the past is not unproblematic from an epistemic standpoint, and this presents a challenge for my account. Our memories of the past are inevitably shaped by our current circumstances and interests, and skeptics about memory will claim that we need to move away from the idea that some of our memories are more truthful or accurate than others. I have claimed, however, that a wholesale skepticism about memory is unwarranted because there are some fairly reliable if not infallible ways of distinguishing between memories that are true of the past and those that are not. Moreover, there is a sense in which this entire chapter is premised on the cogency of the notion of truth in memory. If there was no legitimate distinction to be drawn between true and false memories, a person would be more or less free to make up whatever *past* he wants to take or not to take responsibility for. And this, among other things, would make the topic of this chapter considerably less interesting from a moral point of view.

Finally, it is correct, as far as it goes, that memory gives us access to the past so that it is available to us for responsibility-taking work. However, memory's relationship to taking responsibility is actually not as simple or unidirectional as this suggests. Various current factors shape how we remember the past, among which is our willingness to take responsibility for our past. Those who are willing to take responsibility for their past would likely remember it in a way that those who are not willing to take responsibility would not remember it. For this reason, remembering our past and our taking responsibility for it are not entirely separate processes. (As we will see in the Chapter 3, there is a similar relationship between a collective taking responsibility for its past and its collective memory.) Nevertheless, although our memories are shaped by beliefs about our responsibilities, some of which may expose us to moral or ethical criticism, we have to believe in the possibility of truthful memory and that we can distinguish between the truthful and nontruthful if the task of taking responsibility for our past is to be a morally serious one. Indeed, we can go further than this and say that if we are to take responsibility for our past, then we must treat memory, that is to say, truthful memory, as one of our responsibilities.

NOTES

1. W. Trevor, *Felicia's Journey* (London: Penguin, 1994).
2. Roy Schafer, "The psychoanalytic vision of reality," in *A New Language for Psychoanalysis* (New Haven: Yale University Press, 1976), pp. 42–43.
3. We can think of taking responsibility for past acts (or omissions) that are *not* characteristic of a particular period of one's life or that do not reveal one's past character, as a limit case of the sort of phenomenon that I am centrally interested in here.
4. Galen Strawson, "Against Narrativity," *Ratio 17* (2004): 428–452, at 438.
5. Quoted in Stephan Lesher, *George Wallace: American Populist* (Reading, MA: Addison-Wesley, 1993), p. 502.
6. Lesher, ibid., p. 501.
7. Justin Oakley, *Morality and the Emotions* (London: Routledge, 1992), p. 124.
8. Think here, for example, of the concentration camp inmate who steps forward to take responsibility for something he did not do in order to spare his fellow inmates from execution.
9. These views are distinguished in Angela M. Smith, "Responsibility for Attitudes: Activity and Passivity in Mental Life," *Ethics 115* (January 2005): 236–271, at 238–240.
10. Compare the discussion of taking responsibility in Claudia Card, *The Unnatural Lottery: Character and Moral Luck* (Philadelphia: Temple University Press, 1996), pp. 27–29.
11. Peter French argues that the failure to make behavioral adjustments so as to avoid repetition of behavior that resulted in an untoward outcome can justify holding a person morally responsible for that outcome, even if it was caused unintentionally. See *Responsibility Matters* (Lawrence, KS: University Press), pp. 12–17. It can also justify the judgment that he has not taken responsibility for that outcome.
12. Samuel Gorovitz, "Leaving the Past Alone," *Philosophical Review 73* (1964): 360–371, at 370.
13. Arthur Danto, *Analytical Philosophy of History* (Cambridge, UK: Cambridge University Press, 1965), p. 155.
14. Daniel Schacter, *Searching for Memory: The Brain, the Mind, and the Past* (New York: Harper Collins, 1996), p. 5.
15. See Jerome Bruner, "The 'Remembered' Self," in U. Nesser and R. Fivush (Eds.), *The Remembering Self* (Cambridge, UK: Cambridge University Press, 1994), pp. 41–45; and, in the same volume, M. Ross and R. Buehler, "Creative remembering," pp. 205–235.
16. Extreme accounts of memory – constructivist ones as well as "snapshot" or archival ones – are equally deeply problematic. To say that memory is *entirely* a social or personal construction is to deny that the past is something that is given rather than merely a piece of artifice, and that memory, in some of its operations, seeks to be true to and to do justice to that past. Extreme constructivist accounts would say these beliefs are illusory, but there are good reasons not to follow them in this. For more discussion, see W. James Booth, *Communities of Memory* (Ithaca: Cornell University Press, 2006), pp. 35–36,

67–68. See also Sue Campbell, *Relational Remembering: Rethinking the Memory Wars* (Lanham, MD: Rowman and Littlefield Publishers, 2003), chapter 5.

17. George Herbert Mead, *The Philosophy of the Present* (LaSalle, Illinois: Open Court, 1932), p. 12.

18. I also take up the issue of the accuracy of memory, this time with respect to collective memory, in Chapter 4, Section 6.

19. Maurice Halbwachs, *On Collective Memory*, Lewis A. Coser (Ed. and Trans.). (Chicago and London: Chicago University Press, 1992), p. 38. See also Chapter 1, Section 5.

20. Margaret Urban Coyne (now Margaret Walker) uses the terms "appropriation" and "thematization" to describe two modes of unifying a life in "The Unity of a Life" (Fordham University, unpublished manuscript). Her discussion has helped me in my somewhat different task of setting out conditions for taking responsibility for one's past. Jonathan A. Jacobs makes the following claim about something very much like what I have called appropriation, although I choose somewhat different language to make the point:

> One's own causality is maximally intelligible in understanding and unifying a personal history. The more of my own causality that I impart to my career, the more transparent the determination of it. It is my own authority and responsibility that I apprehend and penetrate. [*Virtue and Self-Knowledge* (Englewood Cliffs, NJ: Prentice-Hall, 1989), p. 38]

21. Roy Schafer, "Claimed and disclaimed action," in *A New Language for Psychoanalysis*, op. cit., p. 146. See also R. Schafer, "Self-control," in *Language and Insight* (New Haven: Yale University Press, 1978), pp. 69–103.

22. Angela M. Smith, "Responsibility for Attitudes: Activity and Passivity in Mental Life," *Ethics 115* (January 2005): 236–271, at 251, 263.

23. See Note 33.

24. See, for example, Carl Elliott, "The Tyranny of Happiness: Ethics and Cosmetic Psychopharmacology," in E. Parens (Ed.), *Enhancing Human Traits: Ethical and Social Implications* (Washington, DC: Georgetown University Press, 1998), pp. 177–188.

25. Peter Kramer, *Listening to Prozac* (New York: Penguin, 1997), p. 259.

26. Carol Freedman, "Aspirin for the Mind? Some Ethical Worries about Psychopharmacology," in *Enhancing Human Traits*, op. cit., pp. 135–150, at 144.

27. For a relevant discussion of the difference between psychopharmacologic and psychoanalytic treatment of depression, see Jonathan Lear, *Therapeutic Action: An Earnest Plea for Irony* (New York: Other Press, 2002), pp. 79–81.

28. Kramer, op. cit., pp. 69–70.

29. Ibid., p. 278.

30. Lauren Slater, "Prozac Mother and Child," *New York Times Magazine* (October 17, 1999), section 6, pp. 115–118.

31. For a thoughtful discussion of how the quest for pharmacologically induced "happiness" devalues memory and threatens personal identity, see *Beyond Therapy: Biotechnology and the Pursuit of Happiness, A Report by the President's*

Council on Bioethics (Washington, DC, 2003), especially chapter 5. The Council identifies a two-fold threat from psychopharmacology:

First, an unchecked power to erase memories, brighten moods, and alter our emotional dispositions could imperil our capacity to form a strong and coherent personal identity. To the extent that our inner life ceases to reflect the ups and downs of daily existence and instead operates independently of them, we dissipate our identity, which is formed through engagement with others and through immersion in the mix of routine and unpredictable events that constitute our lives. Second, by disconnecting our mood and memory from what we do and experience, the new drugs could jeopardize the fitness and truthfulness of how we live and what we feel, as well as our ability to confront responsibly and with dignity the imperfections and limits of our lives and those of others.... Instead of recognizing contentment, pleasure, and joy as appropriate reflections of the richness of human life and inseparable from the fulfilling activities and attachments that are the heart of human happiness, we are invited to treat them as ends in themselves, perhaps one day inducible at will. (212–213)

32. Several authors have related these factors to the devaluation of memory in the contemporary world. According to David Gross, "The dominant tone of life today [in the West] is hostile to memory. On a personal level, the reigning advice now is to let go of and not dwell upon what is absent; "closure" is the new catchword, meaning a willingness to block off or forget what cannot be comfortably assimilated." (See *Lost Time: On Remembering and Forgetting in Late Modern Culture* (Amherst, MA: University of Massachusetts Press, 2000), p. 152). Kenneth Keniston, in his enormously influential book, *The Uncommitted: Alienated Youth in American Society* (New York: Dell Publishing, 1960), gives a diagnosis of American society that is in broad agreement with this assessment. For Keniston, a new type of personality has emerged in our society in response to the collective anxieties arising from that society's worship of technological and social innovation. The defining features of this new personality, he claims, are a concentration on the present and a focus on immediate experience, and although this outlook is particularly evident among the "alienated youth" of our society, it is not limited to them. Indeed, this outlook, what Keniston aptly calls "the cult of the present," is said to be a pervasive feature of our culture, and he explains it in the following way:

When the rate of social change accelerates beyond a given point, or when historical changes are too drastic and discontinuous, the ability to maintain a sense of connection with the past and future disappears, and with it, a progressive view of history. (196)

The psychological implications of this disconnection, he further argues, are profound and disturbing: "a diffusion and fragmentation of the sense of identity," "an experience of [oneself] as amorphous, indistinct, and disorganized" (164). Those who subscribe to the "cult of the present" (and this includes many in American society) are unable to achieve "a clear, unified, and coherent sense of identity" (165).

Similarly, Frank Connerton claims that the "conditions of modernity," its characteristic rhythm and driving force, have had a corrosive effect on how individuals and collectivities relate to their past: "[the very principle of modernity] denies credence to the thought that the life of an individual or a community either can or should derive its value from acts of consciously performed recall" [*How Societies Remember* (Cambridge, UK: Cambridge University Press, 2004), p. 64].

Finally, W. James Booth joins this group when he claims that it is "broadly true that modernity... is suspicious of the social role of memory," and he traces this in a number of ways to "the modern liberal dispensation":

> To advance a [liberal] conception of justice is not something that can be done by reference to the past, or to the (once) unproblematic and uncontested traditions of the life-world of our society. Rather, such claims are sustained by reference to reason and rights.... In that sense... modernity defines itself in opposition to the traditionalist, or weight-of-the-past, view. (*Communities of Memory*, op. cit., pp. 166–167)

These various analyses of how we, or people in the West, stand with respect to the past have some plausibility. None of these commentators is proposing some deterministic view according to which "presentism" is the only option for individuals in the West: cultural norms, economic forces, and political systems constrain, but do not dictate, individual choice. At the same time, as with all generalizations about dominant tendencies, we need to be wary of oversimplification.

33. Freud immediately comes to mind here, since he had a fundamental interest in the ways in which the past can cause symptoms (often pain) in the present, and his conception of neurosis as a self-destructive bondage to the past can help illuminate what is at stake in taking responsibility for one's past. Some of Freud's most important ideas about this subject, within a therapeutic framework, are contained in his short piece, "Remembering, Repeating and Working-Through," in J. Stachey (Trans.), *Standard Edition of the Complete Works of Sigmund Freud* (Vol. 12). (Hogart: London, 1914), pp. 147–156. The aim of psychoanalysis, he says here, can be characterized in either of two ways: "Descriptively speaking, it is to fill in gaps in memory; dynamically speaking, it is to overcome resistances due to repression" (148). Psychoanalysis fills in memory gaps by uncovering resistances which are unknown to the patient and which function as defenses against admission of repressed material into consciousness. Because of these resistances, "the patient does not *remember* anything of what he has forgotten and repressed, but *acts* it out. He reproduces it not as a memory but as an action; he *repeats* it, without, of course, knowing that he is repeating it" (150).

Alternatively, we can say that his compulsion to repeat is "his way of remembering" (ibid.) and that the repressed material is not forgotten at all. It survives below the surface of awareness and is expressed obliquely, often becoming stronger and more disturbing than it was initially because it has been damned up. The goal of therapy, more fully stated, is to turn the patient's compulsion to repeat into a motive for remembering (i.e., for remembering as a process requiring consciousness of the past) through the psychoanalytic work of generating a transference neurosis. The analyzable transference neurosis replaces the patient's ordinary neurosis, thus creating "an intermediate region between illness and real life through which the transition from the one to the other is made" (154). Furthermore, the extent to which *acting out* replaces remembering is a function of the degree of the patient's resistance: the greater the resistance, the greater the extent of acting out, and the more difficult it will be for the patient to "work through" the resistance and for the therapeutic process to have a successful outcome (155).

This working through – a process described much too briefly in Freud's paper – "may in practice turn out to be an arduous task for the subject of the analysis and a trial of patience for the analyst. Nevertheless, it is a part of the work which effects the greatest changes in the subject" (155). If the patient is allowed time, in analysis, to become more conversant with the nature of his resistances, to understand how his defenses have affected his personality, and if he is able to overcome his resistances, he will be freed of the compulsion to act out. And this will have positive effects – in terms of enhanced self-determination and self-esteem and less self-destructiveness in relationships – that will ramify throughout his life, since the compulsion to repeat shows itself not only in the patient's "personal attitude to the doctor but also in every other activity and relationship which may occupy his life at that time" (151). Memory, according to Freud, is what enables the patient to liberate himself from a sort of bondage to the past, a crippling compulsion to enact over and over again what he has forgotten, without knowing that he is doing so. When properly exercised, memory opens up possibilities of individual freedom and personal fulfillment that could never be realized so long as one's mental life is unconsciously shaped or determined by the harmful affects of forgotten events.

Freud's focus in this paper is the technique of psychoanalysis, which, of course, is not why I bring him into the discussion at this point. Moreover, it raises difficult questions about the criteria for claiming that what the neurotic patient is doing is acting out the *very same material* that he has forgotten or repressed, that he is, as it were, acting out the memory. These are not issues that I will pursue here. Nevertheless, we can understand *working-through* as the psychoanalytic counterpart of my notion of taking responsibility for one's past.

David Gross adds an extremely important qualification to the popular conception of Freud as the apostle of memory:

it is not often noticed that Freud suggested yet another way to handle hurtful memories, and that was simply to forget, or "deactivate" them. According to Freud, most of the memories that cause unhappiness are of events that are painful to recall for the simple reason that the events themselves were painful experiences. As a rule, such memories carry no deeper symbolic meanings, nor as they attached to repressed material in the unconscious. They are merely unhappy memories, or what Freud called "disagreeable impressions," which any individual would be better off forgetting, since holding on to them would only do damage to the psyche in the long run. (Gross, op. cit., p. 60)

Thus, Freud allows that forgetting may be an entirely appropriate response to some painful experiences. Sometimes it *is* best not to remember the hurtful past so much or so often. The challenge is to know when and what to remember and when and what to forget. (Recall the discussion of Nietzsche in Chapter 1.) Memory becomes fetishistic when every unhappy memory is regarded as an appropriate subject for psychoanalytic treatment.

There is more on Freud's essay, "Remembering, Repeating, and Working-Through," in Jonathan Lear, *Freud* (New York: Routledge, 2005).

34. Norman Care, *Living with One's Past* (Lanham, MD: Rowman and Littlefield, 1996), p. 14.

35. In terms of Freudian psychoanalysis, he represses but does not liberate himself from his past. The "return of the repressed" compromises his agency.

36. Henry Sidgwick, *The Methods of Ethics* (7th ed.). (Chicago: University of Chicago Press, 1907), p. 334.

37. That is, he will put himself and his accomplishments in proper perspective to the extent that taking responsibility for his past depends on adopting an attitude of humility that gives the past its due. The dependence here is likely to have far-reaching consequences for one's life.

38. For the distinction between these types of accounts for the related trait of modesty, see G. F. Schueler, "Why Modesty is a Virtue," *Ethics 107* (April 1997): 467–485; A. T. Nuyen, "Just Modesty," *American Philosophical Quarterly 35* (January 1998): 101–109.

39. Proponents of accuracy accounts include: Aaron Ben-Ze'ev, "The Virtue of Modesty," *American Philosophical Quarterly 30* (1993): 235–246; Owen Flanagan, "Virtue and Ignorance," *Journal of Philosophy 87* (1990): 420–428; and Norvin Richards, "Is Humility a Virtue?" *American Philosophical Quarterly 25* (1988): 253–259 and *Humility* (Philadelphia: Temple University Press, 1992).

40. Richards, "Is Humility a Virtue?" p. 254.

41. Ibid.

42. Richards, *Humility*, op. cit., p. 5.

43. The accuracy account has been criticized as well. See, for example, Ty Raterman, "On Modesty: Being Good and Knowing It Without Flaunting It," *American Philosophical Quarterly 43* (2006): 221–234. Even if not entirely unproblematic, however, the accuracy account seems to me to capture some of our central intuitions about humility. Moreover, as characterized by the accuracy account, humility is both a valuable trait and one that has links to taking responsibility for the past, so it is worth discussing for these reasons as well.

44. Examples include the rape or incest survivor who holds herself responsible for the earlier violation despite having been only a passive victim. Taking responsibility for the rape or act of incest in this way compounds the original harm and is an all too common phenomenon among its victims.

45. Note that I say "might" here. I am not claiming that one who fails to take responsibility for his past always does this, or that he always lacks humility. I am simply trying to explain what some of the moral concerns having to do with one's relationship to one's past might be.

46. The term "impure agency" is borrowed from Margaret Urban Walker, "Moral Luck and the Virtues of Impure Agency," in D. Statman (Ed.), *Moral Luck* (Albany, NY: State University of New York Press, 1993), pp. 235–250. Among

the virtues of impure agency, she lists *integrity, grace,* and *lucidity.* I would add *humility.*

47. For a lengthier discussion of self-forgiveness and its associated failures, see my "Doctoring and Self-Forgiveness," in R. Walker and P. J. Ivanhoe (Eds.), *Working Virtue* (Oxford University Press, 2007).

48. The distinction between achievement and process is important. Self-forgiveness (process) involves a number of tasks that can restore peace of mind and lead to a state of self-acceptance (achievement). But self-acceptance can also be purchased quite cheaply, without the hard work of true self-forgiveness.

49. Robin Dillon, "Self-Forgiveness and Self-Respect," *Ethics 112* (October 2001): 53–83 at 83.

50. Claudia Card, *The Atrocity Paradigm: A Theory of Evil* (New York: Oxford University Press, 2002), p. 168.

51. Care, op. cit., p. 131.

52. See, for example, Margaret R. Holmgren, "Self-Forgiveness and Responsible Moral Agency," *Journal of Value Inquiry 32,* 1 (March 1998): 75–91. I prefer to speak about warranted and unwarranted self-forgiveness, rather than genuine and fraudulent self-forgiveness.

53. Dillon, op. cit., p. 57.

54. This list of tasks draws from Dillon, op. cit., p. 57; and Margaret R. Holmgren, "Self-Forgiveness and Responsible Moral Agency," *Journal of Value Inquiry 32* (1985): 75–91 and "Forgiveness and Self-Forgiveness in Psychotherapy," in S. Lamb and J. Murphy (Eds.), *Before Forgiving: Cautionary Views of Forgiveness in Psychotherapy* (Oxford: Oxford University Press, 2002), pp. 112–135.

55. *Blind Spot: Hitler's Secretary,* A. Heller and O. Schmiderer (Dirs.). (2002). Quotes taken directly from English subtitles.

56. Traudl Junge, *Until the Final Hour: Hitler's Last Secretary,* Melissa Muller (Ed.). (New York: Arcade Publishing, 2002).

57. Ibid., p. 2.

58. Ibid.

59. Michael Stocker has pointed out to me that an individual may need to deny responsibility for his past to some extent and for some time in order to marshal the inner resources to deal effectively with it. In this way, denial of responsibility can be therapeutic.

60. Holmgren, op. cit., p. 88.

3

DOING JUSTICE TO THE PAST

Memory does not consist in subordinating the past to the needs of the present...for he who looks to gather the materials of memory places himself at the service of the dead, and not the other way around.

– Alain Finkielkraut, *The Imaginary Jew*[1]

1. A HISTORICAL EXAMPLE: THE TULSA RACE RIOT OF 1921

On the evening of May 31, 1921, a crowd of whites gathered at the Tulsa, Oklahoma Courthouse, drawn there in part by a newspaper story implying that Dick Rowland, a black shoeshine man being held there, had assaulted Sarah Page, a white woman, in the elevator where she worked as an operator. When rumors that Rowland would be lynched began to circulate in the city's African-American community, a number of blacks converged at the Courthouse to protect him. Tensions ran high, a pistol went off, and soon a riot erupted. Local units of the National Guard were called in and began working with hundreds of white men deputized by the Tulsa police chief – some of whom were themselves participants in the violence – to quell the riot. Beginning early the next morning, white mobs invaded Greenwood, the prosperous black section of Tulsa, following closely after the guardsmen who arrested every black they could find and took them into "protective custody," leaving their property undefended. Truckloads of whites, often including the special deputies, set fires and shot blacks on sight. When the smoke had cleared, more than 1,400 homes, businesses and churches in Greenwood lay in ruins and anywhere from 100 to 300 people (some estimates put the number as high as 3,000), most of them black, had been killed. Not one of these criminal acts was ever prosecuted or punished by government at any level, municipal, county, state, or federal.[2]

Although the Tulsa race riot of 1921 is now generally regarded by historians as one of the darkest episodes in Oklahoma history, by the end of the decade, public acknowledgment of what had happened practically disappeared, and, as a result, the riot soon faded from the collective memory of Oklahomans. Local newspapers rarely mentioned the riot, the state's historical establishment essentially ignored it, and generations of Oklahoma school children were given a sanitized version of Oklahoma history that either said nothing about the riot or treated it as an unfortunate, but not very significant, event in the state's past.

The shroud of silence that descended over the riot has been explained by historians in a number of ways. The explanations, different but mutually compatible, include the following: many Oklahomans, and particularly Tulsa's white civic and political leaders, eager to attract new businesses and settlers to a young state, regarded the riot as a public relations nightmare to which it was best not to draw attention; official neglect of the riot was part and parcel of the same institutionalized racism that provided fertile breeding ground for the outbreak of racial violence; cities and states, like individuals, do not, as a general rule, like to dwell on their past shortcomings. To be sure, there were occasional efforts by scholars, journalists, and community activists over the ensuing decades to raise public awareness of the riot, but these had only a limited impact, and most Oklahomans and Americans remained ignorant of this part of Tulsa's racial past.[3] It was not until 1997, when the Oklahoma legislature authorized the formation of the *Oklahoma Commission to Study the Race Riot of 1921*, and charged it with conducting a thorough examination of the history of the riot and the complicity and culpability of the various parties involved, that official government action was taken to remedy this situation.

In its final report, issued in 2000, the commission argued that no individual or aggregate of individuals was responsible for the losses caused by the riot, but rather "a collective body" that, "acting as one body – had coldly and deliberately and systematically assaulted one victim, a whole community, intending to eliminate it as a community."[4] To make amends for this wrongdoing, it recommended "restitution to the historic Green-wood community, in real and tangible form," specifically,

> (1) direct payment of reparations to survivors of the Tulsa Race Riot; (2) direct payment of reparations to descendants of the survivors of the Tulsa Race Riot; (3) a scholarship fund available to students affected by the Tulsa Race Riot; (4) establishment of an economic development enterprise zone in the historic area of the Greenwood District; (5) a memorial for the reburial of any human remains found in the search for unmarked graves of riot victims.[5]

The first two recommendations were rejected by the Oklahoma legis-lature. Instead of reparations for the survivors or their descendants, it passed a bill calling for the creation of a Greenwood area redevelopment authority and granting seed money for a riot memorial and a scholar-ship account to be funded by private donations. In taking this position, some lawmakers focused on culpability in the riot, arguing that the state bore no direct legal responsibility to pay reparations and that if any gov-ernmental entity did, it was the city of Tulsa. Some also focused on the injustice of requiring the current generation to pay compensation for historical wrongs, asserting that, regardless of who was responsible at the time, today's taxpayers – many of whom repudiate racism – should not be expected to pay for wrongs committed almost 80 years earlier.[6] Nevertheless, one state representative, who helped launch the Commis-sion, stated that its efforts were still worthwhile despite the legislature's rejection of reparations, because there are various ways of acknowledging past wrongdoing, including fostering economic development, establish-ing a scholarship fund, and erecting a memorial. What is critically impor-tant, he maintained, is that by condemning the history of race relations in Oklahoma and Tulsa and going even part way toward accepting the commission's recommendations, "the government is reaching back into history and saying 'I'm sorry.'"[7]

Publicly acknowledging and apologizing for past wrongs committed by one's predecessors, where such acknowledgment and apology are sincere and not merely intended to mollify the victims or their descendants, is a way of assuming responsibility for those wrongs.[8] This is what the commissioners were doing in their report to the state with respect to the Tulsa race riot. Sometimes the assumption of responsibility is only an *acceptance* of responsibility, by which I mean an admission that one did something for which one might be blameworthy (or creditworthy), possibly accompanied by a willingness to pay some prescribed penalty, typically in grudging response to pressure from the aggrieved parties or those who speak on their behalf. However, the assumption may involve more: a *taking* of responsibility. By this, I do not mean merely a public admission of responsibility, as when a criminal in a plea bargain situation pleads guilty in order to avoid a stiffer sentence. I mean a stance that is not merely reactive to accusations and restricted to answering them, and that includes being creative in devising ways to make amends for the past, and being motivated by a resolve to put things right, insofar as one is able to do so, and to prevent recurrence of past wrongdoing. When a group of people claims to collectively take responsibility for something in its past that it professes to repudiate, these things are expected, including various sorts of reparative action that are real as well as symbolic. When these actions are not forthcoming, the claim rings hollow.

Cutting across this distinction between accepting and taking responsibility is a further one having to do with what a number of people collectively takes responsibility for: it might be confined to particular past events or historical episodes or it might encompass the social, legal, and political conditions that made these events and episodes possible and to which they gave expression. The strong language of the bill passed by the Oklahoma legislature suggests that it thought it appropriate to assume some measure of responsibility, not only for the riot and the death and destruction that followed in its wake, but also for the institutionalized racism that predated the riot and was its main cause.

The story of the Tulsa race riot is not only about large-scale wrongdoing perpetrated by one community against another with the acquiescence and active participation of government. It is also about how this story disappeared from public discourse and from the public record that shapes a community's understanding of its past, so that an analogue of personal forgetting occurred on a collective level. As mandated by the Oklahoma legislature, the Commission's task was two-fold: to develop an historical record of the riot and to make recommendations, including whether reparations can or should be paid. The commissioners saw these as somewhat independent tasks and stressed that the former had value even if their recommendations about reparations were not adopted:

> Whatever else this commission already has achieved or soon will inspire, one accomplishment will remain indefinitely. Until recently, the Tulsa race riot has been the most important least known event in the state's entire history. . . . That is not now and never will be true again.[9]

This shameful event needed to be publicly recounted and collectively remembered. The truth about it needed to be told and the record set straight for current and future generations, even if this did not lead to monetary compensation for the victims or their descendants. The report suggests (without much in the way of argument) that even if the legislature does not back payment of reparations, airing what happened in Oklahoma's past is still a good thing to do and indeed morally imperative in its own right.

The commissioners would no doubt have been dissatisfied with what they had accomplished if the government had not assumed some responsibility and apologized for past wrongdoing. Reconstructing and preserving the historical record is obviously an important part of such a process. However, merely developing an historical record is not sufficient, as the commissioners recognized, because there are complications in settling what that record should contain. Some versions of the past may be controversial, may contain alleged facts for which the historical evidence is meager or ambiguous, and may represent for some parties a distortion of the past, or at best, a partial and highly selective truth. An historical record that is vulnerable to these criticisms cannot do the work it is supposed to do, namely, to provide a commonly agreed upon interpretation of the past with respect to which questions about responsibility for wrongdoing can be debated and resolved, collectively. The point of the historical narrative is not to uncover "the truth" – as if there were some fact of the matter just waiting to be discovered – but to settle, even if provisionally, on a truthful version of the past that permits this collective discourse to go forward. The record must therefore give an account of the past that is shared by and is authoritative for all involved parties, that is, those who are the victims of wrongdoing or who represent them as well as those who are alleged to have some reparative responsibility. The record must be based on evidence that, as far as possible, is verifiable by objective methods. I will say more about this in Section 5.

The case of the Tulsa race riot, like countless other historical examples, focuses attention on one sort of problem about responsibility for the past, namely, the responsibility of a group of persons for past wrongs done to a group.[10] This is to be distinguished from three other kinds of responsibility relationship: individual responsibility for wrongs done to an individual, individual responsibility for wrongs done to a group, and group responsibility for wrongs done to an individual. In the Tulsa example, a governmental body took responsibility, to some extent, for the racism of earlier regimes and the racism they permitted, and the (directly) victimized group was the entire black community of the city. Cases of responsibility of the group–group sort vary in the following respects:

- the group taking responsibility might be a people or a nation or a cultural community or some other association, as well as a state;
- the wrongs for which responsibility is taken might have been episodic or rooted in enduring features of institutional practice or communal life;
- the victimized group might have or lack coherence and unity as a group;
- there may be widely varying degrees of individual responsibility among the members of the collectively responsible group; and
- the consequences of the wrongs might be evenly or unevenly distributed among members of the victimized group.

There are also positive counterparts to each sort of responsibility relationship. Groups, for example, can take responsibility for having benefited other groups or protected them from harm, as well as for having wronged them.

Generally speaking, a group should take responsibility for past wrongdoing, that is, *collectively* take responsibility for it, if there are good grounds for attributing collective responsibility to it and no countervailing reasons that are strong enough to outweigh its taking responsibility. However, as the aftermath of the Tulsa race riot shows – and as history has amply demonstrated – the members of a group may properly be held collectively responsible for wrongdoing and yet, for various reasons, fail to collectively acknowledge and take responsibility for it as they should.

Several questions may be asked about the notions of collective responsibility and collectively taking responsibility for past wrongdoing, including the following:

In order to hold a group collectively responsible for past wrongs, is it necessary to produce criteria of group identity over time, so that it can be determined whether this presently existing group is one-and-the-same agent as the group that committed the original wrong? If so, what criteria should be employed?

How can a group *act* so as to collectively take responsibility for past wrongdoing?

In what sense(s) can we speak of a wrong having been committed against a *group?* Relative to these different senses, how does belonging to a group affect the claims for reparations that persons may properly make and the reparative measures that are most fitting?

How does the fact that the responsible party and the aggrieved party often interpret the past differently, and do not share the same account of who did what to whom, bear on the possibility of taking responsibility for past wrongdoing?

How is a group's understanding of and relationship to its past altered by taking responsibility for it, and how is this connected with the formation of group or collective identity (as I discussed in Chapter 1: not numerical identity over time but the collective analogue of biographical identity)?

Does the case for collective responsibility for past wrongdoing hinge on whether there is such a thing as collective guilt?

Seeing as it is only the members of a group who are morally implicated in the group's responsibility for past wrongdoing, when is an individual to be considered a member in the relevant sense, and what exactly is the connection between group membership and responsibility for past wrongdoing?

An account of what is presupposed by and involved in the claim that a group of individuals does or should collectively take responsibility for past wrongs done to another group should have answers to these questions, and I will say something about all of them during the course of this chapter.

This chapter proceeds as follows. Section 2 seeks to clarify the notion of group–group responsibility by distinguishing among various sorts of groups. Collections or aggregates are distinguished from socially unified and organized groups, the latter being my chief interest. Section 3 briefly rehearses some different senses of collective responsibility and asks how we are to explain the notion of group action, which is presupposed by both collective responsibility and collectively taking responsibility for past wrongdoing. Here, too, I consider whether collective responsibility over generations presupposes group identity over time and note the difficulties of providing criteria for it. Moving next to the victims of group–group wrongdoing, Section 4 discusses the ways in which groups that are unified and organized can be wronged. Wrongful conduct may be harmful or it may be both harmful and profoundly offensive to its victims, and the wrongs for which it may be appropriate to collectively take responsibility can be of these different sorts.

Sections 5 and 6 explore the relationships between collectively taking responsibility for the past and the construction of a shared understanding of history and a collective identity. I argue in Section 5 that collectively taking responsibility for the past is a political act that can only be effective if there is some shared understanding of who did what to whom. But this understanding does not have to be fully comprehensive or immune to contestation: on the contrary, it may leave many issues unresolved and is subject to revision as new accommodations between perpetrators and victims are reached. Moreover, as a political act, there is an intimate connection between taking responsibility for past wrongdoing and the composition and construction of a collective identity, which I elaborate on in Section 6. Rivalry over which version of the past should be authoritative for the society is particularly deep-seated when a group's identity is bound up with how it remembers the past and what it holds itself responsible for.

Identity remains a focus of the next sections. Many, including philosophers, reject the notion of collective guilt, claiming it is morally offensive, if not incoherent. I steer clear of this debate, however, because I am more interested in a much less frequently discussed notion whose cogency and usefulness I proceed to defend in Section 7. Here I propose that the activities of collective responsibility-taking can be justified by appeal to a notion of warranted collective shame. The shame I refer to here is not the shame an individual experiences as an individual or as a member of a group. The shame that is experienced as a member of a group is the shame that derives from an individual's having a collective identity, but I am interested in something else, namely, group shame, which in turn can be understood in different ways, depending on the sense of "group" that is used. I present three accounts of collective shame – *aggregated individual shame, aggregated membership shame,* and *shared membership shame* – and select shared membership shame as the only one that truly brings shame to the collective level. Although the notion of collective shame is rarely discussed in the philosophical literature on collective responsibility, it is likely to seem more morally palatable, and less morally objectionable, than collective guilt, which often is discussed in this context. After all, shame is not as closely tied to blameworthiness as guilt is and can be justified even in the absence of fault. Moreover, collective shame is associated with a notion that helps explain why so much hangs on how groups remember their past and why collective memory is so often the site of controversy and conflict. It is the notion of collective identity, and the discussion of it ties this section to Section 6.

Collective identity is addressed again in Section 8. Here, it plays a critical role in my account of why remembrance of historical injustice is both a legitimate demand of the victims and their successors and obligatory for perpetrators and their successors. Certain harms suffered by members of a group are inseparable from the way the group views its history, and the way a group views its history contributes to the collective identity of the group. This history and the identity to which it contributes call for recognition and memorialization by those who bear responsibility for the wrongdoing. Forgetting a group's history, or remembering it in ways that demean or slight those whose history it is, injures that identity, and this injury constitutes an additional harm to the group and compounds the original injustice.

In demanding that a group collectively take responsibility for its past wrongs, and faulting it for acting unjustly if it does not do so, we expect it to at least acknowledge the wrongs for which it is responsible and, unlike the Tulsans and Oklahomans who for decades either repressed or were unaware of the events of 1921, to remember what happened, why it happened, and to whom. But of course, there is more: we are also demanding that it *do* something to make amends for or repair the wrong done. Although claims for redress of historical wrongs are often expressed in demands for restitution of expropriated property or payment of large sums of money to descendants of the victims, the kinds of response to wrongdoing that can count as reparative are actually quite varied. In particular, remembrance of past wrongdoing not only makes various kinds of reparation possible, but as I argue in Section 8, the fact that some act – be it setting up a scholarship fund, endowing the wing of a hospital, or creating a national holiday – is done *in remembrance* can itself be reparative.

2. TYPES OF GROUPS

In cases of group–group responsibility for past wrongdoing that I discuss in this chapter, a group is the agent of wrongdoing for which it or its successor[11] may or may not take responsibility; and a group is the victim of past wrongdoing and perhaps also continues to suffer from wrongs traceable to the past. Discussions of the ontological nature of groups, and of the distinction between types of groups, have long been a staple of writings in philosophy of the social sciences. The terminology that has been used to mark the distinctions is extremely variable, and different meanings have sometimes been given to the very same expression. The typology I present, therefore, may not exactly match that of others.[12]

(a) *Collections*

A collection is either (a) a random assortment whose identity is exhaustively specified in terms of the identities of its members, so that the subtraction or addition of any individual member entails a different group (sometimes called an "aggregate"); or (b) a group all of whose members have some property or properties in common and whose identity is something more than the aggregated identities of its individual members (sometimes called an "amalgam").[13] Examples of (b) include patients with high blood pressure, residents of the United States, and people over 6 feet tall. The group of people over 6 feet tall, as an instance of (b), would still be this group even if we eliminated Wilt Chamberlain or Abraham Lincoln from it. Further, the possession of common features by the members of a collection does not entail that the group has coherence as an entity in its own right and that its members are unified in some way, for example, by a shared history or joint interests or sense of community. They might not even be aware of each other's existence.

Even though type (b) collections have an identity that is not reducible to the identities of their individual members, truly collective responsibility cannot necessarily be attributed to them. Collective responsibility requires a collective agent and a group that is defined solely by the possession of some common properties is not for this reason a collective agent. Assuming the conditions of collective responsibility have been met, a group can be collectively responsible for harm done to collections of individuals as well as to groups that exhibit some degree of coherence and unity as a group, and this distinction corresponds to different grounds of the reparative claims group members may make.

(b) *Socially unified groups and their importance*

Sometimes a collection of individuals forms a group in a more robust sense: the group members not only have certain properties in common, but there are interrelationships among them and they see themselves as being somehow related to one another because of these properties. For example, the members of a longstanding bridge club comprise a socially unified group, not merely because they have common interests, but because there are various sorts of interrelationships among them. Their common interests are what brings them together and sustains their particular form of social interaction. Meeting for this purpose can also lead to the formation of bonds of mutual concern and affection that deepen their attachment to one other. A somewhat different example is a group of individuals, none of whom knows the other, who attend a dinner party thrown by a mutual friend. The guests are polite and friendly toward one another, as custom dictates, and may have only a rather minimal and transitory sort of social relationship. But it is a sort of social relationship, nevertheless, and this is sufficient to distinguish their group from a mere collection of individuals.

One important type of socially unified group is a *community*. By this I mean a group of individuals whose relationship to one another is mediated by, and partly constituted by, a shared conception of the group to which they belong. Communities can vary in size and degree of intimacy and formality, in the intensity of the dedication of their members, in the importance of the role they play in the members' lives, as well as in other ways. But in all of them, a conception of the social whole that defines the relationship is a component of the consciousness of its members.[14] A baseball team is usually a community in this sense because a represen- tation of the team, as a whole, is a constitutive presence in the relations of its members. Families, military regiments, ethnic tribes, labor unions, and religious sects are other examples.

To take yet another: a neighborhood is not a community simply in virtue of the fact that those who reside there are connected to one another through an extensive web of relationships. It only qualifies as a community when and because, in addition to this, a conception of the neighborhood to which they all belong informs the way in which the residents live and how they relate to others, including how they relate to those who reside in the same neighborhood and those who do not. Successful community activists appreciate this distinction between a neighborhood infused with a sense of community and one that is not. They understand that focus- ing the residents' attention on the ways in which the neighborhood to which they belong informs their lives and relationships is a critical step in organizing the neighborhood for collective action.

Being a member of a socially unified group is significant for self-identity in a way that membership in a mere collection is not. The specific notion of identity to which I am referring here can be clarified by distinguishing between two senses of "group identity." In one sense, we speak of the group identity of a group or community (as, for example, the national identity of Serbs as a people); in another, we speak of group identity as the belonging of an individual to and identification with a group (e.g., the Serbian identity of Slobodan Milosevic). Nenand Miscevic has argued, with respect to national identity, that "many authors move from one [sense] to the other without warning," and that it is essential to keep them apart so as not to beg important questions about the relationship between national and personal identity.[15] The point is well-taken and can be extended to other group identities as well. It is group identity in the second sense that I want to say a word about here; later, in Section 6, I focus on group identity in the first.

When our individual identities are partly made up of belonging to a particular family or ethnic group or faith community, this membership provides us with different standpoints from which to understand the world and our place in it. As forms of identity they are also the source of much that we do and regard as valuable in our lives. When a person belongs to different groups and has more than one identity constituted by such memberships, conflicts may arise, and this is always a matter of serious concern. Although not all of a person's identities are necessarily of equal importance to him or her, an identity is not merely a role that one can step out of or an occupation that one can quit. It is something that is more or less central to one's life and that shapes and constrains how one conducts oneself in a wide range of social situations. It is also, as I argued in Chapter 1, Section 7, internally related to obligations. Furthermore, the identities that we have as members of socially unified groups are typically not created by individual choice or sustained by a decision to retain the identity. We do not *give* ourselves a particular family identity, for example, but we *find* ourselves involved with particular others who have certain expectations of us and of whom we have certain expectations. We acquire a family identity as a consequence of growing up with particular others, sharing experiences and activities with them, drawing on a common fund of memories, and imbibing the customs and traditions that give families their distinctive character. We may question aspects of our identities and work to change a particular identity; we can also choose how much we will organize our lives around a particular identity. However, we can neither discard it right now at will, nor can we adopt a neutral standpoint for assessing some of our identities that is uninfluenced by other identities we possess.

The groups that are involved in the sort of group–group responsibility that particularly interests me in this chapter are socially unified ones (including communities). The victims of wrongdoing can constitute a group in this sense, and so can the perpetrators. In contrast to aggregates, what is owed to the members of socially unified groups is not necessarily what is owed to them as individuals. Moreover, the wrongs done to particular members of socially unified groups can radiate through the group in a way that cannot happen with mere collections of individuals. When the members of a socially unified group are targeted because they belong to that group, when, say, Jews or homosexuals are singled out because they are identified as Jews or homosexuals, and when those who belong to that group interact and interrelate in ways that constitute them a collective body and that are mediated by a conception of community, it is not merely *these* particular Jews or homosexuals who are victimized. Rather, the wrong done to them reverberates through the entire group.[16] Those whose individual group identity is Jewish or homosexual, whether or not they have suffered or are even likely to suffer direct physical harm, will regard the injustice in a particular light, as an assault upon a community that grounds and sustains their sense of self.

When a socially unified group is the agent of wrongdoing, some of those who belong to the group may try to come to terms with the wrongs committed by it. This is likely to be an especially difficult task for those individuals whose identity is bound up with membership in the group. It would not be surprising for anyone having this identity to feel connected, in a particularly intimate way, to that wrongdoing, whether or not they believe themselves to be personally morally blameworthy. If individuals believe that they share responsibility for group wrongdoing because of their group membership and are moved to do something about it, they might work for change in the group's values or goals or try to counteract tendencies within the group to excuse, deny, or forget the wrongs that were done. At the same time, however, each of these measures may carry significant personal risks, because they may encounter powerful resistance from those who committed, actively supported, or benefited from those wrongs.

(c) *Organized groups*

An organized group is a socially unified group with an internal decision structure that facilitates joint action and enables it to achieve collective goals. Organized groups often operate in accordance with formal, explicit decision procedures, but some relaxation of them is possible, although it is difficult to specify when the procedures become too loose for the group to still qualify as organized. E. H. Schein provides the following compact definition:

> An organization is the rational coordination of the activities of a number of people for the achievement of some common explicit purpose or goal, through division of labor and function and through a hierarchy of authority and responsibility.[17]

The decision structure of a formally organized group delineates stations and levels within the organizational power structure, and it subordinates and synthesizes the intentions and acts of various people occupying these positions into an organizational decision. The structure accords certain individuals who occupy positions within the organization the authority to speak for others in the organization and to make decisions that are binding on them, although there may also be avenues open to them for challenging particular organizational decisions with which they disagree. Examples of organized groups include business corporations, governments, military bodies, professional associations, and organized religions, but again not all organized groups have to be as formally organized as these groups.

Organization plays an important role in explaining how groups can collectively take responsibility for past wrongdoing because organization enables individuals to perform actions that they could not perform on their own or that they could not perform as a loose grouping. Members of a group may feel somehow complicit in the wrongs done by their group in the past and may try to make amends in whatever individual or uncoordinated way they can. But collectively taking responsibility for past wrongdoing, the main concern of this chapter, is an instance of concerted collective action, not personal action taken on one's own behalf or the mere aggregate of individual actions. Organization facilitates the collective taking of responsibility to redress wrongdoing, and unorganized groups may with greater or lesser difficulty be able to marshal and coordinate the resources needed to accomplish this by organizing themselves. Moreover, holding an unorganized group collectively responsible for past wrongdoing may motivate it to do this, that is, to organize itself, thereby putting it in a position to take responsibility, and the attribution of collective responsibility can perhaps be justified on this ground.[18]

Sometimes a group is represented by one or more officials who speak for the members of the group and possess legitimate authority to make binding decisions on behalf of the membership. It is sometimes a highly contentious matter, however, which individuals or groups of individuals have legitimate authority to act on behalf of a given group, and there may be a number of contenders, each of whom claims to be its legitimate voice. Furthermore, whether officials issue or refuse to issue apologies for past wrongdoing, and provide or decline to provide compensation or restitution to those who were wronged or their descendants, those on whose behalf the officials claim to be speaking and acting may not regard them as their legitimate representatives and may reject the position they have taken on the particular matter at hand. They may disagree with their representatives concerning the existence and extent of their collective responsibility for past wrongdoing. In general, on this and other matters, representatives may only properly speak for a group if they have been accorded the authority to do so by some process of political legitimation. Without such an authority, officials lack the moral authority to make binding decisions regarding responsibility for past wrongdoing on behalf of the group. The problem of representation, as we may call it, is to characterize the sorts of processes that confer legitimate authority and to define the limits of this authority.

3. COLLECTIVE RESPONSIBILITY FOR PAST WRONGDOING

(a) *Senses of collective responsibility*

Being responsible is not a conceptually necessary condition of taking responsibility because one can take responsibility for something that one is not actually responsible for, but there is an inference that goes in the other direction: those who are responsible for wrongdoing have a special relationship to it such that they are *obligated*, other things being equal, to take responsibility for that wrongdoing. So to determine whether a collective or individual has an obligation to do so, the prior question about responsibility for the wrongdoing must be addressed.

Collective responsibility, in one use of the term, is a species of vicarious responsibility.[19] There are various explanations of vicarious responsibility. One familiar and uncontroversial type derives from the process of authorization, whereby one party, the principal, authorizes another party, the agent, to act in his or her name and assumes responsibility for the consequences of the agent's actions. Another explanation bases vicarious responsibility on the relationship between superior and subordinate within a hierarchical organization, such as the government or the military. In these cases, individuals are responsible for, and answerable for, the harmful consequences of the acts of others with whom they have some sort of relationship. In like manner, when a group is vicariously responsible for the harmful actions of one or some of its members, one party – the group – is called on to answer for the harm caused by another party – individual members. (This does not preclude also singling out some members for individual punishment and blame.)

There is also a sense of collective responsibility according to which a group of people may be said to be directly, not vicariously, responsible for harm. This is the case when group responsibility is distributive, that is, when group responsibility is nothing more than the sum of the individual responsibilities of each and every member of the group. Group responsibility in this sense might be better called "collected" rather than "collective" responsibility, however, and little is gained by speaking of the group at all. In contrast to collected responsibility, the members of a group may be collectively responsible for actions that merit blame, in a manner that does not reduce to the practice of holding individuals morally responsible. And in contrast to vicarious responsibility, there may be circumstances in which the members of a group are not simply responsible for what some of their own have done, but rather for what they, collectively, have done.

Margaret Gilbert, a major contributor to the philosophical analysis of human groups, provides an account of collective agency that has served as a starting point for a great deal of the literature on this topic. In her "plural subject theory," she sets out the conditions that need to be satisfied in order to properly ascribe action and responsibility to a group of persons:

> *There is a group action* if and only if the members of a certain population are jointly committed to pursuing a certain goal as a body, and in light of this joint commitment relevant members (perhaps not all) successfully act so as to reach the goal in question.[20]

The notion of a joint commitment is crucial in this account and, as Gilbert characterizes it, it "is not a set of personal commitments, one for each of the parties. It is rather the commitment of them all . . . to do something as a body."[21] So, on this account, if the members of a group are jointly committed to wrongdoing, and in light of this commitment some members successfully act to achieve the goal, wrongdoing may be considered a group action, and the group may be held collectively responsible for it. Similarly, if *taking* responsibility is a group action, it cannot just be or involve a set of personal commitments by all or most of the members of a group to acknowledge or redress past wrongs. Rather, if they are to redress past wrongs as a group, the members of the group must be jointly committed to the work of moral repair as a body, and certain members of this group must act to achieve this goal in light of this joint commitment. The group can be as small as a family and as large as an entire nation. When the responsible group is large, heterogeneous, and widely dispersed, it will usually be necessary for there to be an organization of some sort that is able to take coordinated action to achieve the appropriate reparative goals. And, once again, in all these cases, plural subject theory holds that the relevant individuals must pursue these measures in light of the group members' joint commitment to make amends for past wrongdoing.

Questions remain about those members of a group who were not a party to any joint commitment to harm another group, who may even have repudiated these actions, and who did not play a causal role in the production of the harm. Can it be claimed that they nevertheless share responsibility for the harm and should take some responsibility for it, even if they did not contribute to it in any way? Certainly, it may be argued, if we think of moral responsibility in this context as justifying guilt, then the individuals who are alleged to share responsibility for wrongdoing must have contributed to it in some way, or if not, at least failed to repudiate it. (Merely having benefited from prior wrongdoing, the argument goes, would not by itself justify guilt; failing to repudiate that wrongdoing might.) Otherwise, they would be faultless and guilt would be unwarranted.[22] Yet, arguably, as I hope to show in Section 7, these are not the only grounds for holding that the members of a group can share responsibility for what their group did in the past. Guilt is one thing, shame another, and even if the guilt is unwarranted, the shame may not be.[23]

(b) *Group identity over time*

When we hold a person responsible for something a person did in the past, it is usually on the assumption that he is the same person as the person who performed those actions. It is natural to suppose that there is an analogous assumption in cases where current persons are held collectively responsible for wrongs committed by a group in the past. That is, the question whether wrongs are attributable to some present group G as its responsibility seems to be intimately connected to the question of whether G is the same group as the group that committed those wrongs. Specifically, if we have a criterion of group identity over time, or a way of telling whether the members of one generation belong to the same group as the members of an earlier one, and if on this basis we decide that they do, then and only then do we have grounds for attributing the earlier generation's acts and omissions to the later generation as acts and omissions for which it is responsible. I will shortly question whether diachronic identity is really necessary in this way. But before doing this, I want to suggest something of the difficulties we face if we accept the assumption and make group identity over time a requirement of collective responsibility for past group wrongdoing. The problems are of two sorts: not only are there difficulties in determining when the criterion has been fulfilled, but there is also likely to be significant controversy about what this criterion should be.

As a starting point, we should agree that a plausible account of sameness over time for groups ought to allow for group change, within limits. Thus, we might stipulate that a group at time t2 is to be counted as the same group as a group at time t1 only if the groups at these two times are defined by *enough of* the same characteristics. Accordingly, in order to decide whether a group retains its identity over time we must first ask what properties identify it as the particular group it is, and then whether enough of these properties have survived as identity-constituting features of the present group. So far, so good. However, among those who hold to the requirement of group identity over time, there may nevertheless be disagreements about collective responsibility for past wrongdoing because of conflicting views about whether enough of a group's defining features have survived in the present group, about the extent to which they have survived, and perhaps also about what those defining features are. What constitutes "enough" is not simply a matter of the number of surviving elements but also of their significance,[24] and one strategy employed by opponents of collective responsibility for past wrongdoing is to deny the continued significance of certain defining features of the group originally responsible for the wrongdoing.

The difficulty of providing a clear-cut and uncontroversial criterion of group identity over time can be readily appreciated. Consider an organized group, a group defined in part by more or less formal structures of decision making and by core values and principles, which, in formally organized groups, are expressed in organizational charters, mission statements, or written or unwritten constitutions. An example of such a group is a political community. The identity of a political community over time depends, in part at least, on the continuity of its constitutional form and its core institutions. On one end of the spectrum, there are cases of radical rupture in institutional continuity that would signal the advent of a new political community. Temporal distance has a bearing on this because there may be less institutional continuity between groups the farther they are removed from each other in time. At the other end, there are incremental changes that, in themselves, are not regarded as signaling a fundamental departure from constitutional principles or institutional arrangements, although this could be the cumulative effect of many of these smaller changes. The addition of amendments to the U.S. Constitution, and the evolution of constitutional interpretation by successive U.S. Supreme Courts, could serve as examples. However, there are many gray areas between these two situations and, what's more, institutional and constitutional continuity, although crucial to establishing the sameness of a political community across time, are not sufficient for it.

The challenge of specifying conditions for group identity over time is particularly evident in the case of a nation, whose modern political embodiment is the nation-state. Nations are historically continuous bodies, but neither the character, nor the enduringness of a nation or national political community can be rooted solely in its constitutional and institutional forms. Consider how Yael Tamir characterizes a nation:

> [a]ll attempts to single out a particular set of objective features – be it a common history, collective destiny, language, religion, territory, climate, race, ethnicity – as necessary and sufficient for the definition of a nation have ended in failure... No nation will have all of them. A nation could thus be understood as a cluster concept, that is, in order to count as a nation a group has to have a "sufficient number" of certain characteristics.[25]

Whether there is one nation over time will depend, then, on whether there is a nation at these two times and they possess enough of the same defining features. There are two sorts of indeterminacy here: one is whether the past and present groups possess a "sufficient number" of the right characteristics to count as nations at all; the other is whether there is sufficient resemblance between these two clusters of characteristics to establish persistence of a single nation over time.

Assertions that a group has persisted over time are interpretive in nature and not straightforwardly or purely descriptive. A complex of distinct but interconnected interpretive judgments is involved in making such claims, concerning matters about which group members and outside observers may reach different, even incompatible, interpretive conclusions. To be sure, there are constraints on interpretation so that not all interpretations are equally admissible or persuasive, but the constraints present challenges of their own. Ronald Dworkin,[26] for example, argues that interpretations are to be evaluated along two dimensions, fit and value: among the interpretations that meet some minimum threshold of fit, selection proceeds along the appropriate dimension of value. Applying this account of interpretation to the problem at hand, one might attempt to defend a claim of group identity over time on the following grounds. First, the interpretation meets some minimum threshold of fit with the past because there is sufficient similarity between the groups past and present; and second, this is the best interpretation that sufficiently fits the facts because it accords with certain substantive moral and political convictions that are appropriately invoked at this stage. These convictions are not formed as consequences of our judgments of group identity over time but provide the basis for these judgments, and, among other things, they reflect moral views about what a group is to be held accountable for.

I have not shown, of course, that the difficulties of determining group identity over time are insurmountable and that an account of collective responsibility for past wrongdoing premised on group identity over time is therefore doomed to fail. There are cases, after all, in which claims of group identity over time are extremely plausible, even if they are denied by those who would then have to take responsibility for past wrongdoing. Still, it may be wondered whether we always have to resolve these difficulties before we can properly attribute such responsibility. That is, we may wonder if, in order to establish collective responsibility for past wrongdoing, we have to establish that the group in question – a nation, say – is the same nation as a nation at an earlier time, the one responsible for the original wrongdoing. Janna Thompson argues that this is not necessary:

> Our concern is not whether a nation at one time is the same or different from a nation as another time, but whether the obligations or entitlements possessed by people of the past have become the obligations and entitlements of their successors. The crux of the matter is not the identity of the agent, but continuity of responsibility for particular agreements or acts. Obligations and entitlements can be passed from the members of one nation to members of the nation that succeeds it.[27]

Thompson would no doubt agree that those who acquire responsibility for past wrongdoing often do belong to the same group as those who committed the original injustice. (The convergence of acquired responsibility and group identity over time is not, in my view, an insignificant fact.) She also notes that group identity is not irrelevant to continuity of responsibility: continuity of responsibility can be upset by far-reaching, systemic changes that produce a different group. Her point is just that responsibility can persist regardless of whether political changes produce a different group because the members of the successor group can formally or tacitly assume those responsibilities from the former, possibly defunct, group. Therefore, in her view, "continuity of responsibility" across groups does not presuppose, so is not a sufficient basis for alleging, group identity over time.

A central question, then, for proponents of the view that people today can be collectively responsible for past group wrongdoing, is how to explain the transference of responsibility (or from another standpoint, the inheritance of responsibility) across generations. Responsibility can be transferred from one group to another group both when the groups exist at the same and when they exist at different times, and for the latter to be possible it is not necessary that the groups be identical to one another. Of course, this does not mean, and it is not the case, that if there is group identity over time, it would play no part in explaining why responsibilities persist.

(c) A note about "different people choices" and groups

It is commonly supposed that there is an obligation to compensate currently living people for the injustices committed against their predecessors if and only if the currently living people have been harmed through the lasting impact of these injustices. Consider this claim in the light of the standard account of harm. According to this account, *harm* presupposes a continuing subject whose existence is not dependent on the harming act or policy. That is, our acting in a certain way at time t1 harms someone only if we cause *this person* to be worse off at some later time t2 than the person was before we acted this way, or would have been had we not acted in this way. But this account of harm cannot ground many claims to compensation made by descendants of people who were wronged in the past, for in many cases, these descendants would not have existed at all had the injustice not been committed. In these cases of what Parfit calls "different people choices," *who* these persons are is not independent of the wrong that was done, and so on the standard account they have not been harmed by past injustice. In order to justify the claim that currently living persons have a moral right to compensation because they have been harmed by past injustice, we would have to provide some other identity-independent account of harm.[28]

However, an identity-dependent account of harm might still be used to justify some claims to compensation for historical injustice if we distinguish between harming the group itself and harming individual members of the group. Even if specific persons would not have existed had the injustice not been done, the existence of the group to which they belong might not be similarly dependent on the injustice having been committed. Thus, assuming group identity over time, a currently existing group may be worse off today because of the lasting impact of injustices committed against it in the past, even if individual members of the group would not have existed at all if the injustice had not been done and so cannot properly demand compensation on the standard account. (I will provide an argument of this sort in Section 8.)

4. WRONGING GROUPS

How can groups, in contrast to individuals, be harmed or wronged? I have so far considered the issue of collective responsibility for wrongs committed against a group mainly from the standpoint of the perpetrators and their successors. I now want to shift my focus and take up the question of what it means to wrong a group. It is important to do this in order to gain a clearer sense of what sorts of past injustices people living in the present can take responsibility for and what would constitute appropriate reparation for them.

Wrongful conduct usually, to at least some extent, causes *harm* to others. According to Joel Feinberg, a *harm* is an invasion of another's interest that thwarts the interest or sets it back; and it is a *wrong* when the invasion inexcusably or unjustifiably violates a moral norm.[29] We can speak of group harm, in one sense of the term, if every member of the group is either directly harmed (i.e., is a primary victim) or, in the manner of family members or friends, is indirectly harmed because he or she loves, cares for, is dependent on, and in this way has an interest in the well-being of the primary victim (i.e., is a secondary victim).[30] On this view, descriptions of harmful treatment of a group are translated into ascriptions of harm to the individuals who happen to make up the group, including primary and secondary victims. Group harm is simply the sum total of all the individual harms.

But of course this is not the only sense in which persons can be harmed as a group: they can also be harmed collectively rather than aggregatively. In common cases of historical injustice in which groups were the victims, the harms they suffered cannot be adequately understood or appreciated simply or solely in the terms of the previous account. The harm inflicted by discriminatory social practices targeted against certain ethnic or religious minorities, say, or by colonial exploitation and oppression of indigenous people, cannot be properly explained merely as the aggregate of the harms befalling individual primary or secondary victims of discrimination or colonization. The harm that is inflicted is based on certain shared group-defining properties, but it is more than this. It is also harm that is directed at the whole group and that is socially pervasive, so that even those who are not victims in this sense are harmed in ways that depend on their membership in the affected group.

To explain: although only certain individuals may directly experience the harmful effects of widespread discrimination and culturally pervasive negative stereotyping, others who are self-identifying participants in the group's traditions and practices, and whose own good is intrinsically a part of the common good of the group, also have a stake in the elimination of these unjust practices. Although only some of the members of a group may be primary or secondary victims, those who regard themselves as members of the group are made worse off with respect to their interest in the well-being of the group than they would be without these practices. There is also such a thing as collective self-respect, which can be damaged by unjust treatment directed at individuals in virtue of their belonging to certain groups. The aggregative account does not give adequate emphasis to the interrelationships among members of the group that explain the collective character of the harm it suffers.[31]

There are other reasons as well why some group harms cannot be made sense of on the aggregative model. When a piece of property is owned communally and this property is forcibly expropriated or destroyed, when institutions that play a significant role in the communal life of a group are attacked,[32] or when public symbols that express in concrete form the shared convictions of a community are desecrated, the members of the community are harmed, not just individually but collectively. In all of these cases, harm is done to individuals, not to some collective person, and the interests that are set back or defeated depend on individuals belonging to or seeing themselves as belonging to a group. We can properly speak of collective group harm to the extent that members of the group have and share this sort of interest.[33]

There is also another kind of group harm that is specific to organized groups. As I discussed in Section 2, such groups have more or less formal decisionmaking methods or structures that make it possible to attribute to them collective intentions and actions as well as collective responsibility. When the structure of decision making is adversely affected, the group's ability to act collectively is damaged or destroyed. It can no longer function, or function as effectively as an organized group and, in its status as an organized group, has been harmed.[34]

The harm inflicted on a group also commonly has expressive meaning in that its members are made the target of actions, policies, and practices that embody and convey insulting, humiliating, derogatory, and degrading messages. The wrongs in these cases can be classified as wrongs of *profound offense*, and not all wrongful harmings of this sort. Conduct can be harmful to a group without being deeply offensive to it, deeply offensive as well as harmful (as, for example, the Palestinians claim about the actions of the Israeli military in the occupied territories), and profoundly offensive even if many group members do not suffer direct harm. In addition to drawing a distinction between harm and profound offense,

Feinberg contrasts profound offenses with mere offensive nuisances,[35] and he lists several distinctive characteristics of profound offenses. First, a profound offense has a particular "tone" for which we use such words as "deep, profound, shattering, and serious."[36] Second, profoundly offensive conduct need not be personally witnessed to offend. Third, profound offense "results from an affront to the standards of propriety that determine one's higher-order sensibilities,"[37] and so believing the conduct is wrong is conceptually prior to being offended by it. Profound offense offends because it is believed wrong; it is not believed wrong because it causes offense. Moreover, its wrongness consists of the violation of standards of human decency, civility, mutual respect, and the like, not merely its causing certain unpleasant states of mind. Fourth, a profound offense is always experienced, to at least some extent, as an impersonal wrong or affront that is independent of its affect on oneself. The member of a profoundly offended group, for example, does not experience the wrong as an entirely personal grievance, that is, he does not only feel wronged on his own behalf by the offensive conduct. Rather, the conduct is, and is experienced as, a wrong done to the entire group collectively, and to himself partly because he identifies with it.

The standards that are violated by profoundly offensive conduct are norms for the expression of evaluative attitudes toward others. In the cases under discussion here, these are norms that prescribe certain evaluative attitudes that should be taken up toward groups, not merely toward persons considered individually or serially. Expressive norms, as Elizabeth Anderson argues, make up a distinct category from consequentialist ones. Consequentialist norms assess the value of persons, actions, motives, practices, and so forth solely in terms of how effectively they bring about the best state of affairs. Expressive norms, by contrast, are noninstrumental and assess actions and practices in terms of whether they adequately express appropriate attitudes toward others.[38]

The attitudes at issue here are evaluative in that they embody modes of valuation. Respect, honor, admiration, and toleration are some of the evaluative attitudes that might be expressed toward others, considered here not as individuals but collectively. More important for our purposes, there are also numerous modes and expressions of group devaluation: humiliation, mockery, avoidance, neglect, and desecration (e.g., of objects of group veneration), to name a few. Often, a number of these attitudes will be expressed simultaneously. Avishai Margalit characterizes one of these, humiliation, as follows:

> Humiliation in all its senses is especially closely linked to the negative justification for respecting humans, which involves the prohibition of humiliation as a type of cruelty that can be directed only at human beings. Taking away a creature's control by tying or locking it up is clearly also a manifestation of cruelty to animals, but what is unique to loss of control as a way of humiliating humans is not merely the cruelty of physical confinement but the symbolic element, which expresses the victim's subordination.[39]

Individuals can be subjected to humiliating treatment, simply as individuals and quite apart from whether they belong to any particular group. Groups of individuals, and individuals insofar as they belong to groups, can also be treated in this way.

P. E. Digeser gives an example of profoundly offensive conduct in his discussion of Simon Wiesenthal's *The Sunflower* (Digeser is chiefly interested in the question whether an individual can have the moral power to forgive wrongs committed against a group of which he is a member, but this is not my concern here).[40] The story concerns a German SS soldier named Karl, whose unit murdered 150–200 Jewish men, women and children on the eastern front, and Digeser takes up the question of who was wronged by these actions. Of course, there are the Jews who were murdered. It might be said that the wrong did not stop there because the actions constituted a threat to anyone identified by others as Jewish. But Digeser rejects this because "it is a stretch to claim that Karl and his unit threatened or potentially threatened all Jews."[41] Many were actually or potentially threatened; some not at all. In his view, Karl's actions as a loyal Nazi did reverberate throughout the entire Jewish community, but in a different sense:

> his actions embodied the standard Nazi message about a master race and inferior beings, and their derogatory, insulting and dangerous character denied the very humanity of a people. The wrong disseminated by the Nazi's message and carried forth in Karl's actions was distributed to every individual in the Jewish community.[42]

So although not every Jew was wronged in the sense of being physically harmed or even threatened with physical harm, every individual who was part of the Jewish community, according to Digeser, was wronged by being the target of a profoundly offensive message.

There are two points to make about this account. First, although Jews were the ones targeted for extermination, they were not the only ones properly offended by the message of hate it conveyed. As Digeser asks, "Was the offense only to Jews? Weren't Karl's actions also offensive to any person with a modicum of humanity?"[43] In general, witnesses to insulting and offensive behavior directed at a particular group may themselves be insulted and offended if they identify with the group's members on the basis of their common humanity; indeed, they should be so offended. However, they are not wronged by these actions in the same way, or to the same extent, as those who belong to that group.

Second, in order to assess Digeser's conclusion that the insult, and therefore the wrong, was "distributed to every individual in the Jewish community," we need to know more about what counts as being "in the Jewish community." If all that is required for being in the Jewish community is that others (let us suppose, correctly) identify you as such, whether you do so or not, then we must ask whether this is sufficient to be profoundly offended – not just harmed – by treatment that targets Jews. Arguably, this is only part of the explanation. Something else is needed: specifically, some sort of *identification with* or *identification as* is necessary for the profound offense (but not necessarily the threats) to be distributed to an individual.[44] This does not mean, however, that one has to have thought of oneself, in some significant way, as a member of the targeted group prior to the offense. Indeed, identification with the group, or as a member of the group, may be a product of being regarded as such by others, in that one would not have internalized the label of being a so-and-so as part of one's individual identity, had it not been that others thought this was a significant fact about oneself and treated one accordingly.

The case of Jean Améry, essayist and Auschwitz survivor, is instructive about how identifications can be induced by how one is categorized by others. In his incisive essay, "On the Necessity and Impossibility of Being a Jew,"[45] Améry recounts his formative years before the rise of Nazism as a fully assimilated Viennese Jew who had no positive identification with Jews and Judaism. Even being a victim of persecution and torture, he relates, could not change this fact and could not establish a "positive

community between me and my fellow Jews" (97). Nevertheless, a kind
of community – "a community of fate" – did develop with his fellow Jews
as a result of his experiences during the war: "The fruitlessness of the
search for my Jewish self by no means stands as a barrier between me and
my solidarity with every threatened Jew in this world" (97). And a kind of
Jewish identity was forged as well, not a positive one, for this was impossible for him, but a negative one, that of the Jewish Nazi victim, which,
for him, was inescapable. This Jewish identity, though "without positive
determinants" (96), and the solidarity that went with it, were sufficient
to render Améry vulnerable to profound offense from demeaning treatment directed at Jews. The identification with other Jews was certainly
unwelcome and not something he would have chosen. But without some
sort of identification, negative though it might be, it is hard to see how
being treated as a Jew could have been profoundly offensive to him.

5. MAKING SENSE OF THE PAST: RECONSTRUCTION AND COMPLICATIONS

A group's understanding of its own history resides in its collective
memory,[46] by which I mean communally shared and socially maintained
memory, not the collection of individual memories of the members of
a group, however similar they may be.[47] As we saw in the case of the
Tulsa race riot of 1921, collective memory of past wrongs may fade or
be repressed and its revival is an integral part of the process by which
a group comes to terms with its past. The truth about the past may be
known initially by only a few historians or investigative journalists, but
it must be widely disseminated and become part of the group's collective self-understanding if the question of responsibility for past wrongs
is going to be taken up collectively. Moreover, it is not just any collective
memory of past wrongs that will do: with respect to coming to terms with
historical injustice, historical accuracy is critically important and morally
required.

These points should not be taken to suggest that there are two entirely
independent stages in the process of coming to terms with the past that
are hermetically sealed off from one another: first a group remembers
the past in a certain way and then it moves on to consider whether the
past, so remembered, is something for which it should take responsibility.

These are not discrete stages as much as interconnected aspects of one complex process. How a group remembers the past, how it considers itself in relation to that past, and whether it considers that past its own past, part of its own history, may already reflect to some extent beliefs about its responsibility for past wrongs and its openness to taking responsibility for them. For example, a group may be motivated to remember the past in such a way as to minimize its responsibility for past wrongs and to project a positive image of itself to the outside world and to future generations.

This possibility should not be surprising because it is now generally understood that there are "reconstructive" dimensions to human remembering in its individual as well as collective operations.[48] There is no such thing as a fully determinate group past just waiting to be recovered if only sufficient evidence of the right sort is forthcoming. Rather, a group's past, like an individual's past, is preserved in, and filtered through, memory, so it has what W. James Booth calls "an uneven topography"[49] whose contours are molded by current needs, interests, values, and preoccupations. A group might not remember past wrongdoing *as* something for which it is responsible because this would give it a burdened history that, for various political or economic reasons, it is not prepared to recognize. At the same time, there are moral (as well as metaphysical) reasons why the past cannot be entirely up to us. There are constraints on how the past is to be remembered – indeed there must be – for otherwise any group that wished to evade responsibility for past wrongdoing could simply construct a narrative of the past that made it reasonable to deny responsibility. (I argue this point more fully in Chapter 4, where I claim that collective memory is vulnerable to and constrained by the discipline of history.) Although it is untenable to think of memory as merely the faithful reproduction of images that correspond to past experiences, and even though there is inevitably an interpretive dimension to how groups remember the past, some ways of remembering may, must, be ruled out as distortions of historical reality. Sometimes a group's account of its own history is so out of sync with the view of its history held by others that this is enough to disqualify it as a credible interpretation of the past. Progress in historical understanding may still be possible, although, among groups with a history and a history that matters to them, the construction of a more credible socially shared historical narrative is likely to be a gradual and often tortuous process. This process, in politically organized groups, will be directed by the shifting balance of political forces over time.

The possibility of conflicting interpretations of the past within a single political community complicates the process of taking responsibility for past wrongdoing, but such conflicts are hardly uncommon. As Iwona Irwin-Zarecka notes, "the social construction of "realities of the past" is frequently a site of intense conflict and debate."[50] Tony Judt is even more emphatic: "Memory is inherently contentious and partisan: one man's acknowledgment is another's omission."[51] A group's interpretation of its past is not merely an academic exercise, motivated, as the "professional" historian is, by a passion for fact, proof, and evidence. It is often an intensely and inherently political enterprise, responding to and reflecting ongoing shifts in collective self-definition and the ordering of political priorities. As an illustration, consider the struggles over collective memory in post-Communist Russia. According to Judt, there was a division within Russian historical memory after the fall of Communism that

> took institutional form, with two civil organizations coming into existence to promote critical but diametrically opposed accounts of the country's Communist past. *Memorial* was founded in 1987 by liberal dissidents with the goal of obtaining and publishing the truth about Soviet history. . . . The founders of *Pamiat'*, anti-Communist dissidents but far from liberal, wanted to offer an improved version of the Russian past: sanitized of Soviet "lies" but also free of other influences foreign to Russia's heritage.[52]

The point is familiar but still bears repeating: collective memories have political uses.[53] They are not disinterested social constructions of the past but are marshaled in the service of political agendas that can be assessed for the values and goods they do or do not promote.[54] This has to be kept in mind as well if normative inquiry about collective memory is not to be dismissed as politically naïve or dangerous or both.

Memory disputes have to be taken seriously because taking responsibility for past wrongdoing cannot just be a unilateral process. It depends, to some extent, on a more-or-less shared understanding between the perpetrators and those who inherit the burden of responsibility, on the one hand, and the victims and those who represent them, on the other, as to who was injured by whom and the nature and extent of the wrong for which it is appropriate to take responsibility and try to make amends. The moral process of repair cannot begin without a basic shared understanding between the parties as to what was done by whom and why it warrants acknowledgment, apology, and reparation, that is, without a stabilized and uncontested record of the past to which the different parties agree. If those who ought to take responsibility for past wrongdoing understand the past in a way that does not do justice to the understanding of the victims or those who represent them, then whatever apology and reparative work the former undertake will be judged by the victims or their representatives to be inadequate. The injured party's sense of justice will not be satisfied and it will seem to it, and may in fact be the case, that the responsible party has not succeeded in taking responsibility for past wrongdoing as it should.

Questions about what should be done to make up for past wrongdoing presuppose identification of the wrong, but identification is a shared or collective task. Predictably, there will be disagreements between the injured party and the responsible party as to what wrong was done, how serious it was, and possibly even whether a wrong was done at all. It might be thought that unambiguously identifying and settling the wrong must come first before moving on to take responsibility for it. However this would be a mistake. It may not be clear initially precisely what wrong was done, by whom or to whom. But, as the state's response in the Tulsa race riot example suggests, a willingness to explore these matters, to air the past and to pursue the evidence wherever it may lead, and to hear the testimony of those who feel they have been wronged, can itself be part of the process of taking responsibility for past wrongdoing.

These efforts neither remove all doubts about the past nor need to do so. There must be agreement on some account of the past for genuine reparation to be possible, but the parties may be open, and it may be publicly known that they are open, to revision of that account as new material facts come to light. In addition, the responsible party and the aggrieved party may continue to disagree to some extent about what happened and about the full extent of responsibility for past wrongdoing. The responsible party may give this as a reason for refusing to take responsibility, but it does not have to do so. It may acknowledge its responsibility even in the face of lingering indeterminacy with respect to what was done and persistent differences in interpretation (within a certain range) between the parties.

Taking responsibility for past wrongdoing, as a moral enterprise, requires not only shared understanding, but also shared responsibilities. The victims and those who speak for them have responsibilities as well, not to exaggerate past events lest it weaken the foundation on which reparative acts will be undertaken. If the injured party is intransigent and makes unreasonable reparative demands, then the responsible party cannot necessarily be faulted if disagreement, between it and the injured party, remains. In such cases, we may say that the responsible party has shown a willingness to take responsibility, but its overtures have been unreasonably rejected by the injured party.

When a group collectively remembers past wrongs as a part of its history and acknowledges the wrongs and takes responsibility for them as it should, it may succeed in *offsetting* or providing adequate *compensation* for them by engaging in reparative actions. But the group is doing something else as well. Robert Sparrow gestures toward this when he notes that "crimes which have been repented for, or for which reparations have been made, are no longer the same crimes."[55] The claim that the crimes are "no longer the same" is easily misunderstood, so it is important to clarify what it does *not* mean. It cannot plausibly be thought that taking responsibility for past wrongs erases them or makes them less bad. The suffering endured by the victims of wrongdoing in the past is not made less grievous because a subsequent generation acknowledges its responsibility for those wrongs and attempts to make amends for them. To express such thoughts and corresponding attitudes in reparative actions is to dishonor the victims: it fails to properly acknowledge their moral subjectivity by making *their* experience of wrongdoing morally decisive. Instead, to quote Sparrow again:

> An apology, if sincere (and accompanied by actions which demonstrate that sincerity) reaches back to the original events and changes their significance by placing them in a historical context which includes the later recognition of the wrong which has been committed.[56]

Collectively taking responsibility for past wrongs cannot change the past in the sense of undoing the wrongs or minimizing their gravity. What it accomplishes is a retroactive change in the *significance* of past wrongdoing, that is, a change comparable to what individuals who take personal responsibility for their past effect in their own lives. The wrongdoing now has a different meaning because it is acknowledged as wrong and responsibility is taken for it. The wrongdoing is not merely followed by apology but is retrospectively transformed by it because of the way the wrongdoing is taken up in the group's collective self-understanding. If, however, past wrongdoing is not acknowledged and responsibility is not taken for it, it stands as an unredeemed wrong: this is what, under these different conditions, it means. Moreover, by accepting the burden of making amends, the responsible group demonstrates its willingness to accept some pain and humiliation for the sake of the victims and, in so doing, symbolically asserts what was previously denied, namely, the moral standing of the victims.

Apology for past wrongdoing, if sincere, transforms the meaning of the past by expressing the responsible party's acknowledgement of the legitimacy of the victim's claim and the wrongness of the prior conduct. It conveys, in other words, the responsible party's shared commitment to the breached ethical principle underlying the past wrongdoing, its dedication to honoring the breached moral value, so that both the responsible party and the aggrieved party can be considered, or can once again be considered, members of the same moral community.[57] Past wrongdoing is repaired, and its significance retrospectively altered, when the norm that has been transgressed is reasserted and the responsible party and the aggrieved party come together around shared moral values. In this way, the past no longer *means* what it meant before the apology: it no longer signifies the subversion of the moral order.

When taking responsibility for past wrongdoing involves apologizing for it, the party issuing the apology must have the moral standing or authority to do so, otherwise the apology will not achieve its proper moral effect and may seem presumptuous to the aggrieved party. Only the offending party – or the party with legitimate standing to act as the offender for purposes of issuing an apology – can renounce its prior commitment to wrong, can promise not to do wrong again, and can restore trust in the aggrieved party that it has nothing further to fear from the offender. We might think that a group – a country, say – only has standing to issue a collective apology if it is the same country as the country that is responsible for the initial injustice. But as I suggested earlier when discussing conditions for collective responsibility for past wrongdoing, this position is too restrictive. It is possible, in other words, for one country to take on reparative responsibilities for past injustices that it did not itself commit, including the responsibility to apologize for those injustices.

6. RESPONSIBILITY AND THE CONSTRUCTION OF GROUP IDENTITY

Group responsibility for wrongs committed by a group in the past is often made to depend, rightly or wrongly, on judgments of group identity over time. A group may attempt to justify its refusal to accept and take responsibility on the grounds that there is not sufficient similarity of the right sort between groups at different times to warrant the ascription of responsibility to it. There is, however, another sense of identity at work in a group's taking responsibility for past wrongs.

Debates about whether a group should take responsibility for historical wrongs are not only debates about what belongs to a group's past; these debates are also about how the members of a group should collectively understand their present in relation to their past. This suggests that, with respect to the issue of identity, the important issues are not, or not only, how to tell whether groups at different points in time are one and the same and whether this has to be determined before we can properly attribute collective responsibility for past wrongdoing. Taking responsibility for past wrongdoing is also related to a group's collective self-conception, its collective identity here and now. The relationship can be viewed as a complex fact amenable to social science description: we can describe how taking, as well as not taking, responsibility for past wrongdoing shapes and partially constitutes a group's collective identity. But collective identity is also related in a normative sense to taking responsibility and has normative implications for those who belong to the group. Specifically, collective identity can impose a collective obligation on them to take responsibility for past wrongdoing, to compensate, to make reparation, or to remember.

A group's collective identity, that is, roughly speaking, the various features of its particular "life-in-common"[58] which contribute to its collective self-understanding and self-conception, is inextricably bound up with the

way it remembers features of its past and what it holds itself responsible
for. (Analogous points were made about the relationship between personal identity and individual memory in Chapter 1.) A good illustration
of this is provided by the debate within post–1945 West Germany concerning responsibility for the crimes of National Socialism. According
to Gerd Knischewski and Ulla Spittler, the question of German national
identity became politicized as a result of controversy in West German society over how the Second World War should be remembered.[59] Post–1945
West German history, in their view, can be divided into several distinct
phases, depending on which of two ways of remembering the war was
ascendant at the time. In one, National Socialism was categorized and
perceived as an unlawful regime that did not have its roots in, and was
not a consequence of, specific features of German national culture. From
this standpoint, the vast majority of Germans are seen primarily as the
victims of Nazi domination and the 12 years of National Socialism are
relegated to the status of an historical aberration. This interpretation,
designed to "foster an unburdened national past," "smoothes the way for
a positive, history-based national identity" and enables Germans to "lose
their negative status in comparison with other nations."[60] The other interpretation emphasized the German origin of National Socialism and the
role that popular consent and mass support played in its successes. From
this standpoint, Germans are viewed as the culprits not the victims of
an aberrant ideology imposed from above, and the effort to reinstate
a positive national identity, unburdened by guilt and the need for constant reminders of the evils of Nazism, is politically counterproductive
and morally insensitive, to say the least. Germans must instead construct
a very different national identity for themselves, one which allows them,
indeed requires them, to take responsibility for National Socialism and
its war. As we can see from this example, it is much too static a picture to
suppose that there is an antecedently fixed identity by reference to which
a group makes sense of its past and determines the extent and nature of
its responsibility for it. Rather, collective deliberation about responsibility
is centrally involved in the formation and constitution of a group collective identity.[61] This collective identity might be constructed on the basis
of partial truths about, or distortions of, the past, that is, on a misreading
of the historical record, and this would warrant normative criticism of
the identity constructed out of these materials.

The failure to take responsibility for past wrongdoing could involve a serious misrepresentation of the past, and a collective identity that is bound up with such a misrepresentation is morally flawed for this reason and to this extent. There is also another normative criticism that can be leveled at the members of group who fail to take responsibility for past wrongdoing: it may indicate that they do not properly understand or honestly face what their collective identity involves and what, burdened with this identity, they are obligated to do. (Identity, to recall a point I made in Chapter 1, is, or can be, a source of values as well as obligations.) That is, taking responsibility for past wrongdoing may be something that they ought to do in part because this is what it takes to properly acknowledge that the wrongdoing reveals in some fundamental way what sort of people or community they are. In such cases, by not taking responsibility for past wrongdoing, they would show that they have failed to grasp that their collective identity morally implicates them in the wrongs of the past and the responsibilities they entail.

The sense of "responsibility" that explains this connection between taking responsibility for the past and group identity is not the same as the familiar sense of responsibility that connotes fault and liability to sanction or self-directed remorse or guilt. In some respects, it is closer to what psychoanalysts have in mind when they say that the analysand must learn to take responsibility for aspects of his self that he has hitherto regarded as foreign to his true nature. As Roy Schafer puts it, "what one presented before as an alien "it" – the aggregate of impulse, defense, conscience, problematic past and future, and external necessity – one now presents as defining aspects of oneself."[62] Taking responsibility here means something different from acknowledging that one is at fault for having caused harm and being disposed to blame oneself for it, although admission of fault and self-blame might be consequences of it. It means rather owning up to these aspects as truly one's own. Similarly, when a group takes responsibility for past wrongs in this sense, it appropriates those actions as it own and acknowledges that they are bound up with its collective identity. It does not disown that part of its past, although of course it may *repudiate* it as a shameful episode and attempt to make amends for it. The parallels with the analysis of taking responsibility for the past, presented in Chapter 2, should be apparent.

This sense of responsibility gives us a way of responding to a familiar argument for denying responsibility for past wrongdoing. The argument goes something like this: the current members of a group cannot be collectively responsible for, in the sense of being at fault for, the crimes of their predecessors, because none of the current members were even alive when the crimes were committed. And if they are not collectively responsible, then barring some exceptional circumstances, there is no moral imperative for them to collectively take responsibility. There are several problems with this argument, but the response I want to make here is that responsibility for wrongdoing is not only linked to fault, guilt, and liability to punishment. Drawing on the appropriative sense of responsibility, we can say that it is possible for a group of people to collectively take responsibility for past wrongdoing for which they are not to blame and for which guilt would not be warranted, and what's more, to reasonably believe that they ought to do so. This is because, irrespective of whether it can be established that a group is collectively at fault for certain wrongs, or that there is an intelligible basis for speaking of a group's blameworthiness for them, the group can still collectively take responsibility for the wrongs in the sense of owning up to them. Understanding responsibility in this way, a group of people that takes responsibility for past wrongs regards them as revealing some fundamental fact about their collective identity, and on this basis they commit themselves to reparative actions. These connections to group character and identity also help to explain why it makes sense to think of responsibility in relation to shame and not just guilt, a topic to which I turn in Section 7.

Although responsibility in this sense is distinguishable from moral responsibility as commonly understood, there is nevertheless a strong link here, as in cases of fault, between the concept of *responsibility* and the idea of agents having a duty to be *responsive* to those who have been wronged. These "duties of response," as Linda Radzik calls them, can be fulfilled in various ways: by "apologizing, expressing regret and shame, offering help, and actively condemning the ones with blood on their hands.... [s]imply telling the truth about history."[63] In general, in collectively reaching back to the past to lay claim to historical wrongs, a group enlarges the scope of collective agency to include them, and undertaking to fulfill duties of response is one aspect of this. Moreover, by extending the reach of collective agency, a group's history enters into critical engagement with its future and becomes something other than just an inheritance that is added to, an accretion of historically significant events.

A comparison with the personal case, discussed in Chapter 2, may help illuminate what is at stake here. With respect to individuals taking responsibility for their personal past, those who ignore, suppress, falsify, or deny the past do not necessarily free themselves of its influence. On the contrary, the past is likely to continue to exert its influence in unacknowledged and unappreciated ways, and because agency is facilitated by an understanding of its prior operation and the impact of formative influences, when that is precluded by the failure to come to terms with the past, agency is likely to be compromised. Unrealistic, distorted, self-deceiving conceptions of the past also condition an individual's projection of himself into the future, effectively limiting the range of imagined alternative futures to those that repeat the problematic features of the past. Appropriating the past, however, gives one control over how the past informs the present and is carried forward into the future. Collective appropriation of the wrongs of the past is similar in the following (limited) respect: it opens up possibilities for managing the influence of the past and enables the construction of a future that is not merely an uncritical recapitulation of the past. Furthermore, although it may be unfair to blame a group for wrongs done in the past, we may be justified in blaming that group for failing to collectively exercise its capacity to determine what its influence and significance will be and for failing to fulfill its duties of response.

7. COLLECTIVE GUILT AND SHAME

The notion of a genuinely collective guilt has not sat well with many philosophers. Guilt, they have argued, can only properly accrue to individuals, and only in virtue of their individual faulty acts or omissions. Deniers of collective guilt can allow that there may be group guilt in an aggregative sense, that is, the aggregate of each member's individual guilt, but in the context of this debate, this is a modest concession. (Using the terminology I introduced before, this is more accurately called "collected" rather than "collective" guilt.) On the other hand, it would obviously get us nowhere to claim, in defense of the deniers' view, that personal guilt attaches only because of what the individual has done or failed to do and not because he or she is a member of a group. For the question would then simply shift to whether there is only personal guilt in this sense and not collective guilt as well.

Claims about collective guilt are often thought to imply that individual persons ought to feel responsible for or guilty about wrongs of their group even if they have in no way contributed to them. It may be held that there is no moral ground for noncontributing individuals to feel this way, because they are innocent of the wrongdoing. There are different responses to this. One is to argue that even if collective guilt does imply this, guilt feelings may still be morally appropriate because there is such a thing as "blameless guilt."[64] Another response is to define and defend a type of guilt – call it "membership-guilt"[65] – which individuals may have to varying degrees and which does not imply individual fault. Whether these arguments succeed in showing that there can be genuinely collective guilt depends on whether we can distinguish the guilt of a group from the moral fault or blameworthiness of its individual members. If we can, then it is possible for there to be collective guilt even though individual members bear varying degrees of personal (nonblameless) guilt, or no personal guilt at all.[66]

I do not intend to pursue the issue of collective guilt here, however. Instead, I want to focus on a moral emotion usually paired and contrasted with guilt, namely, shame, and on one manifestation of this emotion that is closely related to the notion of group identity discussed in the previous section, namely, collective shame. I do this partly to sidestep questions about fault that have generated much moral criticism of collective guilt: shame is not as closely linked to fault as guilt usually is and, uncontroversially, can take a wide variety of conditions, actions, and states of affairs as its object. I also do this because it seems natural for people to feel shame or something like it when their group has committed wrongdoing in the past, even if they are personally innocent of it. A literary example might help set the stage for what follows.

Bernard Schlink's novel, *The Reader*,[67] relates the unsettling story of the relationship between two Germans from very different backgrounds, Michael Berg and Hanna Schmitz. It begins in postwar Germany as a romantic and quite hopeless relationship between a young boy and an illiterate older woman. They part ways, but years later, in the 1960s in the throes of the German student movement and its condemnation of their parents' generation, Michael encounters Hanna again, now on trial for her participation in Nazi atrocities, a participation that he was unaware of during their earlier romance. It is Michael's reaction to this revelation, specifically, the self-directed emotions that it arouses in him and the connections he draws between his personal relationship to Hanna and the larger relationship between his generation and that of his parents, which make this story relevant to the discussion here.

Reflecting on his involvement with Hanna, Michael cannot escape a sense of personal responsibility:

> I had to point [the finger of guilt] at Hanna. But the finger I pointed at her turned back to to me. I had loved her. Not only had I loved her, I had chosen her. I tried to tell myself that I had known nothing of what she had done when I chose her. I tried to talk myself into the state of innocence in which children love their parents. But love of our parents is the only love for which we are not responsible. And perhaps we are responsible even for the love we feel for our parents. (170–171)

He relates his story to the predicament of his contemporaries:

> These thoughts did not come until later, and even later they brought no comfort. How could it be a comfort that the pain I went through because of my love for Hanna was, in a way, the fate of my generation, a German fate, and that it was only more difficult for me to evade, more difficult for me to manage than for others. (171)

Although Schlink describes it in different ways, the "pain" that Michael experiences is not, it seems pretty clearly, the pain of guilt, properly understood.[68] Had he known Hanna served as a guard in a concentration camp, he could not have loved her. But he did not know, and he cannot be faulted for not knowing or for his loving her. The weight of the past is also born by his generation – it is, he says, the German "fate" – though it too cannot be faulted for the wrongs committed during the war. What is this pain, personal as well as generational, if it is not the pain of guilt? At one point, Schlink puts it this way: "Pointing at the guilty parties did not free us from shame" (170). What he is attributing to Michael as well as the German youth of the 1960s is best thought of this way, as shame, personal as well as collective.

How, then, should we explain collective shame and under what conditions is it morally justified? First, a brief word about, how it should *not* be explained. One who believes in the existence of collective shame is not committed to the existence of any mysterious entities, or to the view that feelings of shame can be experienced by some kind of collective consciousness that exists independently of human minds. On the contrary, on any plausible construal of collective shame, it is a function of the understandings, psychological resources, and common knowledge of the members of a group, and feelings of shame only exist in and through the experiences of particular individuals.

Accounts of shame usually contrast it with guilt, so I will start here. Gabriele Taylor expresses the common understanding of the difference between them as follows:

> ... feelings of guilt are localized in a way in which feelings of shame are not localized; they concern themselves with the wrong done, not with the kind of person one thinks one is. This difference is brought out quite well by a distinction drawn by some sociologists between 'primary' and 'secondary' deviance. 'Primary deviance' applies to those cases where a person accepts that he has done wrong but does not think of this wrong-doing as affecting his overall standing as a person.... The secondary deviant, however, now sees himself not just as a man who at some point, for instance, committed a burglary, but rather sees himself as a burglar.... This second view is appropriate to shame, the former to guilt.[69]

To be sure, a person can feel guilty about having done wrong and also ashamed of having acted this way. But this does not alter the main point: he feels guilty about *an act* and ashamed of doing this because of what he believes it expresses about *himself*, about his character or identity. It is not necessary, contrary to what Taylor suggests, that when one is ashamed of oneself, one is ashamed of oneself as a whole, of all of oneself. One might only be ashamed of some aspect of oneself which was expressed by one's acting wrongly. Accounts of shame also typically include that shame is evoked by the belief that one has violated some personal ideal – that one has fallen short of what one expected or might have hoped of oneself.

Taylor makes two other claims about the distinction between guilt and shame that I want to comment on. First, she argues that the notion of repayment, of some way of "making up" for what was done, is "appropriate to guilt but not to shame."[70] Bernard Williams makes a related but somewhat weaker point:

> What arouses guilt in an agent is an act or omission of a sort that typically elicits from other people anger, resentment, or indignation. What the agent may offer in order to turn this away is reparation. . . . What arouses shame, on the other hand, is something that typically elicits from others contempt or derision or avoidance. . . . Shame may be expressed in attempts to reconstruct or improve oneself.[71]

Taylor is wrong to link repayment or reparation exclusively with guilt and Williams's characterization of the difference between shame and guilt is overstated. Offering reparation, trying to make amends, seems quite naturally associated with shame, and self-improvement is quite naturally allied with guilt: one way to acknowledge one's guilt is to commit oneself to self-improvement. Second, Taylor remarks that "it is natural to assume that guilt is related to responsibility in a way in which shame is not. Normally we are held responsible for what we do in a way in which we are not held responsible for what we are."[72] The last sentence seems right, but I would like to slightly rephrase it: the relationship between shame and responsibility that I am chiefly interested in can best be expressed not as 'holding us responsible for what we are' but rather 'holding us responsible for owning up to what we are'. Further, if owning up to what we are involves *responding* in appropriate ways to those who have been wronged, then shame no less than guilt can be associated with responsibility to others.

I turn now to the main issues: what collective shame is and when it is morally warranted among a group of people.[73] To begin, collective shame, if such a thing is possible, should not be characterized in the following way:

> *Aggregated individual shame: collective shame is the aggregate of individual instances of shame experienced by people who happen to be members of the same group.*

This is plainly inadequate as an account of *collective* shame because there is no mention of what the individuals are ashamed of and the significance of the sense of group membership to the shame experienced by them. What is missing is the notion of *being ashamed of being a member* of the group, not necessarily in a blanket way but at least in respect of certain of its policies or practices. It is not required for this that the individual be linked to some group wrong by any directly contributing act of his own. He may have done nothing to create, encourage, or perpetuate it and still have reason to be ashamed of being a member. He may even have dissociated himself from the policies and past practices of his group. Nevertheless, as a functioning member of the group, he retains the advantages of group membership, some of which may be inseparable from the wrongs committed by it, and he may be ashamed of benefiting from its wrongs in this way. Arguably, being ashamed of being a member of the group does not even require this much to be justified.[74]

Let us call *membership shame* the shame that is experienced by the member of a group in virtue of his identification with the group.[75] Membership shame is a type of identificatory shame, that is, shame felt over, or because of, something with which the individual identifies. In this case, it is the group to which he or she belongs and, as a consequence of this, what it has done. Moreover, membership shame is to be distinguished from, and is consistent with allowing, a further sense in which individuals may experience shame because of collective wrongdoing: some members may be ashamed of the active part they played in what the collective did. This might be called *enactor shame* as distinct from membership shame.

Membership in a group covers a range of cases, of course, and not every so-called member will or should be disposed to the same degree to feel membership shame over what his group has done:

(1) Consider the case of guest workers who take up temporary residence in a foreign country in order to earn enough money to help their struggling families back home. They are "members" of the host country in the sense that they are expected to adhere to its laws and are entitled to whatever benefits and protections the host country affords persons with their noncitizen status. But membership has for them only instrumental value. They have no particular feelings of kinship with the host country, they are not expected to have feelings of kinship, and they do not identify with the host country. If the host country has a history of wrongdoing against some group, they will not experience membership shame because of it. It would also not be reasonable to claim that

they ought to experience membership shame. Clearly, such cases must be a small minority in any well-functioning socially unified group.

(2) Consider next naturalized citizens and their descendants. Unlike guest workers, those who take an oath of citizenship embrace the collective values of their adopted country, including the values of participating in a common culture and set of political institutions. They identify themselves as citizens, but their identification with their new country may not yet have had time to take root and permeate their lives. However, through prolonged contact with its traditions and history, its customs and social institutions, their children and their children's children will usually come to identify to some extent with the larger national identity. Acculturation will inscribe them in the collective identity of the group. If their country committed injustices in the past, but this predated their ancestors' arrival on its shores, membership shame would still be quite natural and appropriate.

(3) Finally, there are the descendants of those responsible for wrongdoing. The descendants may have little sympathy with the wrongdoers and may repudiate what they have done. However, they (the descendants) may still feel membership shame at the collective crimes perpetrated by their forebears in the name of a group to which they (the descendants) belong, and such shame may be quite warranted. If they identify with the group, so that their identities are partly constituted by their membership in it, they will have good reason to feel morally implicated in and tainted by these crimes. And their membership in the group will be a source of shame in a way that it is not for the descendants of later arrivals.

An account of collective shame that centers on membership shame seems promising, and for this reason it is important to unpack the notion of membership and mark its different senses. We might at this point be inclined to propose the following account:

Aggregated membership shame: collective shame is the aggregated membership shame experienced by members of the group in relation to some (the same) action or practice of it.

Collective shame, on this account, is just a generalized feeling of membership shame. There are two points to make about this. First, as we have seen, there can be exceptions because there may be members of the group who are not (much) disposed to experience it and who are not necessarily to be criticized for this reason, even if other members should be. Second, and more important, on this account there can be collective shame even if only a few, or none of the members, who do experience membership shame publicly express it, and even if there is no common knowledge within the group that the members feel or are disposed to feel membership shame. These possibilities should generate doubts about the adequacy of this aggregative model as an account of collective shame.

An account of collective shame in terms of aggregated instances of individual shame will not suffice because it does not even mention that it is an action of the group that prompts the shame. An aggregated membership shame account is an advance in this respect, but even it is lacking.[76] For what cannot be captured by *any* aggregative account, including the aggregated membership shame account, is shame over the actions of the group that is shared among the members of the group, that unifies the group, and that expresses a sense of community. Truly collective shame has these features: it is shame that is openly communicated and communally shared. At the same time, truly collective shame is consistent with allowing that the members of the group may experience membership shame to varying degrees, and, for some, perhaps not at all, because "membership" covers a range of conditions. For some, group membership may play a larger or more significant role in their lives than for others. If identification with the group is weak, as it may be for members who have been exploited or marginalized by society, membership shame will be weak also. It is necessary for collective shame, however, that some substantial number of members of the group experience (or are disposed to experience) membership shame over the group's actions.

The account of collective shame that I propose also draws attention to its intimate connection with collective identity. In general, the object of shame is one's self. Even when shame is prompted by wrongdoing, it is because of what this wrongdoing reveals about some aspect of one's self, in the light of which one regards oneself as a lesser person, or perhaps a worthless one. Typically the actions and memories that prompt shame highlight one's normative self-conception, that is, the self-conception that contains the moral and nonmoral ideals one aspires to and the standards to which one holds oneself. Similarly, actions and practices that occasion collective shame throw a strong light on the group's collective normative self-conception, casting doubt on its commitment to the ideals and standards it professes. "Are we really the people or community we take and have taken ourselves to be?" is a question that is apt to surface in the face of acknowledged collective wrongdoing, and collective shame is a reasonable response when the answer is "no."

Taking these points into account, I offer the following account:

> *Shared membership shame: group shame is truly collective when and only when there is shame over something the group has done that is widespread among the members of the group, the shame is publicly expressed and socially unifying, and it is aroused by actions or practices that call into question the group's fidelity to its collective normative self-conception.*

Shame may be evoked by the harmful behavior of one's group, either on a specific occasion or repeated over time, as well as by the profoundly offensive attitudes of one's group. As to whether individual members of the group have engaged in wrongful actions that they should be personally ashamed of, the account leaves this question open.

As I have said, the notion of collective shame, as here explained, presupposes the existence of group standards or ideals that the group may dishonor or violate. Group standards or ideals exist in the public realm. They provide common viewpoints from which to assess the behavior and attitudes of the group; they express the group's expectations and hopes for itself; and they characterize the group for outsiders. It is not necessary that each member of the group embrace these ideals for it to be appropriate to attribute them to the group because it is not required that each member of the group have a group identity in order to be able to attribute a group identity to the group.[77] For example, democratic values of freedom and equality are part of the collective self-conception of the American people, although to a limited extent individuals and groups of individuals may be members of this collective even if they do not share these values. However, no social group can survive except in a debased sense if the majority of its members only attribute instrumental value to group membership and do not endorse the basic values and ideals that define its character as a group.

So far I have presented various accounts of collective shame as a social psychological phenomenon, but while interesting in their own right, their ultimate purpose is to facilitate examination of certain normative issues related to collectively taking responsibility for past wrongdoing. Collective shame can provide a moral argument in favor of taking responsibility for past wrongdoing only if that shame is warranted or would be warranted in the particular historical circumstances. We have to distinguish, therefore, between shame's objective moral grounds and its subjective manifestations. In one sort of case there may be no collective shame even though, in light of existing identifications and the bearing of past wrongdoing on the collective identity of the group, collective shame would be fitting and perhaps even demanded. Collective memory of past wrongdoing may be threatening to the group's normative self-conception; the memory may compete with powerful self-protective group sentiments and the group's collective wish to put the past behind it and get on with social and political life, as well as other factors. Once hidden or absent from the collective consciousness of the group, past wrongdoing is not available to it as a reason for feeling collective shame. Or it might not be entirely hidden but exist only at the margins of group self-consciousness, in which case collective shame will not be sufficiently galvanizing to play the moral role that it ought to in public life. And there are morally criticizable failings in the other direction as well, in the direction of excessive, unreasonable collective shame, although these are less common than the deficiencies.

Whatever may be called for in specific instances of historical injustice, we can say this much: because the appropriateness of shame, unlike guilt, does not always depend on whether the subject is morally responsible for wrongdoing, in the sense of "responsible" that is linked to fault, blame, and punishment, group shame may be called for whether or not the group in question is collectively blameworthy for past wrongdoing or properly punishable for it. The conditions of justified collective shame among the members of a present community over the actions or attitudes of the same community in the past are different from those of justified collective guilt for past group wrongdoing.

In conclusion, members who identify with a group whose previous members committed wrongdoing may properly experience membership shame over these wrongs, even if they are in no way personally or causally responsible for them. Because they identify with and to a significant degree take themselves to be part of the group, they have reasons that those who do not identify with it lack for experiencing shame: unlike the others, they see their group in a particular, and particularly negative, light. If collective shame over these wrongs is or would be justified, because they are morally implicated in those wrongs, then they should be willing to collectively take some responsibility for them. Obviously, it is not a sufficient explanation of collective responsibility for past wrongdoing to say that the members of a group collectively feel shame over what their predecessors did. The shame itself must be justified by independent argument, an argument that, I have suggested, draws a connection between acquiring a group identity and being morally implicated in the actions of that group. That said, the account in terms of collective shame at least permits discussion of collective responsibility to proceed on a less morally contentious basis than collective guilt.[78] And it also captures important features of the phenomenology of moral response to historical injustice that might otherwise be overlooked.

8. DOING JUSTICE TO THE PAST: THE ROLE OF MEMORY

(a) *Memory and the demand for recognition*

One common defense of the historical entitlements of the descendants of those who were wronged in the past is to claim that the descendants have themselves been injured by the wrongs done to their predecessors. In this view, the normative significance and relevance of past wrongs depends on their causal relation to disadvantages suffered by currently living people, the descendants of past victims. Thus, if it can be shown that the descendants of the victims of past injustice lack opportunities or resources that they would have had if the injustice had not been done or that in some other way they are adversely affected by the suffering of their predecessors, the descendants are owed reparation or compensation. However, arguments that base claims to compensation or reparation on causation of harm are problematic.

One problem, which I briefly discussed in Section 3, is that the descendants would never have been born if the injustices to their ancestors had not been committed. Assuming this problem can be resolved,[79] or setting it aside, another is the difficulty of establishing causal linkages between present injuries and specific past wrongs. As Janna Thompson notes, "the disadvantages that descendants presently suffer are the result of a long chain of causes reaching back to, and through, more than one historical injustice."[80] The disadvantages suffered by descendants are the result of the choices and deeds of existing people as well as of those who existed between the present and the time of the initial injustice, and it is an enormously complicated task to tease out the causal contribution of the initial injustice from the array of present and past factors that have also contributed to these disadvantages, especially when the initial injustice took place in the more distant past.

Another, and for my purposes, more important criticism is that the causal argument for reparative claims tends to collapse into a different sort of argument, one in which the fact that injustice took place in the *past* actually does no work in justifying the entitlements of descendants. In other words, because it is the causal connection to *present* disadvantage that is the crux of the argument for reparation, it is hard to see why the historical character of some wrongs – wrongs which are inextricably intertwined with the way people construe their history – should itself be normatively significant with respect to what is owed currently living people.

Thompson makes this point in discussing Boris Bittker's case for reparations for African-Americans. According to Bittker, blacks would not be owed reparations had reforms in the Southern states after the Civil War been successful in achieving equality for blacks and had Southern states not introduced a system of oppression and segregation instead. Because these reforms were not allowed to continue and a system of oppression and segregation was introduced instead, the legacy of slavery persists to the present day. But then, Thompson notes, it is "the persistence of segregation into recent times," not past slavery, that needs to be redressed. "Historical injustices... have dropped out of the picture as far as his defense of reparative claims is concerned."[81] The argument that currently living people are owed reparation for *past* injustices to their predecessors easily collapses into an argument based solely on principles of distributive justice applied to currently existing social conditions, as we see in the following:

(1) Descendants of the victims of injustice would not be owed reparation for harm done by past wrongdoing if that harm did not continue into the present.

(2) What matters is the continuation of that harm in the present; i.e., it is this that grounds currently living persons' claims to rectificatory justice.

(3) Therefore, in the account of what is owed to them, the fact that they are *descendants* is not morally relevant, as such, but only because it explains why they continue to suffer injustice today.

The reason that historical injustices drop out of the picture is that harm is here essentially understood ahistorically. There is no acknowledgment that because harm may have an historical dimension, that is, might be an inseparable part of the legacy that has been passed down to currently living people by their forebears, this history should perhaps be addressed in some direct manner by reparative measures. The historical roots of current injustice, on this account, do not matter as such, because injustice should be corrected however it came about.

Not all arguments for repairing historical injustices end up taking this position on the normative significance of the past. If the entitlements of descendants are based on their rights of inheritance rather than on their suffering harm, for example, reference to the past clearly plays a normatively significant role. If their forebears were unjustly deprived of possessions that would have been passed down to them if the injustice had not been done, then the injustice has violated the descendants' right to possession. The reparation that is owed in this case is restitution, and the descendants may make claims for restitution even if they have not been harmed by the expropriation of their forebears' property (that is, not harmed in any other way than by being deprived of their inheritance).

The argument from inheritance is backward-looking and so focuses attention on the past in a way that the argument from causation of harm does not (it does not in the sense that the argument from causation of harm tends to collapse into a nonbackward-looking argument for rectifying current injustices). However, the former argument has only limited application: it can only justify reparative claims when the past injustice is due to violation of the right to possession, whereas descendants of the victims of injustice often base their claims to reparation on other kinds of injustice as well. Moreover, as Thompson points out, the argument from inheritance can justify reparative claims even when the past dispossession is not caused by injustice.[82] This is problematic because it is specifically the *injustice* done to past victims that drives many demands for reparation made by their descendants and that the descendants want the responsible party to acknowledge. Nevertheless, the argument from inheritance has moved the analysis in a direction that I want to pursue. Can we give a backward-looking account of descendants' claims to reparation that does not depend on rights of inheritance? And to return to a theme introduced earlier in connection with the Tulsa race riot Commission, what role does remembrance play in honoring these claims?

Before going into the details of the argument, let me clarify what sort of argument it will be and some of the assumptions I will be making. First, the argument is backward-looking and group-based, where by "group" I mean a socially unified group, as discussed in Section 2. In such a view, although it would ultimately be individuals who receive some form of reparation, reparation could be characterized as something owed to the group to which these individuals belong and which individuals receive only because of their membership in the group. Second, I make two assumptions. I argued in Section 4 that a group can be wronged and, in Section 3, I commented on the difficulty of specifying criteria for identifying whether a group at one time is the same group as a group at an earlier time. In what follows, I will assume that these matters are not in dispute, that is, that some group has persisted over time, and that it was wronged by injustice in the past. My questions, therefore, have to do with what is owed currently living people because they belong to a group whose members have historically been the targets of unjust treatment (to simplify matters, I refer to the current group as "descendants" of the historical group).

We can begin to construct a backward-looking argument of this sort for the reparative claims of descendants by considering the role that a history of victimization plays in the collective self-understanding and identity of a group. The group-based murder, torture, or abduction of one's forebears, or the disrespect shown to them as persons, is not merely registered by the descendants as a piece of historical information whose psychological effects are no different than those they experience when they reflect on similar crimes committed against other groups. Rather, the injustices suffered by their forebears are part of their shared history, assuming they can be said to have a shared history, and if they are retained in the collective memory they are experienced in a way that similar injustices elsewhere are not. Because their collective identity is constituted in part by the historical narratives that connect past and present members and give them a place in a larger intergenerational story, the injustice done their forebears informs and partly determines how they collectively understand themselves. Commonly they will express their solidarity with the victims of past injustice in such terms as, "Our people have (or our community has) suffered terrible injustices in the past."

Descendants demand reparation not only because they have been harmed by past injustice as this is understood by Bittker and others like him, and not only because they have been deprived of their rightful possessions by past injustice. The harm and inheritance arguments no doubt play important roles in debates about reparations, but as presented they do not capture something that is central to and that drives many reparative claims, namely, the meaning that a particular history possesses for those whose history it is. What they do not convey, in other words, is this: often descendants make claims for reparation because it matters to them what their collective history contains and because getting others (particularly those who are responsible for the wrongdoing) to address this in appropriate ways, including reparative actions of various sorts that acknowledge the historical character of the injustice, is crucial to the self-respect of those who inherit the legacy of past injustice.

Remembrance plays different roles in relation to historical injustice. For one thing, forgetfulness can itself be seen as a kind of capitulation to and perpetuation of the earlier injustice: not only are the original victims dead, but there is not even a trace of them left behind in the memories of those who came after. Remembrance therefore can have powerful symbolic significance for the descendants of the victims of injustice in that it serves as a form of resistance to the triumph of injustice and the nullification of its victims. For another, the significance of some part of the past for a group depends on the particular place that it occupies in the group's collective self-understanding, and this is shown among other things by the manner in which the group remembers or is able to remember it. How and whether historical injustice in particular is remembered and by whom thus helps to (re)configure collective identity. A nice illustration of this phenomenon is the ceremonial reburial of ancestral remains by indigenous peoples.[83] These remains were once treated as mere objects of scientific curiosity by white scientists who were intent on proving their racial inferiority. Today, however, museums across the world are taking steps to return these remains to their descendants. The ceremonial reinterment of these remains is, for the descendants, a profoundly important commemorative act through which they reconnect with their past and reclaim lost or neglected identities.

Jeremy Waldron also remarks on the link between historical remembrance of injustice and collective identity:

> Each person establishes a sense of herself in terms of her ability to identify the subject or agency of her present thinking with that of certain acts and events that took place in the past. . . . But remembrance in this sense is equally important to communities – families, tribes, nations, parties – that is, to human entities that exist often for much longer than individual men and women. To neglect the historical record is to do violence to this identity and thus to the community that it sustains.[84]

"Only the deliberate enterprise of recollection," he claims, "can sustain the moral and cultural reality of self and community."[85]

We need more than a connection between memory and identity, however, to justify the reparative *claims* of descendants of victims of injustice. For even if remembrance of a past that contains injustice is important for the descendants because it is intimately bound up with their sense of who they are, this does not, by itself, show that remembrance is *owed* by present and future generations to these descendants or that the latter have a *right* to demand it of the former. To do this, we need to consider another role of remembrance in relation to historical injustice.

I suggest that in many – though not all – instances, the demand for remembrance of past injustice by current members of the wronged group can be thought of and legitimized as a demand for *recognition* (to use Charles Taylor's term) of the group's distinct identity and history. The harm to its identity caused by a history of injustice makes it appropriate for the group to demand recognition of that violated identity and the harm done to it, and for the successors of the perpetrators to fulfill that demand. As Taylor argues, what others are being asked to recognize by those demanding recognition

> is the unique identity of this individual or group. The idea is that it is precisely this distinctness that has been ignored, glossed over, assimilated to a dominant or majority identity.[86]

Fulfilling the demand for recognition requires acknowledging that history of injustice publicly in memorial activities. In relation to this objective, remembrance obviously cannot be a project for the victims and their descendants alone. Because remembrance fulfills a demand for recognition, it is a project that by its nature requires others, and it ought to be engaged in jointly by the descendants as well as by those who are or should be willing to take responsibility for the past wrongdoing. Making remembrance a joint project is a way of publicly recognizing and affirming the value and significance that a group's past has for the group, and because a group's conception of itself is bound up with its understanding of its history, of recognizing and affirming the group's collective identity. It represents a commitment by those who have inherited the legacy of responsibility to, in Waldron's words, "respect and help sustain a dignified sense of identity-in-memory for the people affected."[87]

We might put the argument this way: remembrance is owed to the living descendants of the victims of injustice on the grounds that the current group is entitled to have its own understanding of its past validated by society and properly reflected in the historical record. If social justice partly concerns the degree to which a society establishes and supports the institutional conditions necessary for the recognition of collective identities, then institutionalized public remembrance of past injustice is owed to the descendants as a matter of social justice.[88] But a group's own understanding of its past may have been deformed and corrupted by the treatment is has historically received from others, and this leads to an importantly different way of construing the argument from recognition. The crucial insight here is that a group's understanding of its past, and the identity to which it contributes, are not merely a function of what the group does on its own. They are themselves dependent on and formed through processes of recognition or lack of recognition by others. Collective identities, like individual ones, do not develop in isolation but "crucially depend on dialogical relations with others,"[89] in Taylor's words. So with this in mind, we can reformulate the argument. What the argument from recognition demands is not merely recognition of a group's understanding of its past, whatever the quality of that self-understanding may be and however it was formed. It demands rather that recognition secure for the current group an understanding of its history that supports a sense of its own worth and a dignified sense of its collective identity. This is the role that the argument from recognition assigns to remembrance.

Failure to publicly acknowledge past injustice and commemorate its victims is frequently but one aspect of the continued marginalization, oppression, and domination of groups whose history of injustice is ignored or denied. Indeed, ignoring or denying the injustice suffered by a group in the past often stems from the same pernicious attitudes and social conditions that explain continued maltreatment of the group in the present and serves to perpetuate it. These forms of maltreatment harm the members of these groups, but the injustice of not remembering or properly remembering a group's past is distinct from them, so that even those groups that are not disadvantaged by political, social, and economic inequalities may still have legitimate grievances on the former grounds. We can use the language of harm – as I have been doing – to describe the effects of being denied due public recognition of their past. But then we must be clear that the harm in question is, in Thompson's words, "intrinsically historical – which cannot be separated from the way people view their history."[90]

When the failure to remember the victims of past injustice amounts to a failure of recognition of the wronged group's identity, the former compounds the original injustice. Groups, however, are seldom quick to take responsibility for past injustices and to engage in acts of commemoration and atonement. They may for various reasons not want to or be able to look too closely at the historical record,[91] and this is particularly true with respect to injustices that occurred in the more recent past.[92] The time lapse between the commission of wrongdoing and the eventual taking of responsibility for it (if indeed this occurs) is itself something for which the responsible party should take responsibility. Adam Nossiter relates how, in the years following World War II, the French people embraced a version of what happened during the Occupation that obscured the truth about their wartime collaboration with the Nazis:

> The country was moving forward; de Gaulle, as everybody knew, had triumphed in those war years, incarnating the essence of France with his refusal to collaborate.... [As noted by the French historian Henry Russo], "France was now cast as a nation that 'forever and always resists the invader,' whatever uniform he might wear."[93]

It would not be until 50 years after the end of the war that the French president and clergy would publicly disavow this version of history, declare that Vichy was the French state, and apologize to the victims and their descendants on behalf of the French people.[94] But an apology for the treatment of French Jews during the war does not repair the injustice because it does not address the fact that the apology was so long in coming. The delay in issuing an apology for past injustices should also be publicly acknowledged as a case of justice delayed and efforts should be made to repair the damage caused by it.

(b) *Symbolic reparation and memory*

Waldron argues that various sorts of reparative action may symbolize society's commitment to remember and publicly acknowledge past wrongdoing, and thus may be construed as "symbolic gestures." Although he distinguishes between genuine and symbolic compensation for past wrongdoing, the distinction, he emphasizes, should not be taken to suggest a ranking in terms of value:

> Quite apart from any attempt genuinely to compensate victims or offset their losses, reparations may symbolize a society's undertaking not to forget or deny that a particular injustice took place. . . . A prominent recent example of this is the payment of token sums of compensation by the American government to the survivors of Japanese-American families uprooted, interned, and concentrated in 1942. . . . The point was to mark – with something that counts in the United States – a clear public recognition that this injustice did happen. . . . The payments give an earnest of good faith and sincerity to that acknowledgment. . . . It is no objection to this that the payments are purely symbolic. Since identity is bound up with symbolism, a symbolic gesture may be as important to people as any material compensation.[95]

Symbolic reparation is particularly appropriate in response to a group's claims for recognition of its distinct identity and history. Although it can take different forms, one important type of symbolic reparation is accomplished through remembrance. Here actions are intended and perceived as acts *in memory of* wrongdoing, as embodiments of collective or communal remembrance. What's more, this is essential from the standpoint of the demand for recognition. These symbolic gestures are not just poor substitutes for something of greater value to the descendants. On the contrary, they can powerfully convey to a group with a history of injustice that society is prepared to accord it the dignity and respect it deserves.

And symbolic acts can be reparative even when actual compensation for past injustice is not possible because there is no one still alive to compensate, or the injustice is of such a nature and magnitude that it is not truly compensible. Even if actual compensation is possible it may be ethically problematic because, as Waldron points out, it involves the commission of further injustices, and symbolic acts of reparation may raise fewer ethical objections in these cases.

For the successors of the perpetrators of wrongdoing, being honest with themselves about a problematic part of their collective past and telling the truth about it are aspects of owning up to it. Truthfulness about the past, it might be said, is important not only for the victims of wrongdoing and their descendants, but also for those who are responsible for (or bear some responsibility for) that wrongdoing. For the descendants, no symbolic reparation is likely to be satisfactory if it is not accompanied by or expressive of a commitment to tell the truth about what happened, to set the historical record straight. Otherwise, the symbolic gestures will appear to be primarily for the benefit of the responsible parties – a way of assuaging their collective guilt or shame – and may only compound the original offense and fuel resentment on the part of the descendants. Even if their motives are not suspect, the descendants may believe that the particular form of symbolic reparation that is offered is inadequate, that more or something else should be done to acknowledge the suffering of their predecessors and the group's distinct history. Disagreements about what constitutes adequate recognition, like disagreements about what actually happened, may linger. However, even if the final resolution of differences is beyond reach, evidence of good faith and sincere self-reproach on the part of those offering reparation, a manifest willingness on their part to engage in dialogue, to negotiate, and to compromise, can do much to repair relations with the aggrieved party.

It may nevertheless be tempting to belittle the value of symbolic reparation because, as is often said, it does not and cannot really "make up" for injustices committed in the past. There are senses, of course, in which this is true. At the same time, it is surely implausible to hold that acts of reparation are solely or chiefly to be graded as better or worse depending on how nearly they restore the victims to the position they were in before the injustice was done, and that the *attitudes* the acts express are of little or no importance in themselves. On the contrary, the value of the good produced by reparative acts importantly depends on and varies with the intentions and expressive meanings of those acts. Descendants of the victims of injustice typically care about what is expressed by reparations, about whether, for example, they are given in a spirit of seeking forgiveness or out of respect for their history or out of less creditable motives.

Those currently living people who are serious about repairing past wrongdoing must make a number of complex and sensitive decisions. Even if the reparation is "only" symbolic, they have to consider not only what measures should be employed (a monument or museum? or an official day of public remembrance? or a scholarship fund in honor of the victims?), but also the circumstances under which to engage in such acts, the potential reactions of their intended beneficiaries, and the prominence that commemoration of the victims of past injustice is to be given in the life of the community. For these reasons, an ethics of memory is also necessarily in part a politics of memory.

Among other things, a politics of memory has to address a problem that I discussed at some length in Chapter 1, what Omar Bartov calls "the surfeit of memory,"[96] that is, an excessive preoccupation with the past that clouds judgment, prevents constructive engagement with contemporary injustices and social needs, and impedes the realization of other important social goods. To be sure, the most vocal advocates of the merits of forgetting are often the perpetrators of wrongdoing who do not want their complicity in injustice to be publicly exposed, or those who continue to benefit from it, and it is more likely that past atrocities will be covered up than dwelled upon. Nevertheless, in order to determine how the current generation should remember the victims of past injustice, the possibility of negative social consequences is certainly a relevant (if not dispositive) consideration. Indeed, such consequences will render a particular mode of symbolic reparation self-defeating, if it generates such hostility or resentment that public attention is actually deflected from acknowledgment of the suffering of past victims.

Finally, the Taylor-inspired account that I have presented presumes that a currently existing group has a history that includes injustice to its predecessors. If the victimized group has died out or undergone such transformation that the injustice done to it cannot be considered part of the successor group's own history, then this particular argument will have no foothold. However, even in this case, it might be alleged that the dead should not be forgotten and that doing justice to the past requires that they and their sufferings be remembered. Indeed, although I believe that the argument from recognition of a distinct history and identity is compelling, I do not want to suggest that it is the only justification that can be given for memorial duties regarding the past victims of injustice, and that any such justification must presume a currently existing group whose history includes injustice done to earlier members of that same group. In fact, as I will argue in Chapter 4, I believe there are other grounds for these duties and that they are not solely based on the obligation to make reparation for wrongdoing. And in Chapter 5, I will take up arguments for duties to remember the dead that do not rest on or importantly involve their having been victims of injustice at all.

NOTES

1. Alain Finkielkraut, *The Imaginary Jew*. K. O'Neill and D. Suchoff (Trans). (Lincoln, NE: University of Nebraska Press, 1994), p. 54.

2. "Final Report of the Oklahoma Commission to Study the Tulsa Race Riot of 1921," compiled by Danney Goble, www.tulsareparations.org/ FinalReport.htm; also Alfred L. Brophy, "Assessing State and City Culpability: The Riot and the Law," www.tulsareparations.org/Culpability. htm. See also James S. Hirsch, *Riot and Remembrance: The Tulsa Race War and its Legacy* (New York: Houghton Mifflin, 2002).

3. John Hope Franklin and Scott Ellsworth, "History Knows no Fences: An Overview," www.tulsareparations.org/HistoryNoFences.htm.

4. "Final Report," op.cit.

5. Ibid.

6. See Ben Fenwick, "Oklahoma closes race riot probe, no reparations," www.agrnews.org/issues/124/nationalnews.html.

7. Ibid.

8. As noted in Chapter 2, there may be situations in which a person takes responsibility for something that he was not responsible for. In such cases, if wrongs were committed, he could apologize, but it would be on behalf of the one who is responsible. In addition, he can fail to follow through on responsibilities that he acquired as a result of taking responsibility, and he might apologize for these failures.

9. "Final Report," op. cit.

10. The cases usually discussed in the literature on historical injustice are those in which questions about actual collective responsibility for past wrongdoing

are raised. Even if such responsibility is lacking, however, those who are not responsible can still collectively *take* responsibility for that past wrongdoing, and there may be good reasons for them to do so. (I made a similar point about individual responsibility and responsibility-taking in Chapter 2.) See also Note 8 in this chapter.

11. I will say more in Section 3 about what counts as a "successor" to a group.

12. This typology is incomplete. The violence of the Tulsa race riot, for example, was perpetrated by a mob. However, the category of collective moral responsibility can also be applied to mobs. See Larry May, *The Morality of Groups* (Notre Dame, IN: University Press, 1987), pp. 73–83.

13. These two sorts of collections are referred to as "aggregates" and "amalgams" by Marilyn Friedman and Larry May, "Harming Women as a Group," *Social Theory and Practice 11*, 2 (Summer 1985): 207–234. Similarly, P. E. Digeser distinguishes between "random aggregates" and "nonrandom aggregates" in *Political Forgiveness* (Ithaca, NY: Cornell University Press, 2001), pp. 111–115.

14. I take this conception of community from Ross Poole, *Nation and Identity* (New York: Routledge, 1999), pp. 10–13.

15. Nenad Miscevic, "Is National Identity Essential for Personal Identity," in N. Miscevic (Ed.), *Nationalism and Ethnic Conflict* (Chicago: Open Court, 2000), pp. 239–257, at 242–243.

16. More on this in Section 4.

17. E. H. Schein, *Organizational Psychology* (Englewood Cliffs, NJ: Prentice Hall, 1965), p. 8.

18. Philip Petit calls this the "developmental rationale" for ascribing collective responsibility. See "Responsibility Incorporated," *Ethics 117* (2007): 171–201.

19. See Joel Feinberg, "Collective Responsibility," in *Doing and Deserving* (Princeton, NJ: Princeton University Press, 1970), pp. 222–251.

20. Margaret Gilbert, "The Idea of Collective Guilt," in *Sociality and Responsibility* (Lanham, MD: Rowman and Littlefield, 2000), pp. 141–153, at 148.

21. Ibid., p. 147.

22. Ton Van Den Beld argues that it is a fatal problem for Gilbert's account that it allows responsibility in the absence of fault in "Can Collective Responsibility for Perpetrated Evil Persist over Generations?" *Ethical Theory and Moral Practice 5* (2002): 181–200.

23. They may have been innocent of the original wrongdoing but, according to Daniel Butt, still be responsible for a subsequent injustice, namely, the injustice of failing to take steps to rectify the original injustice. In this way, the current generation in implicated in *current* wrongdoing, a wrongdoing that perpetuates and compounds the original one. (I say more about this in Section 8.) Butt explains why those living in the present should do something about past wrongdoing by introducing the notion of "overlapping generations." The idea is roughly that because of overlapping generations, changes in the composition of a nation over time are responsibility-preserving. Butt's account raises a number of questions, but what stands out for me is that it is focused solely on the *guilt* of those who belong to the

current generation, on their continuing to be at fault. See "Nations, Overlapping Generations, and Historic Injustice," *American Philosophical Quarterly 43* (2006): 357–367.

24. See P. E. Digeser, *Political Forgiveness* (Ithaca, NY: Cornell University Press, 2001), pp. 161–167.
25. Yael Tamir, *Liberal Nationalism* (Princeton, NJ: Princeton University Press, 1993), p. 65.
26. Ronald Dworkin, *Law's Empire* (Cambridge, MA: Harvard University Press, 1986).
27. Janna Thompson, *Taking Responsibility for the Past* (Cambridge, UK: Polity Press, 2002), p. 74.
28. Several authors have attempted to respond to Parfit's "different people choices" problem. See George Sher, "Compensation and Transworld Personal Identity," *Monist 62* (1979): 378–391; Dan W. Brock, "The Non-Identity Problem and Genetic Harms – The Case of Wrongful Handicaps," *Bioethics 9*, 3/4 (1995): 289–295; Lukas Meyer, "Past and Future – the Case for an Identity-Independent Notion of Harm," in *Rights, Culture, and the Law: Themes from the Legal and Political Philosophy of Joseph Raz* (Oxford: Oxford University Press, 2003), pp. 143–159.
29. Joel Feinberg, *Harm to Others* (New York: Oxford University Press, 1984), p. 34.
30. Trudy Govier distinguishes between types of victims in "Forgiveness and the Unforgivable," *American Philosophical Quarterly 36*, 1 (January 1999): 59–75.
31. See Friedman and May, op. cit., Note 13.
32. Consider, for example, the destruction of synagogues and other communal institutions by the Nazis, or the expropriation of Native Americans' historical lands by the U.S. government.
33. For more on collective harms, see Gerald J. Postema, "Collective Evils, Harms, and the Law," *Ethics 97*, 2 (January 1987): 414–440.
34. See Larry May, *The Morality of Groups*, op. cit., pp. 143–144.
35. Joel Feinberg, *Offense to Others* (New York: Oxford University Press, 1985), pp. 57–60.
36. Ibid., p. 58.
37. Ibid., p. 59.
38. Elizabeth Anderson, *Value in Ethics and Economics* (Cambridge, MA: Harvard University Press, 1993), especially pp. 30–38. I return to Anderson's distinction between expressive and consequentialist norms in Chapter 5 in this volume.
39. Avishai Margalit, *The Decent Society* (Cambridge, MA: Harvard University Press, 1996), p. 146–147.
40. Digeser, op. cit., pp. 112–116. See also the discussion of whether Wiesenthal should have forgiven Karl in Claudia Card, *The Atrocity Paradigm: A Theory of Evil* (New York: Oxford University Press, 2002), pp. 181–187.
41. Ibid., p. 114.
42. Ibid.
43. Ibid., p. 115.

44. "Identification as an L," where L is a label for a group, is a necessary element of having a social identity, according to Anthony Appiah. It means "thinking of yourself as an L, in ways that make a difference: perhaps thinking of yourself as an L shapes your feelings... perhaps it shapes your actions, so that you do something as an L." As I argue, one might not have identified as an L in the absence of being treated as an L by others. See *The Ethics of Identity* (Princeton: Princeton University Press, 2005), pp. 65–71.

45. In *At the Mind's Limits* (Bloomington, IN: Indiana University Press, 1980).

46. Constructivist accounts of memory hold that the elements of an individual's personal history, as recorded in his or her memory, are ordered according to their felt importance in that person's life. Similar points can be made about a group's history, as interpreted by later generations and preserved in collective memory. For more on the relationship between collective memory and history and the complexity of the notion of historical accuracy, see Chapter 4 in this volume, especially Sections 3 and 6.

47. See Iwona Irwin-Zarecka, *Frames of Remembrance: The Dynamics of Collective Memory* (New Brunswick/London: Transaction Publishers, 1994).

48. For more on "reconstructivist" understanding of memory, see Sue Campbell, *Relational Remembering* (Lanham, MD: Rowman and Littlefield, 2003). I discussed this feature of memory in relation to taking responsibility for one's personal past in Chapter 2, Section 4(a).

49. W. James Booth, *Communities of Memory: On Witness, Identity, and Justice* (Ithaca: Cornell University Press, 2006), p. 23.

50. Iwona Irwin-Zarecka, opt. cit., p. 67.

51. Tony Judt, "From the House of the Dead: On Modern European Memory," *New York Review of Books* 52 (October 6, 2005): 12–16, at 16.

52. Ibid., p. 14.

53. Many studies document this point. To cite just a few: Eric Foner, *Who Owns History?* (New York: Hill and Wang, 2002); J. H. Plumb, *The Death of the Past* (New York: Palgrave Macmillan, 2004); and Alan B. Spitzer, *Historical Truth and Lies about the Past* (University of North Carolina, 1996).

54. See Chapter 1, Section 4(a), where I try to make sense of the notion of "too much" collective memory. As I note in Chapter 1, collective memory has to be assessed for its implications for social and political goods like peace, stability, democracy, and distributive justice.

55. Robert Sparrow, "History and Collective Responsibility," *Australasian Journal of Philosophy* 78, 3 (September 2000): 346–359, at 359.

56. Ibid.

57. See Nick Smith, "The Categorical Apology," *Journal of Social Philosophy* 36, 4 (Winter 2005): 473–496.

58. The term comes from Booth, op. cit., pp. 14–15.

59. Gerd Knischewski and Ulla Spittler, "Memories of the Second World War and National Identity in Germany, in M. Evans and K. Lunn (Eds.) *War and Memory in the Twentieth Century* (Oxford: Oxford University Press, 1997), pp. 239–254.

60. Ibid., pp. 246–247.

61. Another example relates to how France understood the significance of Vichy in the aftermath of World War II. De Gaulle's refusal to take responsibility for French collaboration with the Vichy regime and to acknowledge French complicity in the deportation of Jews was based on the conviction that France was identical, not with Vichy but with a certain idea of France, namely, that of a free, Republican France. From this standpoint, Vichy was but a temporary aberration, a brief interruption in the continuous history of the Republic. French national identity under de Gaulle was shaped by this way of understanding French history, by a refusal to acknowledge complicity in and take responsibility for the crimes of the Vichy regime. See Note 93.

62. Roy Schafer, "Claimed and Disclaimed Action," in *A New Language for Psychoanalysis* (New Haven: Yale University Press, 1976), pp. 127–154, at 147.

63. Linda Radzik, "Collective Responsibility and Duties to Respond," *Social Theory and Practice* 27, 3 (July 2001): 455–470.

64. See Claudia Card, *The Atrocity Paradigm*, op. cit., pp. 202–206.

65. Margaret Gilbert, "Group Wrongs and Guilt Feelings," *Journal of Ethics 1* (1997): 65–84.

66. See Margaret Gilbert, "Collective Guilt and Collective Guilt Feelings," *Journal of Ethics 6*, 2 (2002): 115–143. For a defense of the notion of collective guilt that takes a different tack than Gilbert, see Deborah Tollefsen, "The Rationality of Collective Guilt," in P. French and H. Wettstein (Eds.) *Shared Intentions and Collective Responsibility* (Boston: Blackwell Publishing, 2006), pp. 222–239.

67. Bernard Schlink, *The Reader*, Carol Brown Janeway (Trans.). (New York: Vintage Books, 1997). Page numbers in the text are to this edition.

68. I assume that whatever he is experiencing, it not irrational or pathological.

69. Gabriele Taylor, *Pride, Shame, and Guilt* (Oxford: Clarendon Press, 1985), p. 89–90.

70. Ibid., p. 90.

71. Bernard Williams, *Shame and Necessity* (Berkeley, CA: University of California Press, 1993), pp. 89–90.

72. Taylor, op. cit., p. 90.

73. To make clear what I am doing: I will be working my way toward an account of shame as a collective phenomenon, *not* the shame of an individual as a member of a group. And when I speak of collective identity in relation to this, it is *not* the collective dimension of individual identity to which I will be referring.

74. See Radzik, op. cit.

75. Or, alternatively, membership shame is the shame that is experienced in virtue of one's identification with others on the basis of certain group-defining properties one has in common with them.

76. Those familiar with Margaret Gilbert's work will recognize that my distinction between different accounts of collective shame parallels her discussion of collective remorse. I do not end up exactly where she does, however, because I do not employ the notion of a "joint commitment to" have some feeling. See Gilbert, *Sociality and Responsibility*, op. cit., chapter 7.

77. Recall the distinction made in Section 2 between the group identity of a group and the group identity of an individual who belongs to the group.

78. In the course of commenting on Habermas' contribution to the so-called historians' debate in Germany, W. James Booth takes issue with his claim that "collective shame" is an "archaic" sentiment:

   Perhaps, though, it is not so archaic. For shame, as we saw, is bound up with the wholeness of a life, and not the narrower connection between agent and act. At the level of the community, the sense of shame (or pride) in the deeds of one's family or fellow citizens points to a shared community of fate and memory, something that is enduringly ours. (Booth, op. cit, p. 64)

   Booth, as I do, argues that shame points to a sense of responsibility whose conditions are different from those required for guilt. (See also Booth, pp. 39–44.)

79. See Note 28.

80. Janna Thompson, "Historical Injustice and Reparation: Justifying Claims of Descendants," *Ethics 112*, 1 (October 2001): 114–135, at 117.

81. Ibid., p. 119. Thompson notes that recent injustices do not drop out of the picture, but she distinguishes between reparation for historical injustice and reparation for recent injustice. Like her, I am interested in reparation for historical injustice.

82. Ibid., p. 120.

83. See *New York Times*, "Mocked in Europe of Old, African is Embraced at Home at Last," May 4, 2002.

84. Jeremy Waldron, "Superseding Historical Injustice," *Ethics 103*, 1 (October 1992): 4–28, at 6.

85. Ibid.

86. See Charles Taylor, "The Politics of Recognition," in A. Gutmann (Ed.) *Multiculturalism* (Princeton, NJ: Princeton University Press, 1994), pp. 25–73. See also, Iris Murdoch Young, *Justice and the Politics of Difference* (Princeton, NJ: Princeton University Press, 1990), especially chapter 6.

87. Waldron, op. cit., p. 6.

88. As I go on to suggest, groups can also be denied recognition by deliberate efforts to suppress group self-consciousness and collective memory. When this is successful, it undermines a group's shared memory of victimization and with it the basis for pressing reparative claims against those responsible for historical injustice. The account presented here, therefore, cannot stand alone, for otherwise the reparative obligations of the wrongdoers and their descendants could be erased by further acts of injustice against the wronged group. For more, see Samuel C. Wheeler III, "Reparations Reconstructed," *American Philosophical Quarterly 34*, 3 (July 1997): 301–318.

89. Taylor, op. cit., p. 34.

90. Thompson, *Taking Responsibility for the Past*, op. cit., p. 66.

91. As illustrated by the nearly 80 years of silence that followed the Tulsa race riot.

92. Historical distance is of course no guarantee that the truth about the past will finally be publicly acknowledged, but it may permit a more detached and less defensive accounting of responsibility for historical injustices.

93. Adam Nossiter, *The Algeria Hotel* (Boston: Houghton Mifflin, 2001), pp. 4–5.
94. See Note 61.
95. Waldron, op. cit., pp. 6–7.
96. Omar Bartov, "Intellectuals on Auschwitz: Memory, History, and Truth," in M. Morgan (Ed.) *A Holocaust Reader* (New York: Oxford University Press, 2001), pp. 292–294. See also my discussion in Chapter 1.

4

ETHICS, TRUTH, AND COLLECTIVE MEMORY

Modern shared memory is located between the push and pull of two poles: history and myth.   – Avishai Margalit, *The Ethics of Memory*[1]

1. MEMORY AND HISTORY/HISTORY AND MYTH

"Memory," says Kerwin Lee Klein, "is replacing old favorites – *nature, culture, language* – as the word most commonly paired with history"[2] in academic and to some extent in popular discourse. Memory, more precisely collective or social memory not individual memory, has become a preoccupation of contemporary historiography. However, to say that memory is now commonly paired with history is a simple way of conveying a rather complex truth because there is considerable variation in how these terms are understood and in the point of the pairing. Here are some of the claims about collective memory, history, and their relationship that those who link history with memory make.

Historians Pierre Nora[3] and Yosef Yerushalmi,[4] two of the fathers of the current "memory boom" in historical studies, pair "memory" and "history" in order to emphasize their opposition. "Real memory," says Nora, has an "affective and magical" quality that distinguishes it from the dispassionate analytic approach of history. Collective memory, in its true sense, has largely disappeared from the world and been replaced by new kinds of memory, by what he calls "archive-memory" and "duty-memory."[5] Others want to criticize, as naïve, views that give preference to memory over history on the grounds that memory is somehow more authentic or truer to the past than the alleged contrivances and manipulations of history. Rather, they suggest, each is a way of preserving the past for current and future generations, and it is only relative to specific purposes and within particular contexts that we can privilege memory over history or, for that matter, history over memory. For French historian Jacques Le Goff, memory should be paired with history because memory "is the raw material of history. . . . the living source from which historians draw."[6] This view may or may not be accompanied by the further claim that memory is history at an elementary stage of development, a kind of nascent history. Le Goff and others also note the interdependence of history and memory: history draws on, and is sometimes contested by, collective (and personal) memories and, conversely, collective memory is informed by the findings of history. A further point about the relationship between history and memory concerns the notion of *truth*, specifically truth about the past. There are various accounts of how history and memory are related to truth. It might be said that there is a kind of history which is just the collective memory of a group. This kind of history has a tenuous relationship to truth because what is called "collective memory" is often only a fabricated narrative in the service of social-ideological needs. History in this sense is often contrasted with the "historians' history," to quote Paul Veyne, the kind of history that "bases itself on an ideal of truth" and that is judged by the yardstick of truth.[7] Against this, postmodernist critics of a certain conception of history such as Hayden White[8] and F. R. Ankersmit[9] deny that historical narratives refer to reality at all: truth, in their view, is not the norm of history any more than it is that of memory.[10]

Because this last issue is so central to the concerns of this chapter, I want to say a bit more about it at the outset. With respect to the question of truth, history – that is, inquiry into past events, acts, and so forth, not the events themselves – is written from so many varied interpretive standpoints that any aspiration to truth in this domain may seem doomed to failure. There is so-called official history, history written or endorsed by political regimes, religious authorities, and so forth, that often involves deliberate manipulation and obfuscation of the historical record in order to shore up and legitimate their authority. Even when historical inquiry is able to remain somewhat independent of political and other powers, "the recognition that the historical fact is constructed and that documents are not innocent has thrown a glaring light on the manipulations that manifest themselves at all levels of the construction of historical knowledge."[11] These points may seem to support, even confirm, the extreme

postmodernist position. Against this, however, much contemporary historiography and philosophy of history has been taken up with arguing
that it does not follow from the inevitable selectivity and frequent manipulations of history that we can or should dispense with a notion of *the
truth* in history.[12] This is the position I adopt. Indeed, it is a fundamental
assumption of this chapter that truth is the regulative ideal of history, as it
is of science, and that accuracy in what is said about the past is the primary
criterion for assessing the quality of historical research and the achievements of historical inquiry.[13] (Plainly, this oversimplifies: more needs to
be said about (1) what the aim of truth, with respect to history, commits
one to and (2) how the discipline of history is regulated by truth.) This
has important normative implications for collective memory as well. For
as explained later in this chapter, collective memory does not entirely
retreat from history, and therefore collective memory becomes vulnerable to correction by history. And because truth is the normative aim of
history, collective memory is vulnerable to correction by truth about the
past as well.

Memory finds its meaning, in large part, through key concepts with
which it is paired and from which it is distinguished, but *history* is only
one of these concepts that shape our understanding of collective memory.
History is also distinguished from, and opposed to, *myth*, and the opposition that is sometimes asserted between collective memory and history
may be partly explained in terms of the features or functions that collective memory shares with myth. Nora's locating "real memory" within
"so-called primitive or archaic societies," where collective memory links
the group "to the undifferentiated time of heroes, origins, and myths,"[14]
suggests this explanation. Historian Niall Ferguson, commenting on a
series of lectures given by the English historian J. H. Plumb in 1968, also
sets up a contrast between the discipline of history and myth that appears
to align collective memory to a large extent with myth:

> ... These signs of the swinging times are not really what Plumb means
> by the 'death of the past'. Rather, the question he addresses here is one
> which is as important today as it was thirty-five years ago. It is whether
> or not academic history, in dismantling our received notions about the
> past [i.e. notions retained in the collective memory], is essentially a
> destructive enterprise, capable of dislodging but incapable of replacing
> the largely mythical but socially functional 'past'. In worrying about

the antagonism between a past which enhanced social cohesion and a consciously revisionist history produced by professionals, Plumb was in many ways prescient.[15]

The past that enhances social cohesion is largely a mythical past, this suggests, and the worry referred to here is that our received notions about the past – those we accept more or less unreflectively and uncritically and that orient and anchor our lives – will not be able to survive the corrosive effect of professional history and continue to perform their social function.

My own view, the grounds for which will become apparent in what follows, is that history cannot replace collective memory because collective memory is not just bad (inchoate, naive, etc.) history. Collective memory has other vital functions that are truth-independent and so not among those that belong to history. Of course, history too – or more precisely, the public use of history, not just historical scholarship – like memory, has a social function. As Lucien Febvre notes,

> it is in relation to its present needs that history systematically harvests, and then classes and groups, past facts. . . . To organize the past in relation to the present: that is what one could call the social function of history.[16]

But this is only a potential social function as long as history is just a third-person (a view from the outside) narrative of a society's past. To realize its social function, history must have a public use and an impact on collective memory, that is, be taken up by it, enter into its construction, and become the society's possession. It may or may not do so. In any case, collective memory is answerable to history in this sense: good remembering has truth as one its values, and truth is, or ought to be, the concern of history.[17]

Even if history cannot replace collective memory, history is not irrelevant to it either, and this, along with the alignment of collective memory with myth, suggests that there is a tension within collective memory, or within good collective remembering. It is a tension one of whose aspects is alluded to by Plumb's dramatic phrase, "the death of the past": if the past of collective memory is largely a mythical past, can it survive correction by the discipline of history? We can think of this as a tension between memory's *values* too: on the one hand, the value of the past continuing to fulfill its "mythical" social function; on the other, the value of truth, for which collective memory is answerable to the discipline of history.

Truth, however, is not just one of the *values* of remembering. In some circumstances, recording, telling, and disseminating the truth about the past is also memory's obligation, a moral imperative of memory. Certain past events ought to be remembered, but more than this, it is morally imperative that efforts be made to remember them accurately, to expose fabrication, obfuscation, and manipulation, and to preserve for and pass on to succeeding generations the truth about what happened. In this connection, the discipline of history obviously plays a critical role. Public debate and public discourse need to be informed by this discipline if people are to discharge their moral obligations of collective remembrance.

This is one part, but only one part, of an account of the imperatives of collective memory. Sometimes it is desirable and imperative for the members of a group to remember aspects of their past because of the role remembrance plays in sustaining their collective life. Remembering might serve to maintain or enhance social cohesion, might express and strengthen the bonds linking members to one another, and it might be imperative for these and other reasons, apart from whether remembering also preserves and transmits the truth about the past. In saying this, it should be noted, we are tacitly asserting certain similarities between collective memory and myth. In fact, as I will show, a number of important functions of collective memory can be illuminated by reflecting on functions of myth. These functions of collective memory are related to imperatives having to do with social cohesion, communal ties and values, and identification with the group and its past, and they are different from the imperatives that critical history enables collective memory to fulfill.

Following on Chapter 3, this chapter has collective memory as its focus and seeks to enlarge our understanding of it in various ways. I begin, in Section 2, with a general account of collective memory, its complex relationship to individual memory, and the various functions (political, moral, and affective) that collective memory performs in the life of a socially unified group. I also give a brief catalogue of the various means whereby memories are passed collectively from one generation to the next, including but not limited to the transmission of beliefs about the past. Sections 3 and 4 further develop the account of collective memory by examining what I claim is its characteristic *bipolarity*. On the one hand, in the modern world, where historical inquiry is widely regarded as essential to our understanding of the past, it is thought legitimate to criticize custodians of the collective memory who lack the proper concern for truth and accuracy. That is, collective memory, to some extent, is supposed to preserve and transmit knowledge of the past. But collective memory does much more and something different as well. It binds the members of a community to one another, inspires collective action, and encodes the values that give meaning to its collective pursuits. These functions more closely resemble those usually associated with myth than those attributed to history. I characterize these different sorts of functions and distinguish them from one another, chiefly in terms of the appropriateness of demanding truth from them, in Section 3. Section 4 continues the discussion of collective memory in relation to history and myth, here focusing on the tension between these and the possibilities of integrating its historical and myth-like functions.

Sections 5, 6, and 7 take up normative issues. Section 5 discusses some of the views presented in Avishai Margalit's recent book *The Ethics of Memory*, which I use as a stepping off point for the analysis in Sections 6 and 7. This is an important and provocative work that, while occasionally frustratingly vague, pushes us to think more deeply about the normative dimensions of collective and individual memory. Margalit, echoing Bernard Williams, Michael Walzer, Charles Taylor, and others, draws a contrast between the domain of morality and the domain of ethics and between two forms of obligation: the moral and the ethical. I take this to be a useful distinction, if we understand the terms "moral" and "ethical" to mark not a bright line dividing two separate normative domains but different aspects of a single domain without sharp internal demarcations of this sort. As I understand these notions, morality is concerned with our relations to human beings, as such, and the responsibilities we have to them; ethics is concerned with personal and communal relationships and the responsibilities we have in virtue of them. The term "obligation" can be employed to designate either type of ought, the moral or the ethical. With the morality/ethics distinction in hand, I give an account of both sorts of obligation as they relate to and constrain collective memory: moral obligations in Section 6 and ethical obligations in Section 7. These obligations have different sources and embody different understandings of the value of collective memory in relation to others. Moral obligations of remembrance arise from our shared humanity; the ethical ones have a narrower scope and are associative in nature. In applying this framework, I draw attention to correspondences between the two sets of distinction around which this chapter is organized, the history/myth and the morality/ethics distinctions.

2. COLLECTIVE MEMORY AND INDIVIDUAL MEMORY

Before going any further in this discussion of collective memory, I need to take up a task that is probably long overdue, namely, respond to concerns that might be raised about whether the very notion of collective memory is not somehow confused or incoherent, perhaps an illicit extension of the concept of individual memory, or at best merely metaphorical. Some of these worries might be allayed by making explicit that collective memory does not imply belief in a group mind: if there is such a thing as collective memory, it resides in the minds of individuals, not in some mysterious mental entity that exists independent of individual human minds.[18] Still, skepticism about collective memory, about whether memory can be truly *collective*, might remain, so I want to say something about why there is nothing terribly problematic about it at all.

One way in which it will be true that collective memory resides in the minds of individuals is when it is taken to be nothing other than the aggregate or sum of individual memories. In this view, collective memory is reducible to individual memory and is not distinguishable in any fundamental way from it. To be sure, this aggregative or summative conception of collective memory can assign a significant role to the social dimension. It can acknowledge that in order to understand how people come to exercise their individual capacities to remember, or to explain the content of their memories, the influence of social factors, of social context, must be taken into account. This is what David Middleton and Derek Edwards call the "'single-minded approach," which "treat[s] the social as only situational to, or at best facilitative of, a person's memory."[19] However, on the single-minded approach, collective memory is not socially constituted, not an inherently social activity.

Collective memory, which resides in the minds of group members, is only inherently social if an accurate description of the memory activities of these individuals would have to indicate that they are doing them *as* part of a group. Among other things, this implies that whatever it is that they remember, the group members *remember together*. Middleton and Edwards highlight this feature in the following example:

> ....when people reminisce about family photographs, or recount shared experiences of times of happiness and trauma at weddings and funerals, what is recalled and commemorated extends beyond the sum of the participants' individual perspectives: it becomes the basis of future reminiscence. In the contest between varying accounts of shared experiences, people reinterpret and discover features of the past that become the context and content for what they will jointly recall and commemorate on future occasions.[20]

Remembering together is a common activity of groups that is genuinely collective in nature, and there is nothing particularly mysterious or suspect about it.

With respect to memories that are truly collective, the members of a group jointly recall and jointly (re)construct the past, and through these joint activities bind themselves together in particular ways. Depending on how significant the memories are, they constitute themselves as a community of memory with more or less reach and endurance. Thus, *we* remember the day the World Trade Center was attacked; *we* remember the landing on the moon, and so forth, meaning not just that we all remember the same thing, or even that we pool our individual memories, but rather that the memory belongs to *us*. And for this to be true, it is not necessary that everyone who shares in the collective memory actually experienced first-hand the event remembered: others who did not experience it, who know it only by description, can join in. Collective memory can also be passed down through many generations, with each generation creating new context and content for what will be jointly recalled by subsequent generations.

Enough has been said, I believe, to show why this is a false dichotomy: either the notion of collective memory is interpreted in such a way as to deprive it of a truly collective character, or it must somehow be incoherent or hopelessly confused. There is a third possibility, namely, there is nothing particularly mysterious or muddled about the notion of a genuinely collective memory, and this is presupposed by what follows.

I turn next to the manifestations and modes of embodiment of collective memory, which are extremely varied. Collective memory, like individual memory, obviously involves beliefs. In the case of collective memory, these are *shared beliefs* about the group's past, about injustices committed or suffered, reparations made or denied, contributions to human civilization, glorious victories and humiliating defeats, noble beginnings and spiritual trials, traditional and modern communal practices, and so forth. These beliefs can be set alongside the results of critical historical inquiry and assessed for truth, as an historian might, but this is only one perspective from which to evaluate them. Their import for the collective and their role in the collective life are not exhausted by an examination of their truth-value or adequately explained in these terms.

Nevertheless, to focus only on beliefs, or on discursive productions that can be assessed for truth or historical accuracy, is to overlook the variety of other means by which the past and its significance are transmitted from one generation to another. Two significant categories that cover a range of such means are what I will call *memory activities*[21] and, following Pierre Nora, *memory places* [*les lieux de memoire*].[22]

Traditional practices, that is, practices that are engaged in by the members of a collective as prescribed by tradition and typically with the more or less self-conscious purpose of perpetuating tradition, can be said to embody collective memory,[23] and there are other types of collective memory activity as well, such as public commemorative ceremonies and, in smaller groups, coreminiscence.[24] Yosef Yerushalmi, discussing the relationship between what he calls "memory" and modern historiography, speaks about Jewish collective memory in terms that emphasize the important role of social memory activities:

> The collective memories of the Jewish people were a function of the shared faith, cohesiveness, and will of the group itself, transmitting and recreating its past through an entire complex of interlocking social and religious institutions that functioned organically to achieve this.... [There was a] common network of belief and praxis through whose mechanisms . . . the past was once made present.[25]

This observation draws attention to important aspects of collective memory in general: to adequately understand collective memory, we have to consider the diverse and interlocking means by which a group preserves and transmits the memory of its past, the various activities of collective memory in which the past does not always figure as an explicit object of attention but in which it is preserved, nonetheless. Although these activities do involve beliefs and assertions about the past to some extent, these may play a relatively minor role in expressing the significance of the past. Indeed, it will sometimes betray a misunderstanding of the nature and import of the activity to be much concerned about what claims it is making about the past and how these stand with respect to truth. And even when it is appropriate to be concerned, as it is for narrative activities, we need to understand much more than this to appreciate their function and their value as social activities. Sue Campbell emphasizes the need to consider more than the accuracy of memory claims in evaluating memory:

It is a mistake to try to understand the importance and structure of memory by attending solely to cognitive mechanisms or to the content of memory experiences without attending to the occasions of memory activities, including the occasions of narrative activities.[26]

Collective memory is also embodied in places, and, according to Nora, the centrality of places in the collective memory is one of the defining features of what he calls the "new collective memory." The term "places" [les lieux], as Nora uses it, ranges widely, and although it includes memory activities, it covers much more:

topographical places, such as archives, libraries, and museums; monumental places, such as cemeteries or architectural edifices; symbolic places, such as commemorative ceremonies, pilgrimages, anniversaries or emblems; functional places, such as manuals, autobiographies, or associations: these memorials have their history.[27]

These places, many of which, such as libraries, museums, and historical monuments, are familiar parts of our everyday social world, are inextricably tied up with memory and are centrally involved in sustaining it. They are intentionally created, in part at least, in order that they might help us to remember, or not to forget. These include material objects (such as tombstones, commemorative plaques, and statues honoring important persons) whose transitoriness as memory aids is well-known, as well as repositories of artifacts or documents (such as museums and archives), which are often rich resources for social memory.[28] Margalit notes the important role that places play in modern shared memory:

> Shared memory in a modern society travels from person to person through institutions, such as archives, and through communal mnemonic devices, such as monuments and the names of streets. Some of these mnemonic devices are notoriously bad reminders. Monuments, even those located in salient places, become "invisible" or illegible with the passage of time. Whether good or bad as mnemonic devices, these complicated communal institutions are responsible, to a large extent, for our shared memories. (54)

Other places of memory, such as pilgrimages and anniversaries, are not just made to evoke memory but are themselves ritualized acts of remembering. They are not, therefore, places of memory in quite the same way that museums are. And, finally, there are institutional sites of collective memory, that is, repositories of institutional memory. The notion of institutional memory refers to the fact that organizations can create stocks of knowledge that tend to be embodied in relatively durable organizational objects, such as databases and archives, established routines, organizational symbols, and so forth. These objects survive the individuals who create them and are available to later members of the organization to provide historical context for their decision making.[29]

These remarks about memory activities and places give some idea of what a group does, and also what it needs to do, to constitute itself as a community of memory, even if only a very limited one. Collective memories can become objects of historical investigation once they have lost their power to inspire and unify social groups. But if they are to perform their important and distinctive social functions, they must be part of the ongoing life of the group, and this happens when they are expressed in memory activities and embodied in memory places.

The relationship between collective and individual memory is complex. Collective memory exists in the memories of individuals, and it does not exist there in exactly the same way, with the same nuances and emphases, and inclusions and exclusions, in each person. Individual experiences and memories color the memories one shares with others. But the memory of an individual is not the same as an individual memory, and as I have already said, collective memory does not simply exist as, is not simply reducible to, an aggregate of individual memories. As for individual memory, about which I have said little so far, it, in turn, has a social or collective dimension. Although individual memories are personal, are linked to other memories of the individual and woven into his or her life in unique ways, and have particular meaning for that individual, they also draw on, and are shaped by, collective understandings of the past. This is especially clear, perhaps, in the case of persons who belong to distinct cultural or ethnic or other similar groups: what members of these groups select to remember of their own pasts and what they attend to as needing remembering in their own lives, depends to a significant degree on what is salient for the group to which they belong and what is memorialized in its practices of collective memory. But the dependence of individual memory on collective memory is not confined to contexts where there is a strongly defined group identity among its members. There is also a dependence that is, in a sense, more fundamental than the example of ethnic or cultural identity suggests, for we can remember our own individual pasts only insofar as we can locate them in a world that we share with others and whose past is our past as well. It is only on the basis of a kind of "memory that pervades our lives-in-common"[30] and that is embodied in the institutions, practices, and civic habits that constitute our shared world, that individual recollection is possible at all.[31]

Collective memory, which I understand as a nonaggregative phenomenon of remembering together, has various roles. There are the *political* ones, which I alluded to in Section 1: collective memory is used and manipulated to strengthen and serve the authority of the ruling powers or to challenge that authority. Collective memory, as LeGoff puts it, is "an instrument and an objective of power."[32] There are also important *moral* uses. Ross Poole argues that one "role of memory in both the individual and the social case is . . . to provide a route by which responsibility for past events is transmitted to the present, and thus to identify a locus of present responsibility for these events."[33] This is one justification for speaking of memory not only as an individual phenomenon but as a social one as well, because groups can have responsibilities that are transmitted this way too. Besides transmitting responsibility, there are other explanations of collective memory's moral significance: it is a conduit for the transmission of privileges and rights, including rights to reparation, from past to present. Collective memory also helps constitute the identity of groups, as it does of individuals, and as discussed in Chapter 1, identities are a source of values and internally related to obligations.

Finally, there are functions related to the fact that both collective memory and individual memory are affective phenomena.[34] Individual memory enables us to reconnect with parts of our own past, and one aspect of this reconnecting is the recollecting of past emotions, positive as well as negative. Just reconnecting itself, for example, reconnecting with people, places, and experiences in one's past, is often a source of enormous pleasure and delight, and sometimes of pain, sadness and regret, for the rememberer. Similarly, collective memory reconnects a group with events in its collective past, and this reconnection with the past can be an occasion for communal celebration, for an outpouring of communal grief, a source of communal pride, and so forth. Both individuals and communities have emotional lives, and collective memories are an essential part of them.

3. HISTORY, MYTH, AND COLLECTIVE MEMORY

Pierre Nora sets up an opposition between archaic collective memory and history (that is to say, history in the modern sense of the word): he characterizes archaic collective memory as having an "affective and emotional quality" that sharply distinguishes it from the lifeless intellectual work of historians. This would not be an accurate description of collective memory in the modern world, however. Modern collective memory does not have the same relationship to the past that the historian has, of course, but it, nevertheless, has a historical function in the following sense: inter alia, it is supposed to preserve a record of the past in a way to which it is thought that historians can make relevant and significant contributions. And by history in this connection, I mean the discipline that attempts to make sense of the past by the application of more or less scientific methods. At the same time, collective memory has very different functions, which are not historical in nature and are not wholly governed by the norms of historical discourse. These functions are in tension with, but not necessarily incompatible with, its historical role, and they hark back to some extent to qualities of premodern forms of collective memory. Speaking of these nonhistorical functions, Kerwin Lee Klein claims that we expect collective memory "to re-enchant our relation with the world and pour presence back into the past."[35] This may not be the most helpful way to characterize what, apart from its historical uses, we expect from and value about collective memory.[36] But it does suggest the following important observation: what differentiates collective memory from history are qualities of collective memory that are frequently also associated with myths.

In this section, I make a number of claims about certain qualities or functions of myths in order to illuminate the complex nature of modern collective memory, but because there are various social constructs to which the label "myth" is attached, I need to clarify how I am using the term. Here are some of the ways it is used:[37] a myth may be an imaginary creation that is believed but is irrational, fictitious, and false; or an ideological construct by means of which a ruling elite deceives the ruled; or a story that takes place in an imagined, remote, timeless past and tells of the origins of humans, animals, and the supernatural; or a myth may be a parable or an allegory. The list could go on. My interest here is the functions of myth – what makes myths meaningful and valuable for those who believe them – and I do not claim that what I say about this holds for all the different sorts or senses or "myth."

If there is one kind of myth whose functions come closest to those I describe here, it is what is known as a *foundational myth*. Foundational myths loom large in the life and study of societies past and present. A foundational myth, to quote Mircea Eliade, "supplies models for human behavior . . . it expresses, enhances, and codifies belief; it safeguards and enforces morality . . . and contains practical rules for the guidance of man."[38] Foundational myths may also be religious in nature, or transmitted mostly through oral tradition, but, for my purposes, these are incidental features and I will not highlight them. What I do want to emphasize, however, is a distinction between accuracy and normative significance in relation to foundational myths. That is, although foundational myths may not present a strictly accurate historical account of the past, they preserve the significance of the event for successive generations.

Drawing on characterizations of this specific but important kind of myth, let us consider some of its critical social functions and how well they coexist with collective memory's other, historical functions.[39]

Bernard Williams, in his final book, *Truth and Truthfulness*,[40] discusses the nature of myth and its relation to truth. "What responsibilities," he asks, "does one take on by telling a tale in what, at this stage, we may call the mode of truth rather than in the mode of myth?"[41] The responsibilities are different, he answers, because

> in the mode of myth, the question whether the story should be told is just the question whether the story is appropriately directed to its audience, whether, as I put it before, it will suit them,

whereas "truth is not audience-relative,"[42] and this alters the standards to which we hold the teller. Williams follows Paul Veyne who, in *Did the Greeks Believe in their Myths?*, characterizes the sort of "truth" that myths possessed for the ancient Greeks. His remarks have wider application:[43]

> The Greeks often seem not to believe very much in their political myths and were the first to laugh at them when they flaunted them on cere-monial occasions. Their use of etiology was formal; in fact, myth had become rhetorical truth. . . . Hence, a special modality of belief: the con-tent of set speeches was perceived not as true, or moreover, as false, but as verbal. . . . Nevertheless, interested parties were not against it, for they could distinguish between the letter and the good intention: although it was not true, it was well said.[44]

Generalizing this description, we can say that if myths possess truth at all, it is "rhetorical" or "verbal" truth, that is, truth in the sense of *aptness*. Something may be aptly said because it evokes certain emotions, or just fits the time and place, or perfectly captures the style of another author or period, or rouses the audience to needed action, or for any number of other reasons, quite apart from whether what is said is true. (It is aptness that we chiefly seem to mean when we say, "A truer word was never said.")

In sharp contrast to this, historical accounts are not to be judged by their aptness but by their truth, and "truth is not audience-relative." The claims of the historian can be assessed, at least in principle, as either true or false, whereas those of the maker or transmitter of myths are embraced by a different and "special modality of belief." So, to the general form of the question Veyne asks, Do people really believe in myths? We should answer with him that "They believe in them, but they use them and cease believing at the point where their interest in believing ends."[45] Both their believing and their ceasing to believe are not to be judged by the very same criteria that we use to judge belief in what historians tell us.

The contrast drawn here between myth and history is not, say, between truth that is obscure and truth that is transparent. This gets it wrong about both myth and history. It gets it wrong about myth because it is not a kind of truth that myth aims for, where "truth" is what most of us understand it to be in the study of history and elsewhere. Truth is simply not its object. It gets it wrong about history because, as most historians who are reflective about their craft readily acknowledge, there is no simple notion of fidelity to the past that constrains the construction of historical narratives. A naive empiricism about the past, according to which the veracity of historical accounts is to be assessed by means of a simplistic appeal to "the facts," fundamentally misconstrues the nature of historical inquiry. Whether or not individual historians acknowledge it, historical inquiry is essentially a theoretical and interpretive enterprise. They adhere, with varying degrees of explicitness, to sets of presuppositions – about what is worthy of being an object of historical investigation, about how to define who are the key historical actors, about how to explain the facts that have been selected for study, and so forth – that reflect diverse theoretical commitments as well as political and moral sympathies and standpoints.

There are difficult and important questions about what exactly *historical truth* consists in, some of which I will take up in Section 6. There, I link the discipline of history with a norm of *accuracy* in recounting past events, but I maintain that questions about historical accuracy are about much more than whether a historical account gets the details of the past right. For now, however, I want to reiterate and expand a bit on the basic point I made in Section 1, namely, the undeniable fact of diverse interpretations of past events is compatible with there being truth about the past, or rather truths about it, and it is truth that is normative for the discipline of history. Even if historians must operate within the constraints of particular interpretive frameworks, they can formulate truths about the past – not just those they "recover from the record" but also what they "fill in"[46] – that have critical force against the claims that they and other historians make.

The best I can do here is to mention a few of the philosophers who have defended, in different ways, the possibility of historical objectivity and truth. Arthur Danto, for example, notes that some have taken the existence of varying sets of presuppositions – or varying criteria for their acceptability – among historians as a basis for skepticism about history's claims to knowledge. He goes on to dismiss such skepticism on the grounds that any empirical inquiry, including science, always takes place in the context of certain preconceptions and organizing principles that go beyond what is given.[47] Chris Lorenz defends a position in the philosophy of history between an objectivism that discounts differences of historical perspective and a relativism that rejects historical knowledge, a position which he calls, following Hilary Putnam, "internal realism." The existence of a plurality of viewpoints does not defeat history's claim to knowledge, on his view, because the question "'what is true or real?'" is always dependent on and *internal* to the specific linguistic framework in which reality is described,"[48] and this sort of dependence is not damaging to the objectivity of the historical enterprise. In a similar vein, Mary Fulbrook argues for a "more theoretically sophisticated notion of history which, while recognizing the degree of contemporary construction and imagination involved in the practice, still retains a belief in the possibility of searching for more adequate representations of the past."[49] She, like the others, wants to distance herself, on the one hand, from a crude empiricism that neglects or denies the importance of theory and interpretation in historical inquiry, and on the other, from the postmodernist position that concludes from our reliance on "frameworks" and "perspectives" that history is merely another kind of fiction.

Truth-deniers commonly claim that historians are captives of interpretive practices or viewpoints that reflect and are dictated by social, political, and other needs and interests. For example, Anita Shapira, defending this relativist position, argues that professional historians, along with politicians and social elites, belong to "a whole line of 'memory agents' that shape the picture of the past according to the needs and agonies of the present." Historical scholarship, therefore, merely "pretends to be based on impartial research." In reality, historians "seek to shape a certain historical memory" rather than reconstruct the past.[50] Against this, the arguments referred to in this section, which are representative of a viewpoint found among many historians and philosophers of history, grant the interpretive nature of historical explanation but deny that it implies historians are enmeshed in their interpretive frameworks in such a way that neither they, nor we can properly assign truth-values to their claims about the past.

These are extremely contentious issues, of course, and it would be too much of a digression for me to pursue them here. My own position is that it is possible to reconcile the contingent, historical, culture-bound nature of historical inquiry with the ability of historians to make assertions about the past that are not merely different from, but better because more accurate than, the claims of those who do not adopt a scientific approach to the past that involves rigorous investigation of primary sources. If doubts remain about this, what I say about history in the rest of this chapter can be read conditionally: 'if truth is the regulative aim of history, then. . . . ' Where I think there will be few doubts, however, is with respect to myths. Here relativism seems to be quite unproblematic because myths are not constrained by the past in the same way as critical history. The relevant question about myths is not whether they are true but whether they are appropriately directed to their audience, and this will depend on features that are peculiar to the particular audience addressed.

The last point leads to a question about myth and memory: myths may make some sort of reference to the past, but are they actually ways of *remembering*? Consider, first, history. Historical inquiry, properly conducted, seeks to establish truths about the past, not simply to serve present social interests and needs. The historian addresses his interpretation to an audience, a society or community or smaller group like a family, and if he is able to convince it that he has fairly and accurately represented and explained the past, his interpretation may become part of that audience's collective memory. The audience may come to have a different understanding of its own past and perhaps of the role it played in some historically significant event. Myth, by contrast, does not have the same function. It too is addressed to an audience, but it does not aim to enlighten it as to what actually happened, and "what actually happened" does not have the same regulative role here that it has in historical inquiry. Myths, typically, dehistoricize their contents.

If we think of memory – individual as well as collective – as purporting to be about events that have actually occurred in the past and as aiming for truth, then insofar as collective memory functions like myth, it may be misleading to say that what we are dealing with is really collective "memory." Myths may affect collective memory in various ways, for example, by weakening (or strengthening) the confidence of tradition-minded people in the veracity of their memories. But what they do not do, and do not aim to do, is faithfully record and preserve the actual past, and whether an audience adopts a myth may not have very much to do with a claim to historical truth or historical accuracy on its behalf. Or if truth does play some role, an audience's acceptance normally depends on many facts about that audience and the fit between it and the story that are independent of the story's veracity. All this I grant. However, it is not necessary to resolve the issue of whether mythic thinking can properly be regarded as a type of collective memory, because in the context of the present discussion, worry about the appropriateness of speaking of collective "memory" is misplaced. Even if myths are more an embodiment of a group's sense of itself than a way of remembering its past, this would not contradict the claims I have been making about the relationship between myth and collective memory. For I have not been arguing that collective memory is no different than myth, only that (in a sense to be explained) collective memory has myth-like functions.

Plainly, we do not value myths, if we do value them, because and to the degree that they give us a true account of the past. Why, then, do we value them? Williams suggests that we value them for the same general reason that we value historical inquiry: there is a need "to make sense of one's situation, and that requires an appeal to the past" (263), *our* past to make sense of *our* present, and there are various ways of satisfying this need. The construction of myths – not all myths, certainly, but those like foundational ones – is one way of doing this. Taking this suggestion as a point of departure, we may hope to better understand the nature of collective memory by considering similarities between its features or functions and those of myth.

Myths in my sense are bound up with the identity of socially unified groups, that is, with the identity that is shared among its members, and they play an important role in individuals' understandings of what membership involves. Like foundational myths, which in heroic societies include those embodying ideals of honor and nobility and, in democratic societies, ideals of liberty and equality,[51] they encapsulate a cluster of shared values and guiding beliefs that constitute a framework of meaning within which members of a society live their lives. Of course, myths are not immune to criticism, external as well as internal. Myths may be challenged from within by those who do not find in them a reflection of their own personal or collective values, or who believe that the myths are merely ideological constructions designed to mask oppressive and unjust social conditions, and so forth.[52] But myths, those that are or resemble foundational ones, remain critical, perhaps indispensable, artifacts of many forms of organized social life, in that they serve as means by which individuals form and express a sense of themselves as participants in a common heritage.

We can expand on these points as follows: a myth encapsulates and confers special status on those of its features that correspond to our sense of what presently matters to us and makes us who we are as a collective body. Steven Knapp makes the following observation which, though offered for a somewhat different purpose, is relevant here.

> If an event in the past... *resembles* one in the present, it may indeed provide us with "symbolic resources" – ways of representing our present values and intentions so as to shape and motivate our present actions... in that case our sense of what is symbolically useful in the past will depend on our present sense of what matters, and the values represented by what we borrow from the past will only be the ones we already have.[53]

We make sense of the present in relation to the past by interpreting it, by seeing what lessons we can derive from it or how it can shed light on the principles, practices, and institutions that constitute our shared life. This is what (some) myths do: they tell a story in which the past (or particular past events or episodes or periods) functions as a symbolic resource for, or as an analogue of, the present. What is important in and distinctive of these mythic narratives is the symbolic resonance that the past possesses for the present, rather than its causal relationship to the present. If the myth is relevant to and resonates with significant aspects of current social life, we may say that it possesses a kind of "truth." But we do not expect the myth to be true in the same sense that we expect history to be.

Myths provide symbolic resources for the present, but symbolic representations relating to the past have other uses as well. Symbolism is employed in artistic representations that provide a mode of access to past events that historians cannot provide. They have the power to affect an audience in emotional ways, frequently by nonnarrative means, and this is something that stories in the mode of history usually cannot match. Sometimes the symbolism is intended to work in concert with prevailing historical understandings. In other instances, it is used subversively to interrogate dominant assumptions about the past and challenge an audience to re-examine them. The representation becomes, in Dora Apel's vivid expression, a "site of resistance."[54] These ways that artists engage with the past are clearly different from those the historian employs. The artistic engagements also differ from, but may operate in conjunction with, the symbolic representations of myth.

We do not yet have a complete account of the social functions or normative significance of myth, however. If myths only supplied symbolic resources, then a question like Knapp's would be quite apposite: "why not turn to other people's histories . . . for symbolic narratives as good or better than the ones our own tradition happens to provide?"[55] Why, that is, should the stories of *our* past have any greater weight or meaningfulness for us than the stories of *other people's* pasts? Does it matter whose past provides symbolic resources for us, as long as it is symbolically relevant and analogous to our present?

It does matter, and a great deal. A myth, as I understand it, just is the sort of story that has the significance it does for a group precisely because, in part, it is a story of that group's past and not another's, or if another's, then that other's as well. It is not merely some story about the past that happens to meet certain criteria of symbolic relevance, and not just any such story will do. The narrated events or episodes that provide symbolic resources for *us* must be located by us in *our* collective past, although, once again, myths make no pretense of giving an accurate description or account of what actually occurred. Furthermore, their belonging to *our* collective past is explained by the fact that these stories are passed down from one generation to another by us and our predecessors and successors and are taken up as part of the common heritage with which we, and they, identify. As the historian David Lowenthal notes, "Heritage *distinguishes* us from others; it gets passed on only to descendants, to our own flesh and blood."[56] So in our explanation of how myths – the ones resembling foundational ones – make sense of the present in relation to the past, we should not overlook this proprietary feature. Myths refer to and draw upon aspects of the past that are particularly significant to a group in part because that past belongs to it, and, belonging to it, they provide resources for representing features of that past that are held by that group to contribute to its self-understanding and identity. Indeed, this proprietary relationship to the past helps explain why myths can be so motivating. Citing the past in myth is often a way of reinvigorating commitment and generating collective rededication to certain group values or an endangered way of life, and it is able to do this because it draws upon the group's *own* past, not some other group's past, for inspiration.

These remarks suggest a distinction between myth and history, and therefore also between collective memory and history. Although the historical account of one group's past cannot substitute for the historical account of another's because these groups have different actual histories, narratives of this sort are appropriately appraised from a standpoint outside that of any particular group.[57] To properly assess whether myths do their work, by contrast, it is necessary to consider them in relation to the collective life of the target group. A standpoint that is not relativistic in this sense is not appropriate for myth.

The characteristic of myth that I have just described has to do with the way in which it presents the past, as belonging specifically to the group to which the myth is addressed and not borrowed from another. Related to this is another characteristic, which might be described as its socially integrative function. This feature of our understanding of myth bears traces of what Andrew Von Hendy claims are the "romantic roots" of the modern concept of myth; indeed, it resembles "one of the principal corollaries of the romantic definition [of myth] – that myth is a belief around which a culture coheres."[58] Its having this function is partly due to the fact that myths serve as resources for the articulation and validation of values, principles, and ideals that underlie a wide range of social practices and cultural expressions. Myths, in other words, or myths of a certain kind, are stories that a group uses to express the basic norms that unify, but are often obscured by, the diversity of its cultural and social forms. In addition, myths are socially integrative narratives in that they *bring people together* by fostering loyalty to the group as a whole and a sense of common purpose among its members. The capacity of myth to inspire (re)dedication to fundamental values and to galvanize collective action, in general, to resonate emotionally with the group's members, are among its most noteworthy characteristics.

In summary, I have focused on three interrelated features that are characteristic of a socially significant and widespread kind of myth in order to draw out salient features of collective memory.[59] Myths of this sort provide symbolic resources for underwriting present identity-constituting values, institutions, ideals, and so forth; they connect a group to its own past and help to distinguish it from other groups in the eyes of group members; and they embody norms that serve as organizing principles of social life, norms that are capable of generating not only intellectual assent but emotional commitment. These features are all essentially independent of the historical truth of what the myths relate, and they explain both the value and the peril of collective memory. Simply put, on this conception, a myth is a story about the past that has various sorts of truth-independent normative significance for a particular group of persons.

I acknowledge that there is some overlap here between myth and history and that the distinction between them is not as sharp as my remarks may have suggested. History, as well as myth, can inspire collective action, depending on how it is marshaled, and both can fail to do so; history, as well as myth, can contribute to and shape group identity, again depending on the uses to which the former is put; stories in the mode of history and stories in the mode of foundational myth are both accounts of a group's past, that is to say, narratives in the past tense. But these similarities should not obscure the fundamental difference between them, which has to do with their respective conceptions of and relations to truth. Historical interpretations are intended to be of actual past events and they are governed by different norms than myth.

We can put the difference this way. A historical account may or may not be taken up by the group to which it is directed, but this is a separate matter from whether the account passes muster as a piece of critical history, that is, from whether it satisfies the criteria of methodological rigor and explanatory adequacy that historical interpretations must satisfy. With respect to myth, however, there are different criteria of assessment because myth does not aspire to (this kind of) truth. The question for myth is whether it should be told, and this, Williams tells us, "is just the question whether the story is appropriately directed to its audience, whether, as I put it before, it will suit them." There may be good reasons why a story in the mode of history should not be told. For example, telling it may disrupt a society's efforts to put its authoritarian past behind it and build the foundations of a future democratic society, as the governments of countries making the transition to democracy often allege. But history that shouldn't be told is not necessarily bad history, and may in fact be very good history; and history that is relevant in respects not well-suited to those whose past it relates is not, for this reason, defective as a piece of history. It is critical to the assessment of myth, in contrast, to identify criteria of suitability and then determine whether the story it tells is well-suited to its target audience according to these criteria. If it is not, if, say, it fails to win adherents or is harmful to some or no longer seems relevant to the audience's concerns, then criticisms of different sorts may appropriately be leveled against it: it is ideology in the service of the interests of an elite, or a relic from the past, or wishful thinking, or socially divisive, and so forth.[60]

4. THE INTERPLAY OF HISTORY AND MYTH IN COLLECTIVE MEMORY

Collective memory, as it operates in our world, is not totally discontinuous with its much earlier, more primitive manifestations: like its archaic version, it can have myth-like qualities that are truth-independent. But modern collective memory is characteristically more complex because it distinguishes itself from myth pure and simple and so is answerable to the discipline of history. That is, to some extent collective memory purports to concern itself with the past as it was, and so makes claims about past events that are subject to confirmation, modification, or rejection by the methods of scientific history. When its claims about the past cannot be validated by the standards of critical history, there is often some pressure, both from group members and from outside the group, to revise or withdraw its claims. There is no guarantee, of course, that this pressure will succeed; political and economic forces may be marshaled against it and be too powerful to overcome.[61] But it is instructive that even then, the controversy is typically portrayed by all parties involved as being about which account of the past is the true one or the more accurate one, not about whether the truth of what is collectively remembered matters at all. Vulnerability to the claims of history could only be avoided in fact if collective memory retreated from the actual past and withdrew completely into the realm of myth where questions about the truth of the narrative are largely beside the point. Revisionist history may sometimes retreat so much from the past as to verge on myth, yet it still professes to be history and so cannot very well simply flout widely accepted criteria of acceptability for historical claims.

So much for the different sides of collective memory considered separately. We now need to bring them together. The discussion so far has not considered the implications of what I call collective memory's bipolarity: the predicament that collective memory is caught in a kind of tug of war between history and myth that gives it an unsettled, internally divided quality and makes it a site of contestation. This is because the myth-like attributes of collective memory cannot easily be reconciled with historical truth. Collective memory is drawn into history and does, in fact, take account of it to some extent.[62] However, because history can also threaten its capacity to fulfill its myth-like functions,[63] collective memory pulls back from history. These are not normative but sociological claims about the peculiar character of modern collective memory, and I take it that they can be defended on the basis of evidence that history itself provides. But in addition to this, the bipolar character of collective memory has normative implications and gives rise to normative conflicts.

The difficulty facing collective memory cannot simply be chalked up to its vulnerability to abuse. Of course, collective memory has often been manipulated to serve the interests of ruling elites or to protect entire societies from having to take responsibility for the past. (The study of these processes belongs to the *politics*, as distinguished from the ethics or the morality of memory.) Historical truth has been, and will continue to be, sacrificed and distorted in the service of narrow utilitarian ends, and narratives of the past for which there is little credible evidence will still prove highly resistant to historical criticism and correction. These observations about the resistance to bringing critical history fully to bear on collective memory are familiar and important. However, other problems beset collective memory even when it is functioning more or less unexceptionably, that is, even when there are no such deliberate processes of manipulation and falsification at work and no crassly self-serving motives operating. In these cases, collective memory is nevertheless caught between history and something like myth, and this is because collective memory, although not entirely discounting the relevance of history to its understanding of the past, also involves a fundamentally different way of making sense of the past and of social reality, similar to the way of myth.

There are tensions within collective memory arising from the clash of these different stances toward the past. Despite this, I am not prepared to claim that collective memory cannot continue to function in myth-like ways as major truths about the past become known and widely disseminated in the group. In other words, it may be that collective memory can absorb the revelations of critical historical inquiry without, for example, losing its ability to forge a sense of belonging and community and to generate the emotions it involves. Of course, collective memory may well be revised and reshaped as a result of these disclosures, but the claim – and the hope – is that they need not be so socially polarizing that the collective memory is shattered into a number of warring parties, each embracing a different representation or construction of the past.[64] Whether or not this is so for a particular society at a given point in its history is an empirical matter, a matter of group psychology, and an outcome in which community is preserved and history properly acknowledged is obviously not assured. The integration of history into collective memory may be a very difficult and wrenching process for a particular society, and its social and historical circumstances may not permit it, or may only permit it to a limited extent, at least for the short term. If in a particular case significant social disruption would result from the attempt, a choice will have to be made between the pursuit and dissemination of historical truth, on the one hand, and other important social goods and obligations, on the other.

Supposing that collective memory can both be responsive to history and continue to fulfill its myth-like functions, however uneasily, what impact can the operation of collective memory be expected to have on the contributions of history? Collective memory, I have argued, is not simply engaged in preserving true accounts of the past, where "true accounts of the past" refers to the products of critical historical inquiry. Collective memory is not to be assessed solely by the same standard we apply to historical narratives, according to which the actual past is, at the most basic level, the central constraint on them. A particular historical account of events in a group's past may be clearly favored by the balance of evidence and may be widely accepted as true at least by those who are qualified to make this determination. Yet, that account may have little significance or value for the members of that group. This changes when the events are taken up in the collective memory of these individuals, assuming that the collective memory is sufficiently robust to play the role I have attributed to it. When these events are taken up, they are given a particular place and integrative role in the lives of the members in virtue of the importance they acquire for them. The historical account may influence their collective self-understanding and contribute in profound and lasting ways to the group's sense of identity. In addition, collective memory imbues accounts of the actual past with symbolic meaning and finds in the historical events normative resources for promoting, reinforcing, or challenging particular ethical and political conceptions, collective aspirations, and social policies. In short, historical narratives, absorbed by and integrated into collective memory, can shape the collective self-conception and become constitutive ingredients of the shared life of a group, and they are laden with meanings that give past events various sorts of normative significance for the present. Collective memories also belong to persons who are members of a community conceived in intergenerational terms, and when collective memory is informed by history, history itself becomes part of the legacy that is passed from one generation to another. These are ways in which, by taking up history, collective memory transforms it, and it does so because collective memory characteristically has qualities that resemble those of living foundational myths.[65]

All this, as we might put it (a bit misleadingly, to be sure), is what memory adds to history. Distortion and falsification are certainly possibilities here, but they do not seem to be inevitable. Moreover, it has not been settled – as I have already remarked – that the myth-like qualities of collective memory are incompatible with objective or historical truth and that collective memory can only be sustained by retreating from history. For this reason, I do not insist on an opposition between collective memory and history, as some writers have done.[66] It remains true, however, that the bipolarity of history and myth presents a serious challenge for collective memory in the modern world, and the possibility of historical and social progress may depend on how successfully it is met.

Yerushalmi, like Nora, asserts that memory and critical history "stand, by their very nature, in radically different relations to the past" (94), and although I do not follow him in this, he makes an observation that I can use for my purposes to explain what collective memory adds to history. He asserts that "those who are alienated from the past cannot be drawn to it by explanation alone; they require evocation as well" (100), and he connects this point, in the case of the Jewish people, to what he characterizes as "an eroded group memory," "the decline of Jewish collective memory in modern times." (94) Again, as before, I take his claims to illuminate the nature of collective memory more generally. History can provide causal explanations of past events and of their relations to the present, but this is quite compatible with a group's not *caring* about its history, caring about it enough and in such a way that those who belong to it seek to actively transmit what they know of the past to their posterity and accept the past as a significant resource for the present. For those who do not care, or who have stopped caring, historical explanation by itself is impotent to overcome their alienation from the past: "the past it retrieves is indeed a lost past, but it is not the one [they] feel [they] have lost" (114). They may understand this as their past, but it will not be a past with which they collectively identify, and it will not play an important role in forging a sense of group identity. For this to happen, historical narratives, which are themselves the products of a kind of memory work, must be incorporated within collective memory. Past events described and explained by history must be appropriated and preserved by collective memory which, in virtue of what I have called its myth-like qualities and operations, is capable of generating identification with the past and imbuing the past with value and motivational efficacy.

There are good reasons to strive for the assimilation of history by collective memory and to hold collective memory to the standard of consistency with what is known or justifiably believed about the past, as determined by the best methods currently available for discerning this. If there are valuable lessons to be learned from the past, if the only way of achieving moral progress and preventing future evils is by facing the past honestly and rendering it accurately, then collective memory, unrestrained by a commitment to the truth, is free to invent fictive pasts "in the service of the powers of darkness."[67] Falsification, distortion, obfuscation, omission, and the like, left unchecked, will subvert truth even as they are, indeed because they are, presented as conveying what actually happened.

Truth-subversion should be distinguished from truth-independence, however. There is another type of narrative that, although it does not chiefly seek to conform to the norms of truth-telling, does not necessarily subvert the truth either, and this is myth, understood to refer to a story about the past that reflects and incorporates the historic values and visions that define the character of a society. Although collective memory's socially integrative and motivating functions diverge from a concern with the truth of the past, these myth-like qualities of collective memory are not necessarily a prescription for wrongdoing. They are not, that is, if it is not unrealistic to suppose that these qualities can be coherently combined with a proper appreciation for historical truth.

They cannot always be coherently combined, of course, and there are different reasons for this. For one thing, there is a tendency for myths of this sort to evade explicit and self-conscious reconsideration by each new generation and adjustment to altered social realities. In addition, political players often seek to shield myths from societal scrutiny because their continued power depends on widespread adherence to a particular static vision of the past. And then too, some myths purport to have some connection to real historical events or persons, although the connection is a tenuous one. If it were learned that these events never happened or that these persons never existed, the myths might be shattered and their integrating and motivating functions undermined. For these various reasons, the relationship between myth and history is an uneasy one at best, and this gives rise to the peculiar vexed character of modern collective memory.

5. MARGALIT ON THE ETHICS AND MORALITY OF MEMORY

I turn now to questions about the responsibilities or obligations of collective memory. To introduce this topic, I will discuss a critical distinction in Avishai Margalit's book, *The Ethics of Memory*, and the use he makes of it to clarify these normative dimensions of collective memory. The key sentence from Margalit is this:

"Memory belongs primarily to ethics, not to morality." (38)

I will argue later, in Section 7, that it is the myth-like attributes of collective memory that help explain why, and the extent to which, this type of memory is properly located within the domain of ethics as distinguished from morality. But first let me say something about the distinction itself and what Margalit does with it.

Some sort of distinction between ethics and morality and their corresponding responsibilities and obligations has been drawn by numerous philosophers and does not require extensive discussion here.[68] The distinction, as Margalit spells it out, corresponds to a distinction between "thick" relations (ethics) – those which invoke or involve a community founded in a shared past and unified by collective memory – and "thin" relations (morality) – those which we have with strangers and which are entailed by a shared humanity. Moral concerns and constraints guide behavior "toward those to whom we are related just by virtue of being fellow human beings" (37), whereas ethical concerns and constraints govern how we relate to those connected to us in more full-blooded ways, such as a "parent, friend, lover, fellow-countryman" (7). In general, ethics encompasses a set of evaluative concerns or modes of thought that are distinct from those that fall within the ambit of morality: the concepts that define the domain of ethics include care, relationship, and partiality, while to the domain of morality belong the concepts of right and obligation, impersonality, and impartiality.[69] Neither perspective, in Margalit's view, is reducible to or replaceable by the other, because not all concerns related to how we should live or act can be translated into just one of these outlooks. Rather, there is an appropriate place for both ethics and morality in assessing how we relate to others and, through memory, to those who are absent or have died.

There are other ways to construe the subject matter of morality, and we might pause at this point to ask whether Margalit has correctly understood or helpfully characterized its nature. Many philosophers would not make as sharp a distinction between ethics and morality as he does[70] would argue that the domain of morality encompasses the concerns claimed to be distinctive of ethics,[71] and perhaps as well that there are untapped resources within traditional moral theory for addressing these concerns. Others claim that there are strong reasons for linking moral thinking with impartialist thinking and using "moral" the way Margalit does.[72] I do not want to pursue this debate, however, because it can quite quickly become unproductive. The core idea and what I believe that moral theorists of various persuasions – Kantian, utilitarian, and virtue – can agree on, is that there are different kinds of reasons for action: some are provided by evaluative concerns and constraints governing thick relations, and others by concerns and constraints governing thin ones. These various normative factors interact with one another in complex ways and there are difficult questions about how they are to be weighed against each other in cases of conflict. There may also be different sorts of thin and thick relations, requiring further reflection on their normative implications. But, arguably, the basic distinction can be useful in helping us to tease out the different strands of our normative thought.

Whether we distinguish between ethics and morality, as Margalit and others have done, or between different dimensions of the moral or the ethical, is ultimately less important than the recognition that there is a plurality of considerations bearing on how we should live, on what makes for a good human life, including but not limited to those associated with a narrow conception of moral obligation. The various considerations marked by the contrast between ethics and morality also illuminate different normative dimensions of memory.

There are, as we will see in Section 7, distinctively ethical obligations or responsibilities of memory, where "ethical" has the particular meaning Margalit gives it. In addition, memory plays an indispensable role in sustaining claims about those relationships that are of central concern in this normative domain. It is a mark of close personal relationships, such as friendships and family and love relationships, that one does not (too quickly) forget the person to whom one is attached when he or she is absent or dies and, moreover, that one makes an effort to resist forgetfulness. Memory will often fade with time, of course, despite our best efforts to keep this from happening, and we are not locked into maintaining a personal relationship regardless of our interests and inclinations. But memory is a test of caring in the sense that forgetting can – and within a certain time frame, normally will – retrospectively cast doubt on whether and how deeply one actually cared about the person to whom one professed a close attachment.[73] Margalit puts it this way: "If I both care for and remember Mira, then my remembering Mira is inherent in my caring for her. I cannot stop remembering Mira and yet continue to care for her." (30)

Caring looms large in Margalit's account of the evaluative norms pertaining to memory, for he bases his claim that memory belongs mainly to ethics on what he sees as memory's particular affinity with caring. (See 27.) "Caring," in turn, is said to be or involve "attentive concern for the well-being" of others (32), a "demanding attitude toward others" (33), and "unselfish heed to the particular needs and interests of others" (33). Personal and relatively intimate relations are obvious examples of relations of care, but, significantly, Margalit sees care operating across a much wider field.[74] This is clear from his discussion of "natural communities of memory" (69), communities which he regards as the most promising candidates for projects of collective memory.

Margalit acknowledges that it is "conceptually" possible to care about others just in virtue of their being "fellow human beings," which suggests that there can be some overlap between morality and ethics. But he thinks it is exceedingly difficult to generate and sustain such caring, and hence to transform humanity into "an ethical community of caring and of shared memory."(77) In view of this difficulty, he suggests that we might lower our sights and aim for "a second best" (78) sort of community whose task it is to remember our fellow human beings. Such a community engages in a type of remembrance that enacts a sense of obligation rather than one founded in care for and a sense of concrete connection to those who have died or are absent. Those who belong to this community understand that morality obligates them (under some conditions) to remember others qua fellow human beings, regardless of the limitations of their capacities for care. A community of memory constituted on the basis of acknowl-edgment of "a minimal obligation to remember" (47), where persons are bound together in recognition of what they, as human beings and not as members of this or that particular group, ought to remember, is a *moral,* not an *ethical,* community. By contrast, because features of human psychology restrict the scope of our capacity to care, care is constitutive of less encompassing forms of social relation and expected in more local set-tings, and here memory is regulated centrally, although not exclusively, by ethics.

In the end, however, Margalit does not appear to hold out much hope that humanity at large will even be able to constitute itself a moral com-munity of memory, let alone an ethical one. Both of these aspirations he calls "utopian universalistic projects," (82), neither of which is likely to bear fruit in terms of shared memories that have the power to motivate collective action.[75] Much more promising as loci of collective memo-ries, in his view, are the "natural communities of memory," those groups, like "families, clans, tribes, religious communities, and nations," that, when "left on their own, are very likely to become communities of mem-ory, usually quite spontaneously and sometimes with the help of manip-ulation."(70) Although humanity may *have* moral obligations of remem-brance, it is much less likely to coalesce around them and to stay coalesced than are the smaller groups whose members are bound to one another and to the group as a whole by affective ties and sentiments of loyalty and patriotism.[76]

But if it is utopian to believe that humanity at large can become a community of memory, reliance on these smaller natural communities for the preservation and diffusion of collective memory carries significant risks, as Margalit is well-aware. Ethnic, religious, tribal and national identities are partly constructed by means of stories about the past that are preserved in the community's collective memory, and these shaping narratives can also, and often do, sharpen group conflicts. Throughout history, natural communities have fabricated stories about the past that legitimize their possession of or claim to power and dominance; socially sanctioned as collective memories, these stories have served to justify and galvanize collective actions that promote the self-perceived interests of the community at the expense of the rights and legitimate interests of those outside it. Consider, as one recent example, Serbian inventions of an ethnic history supposedly distinct from or opposed to that of the Muslims and Roman Catholics, Bosnians, Kosovans, and Croats, and the devastation and mass slaughter this "collective memory" helped to legitimize. So if we have little choice but to rely on natural communities to discharge the responsibilities of memory, we must at the same time recognize and take steps to counteract the powerful self-interested and chauvinistic motivations that are indifferent or hostile to the constraints of morality. Although it may be too much to hope that a universal ethical or moral community will supplant the memory work of natural communities, international organizations founded on mutual self-interest may at least be able to achieve some success in curbing their most egregious abuses of memory.

Group narratives that locate the present in the context of the past may provide a pretext for collective action that violates moral norms against murder, torture, expulsion of populations from their lands, and the like. In these cases, collective memory constructs a social reality and a collective identity that aggressors use to justify violations of these norms, norms that are external to collective memory in the sense that they are not norms *for* or *of* collective memory itself. There are norms of the latter sort as well. Among these are moral norms that govern the content and practice of collective memory and that specify what should be remembered and the forms that commemoration should take. Communities can, in various ways, violate these norms as well. As Margalit conceives of these moral obligations of remembrance, they have as their objects actions and practices that fall within a quite specific and limited domain of human conduct:

> So what should humanity remember? The short answer is: striking examples of radical evil and crimes against humanity.... The source of the obligation to remember, I maintain, comes from the effort of radical evil forces to undermine morality itself by, among other things, rewriting the past and controlling collective memory. (78, 83)

Moral obligations to remember are binding on all of humanity, and they come into play in cases of large scale and gross violations of human rights – violations that, in their extreme nature, call the very authority of moral standards into question. This, Margalit says, is the "short answer," but the long answer, unfortunately, he does not provide. In addition, there is little discussion of humanity's moral obligations to remember anything else, including deeds of extraordinary self-sacrifice and courage and, generally, acts of exemplary virtue, whether in opposition to injustice or in pursuit of other worthwhile ends. Margalit claims that there is an asymmetry here – there are obligations to remember "moral nightmares" but not "moments of human triumph" – but he provides no argument for it. (82–83)

Because of his pessimism about mankind's ability to constitute itself as a moral community of memory, Margalit turns to natural communities of memory to act on its behalf: projects of shared memory are most likely to succeed, he says, when they "go through" such communities (82). But how is this supposed to work and what are its implications for the members of these communities? Susie Linfield objects to the claim that mankind, or these natural communities, can and should remember extreme violations of human rights:

> Margalit . . . argues that humanity as a whole should remember "striking examples of radical evil and crimes against humanity, such as enslavement, deportations of civilian populations, and mass exterminations." Yet this seems to pose more questions than it answers: Why, and how, should a victim of the Rwandan genocide remember those of the Gulag? And why should a comfortable 25-year-old citizen of, say, Amsterdam – or Cairo or Beijing – remember either? What, in such cases, would "remembrance" mean, and how would it manifest itself?[77]

To be sure, these are reasonable questions, but we can see how Margalit would respond. Presumably, natural communities have obligations to remember radical evil because, from a realistic standpoint, it is only through them that the general obligation can be discharged. The obligations, therefore, are to be construed as devices whereby the obligations imposed globally on mankind are assigned to particular communities. As to what the shared memory of a natural community involves, Margalit does not make specific claims about what particular members of natural communities, be they survivors of the Rwandan genocide or comfortable citizens in Amsterdam or elsewhere, are obligated to do. He does stress, however, that the responsibility to remember is a collective one and that to fulfill it there must be a "division of mnemonic labor" within the community, a notion which he explains as follows (and which deserves greater elaboration than he provides):

> ... the responsibility over a shared memory is on each and every one in a community of memory to see to it that the memory will be kept. But it is not an obligation of each one to remember all. The responsibility to see to it that the memory is kept alive may require some minimal measure of memory by each in the community, but not more than that. (58)

It is in terms of such a division of labor that we are to understand how a community can discharge moral obligations of remembrance, and this holds as well for the other sort of obligation that Margalit discusses: ethical obligation. It is ethical obligations, not moral ones, which Margalit is chiefly interested in because in his view, "memory belongs primarily to ethics, not morality."

In his view, ethical obligations of memory are not imposed on all of humanity or owed to others in virtue of our common humanity, but are only imposed on and owed to the members of particular familial, tribal, religious, or national communities,[78] and they chiefly concern civic virtue, affective ties, and the good of the community. These ethical oughts are similar to what Ronald Dworkin refers to as "associative obligations."[79] Obligations of this sort arise only because we are joined together with certain others in particular associations, including so-called natural groups, such as family, ethnic, and national groups, and the obligations differ because they are contingent on the particular character of the association in question. Whereas moral obligations to remember do not depend on the existence of any associative connection between ourselves and other persons, there will be much else besides that *we*– that is to say, we who are associatively connected to others with whom we share a common past – ethically ought to remember about our past, because of this connection.

In summary, according to Margalit's classificatory scheme, obligations of memory are both moral and associative (or ethical), rooted in our common humanity as well as in our particular associations and affiliations. Furthermore, natural communities are assigned the task of discharging both sorts of obligations because it is utopian to suppose that any substantial portion of mankind will be able to do so. In Sections 6 and 7, I will adopt this distinction between types of memorial obligations and try to explain, with more argument and clarification than Margalit provides, a basis for each. Margalit has made a valuable contribution to the normative study of collective memory by getting us to think about the oughts of remembrance in *both* of these ways and pointing out their differences, but what follows is not intended to be a reconstruction or a defense of all aspects of his views. I do not, for example, connect ethics and caring as tightly as he does, in part because there are various definitions of care and connecting them this way could lead to confusion and misunderstanding about the nature of ethical imperatives of collective memory. I also want to distance myself from his claim that memory *primarily* belongs to the ethics side of the divide because, in my view, memory is implicated to an equally significant degree in both the ethical and moral domains. And then too I do not necessarily subscribe to all the ways in which he marks the distinction between morality and ethics.

6. MORALITY AND COLLECTIVE MEMORY

I have to this point introduced two distinctions relating to collective memory: myth/history and ethics/morality. In Sections 3 and 4, I claimed that (a) collective memory, concerned as it is with the past that actually happened, is answerable to history and to the truths that it conveys, and also that (b) collective memory has myth-like integrative, identity-constituting, and motivating functions that are truth-independent and that do much to explain the social value and significance of collective memory. In Section 5, I used Margalit to introduce a distinction between

morality and ethics as it pertains to obligations of collective remembrance. I now want to examine the nature and grounds of these obligations and how they link up with the distinction between history and myth.

Ethics, I have stipulated, concerns itself with particularistic attachments
and loyalties and special responsibilities: the imperatives of ethics are not
general duties that we have toward one another. This conception of ethics
seems to fit quite well with a conception of collective memory as having
certain myth-like attributes, because it is these attributes that give collective memory a particularistic character. Moreover, because collective
memory involves or expresses particularistic attachments and is the sort
of phenomenon described in (b), it would be surprising if there were
no obligations that reflected or presupposed these features, that is, no
obligations that are ethical in nature. Morality, by contrast, takes up an
impartialist point of view and justifies general duties that do not necessarily tie us to particular others or to a particular community, including
our own. Is there some connection between morality and the claim about
collective memory made in (a)?

If there are obligations of collective memory that are moral in nature,
the content of these obligations should be such that we can see why they
ought to be so classified. Truth, I suggest, or more precisely, discerning
and telling the truth about certain events and people in the past, seems
to be the sort of thing that can be owed to others as fellow human beings.
It is not just owed to those with whom we are associatively connected or in
virtue of being so connected. Moral imperatives, unlike ethical ones, do
not have to satisfy a particularity requirement, and imperatives of truth
about the past seem to fit the bill because they are not necessarily conditional on the existence of special ties. Another way to state the point is
this: moral imperatives obligate us to do *justice* to the past, which can only
be done by bringing the truth about it to light and keeping it illuminated.
History plays a critical role here because truth is its governing norm. Of
course, this can only be part of the explanation of the moral imperatives,
for even if we accept that they have to do with truth about the past, there
can be no moral obligation to know and convey *all* such truths. For
one thing, there are too many truths to know. For another, not all truth
about the past is normatively significant for people in the present.

I want to approach this suggestion about the link between collective memory's historical role and collective memory's moral obligations

by considering the responsibilities that historians as a group have with respect to truth about the past. Paul Ricoeur, in *Time and Narrative*, makes the following remark about the historian's relation to the past: "[The historian's] relationship to the past is first of all that of someone with an unpaid debt, in which they represent each of us who are the readers of their work."[80] The importance of the historian's investigation of the past, in Ricoeur's view, is chiefly to be understood through the idea of an unpaid debt, a debt that can only be discharged by giving or attempting to give a faithful account of the past. Similarly, though without using the language of debt to express the point, David Cockburn maintains that the attempt to render the past faithfully, which is a defining characteristic of the practice of history, is "itself the expression of a recognition . . . of what we owe to those past lives," that "we owe it to past individuals and societies to remember them," and that remembrance is a moral requirement.[81] In the same vein, Yerushalmi speaks about "the essential dignity of the historical vocation" and "its moral imperative," an imperative that is "now more urgent than ever. . . . against the agents of oblivion, the shredders of documents, the assassins of memory, the revisers of encyclopedias, the conspirators of silence."[82]

The moral imperative to which these authors draw attention – and to which collective memory is subject because collective memory is answerable to history – is not simply the obligation to remember past lives or societies or events. Linked as the imperative is to the vocation of the historian, it is more specifically an obligation to remember accurately, to be conscientious in remembering and to strive to discover (or uncover) and, without distortion, obfuscation, and the like, convey the truth about the past. Accuracy, in this context, is a complex notion that calls for careful examination.

The first point of clarification is that we are talking about accurate representations that are also true. Accuracy is not always as tightly linked to truth as this: a fictional story of life on a whaling ship, for example, might give a very accurate impression of it, perhaps more accurate than some true accounts of that life. But with respect to accounts presented within the discipline of history, the accuracy we are concerned with cannot be so detached from the truth of what is accurately depicted. Furthermore, historical accuracy is a matter of *getting it right* about the past, and one does not usually get it right in the sense at issue here simply by collecting and recording a bunch of individual facts, even if these are not just any facts about the past but historical facts that are believed to have significance for the historical process.

Adam Morton offers the following as a "tentative definition of accuracy":

> One story is a more accurate depiction than another of an actual situation when there are more elements of the one that are true descriptions of aspects of the actual situation than there are of the other.[83]

On this definition, one historical account is a more accurate depiction of a past event than another if it contains more true descriptions of aspects of that event than the other contains. But although comparative assessments of accuracy are sometimes made in this way, it would be a mistake to suppose that striving for historical accuracy is simply a matter of accumulating more and more details and facts about something that happened in the past. The norm for historical accuracy involves as well putting the facts together in a certain way in order to convey their import, moral, political, cultural, and so forth.[84] An account that does this may be a more accurate account, according to this conception of historical inquiry, than an account that contains more true descriptions, but that does not connect them in a manner that makes sense, or a good sense, of the events described. One account may provide more details than another and, depending on the purpose of the account, sometimes the more details the better; but it is less accurate to the extent that it does not do as well in terms of giving appropriate significance to those details. So a historical account may be inaccurate, not only because it contains false statements about the past or omits critical details, but also because it assembles truths about the past in misleading ways, or in ways that trivialize what happened or that exaggerate its significance to the present and future.

To help clarify the operative notion of historical accuracy, consider, as an example, differing claims about exactly how many Armenians were killed by the Ottoman Turks in the early twentieth century. Was it was actually 1.5 million as is commonly reported or some smaller or larger number? The question is not without historical interest and importance; although it is certainly not mere historical curiosity that explains the intensity with which individuals stake out positions on this issue. To be sure, as a general matter, empirical accuracy – that is, establishing "true facts" about the past, discarding false assertions and exposing lies, distortions, and half-truths – is a vital prerequisite to the production of adequate historical knowledge. But such debates, insofar as they are narrowly focused on the "facts," are neither directly about what accuracy, in the larger sense of the term, requires, nor, as a consequence, are they about how the Armenian genocide ought to be remembered. Another point about the role of facts in such debates is that challenges to the factual accuracy of claims about the past often reflect, and serve as surrogates for, differing political and moral agendas. It is frequently those who want to downplay or divert attention from the moral gravity of past events (Holocaust deniers come to mind) who are the most insistent about getting the facts right and who become embroiled in disputes about what "exactly" happened, as if this would by itself settle the accuracy of the historical account. However, insistence on factual accuracy can have another motivation too: it can compel a reassessment of past events in the other direction and thereby further the cause of reparative justice.

Moral obligations of remembrance, in the sense in which I am discussing them here, are obligations of collective memory that center on, that support and preserve, truth about the past. Margalit's notion of a division of mnemonic labor is a helpful way to begin thinking about what this requires of the members of a community. "The responsibility over a shared memory," he explains, "is on each and every one in a community of memory to see to it that the memory will be kept." Obviously, it would be absurd to expect everyone in the community to be an historian or an archivist or a memoirist or a designer of monuments, and the like. Communities of memory would be very small indeed if the only way of fulfilling one's responsibilities as a member of such a community were to engage in occupations of this sort. But it is not, and there is much besides this that the members can do "to see to it that the memory will be kept alive." They can, for example, work to expose and oppose processes operating on the group level that prevent acknowledgment and retention of truths about the past. Specifically, they can advocate for the establishment of truth commissions; contribute money and/or time to organizations that do memorial work; provide testimony about past victimization; educate themselves and their children about historically significant events; and more. What and how much individuals do in the division of memorial labor naturally depends on their particular backgrounds, temperaments, interests, and talents. What's more, this diversity of contributions to the work of collective memory fortifies and enriches the social practice of remembering.

The historian, according to Ricoeur, plays an indispensable and distinctive role in this division of labor: he does not merely respond to a debt which he owes to the past, but speaks for or represents us in a particular way in relation to the past. He can help shape collective memory through the techniques of historical inquiry, which involve the persistent use of investigative methods to ferret out evidence, the application of methods of inquiry that are, in Williams' expression, "truth-acquiring"[85] in the manner appropriate to this type of inquiry. Constraining such investigative pursuit, however, is the fact that the process of acquiring true beliefs, about the past or quite generally, is not cost-free: time is spent, energy expended, opportunities lost, perhaps risks run. Historical inquiry, like other kinds of inquiry, involves an "investigative investment,"[86] and there is no simple or single answer to how much we should be prepared to invest in our own or others' investigations, especially because it will often be unclear how much we stand to gain by further inquiry.

There are often obstacles to the discovery of truths about the past, and these are of different sorts. Some of them are internal to inquiry, such as self-deception and wishful thinking, which may consist in denial or neglect of difficult truths about one's predecessors or the portrayal of past deeds in favorable terms that bear little relation to reality. There are also external obstacles deriving from inquiry's dependence on objective evidence: evidence may have disappeared or be inaccessible, sometimes because of deliberate efforts of concealment, sometimes simply as a result of the passage of time. The imperative to remember accurately requires efforts to resist and overcome both sorts of obstacles. Moreover, as expressed by the notion of a division of mnemonic labor, there are diverse ways in which the members of a community can participate in these efforts.

The moral imperative to remember accurately and to tell the truth about the past so remembered is a general duty that is assigned to particular communities because they are best able or most qualified to discharge it.[87] Of course it is one thing to establish the existence of this general memorial obligation and the role of particular communities in discharging it, and something else to specify which lives or events or deeds are to be included within the ambit of this obligation. The moral obligation to remember the past accurately presumes an obligation to remember it in the first place, and as noted earlier, it is absurd to suppose that there can be an obligation to remember the past just as such, or even everything of historical significance in the past. Even when there is an obligation to remember something in the past, we do not necessarily place a premium on historical accuracy in all such cases. But sometimes we do, and we need some criteria for identifying the cases where it matters. For example, it is critically important for humanity to remember accurately "striking examples of radical evil and crimes against humanity, such as enslavement, deportations of civilian populations, and mass exterminations,"[88] and there might be widespread agreement on this. We might also want to claim the same about striking examples of human goodness and self-sacrifice. But there may be areas of controversy where the moral importance of remembering accurately is in dispute.

One question, therefore, about the scope of the moral obligation is what sort of events or acts are included within it. Margalit restricts the obligation to instances of large scale wrongdoing – to genocide, crimes against humanity, mass deportations, and the like – but he does not say what there is about large scale wrongdoing that should be remembered. It is implausible to suppose that there is only a general duty to remember the *victims* of the Holocaust, say, for what about those individuals who risked their lives to protect Jews from Nazi extermination? Is there not also a general duty to remember them? And perhaps there is also a general duty to remember some persons for their extraordinarily praiseworthy actions, whether or not they were undertaken in response to injustice.

A second question, no less important, has to do with the temporal dimension, with how far into the past collective memory should reach. Should this extend only to the recent past? To the remote past as well? If so, then how remote? Plainly, we need another principle of selection here in order to set some limits because temporal distance has a bearing on how normatively significant even historically significant catastrophic events are for those in the present. Some past wrongs are incontestably of historical importance for particular societies or peoples and the world at large, and professional historians, as historians, are and ought to be interested in them. But it will often be extremely unconvincing to claim that people today have a moral obligation to remember those wrongs. It seems unlikely, for example, that there is a moral obligation to remember major injustices committed, say, a thousand or more years ago, even assuming that we know what commemorating such injustices would involve. The reason appears to have to do with the fact that the societies or worlds in which such wrongs took place are not just far removed from us in time, but are so distant from our present social situation that either they are not relevant to it or we could not, to quote Bernard Williams, "live inside [their outlook] in [our] actual historical circumstances and retain [our] hold on reality, not engage in extensive self-deception, and so on."[89] A number of questions remain, of course, about the meaning and application of this principle: about what is involved in taking on the outlook of a past society or world, whether it is possible for a given people under given historical circumstances to do so, and the criteria of relevance.

Even with respect to pasts that have the right sort of content and that are near enough to us in time to be candidates for collective memory, there will still likely be too much for even the combined efforts of particular communities to properly commemorate. The moral obligation is thus best construed as imperfect, that is, as an obligation whose principles allow some freedom to choose which events will be remembered and which events will go unremembered, even though the latter events fall under the principle.[90] It is important to note as well that memory has many functions besides that of preserving and disseminating the truth about the past, and that there may be good and compelling reasons why we ought to remember that have little or little directly to do with truth.[91]

In my account, the moral obligations of collective memory are explained in terms of respect for the truths of history, that is, as duties to remember (some of) the past accurately, to find out, preserve, and relate the truth (or certain truths) about it. These general obligations get applied to particular communities, and their obligations derive moral force from the moral force of the general obligations. Furthermore, there may be features of a group's relationship to particular dead persons or past events that make it especially appropriate to apply the general obligation to a particular community. These special relational features include collective responsibility for historical injustice. That is, a collective that is responsible for injustices committed against groups or individuals in the past has, among its other duties, duties of accurate and truthful remembrance of those injustices and their victims. It has these because, in order for the collective to take responsibility for the injustices that have been committed, accurate remembrance is essential, both as constitutive ingredient and as first step, and the collective cannot provide appropriate reparation without it. The members of the collective, therefore, have memorial duties in part because the collective is legitimately held responsible for those injustices. In another type of situation, certain events may qualify for a general moral obligation to remember, but the members of a particular group should be singled out for a special responsibility, not because of prior injustices for which the group to which they belong is accountable, but for some other reason, say because it was their fellow members who were targeted and victimized by outside parties (e.g., it is especially appropriate for Americans, and more particularly, New Yorkers, to collectively remember the 9/11 terrorist attack on the World Trade Center; for Israeli Jews to collectively remember the suicide bombings targeting innocent Israeli citizens).

Because moral obligations of collective remembrance are general in nature, that is, owed by us to others in virtue of our common humanity, the moral obligations of particular communities to remember are not in any deep sense particularistic. Consider, for example, what we might say about the obligations of fellow countrymen. I take it that the special obligations that bind compatriots to one another include the obligation to remember and honor those who gave up their lives in a just war against an evil enemy. Although there are no deeply particularistic moral obligations, it may still be the case that, because compatriots are related to the dead in ways that foreigners are not, there is an obligation of accurate and truthful remembrance that the former and only the former have. That is, there may be good reasons for assigning the general duty to compatriots alone or to them especially. Nevertheless, to repeat the point, even if there are good reasons, this does not imply that the moral "ought" has simply been transformed into an ethical ought. On the contrary, these "oughts" have different grounds and remain distinct.

A final issue to be addressed in connection with the imperative of accurate and truthful remembrance is to whom it is owed, and this leads to a discussion of the moral status of the dead and the role, if any, that this notion plays in the justification of the imperative. A common view is expressed in the slogan, "Those who forget the past are condemned to repeat it": we can only prevent what happened in the past from happening again if we ferret out and tell the truth about the relevant portion of the past, and we owe it to present and future persons to do so. In J. H. Plumb's consequentialist conception of the duty of the historian, for example, the dead serve as a source of moral instruction, which is very different from claiming that the living owe it to the dead to acknowledge them in their thoughts, feelings, and actions:

> Progress has come by fits and starts; retrogressions are common. Man's success has derived from his application of reason, whether this has been to technical or to social questions. And it is the duty of the historian to teach this, to proclaim it, to demonstrate it in order to give humanity some confidence in a task that will be cruel and long.... Historians can use history to fulfil many of the social purposes which the old mythic pasts did so well.[92]

If collective memory must acknowledge the claims of history as imposing constraints on its interpretations of the past, if, that is, collective memory is to some extent bound by the norm of historical accuracy, then the duties of collective memory can be justified in part by the same "social purposes" that historians use history to fulfill. (These purposes include instilling confidence in the possibility of moral progress despite repeated examples of man's inhumanity to man.) To accomplish these purposes, the dead must be invoked, so the duties will concern them or be *with respect to* them. But in this construal, they are not necessarily owed *to* them, and the duties of collective memory will have the same normative structure.

An exclusively forward-looking view that only allows duties with respect to the dead may strike some as inadequate, however. Cockburn, for example, expresses a backward-looking view when he claims that we owe it to past individuals to remember them, and not (only or perhaps even primarily) to those who are still living who have been affected by or can learn from their deaths. The very idea of obligations or duties to the dead, however, has struck some philosophers as bizarre or incoherent.[93] If we can have duties to them, then they can be wronged by our failure to fulfill them. But how can the dead be wronged or even harmed if there is nothing left of them but dust and they are no longer persons? In particular, how can we make sense of the claim that failing to remember the dead, who are incapable of feeling joy or pain and have no functions to be impaired, might, nevertheless, wrong them? The answer to the general question, by those who hold to a backward-looking view, usually proceeds by drawing a distinction between the antemortem person and the postmortem body that is continuous with it: the dead can be harmed by setting back the interests of the living people they once were, and they are wronged if this violates a moral norm. We can make sense of posthumous harm or wrong, on this view, in terms of persons having a stake in what happens to or with respect to them after their deaths.[94] On this basis, we can also make sense of duties of remembrance being owed to the dead, if persons have a stake in being remembered after their deaths. Because persons generally do, indeed have a vital interest in being so remembered, the view that there are such duties is not only intelligible but plausible as well.

I will not pursue this issue here because the connections I want to draw between morality, truth, and collective memory are not materially affected by the choice between a backward- and a forward-looking grounding of obligations of accurate remembrance. Whomever these obligations are owed to, whether to the dead or only with respect to the dead but to the living,[95] the more important point for my purposes is that they are not only owed because of particularistic ties to them but because of a general principle, and that insofar as this is the case, the obligations can be classified as moral ones. We do not owe truth about the past to the living or the dead only when and because we have some special "thick" relationship with them, or when they are *our* dead. In important cases where truth in memory is critical, we owe it under a description that does not contain pronouns denoting relatedness, except perhaps the relatedness that comes from sharing a common humanity.

I should note, however, before leaving this topic, that the notion of surviving interests can also figure in the justification of ethical in contrast to moral imperatives of remembrance. This is because it is not only their interests as once living persons that ground obligations to remember the dead. Also relevant are the particular *relationships* that we may have had with these once-living persons. Persons often have interests in being remembered by *specific* others after their deaths, and this holds for both personal and collective forms of memory. In these cases, it might only or chiefly be these specific others who have an obligation to remember.

7. ETHICS AND COLLECTIVE MEMORY

Collective memory makes itself answerable to history and the regulative aim of history, I have claimed, is truth about the past. Although there is certainly no moral obligation to accurately remember everything in the past that is a proper subject of historical inquiry, there is a moral obligation to remember some of these events in this way. This obligation, moreover, is most likely to be effectively discharged if it is assigned collectively to particular communities. Often one particular community has a special relation to those events, so that it is especially wrong for it to fail to discharge the obligation. But the obligation is nonetheless a moral one, owed to others as fellow human beings, not as persons with whom we have some sort of thick relationship. It is owed as a basic requirement of justice.

Not all obligations of collective memory belong to the moral domain, however. It seems to agree with commonsense thinking about these matters that there are ethical imperatives of collective memory as well, that is, imperatives that flow from and constitute special ties that bind the members of a collective to one another. This is also a view for which there is independent argumentative support, as I will show. Before turning to this, I want to say something about why it is not implausible, at the outset, to think that there are ethical oughts (imperatives, obligations, etc.) of collective memory. We can understand how ethical oughts of collective memory can arise if we shift our attention from history and view collective memory in relation to those characteristics that I have linked with myth.

The properties or functions of collective memory I have highlighted as resembling those of myth are truth-independent. Similar to foundational myths, collective memory is in this respect more interested in symbolic meaning and resonance than in historical accuracy. In this role, it embodies and shapes a community's sense of its identity, draws the community's members together around a shared understanding of their past and its contribution to the present, and is capable of inspiring and motivating collective action. It is not difficult to appreciate how there might be ethical oughts of collective memory when we reflect on these symbolic, identity-constituting, integrative, and motivating functions. Ethical oughts are associative obligations that derive from special ties, and collective memory (in its myth-like capacities) contributes to and partially constitutes special ties, so there is at least an obvious fit between the two, that is, between ethical oughts and these operations of collective memory. This is not to claim, I hasten to add, that the special ties partially forged by collective memory always create or lend support to ethical obligations of collective memory. They may not. My point is rather this: given that ethical oughts are of this nature and, further, that the rituals and other expressions of shared memory play a critical role in binding a group together and shaping and expressing its sense of identity, it is not unreasonable to suppose that there might be ethical obligations of collective memory in some circumstances, that is, ethical oughts that have these memorial practices as their content. Of course, this isn't yet much of an argument for the existence of ethical oughts of collective memory. But it does suggest a way to think about and argue for imperatives of collective memory, namely, in relation to its critical truth-independent, myth-like functions.

To turn then to whether there are such oughts. The main argument for the existence of ethical oughts of collective memory, briefly put, is this: these oughts are internally related to the good of some particular form of collective life and hence to the good of maintaining it. We can begin to understand how this is so by examining the case of friendship. Consider the following claims that Joseph Raz makes about this sort of thick relationship.[96] First, friendship is an intrinsically valuable relationship, that is, it is properly valued not or not only because it is instrumental in providing various goods but for its own sake. Second, part of what it is for two people to be friends is that they have certain duties to one another, duties that are justified by the good of the relationship. In other words, duties of friendship are at once partially constitutive of, and grounded by, the friendship. Third, the special duties of friendship are internally related to the good of friendship, that is, they are part of that good. On Raz's view, in short, friendship is an intrinsically valuable relationship that is specified in part by special duties that are internally related to the good which justifies them.

Although Raz does not discuss it here, we can use his general analysis to explain how memory in particular can be a special duty of friends. It is part of the good of friendship, indeed, part of what it is for two people to be friends, that each is kept in the memory of the other and that experiences and activities they have shared are remembered by them. Friends owe one another certain special forms of care, consideration, and the like, because, without these, the good of friendship would not be realized. Similarly, memory, of one another, of what they have meant to each other, and of their lives together, is a special duty of friends, and not merely because the memory of these things is a means to the end of care and consideration. Margalit argues something similar:

> So, ought we to remember ethically? My answer is yes – if we are, and want to be, involved in thick relations. For the goodness within the relation, memory is crucial. It is crucial both as a constitutive part of our typical thick relations and as an affirmation of the relation. . . . But it is not just for the goodness *within* the relation that memory is vital. It is also vital for the goodness *of* the relation. (105–106)

A similar line of reasoning can be used for other kinds of thick relationship, including the relationship among fellow countrymen (about which I will say more in a moment). What role does collective memory play in the life of a community that endures across generations? There are obviously significant differences from friendship, but the example is still instructive. Collective memory, embodied in memorial activities and memorial places of various sorts,[97] is a constitutive ingredient of a community viewed as an intergenerational association. Without a past preserved and passed on in these ways, a community cannot survive intact. Collective memory is normatively significant as well because activities and places of collective memory are partially constitutive of the good of membership in a group. They are part of what makes it good to have and belong to a group and through them the value and importance of participating in the shared life of this enduring association is affirmed. Not all collective memorial activities play this normative role, of course. Some persist but are devoid of their original meaning, mere remnants of once vital communal interests and concerns. Some are coerced, as when a totalitarian regime imposes memorial practices in order to shore up its claim to legitimacy. These activities are not constitutive of the good of membership and there is no ethical imperative to engage in *them*. But when there is an ethical imperative, it is to be explained and justified, in part at least, by its relationship to the good of the collective it sustains.

Even if collective memory plays an essential role in social life and is a core part of group identity, this is not sufficient to generate ethical oughts of collective memory. Ethical oughts of collective memory are justified in terms of the good of (maintaining) some particular kind of thick relationship, a good that is partly constituted by ongoing memorial activities. But whether it is good to maintain the relationship or whether the good of maintaining it is sufficient reason to do so, will at least partly depend on the moral character of the group in question and the relationships among its members. There are certain threshold moral requirements that a group and these relationships must meet if membership in that group is to be able to give rise to ethical oughts of collective memory. Thus, we can imagine a tightly-knit group, on the model of the mafia, say, that systematically engages in acts of murder, extortion, and intimidation, and that is bound together by traditions preserved in the collective memory of its members. To be sure, there may be some good that comes from participating in rituals that sustain this memory. Being part of the group might even form an essential component of the members' identities. But there can be no justification for ethical oughts of collective memory that rests on the good of membership in the mafia. Even if there is some good in having and belonging to such a group, it is outweighed by the group's manifest immorality, and therefore it is disqualified as basis of ethical imperatives. Moral oughts in this way provide a threshold test for ethical oughts.

A particularly important sort of ethical ought pertains to the collective memory of fellow countrymen, and according to the account I have given, ethical oughts are to be justified in this case in terms of the good of the particular form of association that is a political community or perhaps a nation. Patriotism is one form that the sense of belonging to such a community takes, and focusing on this, we might try to justify some ethical oughts of collective memory by considering the merits of patriotism. This is no easy task, however, because, as Stephen Nathanson rather mildly puts it, "patriotism is an ideal that makes many thoughtful people uncomfortable."[98] It makes them uncomfortable because patriotism is not just love for one's country and its traditions. It also involves loyalty and a preference for the well-being of one's own country over others, and historically this preference has often manifested as national chauvinism and blind allegiance, as Tolstoy famously pointed out.[99] And as I noted earlier in this chapter, collective memory has played an undistinguished role in this connection because it has been used and manipulated by its spokesmen to promote devotion to the nation and to whip up patriotic fervor. Nevertheless, I believe, although I cannot properly argue for it here, that a morally acceptable kind of patriotism is possible and, more strongly, that patriotism in some form may even sometimes be ethically imperative.

The connection with patriotism brings to the fore a notion that was implicit in the discussion of duties of friendship, namely, *loyalty*. It is part of the concept of loyalty that it is partial to its objects, and in real-life examples of patriotic and other loyalties, this partiality often takes oppositional and exclusionary forms. Indeed, some have argued that being exclusionary or oppositional is not merely how loyalty happens to play out in the real world but rather a necessary truth. George Fletcher suggests as much:

> A can be loyal to B only if there is a third party C (another lover, an enemy nation, a hostile company) who stands as a potential competitor to B, the object of loyalty.[100]

In other words, to be loyal, A has to favor B *against* C, and if this formulation is accepted, it raises troubling questions about whether and to what extent loyalty ought to be encouraged and complicates its defense. However, there is nothing in the notion of loyalty that requires it to take an oppositional form, and though it often does so in the case of patriotic loyalty, this does not have to be oppositional either. As John Kleinig observes: "My attachment to my country need not involve any comparison with or derogation of others' countries.... I may hope that others feel about their country in the way that I feel about mine."[101] In this view, patriotic loyalties can take affirmative and supportive rather than exclusionary and oppositional forms,[102] and as manifestations of patriotic sentiment, memorial acts can function in the same ways. That is, they can simply serve to express our preferential attachment to and support of our own country rather than a sense of its superiority. Moreover, as with loyalties more generally, the patriotic attachment that is expressed in activities of collective remembrance does not have solely instrumental but also has intrinsic value for us; and we give our support in these and other ways because our country is thought to embody values that are for the most part in agreement with our own.

The point I made a few paragraphs back about moral constraints on ethical oughts applies here as well. Ethical imperatives of collective memory can be justified on the basis of patriotic loyalty only if the people *ought* to be patriotic, and this is not always the case, even if patriotism need not be comparative and oppositional. Some critics, who regard themselves as cosmopolitans, envision a world without patriotism as we know it. They hold that the current division of the world into sovereign states is a moral anachronism and that patriotism will have little or no role to play once a truly enlightened world order is achieved.[103] A less-extreme view is not dismissive of patriotism in this way, but holds that whether people ought to be patriotic depends on the qualities of their particular nation. If a nation lacks the qualities that make it merit loyalty and devotion, then on this view patriotism with respect to it is an inappropriate attitude, and the argument from patriotism for imperatives of collective memory fails. (This conclusion is consistent with Raz's account of the duties that inhere in friendship.) Even if collective memory is a constitutive part of the thick relations that make up the life of a nation, this will not suffice to justify ethical imperatives of collective memory if those relations and the nation are not worthy of being sustained.

According to my account, ethical oughts of collective memory are con-stitutively related to valuable relationships among the members of a col-lective, to relationships worthy of being sustained by them. In this sense, the imperatives are grounded in the nature of the relationships them-selves. Ethical oughts of collective memory, therefore, have a different grounding than moral oughts. Ethical oughts are not owed to others in virtue of shared humanity but by specific persons to others with whom they are bound up in thick relationships, and these relationships can span generations. Because different collectives have different histories, cul-tural and religious traditions, political arrangements, and socially sanc-tioned modes of public observance, these memorial duties are necessarily *particularized* by characteristics of the collective in which they hold. The duties are also particularistic. Although the members of one group may be able to appreciate the vital role that collective memory plays in the collective life of another, their obligation to participate in practices of col-lective memory, by this argument, reaches only as far as the boundaries of their own group. Furthermore, ethical imperatives justified in this way are neither restricted to, nor chiefly concerned with, accurate representa-tions of the past. Their justification consists in placing them in the context of collective life as a whole, where we can appreciate how they help sus-tain that life and are in turn sustained by it. There are many ways in which acts and practices of collective remembrance can sustain collective life even though they do not aim for and do not satisfy the criteria of his-torical accuracy. Their obligatoriness derives not from the demand for fidelity to the past but rather from the good of sustaining a particular valuable form of human relationship.

I want especially to draw attention to the concept of collective *identity* here. I spoke in Chapter 1 about obligations that spring from and define identities, personal as well as collective. My remarks in this section suggest that ethical oughts of collective memory, or at least some of them, are of this sort. These oughts presuppose particular ties among the members of a collective and when they are fulfilled, those ties – ties that bind *us* to one another, not to mankind at large – are affirmed and strengthened. Specifically, among these are ties that are identity-constituting. Ethical oughts, therefore, encompass memorial acts that are significant for the identity of groups, and fulfilling them is an integral part of a group's having a collective identity worth sustaining.

Hopefully, I have said enough now to substantiate my claim that memorial activities people have for ethical rather than moral reasons are activities whose functions more closely resemble those of myth than history.

8. CONCLUSION

Any form of human association that can be an object of loyalty and devotion (including a political community) is only fully worthy of being such an object if it takes its responsibilities seriously, some of which it may have acquired as a result of acts that were done in previous generations. In order to take its responsibilities seriously, in particular to take responsibility for events that occurred in its recent or more remote past, it must of course remember these events. There are obligations of memory partly because memory is needed to make the historical record accessible to the present. Collective memory is also intimately connected with collective identity, in both a moral and a sociological sense of the term. As Janna Thompson notes about the former:

> Remembrance of events that have to do with the obligations and entitlements of a nation is thus part of what could be described as the 'moral identity' of its members. The importance of having such an identity explains why their remembrance ought to be treated with respect, and not as an unfortunate psychological condition subject to treatment or manipulation.[104]

The two arguments suggested here – one linking collective memory to responsibility, the other to identity – provide plausible grounds for claiming that there are obligations of collective memory.

In this chapter, I have added two more arguments to these: one supporting moral obligations of collective memory, the other ethical obligations of collective memory. With respect to the former, I have argued that truth about the past is the yardstick and that this is why critical history is essential to their fulfillment. Wrongs committed in the far distant past can perhaps be used as symbols or metaphors for the edification of present and future generations without raising serious moral concerns. But, in the case of less remote wrongs, especially those of a more serious nature, it would often be a kind of trivialization of the past and an insult to the victims and their memory to do so. To be sure, collective memory, on its more mythic side, is, to a significant degree, permeated with symbolism, and given that activities of collective memory are valuable along several different dimensions, quite apart from whether they accurately represent the past, symbolic use of the past is not necessarily inappropriate. But collective memory has moral obligations for which the contributions of history are essential, and the moral identity that is partly constituted by remembrance must be informed by truth about the past, including the group's own. In order for these obligations to be discharged, those who occupy roles within the division of mnemonic labor must recognize and respect "the essential dignity of the historical vocation," for it is the task or, if you will, duty of history, sometimes a sad but nonetheless a vitally important task or duty, to tell the truth about what actually happened in the past.

We make room for ethical obligations, by contrast, if we recognize that collective memory is not merely a recorder, preserver, and transmitter of historical truths, but has other vital social functions that do not track truth. These functions are what the comparison with myth (or a type of myth) brings out and what I have chosen to retain from the writings of those who have characterized collective memory in the terms of myth. The argument for ethical obligations appeals to the good of the relationship that these obligations partly constitute and sustain, not to what we have reason to do as abstract moral agents. But in order to understand how the ethical obligations could play this role, we first need to appreciate these other functions of collective memory.

NOTES

1. Avishai Margalit, *The Ethics of Memory* (Cambridge, MA: Harvard University Press, 2002), p. 63.
2. Kerwin Lee Klein, "On the Emergence of *Memory* in Historical Discourse," *Representations 69* (Winter 2000): 127–150, at 128.
3. Pierre Nora, "Between Memory and History: *Les Lieux de Memoire,*" *Representations 26* (Spring 1989): 7–25. Nora and Yerushalmi (see Note 4) follow in the footsteps of Maurice Halbwachs. For Halbwachs, true collective memory is carried forward mainly by means of rituals and oral traditions, and it is different from and more vital than "historical memory." Historical memory is the general knowledge of the past that historians give us, and its predominance is explained by the weakness of collective memory. See *The Collective Memory*, Francis J. Ditter, Jr. and Vida Yazdi Ditter)(Trans.) (New York: Harper and Row, 1980), pp. 64, 78–87.
4. Yosef Hayim Yerushalmi, *Zakhor: Jewish History and Jewish Memory* (Seattle: University of Washington Press, 1996).
5. Nora, op. cit., pp. 8, 13–16.
6. Jacques Le Goff, *History and Memory*, Steven Rendall and Elizabeth Claman (Trans.). (New York: Columbia University Press, 1992), p. xi.
7. Quoted in ibid., p. 114. LeGoff not only distinguishes these but claims, questionably, that collective memory is "in reality more dangerously subject to manipulation by time and by societies given to reflection than the discipline of history itself" (xi).
8. Hayden White, *Metahistory* (Baltimore: Johns Hopkins University Press, 1973).
9. F. R. Ankersmit, *Historical Representations* (Palo Alto, CA: Stanford University Press, 2001). In characteristic fashion, Ankersmit asks rhetorically: "Is the historical discipline, taken as a whole, not the modernist text in terms of which we express our relationship to our past?" (260).
10. For more on postmodernist conceptions of history, and a critique of them, see Chris Lorenz, "Historical Knowledge and Historical Reality: A Plea for "Internal Realism," in Brian Fay, Philip Pomper and Richard Vann (Eds.) *History and Theory: Contemporary Readings* (Oxford: Blackwell, 1998), pp. 342–376.
11. Le Goff, op. cit., p. xviii.
12. This is a theme of Le Goff's book and also of Joyce Appleby, Lynn Hunt and Margaret Jacob, *Telling the Truth About History* (New York: W.W. Norton, 1995), to name just two.
13. For more about historical accuracy, see Section 6.
14. Nora, op. cit., p. 8.
15. Niall Ferguson, "Introduction," J. H. Plumb, *The Death of the Past* (New York: Palgrave Macmillan, 2004), pp. xxv–xxvi.
16. Quoted in Le Goff, op. cit, p. 109.
17. I will in fact go further than this: truth is not only one of the criteria by which we assess the goodness of memory but, in some instances, memory's obligation.

18. Noa Gedi and Yigal Elam hold that "the employment of "collective memory" can be justified only on a metaphorical level" on the grounds that a group is not "some integral entity with a will and capacity of its own." Otherwise, we commit "the fallacy of "concrete generalization," namely, of treating a generalization as though it were some concrete entity." For Gedi and Elam, there seem to be only two alternatives: if collective memory does not reside in "a separate, distinct, single organism with a mind," then talk of collective memory must be metaphorical. As I argue here, these alternatives are not exhaustive. See "Collective Memory – What Is it?" *History and Memory 8*, 1 (spring/summer 1996): 30–50.

19. David Middleton and Derek Edwards (Eds.), *Collective Remembering* (London: Sage Publications, 1990), p. 1.

20. Ibid., p. 7.

21. I borrow the term "memory activities" from Sue Campbell, *Relational Remembering: Rethinking the Memory Wars* (Lanham, MD: Rowman and Littlefield, 2003).

22. See Nora, op. cit.

23. Obviously there are embodiments of collective memory that do not in any straightforward or usual way make claims about the past. Nevertheless, they do *refer* to it or, rather, they have to do so in order to count as activities or sites of collective *memory*.

24. For a discussion of coreminiscence, see Edward S. Casey, *Remembering: A Phenomenological Study* (2nd ed.). (Bloomington: Indiana University Press, 2000), pp. 114–115. See also Chapter 5, Section 2 in this volume.

25. Yerushalmi, op. cit., p. 94.

26. Campbell, op. cit., p. 51.

27. Quoted in Le Goff, op. cit., pp. 95–96.

28. For more, see Alan Radley, "Artefacts, Memory and a Sense of the Past," in David Middleton and Derek Edwards (Eds.), *Collective Remembering* (London: Sage Publications, 1990), pp. 46–59. W. James Booth also discusses place and memory in *Communities of Memory: On Witness, Identity, and Justice* (Ithaca, NY: Cornell University Press, 2006), pp. 29–31.

29. See P. M. de Holan, N. Phillips, and T. B. Lawrence, "Managing Organizational Forgetting," *MIT Sloan Management Review* (Winter 2004): 45–51.

30. Booth, op. cit., p. x.

31. See Chapter 1, Section 5.

32. LeGoff, op. cit., p. 98.

33. Ross Poole, "Memory, History and the Claims of the Past," presented at Pacific Division meeting of the American Philosophical Association, March 26, 2004.

34. I owe this point to William Ruddick.

35. Kerwin Lee Klein, op. cit., p. 145.

36. Avishai Margalit invokes Max Weber's notion of "the disenchantment of the world" to explain the particular nature of collective memory and the competing pressures to which he claims it is subject. [See "Science as Vocation," and "The Protestant Sects and the Spirit of Capitalism," both in H. H. Gerth and C. W. Mills (Eds.), *From Max Weber: Essays in Sociology* (New York: Oxford

University Press, 1971.] In Weber's complex analysis of the distinctive character of modernity, modern civilization is characterized by a progressive disenchantment of the world, that is, by the displacement of magical and religious views of the world by the scientific view, according to which the phenomena of everyday life are calculable and, therefore, in principle, are controllable. Weber saw, in the ascendancy of the scientific worldview, the genesis of a profound problem of *meaning*: the deeply rooted human need to believe that worldly occurrences possess significance or meaning becomes ever more difficult to satisfy, because science is not itself a source of meaning that can fill the void left by the displacement of enchanted worldviews. The need for meaning does not therefore abate, however, but actually becomes more acute:

> As intellectualism suppresses belief in magic, the world's processes become disenchanted, lose their magical significance, and henceforth simply 'are' and 'happen' but no longer signify anything. As a consequence, there is a growing demand that the world and the total pattern of life be subject to an order that is significant and meaningful. (Weber, *Economy and Society*, G. Roth and C. Wittich (Eds.). (Berkeley: University of California Press, 1978), p. 506)

Weber's historical sociology, his claims about the scientific worldview and its disenchantment of the world, and his moral response to modernity, raise difficult problems of interpretation and invite criticism in a number of respects, so the wisdom of drawing on Weber to provide an explanatory framework for collective memory may be doubted. Specifically, to suggest, as Margalit does, that myth enchants the world whereas critical history (the discipline or science of history) disenchants it, may only invite questions about which elements of Weber's multifaceted notion of (dis)enchantment Margalit means to carry over into his account of collective memory and about how helpful these various elements are in better understanding its nature.

37. For some of the various senses, see Andrew von Hendy, *The Modern Construction of Myth* (Bloomington, IN: Indiana University Press, 1989).
38. Mircea Eliade, *Myth and Reality* (New York: Harper and Row, 1963), pp. 2, 5–6.
39. One may wonder why I need to introduce the notion of *myth* at all in this context, rather than just directly describe the various nonhistorical functions of collective memory. Isn't "myth" just a convenient shorthand way of referring to these different functions, so that nothing of substance would be lost if it were simply dropped from the discussion altogether? I do not think so. The comparison with myth clarifies and facilitates the exposition. Characterizing some of collective memory's features as myth-like gives the account of them a unifying principle and fits them together in a coherent cluster of traits. These factors are part, but only part, of the reason I frame the discussion in relation to myth. In addition, many writers on collective memory are interested in its mythic aspects and explicitly discuss it in these terms, and they take the notion of myth to have real explanatory value. (See,

for example, Margalit's characterization of collective memory at the beginning of this chapter.) This confers a legitimacy on my use of the category of myth beyond that of mere convenience or organizational clarity.

40. Bernard Williams, *Truth and Truthfulness: An Essay in Genealogy* (Princeton: Princeton University Press, 2002).

41. Ibid., p. 164.

42. Ibid., p. 165.

43. I should make it clear that I am not endorsing Veyne's more ambitious philosophical views about the nature of truth (which have been heavily influenced by the work of Michel Foucault) but only the specific suggestions about the relationship between myth and truth.

44. Paul Veyne, *Did the Greeks Believe in Their Myths? An Essay on the Constitutive Imagination*, Paula Wissing (Trans.). (University of Chicago Press, 1988), p. 79

45. Ibid., p. 84.

46. See Williams, op. cit. pp. 247–250.

47. Arthur Danto, *Narration and Knowledge* (New York: Columbia University Press, 1985), chapter 6.

48. Lorenz, op. cit., p. 351.

49. Mary Fulbrook, *Historical Theory* (London: Routledge, 2002), p. 187.

50. Anita Shapira, "Historiography and Memory: The Case of Latrun 1948," pp. 29, 30, 31.

51. Specific American versions of these democratic myths are myths of the open frontier, the agrarian past, and the self-made man. See David Thelen (Ed.), *Memory and American History* (Bloomington, IN: Indiana University Press, 1989).

52. There is a different sense of "myth" than the one I am focusing on here, according to which a myth is equivalent to a "widely repeated lie" or "a false belief," notions that are closely related to "ideology."

53. Steven Knapp, "Collective Memory and the Actual Past," *Representations 26* (Spring 1989): 123–149, at 130.

54. Dora Apel, *Memory Effects: The Holocaust and the Art of Secondary Witnessing* (New Brunswick, NJ: Rutgers University Press, 2002).

55. Knapp, op. cit., pp. 130–131. The thrust of Knapp's article is skeptical: he argues that people's worries about the fit between what actually happened and received narratives about the past are based on a confusion. I do not think he is correct about this, as I hope to show in this and the next section.

56. David Lowenthal, "Identity, Heritage, and History," in *Commemorations: The Politics of National Identity*, J. R. Gillis (Ed.) (Princeton University Press, 1994), pp. 41–57, at 47.

57. Compare this from Booth, op. cit., p. 93:

> Historiography aspires to move alongside the event, outside and parallel to it. It is linear, chronological, and oriented toward the explanation of change. Memory, by contrast, seeks a fusion with the past, seeks to make the past present as its own, as part of an identity, of the persistence of the same.

The features that Booth attributes to memory are features that some myths possess as well.

58. Von Hendy, op. cit., pp. xii–xiii.

59. Collective memory does not always have these features, of course. My claim is only that it characteristically has them. For an exception, see discussion of the empty formalism of much contemporary commemoration in Chapter 1, Section 3.

60. Margalit (op. cit., note 1) has his own list of characteristics of myth or of what he calls "living myth" (65). The feature he is most interested in is myth's power to "revivify":

> A myth is living if it plays a role in a ritual that intends to revivify events and heroes. . . . Revivification is not resurrection; it brings the dead to life in essence but not in form. A living myth is a sacred story, then, connected with revivifying elements from the past. (65)

I confess that I find this passage puzzling. Margalit emphasizes that he is not talking only about traditional societies, where the notion of myth as a genre of sacred story is most clearly at home, but about "secular modern nation-states" (67) as well. He also explicitly distinguishes this sense of living myth from other senses, according to which a myth is living if it is vivid or if it deeply impresses a community so that its members are willing to shape their lives in accordance with it. Living myths "bring the past to life," not merely by presenting "vivid and animated descriptions" of it (66), which a well-crafted piece of historical writing is capable of doing, but by bringing "the past itself" back, albeit it "in essence" and not in fact. How is this to be understood? Perhaps we can make some headway on an answer by pursuing the connection Margalit draws between living myth and ritual and noting some of ritual's properties. Although scholars offer various theories of ritual and define ritual in different ways, certain features are held to be more or less common. For example, it is generally held that ritual is not essentially a contemplative activity but a type of performance in which thought and action are fused; that ritual, because of its standardized and nearly invariant character over time, serves to link past to present and present to future; and what is especially relevant here, that ritual frequently is or involves a symbolic re-enactment of an original episode or scenario. Assuming that we can thus make sense of the notion of revivification, I am not necessarily opposed to including it among the features that may distinguish myth from history.

It is doubtful, however, that this explanation would be entirely satisfactory to Margalit. In the book he coauthored with Moshe Halbertal, *Idolatry* (Cambridge, MA: Harvard University Press, 1992), and to which he refers in the discussion of myth in *The Ethics of Identity*, the notion of revivification is explained by reference to the doctrine of transubstantiation. "All we require [sic]," they say, "is the idea that the sacrament of the bread and the wine in the appropriate ritual framework is supposed to create not only a symbolic presence but actual revivification" (103). But it is unclear why this particular notion of revivification should be so central to Margalit's account of collective memory and how it is supposed to help us better understand it. Do collective memories actually (typically?) revivify the past in this sense, and what are the criteria by which to determine whether they have done so?

61. Recall the case of the Tulsa race riot discussed in Chapter 3. Despite occasional efforts over the years to set the historical record straight about what happened, the entrenched political and economic interests in Oklahoma were too powerful to permit them a proper hearing.

62. Irwin-Zarecka [*Frames of Remembrance* (New Brunswick, NJ: Transaction Publishers, 1994] discusses the various ways in which the professional study of the past has a formative influence on collective memory:

> The role of historians as advisors to media producers or to commissions in charge of public commemorative works and events, when coupled with the growing interest in nonfiction that gives at least some scholars an unprecedented amount of public exposure, provide for an extensive contribution of historical research to the construction of collective memory. Where that contribution is most crucial, however, is within the educational system proper. (148)

See also Tony Judt's assessment of postwar German memory:

> Only after Germans had appreciated and digested the enormity of their Nazi past – a sixty year cycle of denial, education, debate, and consensus – could they begin to live with it, i.e. put it behind them. The instrument of recall in all such cases was not memory itself. It was *history* in both its meanings: as the passage of time and as the professional study of the past – the latter above all. ("From the House of the Dead: On Modern European Memory," *New York Review of Books* 52 (October 6, 2005): 12–16, at 16)

However, the relationship between history and collective memory remains uneasy. See Note 63.

63. On the problematic relationship between history and collective memory, see Irwin-Zarecka, ibid.:

> History offers a great deal of comfort, inspiration and the essential anchoring for the self. But history can also be a burden, a troublesome obstacle to the sense of common identity and well-being. Even families face this predicament, trying as they might to erase memories of abuse, for example. The presence of the past, for all its fit within the current agendas, is often disquieting. It is not surprising, then, that questions about the "correct" role of remembrance in public life are so frequently subject to intense debate. (99)

Tony Judt makes a similar point:

> Unlike memory, which confirms and reinforces itself, history contributes to the disenchantment of the world. Most of what it has to offer is discomforting, even disruptive – which is why it is not always politically prudent to wield the past as a moral cudgel with which to beat and berate a people for its past sins. (ibid.)

Whereas Margalit thinks of modern collective memory as being internally conflicted, torn between an enchanted and a disenchanted worldview, Judt seems to think of history as operating on collective memory from the outside.

The difference between these different views of collective memory is not very significant for my purposes here, however.

64. An example of a society that seems to have successfully avoided this problem, despite the enormity of the crimes it has confronted, is contemporary Germany, although it has faced new challenges since reunification.

65. On Margalit's notion of "living," see Note 60.

66. As I noted in Section 1, one writer who does so is Pierre Nora. Nora characterizes (true) collective memory and history in such a way that they are "in fundamental opposition." He articulates a number of contrasts. "Memory," he says, "installs remembrance within the sacred; history, always prosaic, releases it again. . . . memory is by nature multiple and yet specific; collective, plural, and yet individual. History, on the other hand, belongs to everyone and to no one, whence its claims to universal authority. Memory takes root in the concrete . . . history binds itself strictly to temporal continuities, to progressions, and to relations between things." See Nora, op. cit., pp. 8–9. Although I have a different understanding of collective memory than the one Nora articulates here, his distinction between universal (history) and particular (memory) authority is especially interesting because it echoes some of what I have to say in Sections 6 and 7.

67. Yerushalmi, op. cit., p. 116.

68. Other philosophers who have drawn a similar distinction include: Michael Walzer, *Spheres of Justice* (New York: Basic Books, 1983); Bernard Williams, *The Ethics and Limits of Philosophy* (Cambridge, MA: Harvard University Press, 1985), chapters 8 and 9; Charles Taylor, "A most peculiar institution," in J. E. J. Altham and R. Harrison (Eds.), *World, Mind, and Ethics: Essays on the ethical philosophy of Bernard Williams* (Cambridge, UK: Cambridge University Press, 1995): 132–155; and Kwame Anthony Appiah, *The Ethics of Identity* (Princeton: Princeton University Press, 2005), chapter 6, especially pp. 230–237.

69. The contrast between these two domains closely resembles one that has emerged in a particularly focused way in Carol Gilligan's work attacking Lawrence Kohlberg's conception of moral maturity. See Carol Gilligan, *In a Different Voice* (Cambridge, MA: Harvard University Press, 1982). Drawing on her empirical research in the moral development of girls, Gilligan claims that there are important aspects of the moral life that have been neglected by the traditional perspective Kohlberg adopts, and she argues for the existence of a moral outlook that is defined by a number of contrasts with it.

70. In Buddhist moral philosophy, for example, the notion of universal compassion seems to combine features of both morality (universality) and ethics (caring). Thanks to Christopher Gowans for pointing this out to me.

71. Harry Frankfurt, for example, says that "morality is most particularly concerned with how our attitudes and our actions should take into account the needs, the desires, and the entitlements of other people." See Harry Frankfurt, *The Reasons of Love* (Princeton: Princeton University Press, 2004), p. 7. For Margalit, and Appiah as well (see Note 68), both ethics and morality

have to do with our relationships to others, so they would be included within morality as Frankfurt characterizes it.

72. See, for example, Susan Wolf, "Morality and Partiality," in James E. Tomberlin (Ed.) *Philosophical Perspectives, 6: Ethics* (Atascadero, CA.: Ridgeview Publishing Co., 1992), pp. 243–259.

73. For more, see Section 1 of Chapter 5.

74. It may be argued that the language of care is most appropriately, perhaps only appropriately, used in the context of personal relationships like love and friendship, and that we normally do not use the term "care" when discussing our relations to fellow countrymen. As I say, Margalit does not limit care to the former, but especially in the light of our usual understanding of care, it would have been helpful had he said more about what care consists in. One philosopher who has written extensively on caring is Harry Frankfurt. See Note 71, and also: Harry Frankfort, *Taking Ourselves Seriously and Getting It Right* (Palo Alto, CA.: Stanford University Press, 2006); and "The Importance of What We Care About," in his collection, *The Importance of What We Care About* (New York: Cambridge University Press, 1988), pp. 80–94.

75. Margalit thinks a moral community of memory is a conceptual possibility, but does not hold out much hope for it. W. James Booth also casts doubt on the possibility of a moral community of memory. Collective memory, in his view, is particularistic, that is, it individuates a community and differentiates it from others. But universal values cannot do this. Therefore, he claims, "the idea of a commonality based on universal values, or of a global or even supranational regional memory seems wrongheaded" (Booth, op. cit., pp. 173–174).

76. Iwona Irwin-Zarecka also speaks about "communities of memory," but she seems to have something different in mind than Margalit. According to Irwin-Zarecka, "In its most direct meaning, a community of memory is one created by that very memory. For people to feel a sense of bonding with others solely because of a shared experience, the experience itself would often be of extraordinary if not traumatic quality." [op. cit., p. 47]. In this sense, for example, the attacks of September 11th created a community of memory among New Yorkers; but this was not a natural community of memory in Margalit's sense. One difference between these senses of "community of memory" is that communities of memory created by memory are likely to be more tenuous and transient than those that Margalit speaks about. They may be less reliable, therefore, as repositories of collective memory over the long term.

77. Susie Linfield, "Memory's Lair," *Boston Review* (Summer 2003).

78. Ethical obligations are restricted to these smaller groupings because caring for mankind in general exceeds human capacities, according to Margalit.

79. Ronald Dworkin, *Law's Empire* (London: Fontana Press, 1986), pp. 199–201. See also the discussion of associative obligations in Yael Tamir, *Liberal Nationalism* (Princeton: Princeton University Press, 1993), especially pp. 99–102.

80. Quoted in David Cockburn, *Other Times: Philosophical perspectives on past, present and future* (Cambridge, UK: Cambridge University Press, 1997), p. 298.

81. Ibid., pp. 298–299.

82. Yerushalmi, op. cit., p. 116.

83. Adam Morton, "Emotional Truth," *Proceedings of the Aristotelian Society* (Suppl.) 76 (July 2002).

84. What Williams says about history is relevant here: "With history as with some everyday narrative, every statement in it can be true and it can still tell the wrong story" (*Truth and Truthfulness*, op. cit., p. 244).

85. Ibid., p. 127.

86. Ibid., p. 87.

87. See the discussion of this point in Section 5.

88. Margalit, op. cit., p. 78.

89. The quote, though relevant, is taken a bit out of context because it occurs in Williams' discussion of what he calls "the relativism of distance." See *Ethics and the Limits of Philosophy* (Cambridge, MA: Harvard University Press, 1985), pp. 160–161.

90. An imperfect general obligation of memory might leave comparatively little latitude for a particular community, however. Consider, for example, the case of Raoul Wallenberg: humanity at large has an imperfect obligation to remember persons of remarkable virtue, and Wallenberg is one such individual; the Jewish community or the survivors and their descendants, by contrast, may have a obligation to remember *him* specifically.

91. I say more about this in Section 7.

92. Plumb, op. cit., p. 142.

93. See, for example, J. Callahan, "On Harming the Dead," *Ethics* 97 (1986): 341–352.

94. For defenders of this view, see Joel Feinberg, *Harm to Others* (New York: Oxford University Press, 1984), pp. 89–92; Michael Ridge, "Giving the Dead Their Due," *Ethics 114* (2003): 38–59; and Geoffrey Scarre, "Archeology and Respect for the Dead," *Journal of Applied Philosophy 20* (2003): 237–49.

95. My own view is that the idea of duties to the dead is both coherent and defensible and that we lose something ethically significant if we discard the idea. But I will not press the point here. For more, see Chapter 5, Section 3.

96. Joseph Raz, "Liberating Duties," *Law and Philosophy 8* (1989): 3–21.

97. See Section 2 in this chapter.

98. Stephen Nathanson, "In Defense of 'Moderate Patriotism,'" *Ethics 99* (1989): 535–552, at 535.

99. Leo Tolstoy, "Patriotism," and "Patriotism, or Peace?" in *Tolstoy's Writings on Civil Disobedience and Non-Violence* (New York: New American Library, 1968; New York: Bergman, 1967).

100. George P. Fletcher, *Loyalty: An Essay on the Morality of Relationships* (New York: Oxford University Press, 1993), p. 8.

101. John Kleinig, *Loyalty and Loyalties* (unpublished manuscript), chapter 1.

102. Similar points are made by Yael Tamir, *Liberal Nationalism* (Princeton, NJ: Princeton University Press, 1993), pp. 100–101.
103. See discussion in Ross Poole, *Nation and Identity* (London: Routledge, 1999), chapter 5.
104. Janna Thompson, *Taking Responsibility for the Past* (Cambridge, UK: Polity Press, 2002), p. 68.

5

THE RESPONSIBILITY OF REMEMBRANCE

For everything, in time, gets lost. . . . But for a little while some of that can be rescued, if only, faced with the vastness of all that there is and all that there ever was, somebody makes the decision to look back, to have one last look, to search for a while in the debris of the past and to see not only what was lost but what there is still to be found. — Daniel Mendelsohn, *The Lost*[1]

1. RAISING THE ISSUES: ABSENT FRIENDS, DECEASED FRIENDS

If ethical norms govern how one is to behave toward others with whom one has a thick relationship, then broadly speaking, the topic of this chapter belongs to what, in Chapter 4, I called an ethics of memory.[2] Specifically, this chapter deals with ethical norms governing remembrance in the domain of personal and intimate relations. What obligations of remembrance do we have to or with respect to the near and dear – friends, lovers, family members, and so forth? More specifically still, what obligations do we have after they have died? I want to approach this question indirectly by first considering remembrance in the context of an ongoing friendship.

Bill and I have known each other for some time, and when I think about my feelings for him, I have no hesitation saying he is a dear friend about whom I care a great deal. Indeed, our relationship has all the earmarks of a very close friendship: there is an enormous bond of trust between us that is expressed and reinforced by mutual self-disclosure; we have great affection for each other and support each other emotionally; we share activities and experiences; and we delight in each other's flourishing and commiserate with each other's misfortune. But then our friendship is put to the test, when Bill, who has been living near me, takes a job in a distant city. At first, I resolve not to let our friendship suffer because of the change. I feel the pain of separation; I think of him often and tell him how much I miss him; I make frequent phone calls and visit him regularly. But time passes and increasingly I fail to do what I have resolved. Perhaps this is because our separation has brought to the surface certain unresolved difficulties in our relationship that we did not address before. Or perhaps, I have just become preoccupied with other interests and responsibilities and neglected to remind myself of how much my relationship with Bill matters to me. In any case, I find myself thinking of him less and less often; the strong desire I once felt to be in his company and to confide in him diminishes; the time that elapses between phone calls grows longer; he gradually comes to occupy a less and less emotionally central place in my life. In the past, before Bill's move and in its aftermath, I took care to remind myself of important events in his life and to acknowledge them with tokens of my continuing concern and affection. I frequently spoke to other people about the times Bill and I spent together. Whenever I engaged in activities that Bill and I had shared and enjoyed together, I would know just how he would act and what he would say were he with me, and this would make me feel close to him, despite the geographical distance between us. Gradually, however, these and other memories fade, and my attachment to Bill grows more and more tenuous.

Have I done anything wrong? More precisely, have I been disloyal to Bill, and have I been an unfaithful friend? In general, friendships can come to an end in all sorts of ways and for all sorts of reasons, and even when one or both of the parties can be said to be responsible for ending their friendship, it is not always appropriate to affix blame. For one thing, the responsibilities of friendship are canceled if, by mutual consent, the parties to the relationship decide to end it. Even without mutual consent, there seems to be no general reason why I should have to maintain a friendship if it has lost its appeal to me, and I can signal my desire to end the relationship in various ways. But now consider the case I am constructing. Bill and I have not in any explicit way come to an understanding about ending our relationship. Moreover, when I do think about the state of our relationship, which admittedly occurs less and less frequently,

I regret what has become of it, the lack of communication, the ever rarer tokens of affection, and the emotional distance. It is not as though I no longer see any reason to maintain the friendship or that it has entirely lost its appeal to me, although I may sometimes wonder if this isn't the case. I still tell myself, on occasion, that I care very much about Bill and that I will work harder to maintain our relationship. I even tell Bill this as well. So Bill, although aware of the changes that have taken place in our relationship, has been given reason to believe that I want to continue to be his friend, and has expectations of renewed sharing and intimacy. Little changes, however, and for a while, Bill feels that I have misled him, and he is angry at me for it. Perhaps he should have known better; perhaps he should have been more perceptive and realized that I had no serious intention of working to maintain our relationship, despite my declarations to the contrary. But perhaps it is unfair to expect this of him, and if so, I ought to feel guilty about not being the friend to Bill that I have encouraged him to believe I am. Presumably at some point, however, it becomes clear to Bill that our relationship will not be renewed after all, and knowing that friendships do not necessarily last for a lifetime, he accepts its demise.

In Bill's case, I will suppose, I let him down as someone professing friendship and wronged him by doing so: I abused his trust in me or at least did not give enough thought to how I might have done so. As not uncommonly happens, our relationship didn't end abruptly or cleanly but persisted in some form for a time. This complicates the assessment of my wrongdoing but does not completely absolve me of blame for having ended the relationship the way I did. To be sure, once it becomes clear to both Bill and me that our friendship is truly over, I can no longer be accused of disloyalty from then on, but this cannot retrospectively justify my earlier conduct. Compare this to a case in which I forget my so-called friend much more quickly. I do not resolve to work on maintaining our relationship after he moves away; I am always too busy or find it too inconvenient to call or visit him; and so forth. In a case like this, we are right to wonder if he was ever really my friend at all.

What these cases suggest is an important fact about the relationship between memory and friendship. Friendship is not merely an affective relationship. Notwithstanding certain philosophical accounts of duty that view it as antagonistic to intimate personal relationships, we recognize that friends ought to treat each other in certain ways under certain circumstances, and reflection on how we think about friends shows the propriety and importance of talk about duties of friendship.[3] Indeed, it has been argued that the very idea of friendship is a normative idea in that we understand the concept of friendship in part by understanding what a good friendship is like and we understand what a good friendship is like, in part, in terms of duties to pay special attention to the other and the other's particular needs, interests, desires, and tastes.[4] Even if, implausibly, the concept of friendship is not itself partly normative, friends do owe one another certain special forms of care and consideration and are subject to moral criticism if such special care and attention are not forthcoming. And depending on the circumstances, one way of failing to show the concern appropriate to friendship is to forget our friends in their absence.

Now suppose that Bill's absence is due not to his departure from my city but to his departure from life. Similar to the previous example, while Bill was alive, my relationship with him had all the characteristics of a close friendship. And, again, as before, I do not suddenly stop caring about Bill because he has died, and as an expression of my continuing affection, I resolve not to forget him. However, my resolve weakens. Obviously, many of the ways of showing that I still care will not be possible now that Bill is dead because I cannot show *Bill* anything, unless Bill survives in some form, a possibility I discount here. And because Bill no longer exists, I cannot hurt his feelings or disappoint his current expectations if I fail to show proper concern. There is also no question of having a duty to Bill to maintain the relationship with him because friendship is a relationship of *mutual* respect, trust, and affection, which is no longer possible now. But Bill was not merely a passing acquaintance: he was a close friend. Should I not be disturbed by the waning of memory, out of a sense that I have done something wrong by forgetting him, by not working harder to keep my memory of him alive? The question is not whether I should be disturbed by the fact that I have gotten over the death of a close friend sufficiently to be able to get on with my life. Completing the work of mourning, psychologists tell us, is a mark of psychic resilience and health, not something to be resisted or regretted or morally criticized, and it does not involve or result in the suppression or obliteration of the friend's memory. The question is rather whether I am somehow being unfaithful to our friendship and to Bill as my friend, and thereby violate an obligation, if memory, and not just any memory but the right sort of memory, does not persist. Perhaps in some circumstances, forgetting, like grief too easily overcome, is a kind of moral failing. More than this, it might retrospectively alter the meaning of our relationship or, at least, raise serious questions about the sort of friendship Bill and I actually shared.[5]

This example differs from the previous one in obvious respects and adds a new twist to questions about the relationship between memory and friendship. In the example of the absent friend, as I noted, the friendship eventually came to an end – something that Bill would probably have realized at some point as expressions of my concern and affection became increasingly rare over time. Because I did not end the relationship cleanly but kept Bill supposing that we were still friends, I misled him and would have this to apologize to him for, even if I did not intend to deceive him. The wrong here is not so much that I stopped caring – certainly we are sometimes permitted to do so – but that I nurtured expectations in Bill that I was not willing or able to live up to because I was not wholeheartedly committed to the relationship. (I was also not sufficiently honest with myself about this). But in the second example, Bill died when our relationship was still close, when we both believed (correctly) that there was a special bond between us. The relationship, but not the caring, ended when he died, with no possibility of further communication between us or evolution in our relationship. Is there an obligation of remembrance grounded in a *past* friendship, a relationship that ended not because of a change of feeling for the other but because of the brute fact of death? If there is an obligation to remember a living friend in his absence, as I have suggested there is, an obligation partly constitutive of the friendship itself, is there not also an obligation to remember a deceased friend that flows from the relationship we had?

When someone who is dear to us dies, Kierkegaard tells us, "it is the most frequent occurrence, the customary thing, that he is remembered" for at least some brief period of time after death. "The survivor – faithful during the first period – says, 'I shall never forget him who is dead.'" But, Kierkegaard goes on, "the loving memory of one dead has to protect itself against the actuality around about lest by ever new impressions it gets full power to expel the memory, and it has to protect itself against time." Remembering the dead, even one dearly loved, is difficult work that must contend with "the multiplicity of life's demands" and the forgetfulness induced by the passage of time.[6] We often forget, despite our firmest resolve not to do so. Nevertheless, it is noteworthy that the resolve not to forget seems to be both a natural outgrowth of the love and concern we had for the living and a token of our continuing faithfulness. Remembering is what we resolve to do and what love seems to demand of us. Indeed, for Kierkegaard, it is our *duty* to remember our deceased loved ones, to resist the encroachment of life's many distractions and thereby the attrition of memory.

I want to investigate our obligations of remembrance in relation to persons we care about, in the sense of care that involves consideration, affection, attentiveness, and individualized knowledge. Friends are one example, but I will be speaking more broadly about those I call the *dear departed*, persons we have loved, cherished, and/or esteemed, and who have not just been significant in our lives but have mattered to us, and who have now passed away. What is the moral or, if we use the language of Chapter 4, the ethical significance of remembering those we loved and cared about who have died? Are we to be faulted for not resolving to remember them or, if we do resolve to remember them, for allowing our resolve to erode over time? Do we have, as Kierkegaard asserts, a duty to remember them? And these evaluative questions aside, what are the different modes of remembering the dead and how does the character of the relationship we had with them affect how we remember and what meaning it has for us?

I begin, in Section 2, with some brief remarks about the phenomenology of remembering the dear departed and then, following the work of Edward Casey, distinguish among different modes of remembering them: reminding, reminiscing, and recognizing. This typology give us some idea of the different ways that are available to us of remembering the dear departed, and it is helpful to know this if, as I argue in later sections of this chapter, remembering them can be our obligation. Section 3 considers whether and how we can make sense of the notion of loving the dead as an instance of the more general question of how we are to understand continuing to care about the dear departed after their deaths. This will prove important for the expressive theory I offer in Section 4, because as I employ it, the theory presumes that we can

do so and so requires some account of how this is possible. With respect
to personal love in particular, I argue that different accounts of love will
yield different explanations of how we can love the dead. The accounts
I prefer share a conception of love as a way of valuing another. Section 4
introduces a critical distinction between different theories of value and
reasons for action and relates it specifically to memory. I label these, following Elizabeth Anderson, consequentialist and expressivist accounts,
and it is the fundamental differences between these general types rather
than the particular versions of each that are my concern. An expressivist
theory, as applied to memory, construes memorial acts or practices as
expressions of certain intrinsically valuable attitudes and emotions and
justifies an imperative to remember in these terms. I argue that such
a theory is needed because a consequentialist theory alone cannot do
justice to the obligations that we have to remember the dear departed.

Three arguments for obligations to remember that are nonconsequentialist and expressivist in nature are discussed in Section 5. The first two,
the rescue from insignificance view and the enduring duties view, hold
that we have obligations of memory independently of whether we want
or choose to have them. The third, the reciprocity view, is in a different category, for it generates obligations conditionally. That is, according to reciprocity, consistency requires that we recognize and discharge
such obligations if we desire or demand that others remember *us* after
our deaths. Because I take it that being remembered after our deaths is
something that is vitally important to many people, in this as well as other
cultures, the argument speaks to a deep psychological need and has a
ubiquitous role in generating memorial obligations. Section 6 deals with
a common occurrence in the lives of adult children, the death of parents,
and its effects on their adult identity. It begins with some general remarks
about mourning drawn from the work of Jacques Derrida and moves on
to discuss the sorts of meaning and value that we can derive from reflecting on our deceased parents and ourselves in relation to them. Parents
are a special case in this regard because their deaths can have a unique
impact on our psychic lives, in ways more profound than that of spouses
and friends. This chapter concludes with a discussion of two issues that,
roughly speaking, concern the relationship between memory and time.
Section 7 returns to the problem that Kierkegaard noted, namely, that
memory of the dear departed, which is an obligation, needs to "protect

itself against the actuality around about [and] against time." Here I show how an understanding of remembrance as having a social or interpersonal dimension can suggest ways of protecting personal memory against these corrosive forces. Specifically, I focus on ritualization as a means of shoring up the fragility of socially unsupported memory. And finally, Section 8 considers the moral implications of our progressively diminishing capacity to sustain care for those who have died. It asks whether we should be ethically or morally troubled by the fact that our memories of the dear departed are as fragile as we know them to be.

I have two final preliminary remarks. In this chapter, I use different words to describe the focus of my inquiry: duty, obligation, responsibility, and imperative. I use these interchangeably, setting aside any distinctions among them which may have been drawn in the philosophical literature and which may be useful in other contexts. Furthermore, I am chiefly concerned with whether there are such memorial duties and what their grounds are, not with duty as motivation; in other words, with acting in accord with duty rather than acting from duty. I take it to be the case that persons only sometimes, and perhaps infrequently, remember the dear departed because they believe they *ought* to. Similarly, parents rarely feed, clothe, shelter, and educate their children out of a sense of obligation, but do so out of love and concern. Nevertheless, parents have duties to do so (or to see to it that others do so), and remembering the dear departed may be morally or ethically nonoptional even though it is seldom done for this reason. If in these circumstances one fails to remember or to make an effort to remember, one opens oneself up to censure or blame.

2. QUALITIES AND MODES OF REMEMBERING THE DEAD

The subject of this chapter, as I have said, is remembrance of persons with whom one had some sort of personal relationship of care and concern involving some reciprocal response of individual to individual. Such relationships include various types of love relationship (filial, parental, erotic), friendship, and (some) teacher–student relationships. A personal relationship necessarily involves deep and detailed knowledge of the other, and these facts about the nature of the relationship have implications for how the dear departed are remembered. Memories of the dear departed have distinctive qualities because they bear traces of and reflect these highly particularistic epistemic qualities. We can of course also remember persons who have died whom we have not known in this way, but qualitatively this is a very different sort of remembrance.

Much of our knowledge of friends and loved ones has a direct and specific sensuous quality, unmediated by any process of inference and irreducible to knowledge of truths. We may come to know an immense amount about a given person from various sources, his likes and dislikes, habits, and virtues and vices, so much, in fact, that other people may say that it is just as if we had known him all our lives. But the "as if" signifies that something crucial is missing: not more facts about him, but the immediate knowledge of this person that comes from close and intimate association. Knowledge of someone we have never met, or met only in passing, necessarily lacks this element: it is predominantly a matter of remembering *that* and takes a propositional form. The sort of knowledge, in turn, conditions the possibilities of remembrance. How we can and do remember those who have died depends on the kind of knowledge we had of them when they were alive: persons known to us only or largely by description (e.g., the grandfather who died before I was born) are remembered differently (but not entirely differently) than those known to us through personal and intimate acquaintance.

In remembering a deceased friend or a loved one or a revered teacher, we remember actions they performed or qualities they possessed. We remember states of affairs with the following structure: x did y or x was (an) a. I remember, for example, that my mother was a committed feminist before it was fashionable; that my mentor was an inspiring role model for all who were fortunate enough to know him; that my father was a deeply unhappy man who died much too young; that my friend and I went to Yosemite together after our graduation from college; and so forth. But there is also, or may also be, a remembering of the person that possesses a directness and sensuous specificity that can only come from the knowledge acquired in and by close association with that person. Beyond the various facts about this person, or what are taken to be facts, we are immediately aware of *this person* in our memories, and this gives our memories a particular poignancy and accounts for much of their emotional power. Although we also remember this person's various doings and beings, these rememberings typically play a different role in remembering the dear departed than in remembering the dead we only know by description. When remembering is of the dear departed, then for some period of time the immediate, sensuous memory of the person has a certain psychological priority over remembering that the person did so-and-so or was so-and-so. It is not surprising, then, that remembering the dear departed often does not require a great deal of remembering that.[7]

Martha Nussbaum's moving description of her grief at the death of her mother emphasizes these features of our memories of the dear departed:

> Grief is not just an abstract judgment plus the ineliminable localizing element: it is very richly particular. Even if its propositional content is, "My wonderful mother is dead," the experience itself involves a storm of memories and concrete perceptions that swarm around that content, but add more than is present in it.... When I grieve for my mother, I *see* her, and the sight is, like a picture, dense and replete. That density is inseparable from the experience: in fact, it is often tiny details of the dense picture of the person one loves that become the focus for grief, that seem to symbolize or encapsulate that person's wonderfulness or salience.[8]

Grief is what we commonly feel at the loss of a close friend or loved one, and even when we do not grieve any longer as we did in the immediate aftermath of our loss, our memories of the dear departed continue for some time to be constituted by these rich and dense perceptions.

The remarks so far tell us something about the texture and feel of our memories of the dear departed. A full account of such memories must also include a description of what (borrowing a term from Edward Casey) we can call their various "mnemonic modes."[9] These are generic modes of remembering, ways of remembering both the living and the dead, and among the dead, both those who were known intimately and those who were not. They are the forms that the distinctive content of our memories of the dear departed can take.

First is reminding. "The work of reminding," according to Casey, "is to induce the actual or potential remindee to do or think something he or she might otherwise forget to do or think.... Remindful thinking of the past is itself a basic way in which we remember the past" (93–94). When I am reminded of my deceased wife by her photo on the mantel, or when I remind myself of my deceased father by lighting a candle in his memory, the person who has died is both evoked by the reminder and referred to by it. The reminder functions in both of these ways as a sign of what or who it reminds me of. In addition, reminding may be something one does deliberately or it may come about quite spontaneously.

A second mode is reminiscing. Reminiscing, Casey asserts, is typically undertaken not for any utilitarian purpose but for the sheer joy of reliving the past. The persons or experiences reminisced about "come[s] back to life (and not just to mind) in the activity of reminiscing, which revives remembered content in a particularly vivid way," and when the reminiscing is "fulfilling or successful, there is . . . a sense of becoming one with what I remember" (109). Reminiscing also has a communal aspect in that it frequently occurs in a social setting and flourishes in the company of others who are engaged with us "in a common enterprise of reliving the past wistfully" (115). Because reminiscing about the dead is done communally, with the reminiscences of others reinforcing and animating one's own, it shows in the clearest way why remembering is not simply an introspective affair carried out in the privacy of the psyche. Furthermore, when we reminisce about the departed, we not only recall facts about the person's life or character or deeds. We insinuate ourselves back into that person's life in a way that brings the person him or herself back to life, and the person's presence is more or less vivid, and felt more or less powerfully, depending on what sort of relationship we had with that person and how intimately we knew him or her. Finally, like reminding, reminiscing can be something that just happens, that we fall into, or something that we set out to do.

A third mode of remembering is recognizing, which takes different forms. One type is *recognizing-in*, an example of which is recognizing my deceased mother in my daughter's physical appearance, temperament, and mannerisms. A second is *recognizing-as*, and there are various ways in which the deceased can be involved in and summoned up by this kind of recognition.[10] For example, I may recognize (as a fact) that I have qualities very much like those of my deceased parents, or that I am repeating with my own children many of the mistakes I believe my parents made in raising me, mistakes I vowed I would never repeat when I became a parent. What I become aware of is what in some sense I already know about my parents, namely, how their qualities or actions relate to my own. Or there may be an immediate recognition of something as being closely associated with a living or dead person, which by virtue of this association summons up and draws attention to that person. I immediately recognize this weather-beaten catcher's mitt, say, as having been my coach's. (Note that this is different from knowing that this mitt belonged to my coach. I might know this without the mitt evoking my coach.) Whatever form it takes, recognition bestows on experiences the stamp of the familiar; it may dawn on us suddenly or gradually unfold, and sometimes we can help it along in more deliberate ways.

Although we sometimes set out to remember and succeed, memory recall is usually not a matter of conscious intention.[11] Indeed, memory recall characteristically has a contingent and random quality: memories just break into consciousness, unbidden by our wills. There is my deceased wife's picture, a picture I have not seen in years. At once, without any conscious or deliberate effort on my part, the memory of my wife comes flooding back. I fall into reminiscing with friends about our college days, and suddenly, without any prompting, we remember George, our deceased classmate, who is not here to join us. My brother calls on the telephone; immediately I recognize my late father's voice in the inflections of my brother's voice, and it is as if I am once again talking to my father. It is not necessarily regrettable that memory often comes to us this way. Memories are not less faithful to what we remember simply because they arise effortlessly, and some of our most moving memories may be ones that come to us without being summoned.

However, we can only properly speak about an *obligation* to remember the dead, and the dear departed in particular, if the having of such memories is attributable to us as our responsibility, and as we usually think about this, this is because there is something we can do to help ourselves remember and to avoid forgetting. Because this may be and typically is indirect, we should not assume that we can usually produce, retain, or eliminate such memories "at will." However, we can fulfill the imperative in other ways. We can, for example, rely on a variety of techniques and practices to assist memory recall.[12] We can also have a kind of negative control over our memories in that we are able to do something to resist their erosion. Indeed, this is normally how we comply with the imperative: simply by its willing acknowledgment and by freeing ourselves of motives that undermine it.[13] And of course, if we can be responsible for our memories in these various ways, so that it makes sense to speak about an obligation to remember, then forgetting may, in some instances, be a moral failing and one for which we can be rightly faulted.

3. EVALUATIVE ATTITUDES AND REMEMBERING THE DEAD: THE CASE OF LOVE

One way of answering the question about how we remember the dear departed is to describe the qualities and modes of remembering. As I have noted, one consequence of the personal nature of our relationship with them is that our memories are not confined to states of affairs in which they were implicated in actions or endowed with qualities. This is an important phenomenological difference between remembering the dear departed and remembering those we know only by description. We also remember the dear departed in various mnemonic modes. We remember them by being reminded of them and by reminiscing about them, and they are present to us more or less immediately in recognition. But the question about how we remember might also be asking about something different, namely, *the emotions and attitudes expressed in remembering.* This is the sense of the question to which I now turn, and I approach it by examining the specific case of remembering the dear departed as an expression of love.

I begin with some commonplaces about love. Genuine love of another, it is said, is independent of love of self; the test of its genuineness is whether the love continues even when there is no possible use of the other as a means to one's own good.[14] If this is correct, then the ideal test would seem to be whether love persists after the death of the loved one, for love of the dead cannot depend on getting anything from them. This, in fact, is Kierkegaard's view: one's relationship to the dead provides the criterion whereby one can test the genuineness of one's love. It is also his view that the most disinterested love is the love that is shown in one's relationship with the dead.

In *Works of Love*, Kierkegaard asserts that remembering the dead can be an expression of love and, furthermore, that "the work of love in remembering the dead is a work of the MOST UNSELFISH love" (320). Love for the living, in his view, usually involves self-interested motivation and is therefore impure. We may have a more or less disinterested concern for the well-being and flourishing of the beloved, but we also want and "hope that at some time he will reward our love" (321), that he will repay our love in some way. The repayment may take the form of material benefits and support and so be "heterogeneous, something different from the love itself" (320); or it may take "the form of gratitude, of thankfulness, of devotion, in short, of requited love," in which case it is "homogeneous with love" (321). Both are forms of repayment, although the second is perhaps less corrupting of love than the former. For many of us our love is so weak, or our self-love so strong, that we need "this encouraging prospect" if our love is to endure.

Kierkegaard makes a number of claims about the relationship between love, death, and memory. The first claim concerns the *conditions* under which truly unselfish love is possible: the love of those who lovingly remember the dead, in contrast to the love of the living, is the most disinterested love because the dead can make no repayment. The second claim is about how to *test* the unselfishness of one's love: the best test of the genuineness of our love is one that we cannot know we have passed until the loved one has died. Our motivations in loving the living are opaque to ourselves; rarely can we be sure that our love is not defective, that we are not deluding ourselves in thinking that our concern for the other is not egocentric. But if our love persists after the death of the beloved, this provides strong, indeed the strongest, evidence that our attitude toward him was not instrumental. The third claim, presupposed by the other two, is that remembering the dead can be a *work of love*.

It is the last of these claims that I find most promising and useful for my purposes, and I will spend the bulk of this section trying to understand how remembering the dear departed can be a work of love. For this task, I do not intend to engage in exegesis of Kierkegaard's views: I employ him merely as a point of departure, a way of posing a problem that needs philosophical analysis. However, before moving on, I want to say a few words in response to his other claims about love.

For Kierkegaard, whose account of personal love is deeply influenced by the Christian notion of agape, claims of the disinterestedness of love are always suspect when love is reciprocated. This may be a popular view, but the depth of the suspicion seems excessive, for there are ways to determine the disinterestedness of one's love that do not depend on the loved one's dying or inability to reciprocate. It is certainly possible, even unremarkable, to be mistaken about our true motivations when reflecting on the quality of our concern for the living person who reciprocates our love. But although it would be wrong to suppose that our motivations are always transparent to us, it would be the opposite error to suppose that someone who takes joy in forms of reciprocity with his or her loved one probably for that reason can't be trusted to stand by the loved one when it requires self-sacrifice. Moreover, self-deception is not only a possibility in connection with living persons whom we profess to love: we may also be self-deceived in thinking that our love for the dead is disinterested because we can get nothing from them. Even though the dead can no longer *do* anything to advance our good, there are various ways in which a loved one can continue to be instrumentally valuable to us even after his death. So, even death does not remove the "taint" of self-interest from our love. In short, the persistence of love after the death of the beloved is arguably not the only true test of the disinterestedness of that love, and love of the dead is not necessarily the most disinterested interpersonal love.

I turn now to the claim about remembering the dead as a work of love. If remembering the dead can be a work of love, then it must also be possible for remembering the dead to be an expression of love. And if remembering the dead can be an expression of love, the love must have a target. But this claim raises questions about who the object of this abiding love is. How shall we understand love for the dead? How can I, or can I, love someone when there is no one to love, when he or she is gone forever? Isn't my saying that I continue to love the dear departed merely an expression of my grief, something that I say because I have not yet come to terms with my loss? We may be tempted to dismiss these questions as little more than philosophers' worries, but I believe they speak to concerns that commonly arise in everyday life as we attempt to deal with the loss of a loved one and as the memory of the departed recedes. Moreover, in trying to formulate responses to these questions, we will have to address the nature of personal love itself, and this is another reason to take these questions seriously.

These worries about what it can mean to love the dead are reinforced by a particular account of the nature of love. Suppose we adopt a conative view according to which love has multiple aims and is constituted by "a particular syndrome of motives – primarily, desires to act upon, or inter-act with, the beloved,"[15] to benefit, to share, and be with, the beloved.

From this it seems to follow that those who claim to express an attitude of love in how they remember the dead – and who hold no theory of human immortality – are either not thinking clearly or are speaking figuratively. For if one does not believe in any sort of survival after death, one must believe that the deceased are incapable of experiencing anything and, therefore, that they cannot interact with anyone or share anything with anyone. This suggests a conclusion about loving, and lovingly remembering, the dead that echoes a criticism some philosophers have made of the notion of posthumous harm and wrong. Joan Callahan, for example, claims that although "we certainly can do things that are wrong which pertain to the interests the dead had as living persons," all arguments for harm or wrong *to* the dead must fail because "there simply is no subject to suffer the harm."[16] The lack of a subject precludes our pretheoretic intuitions regarding harm and wrong to the dead from being genuinely moral convictions and compels us to account for them entirely in psychological terms, or so she and others argue.

Drawing on a conative or desire-based account of love, the notion of love for the dear departed would be explained as follows. Because there is no longer a person to be benefited by our love, to share and be with, continuing to love a person after his death in the way we remember him can only mean the following (again, assuming no belief in an afterlife): we are loving his memory not him, or we have desires that must by their very nature remain unfulfilled, or both. From the standpoint of this account of love, we may say that we love the dead, but because love is constituted by a particular directed set of desires, and these cannot take the dead as their object, we are not really doing what we claim to be doing or, unlike usual cases, we have desires that are for something that is unobtainable, and which we know to be so. According to the first possibility, when we say in everyday conversation that we continue to love S after his death in remembering him as we do, what we are doing is thinking of the dead S as the person he was when alive and cherishing our memories of him. To be sure, sometimes those who remember the dead do say they want to be with them again, perhaps even to join them in death. Remarks like this, common in the early phase of mourning but persisting in some form well beyond it, convey the survivor's deep sense of loss and abandonment, and they may only indicate a desire for things to be as they were before the beloved died, not a belief in an afterlife. This leads to the second possibility. According to this possibility, we very much want things that we know are just impossible for us to have – namely, a relationship with the formerly living or deceased person and all that this involves.[17] Desires that cannot be satisfied may be futile and irrational, but because they are still desires, the conditions of the conative analysis would be satisfied.

We sometimes speak about cherishing the *loved one who is now deceased* and sometimes about cherishing *memories* of him or her. The conative analysis of love either effectively collapses loving the deceased person into cherishing his memory, or it interprets loving the deceased person as constituted by a necessarily frustrating kind of desiring, a desiring for the impossible. I take it that these implications of the conative account show its inadequacies. With respect to the first possibility, intuitively, there is a significant difference between cherishing the person and cherishing our memories of him, so that cherishing the person is not reducible to the latter. With respect to the second possibility, love for the dear departed, as distinct from cherishing his memory, may involve desires for the unattainable, but these desires may wane without endangering the love or diminishing its quality.

Central to the alternative conception of love that I propose, and which the conative analysis leaves out, is love's evaluative dimension. This conception is shared by a cluster of related views, all of which converge on the proposition that love is a way of *valuing* a person. It is not defined by desires to be with, to share, or to benefit, although commonly we do have these desires with respect to persons we love. Love is, as David Velleman puts it, "the awareness of a value inhering in its object ... an arresting awareness of that value,"[18] not inherently an urge or impulse toward anything. There are different accounts of what we are valuing when we love. According to Velleman, what we value is the rational nature of the other, which he clarifies as follows: "a capacity of appreciation or valuation – a capacity to care about things in that reflective way which is distinctive of self-conscious creatures like us."[19] Niko Kolodny thinks the main shortcoming of this account is its inability to explain the partiality of love and argues instead that what we value in love is the relationship we have with the loved one. Because our valuing the other is inseparable from our valuing the relationship, those who love us "cannot respond appropriately to the value of their relationship to us without also valuing us."[20] Both accounts, I believe, are problematic,[21] but I will suppose that the basic claim about love is sound and that a persuasive argument can be given for it. In the context of this discussion about loving the dead, the claim is significant for the following reason: the possibility of continuing to love seems to be unaffected by the bare fact that after death there is simply no subject to enjoy benefits or share our lives with. If love is centrally a matter of valuing, and we can continue to value a person in this way after (indeed, long after) his death, then love can persist even if we cannot have a relationship with the deceased.

An account of love as a way of valuing a person provides the beginnings of a response to worries about what happens to our love when the loved one dies. The dead, as dead, cannot be benefited or harmed by our remembering or forgetting them, or by what we do when we remember them, and we may have few unfulfilled desires of the sort the conative analysis requires. Nevertheless, we can value the dead in the way we remember them. Those we value do survive, psychologically speaking, in our memories of them, in more or less vivid images that we can sometimes summon up or that, perhaps more frequently, we recall without conscious intention. But it is not only the memories of deceased loved ones that we can value and cherish: we can also cherish the *deceased loved ones themselves*, both before death and in lovingly remembering them after death. How is this to be explained?

This can be explained by noting that we are not limited to the following two possibilities for the object of our love in these cases: either (i) the memories of the formerly living person, the person who, in a manner of speaking, lives on in those memories, or (ii) the postmortem person, i.e., the dead body. Possibility (i) would be the correct account if these were the only choices because plainly lovingly remembering the dead is not usually taken to mean loving a corpse. There is a third possibility, however: (iii) the object of our love, and so of our valuing, is *the person now dead as he was when alive.*[22]

Obviously, this third possibility needs to be formulated in a more nuanced way, for the clause "as he was when alive" cannot plausibly be interpreted to mean that the object of our love is the person now dead as he was through his entire life, from birth to death. Rather, the person I continue to love after his death is the person as I knew him; the person who possessed particular qualities that I came to love precisely because they were the qualities of someone I loved; the person with whom

I shared experiences and activities that were stored in our memories and that constituted the narrative history of our lives together; and so forth. The person I continue to love after his death, like the person I loved when he was alive, is this particular irreplaceably valuable person as he is known to me through a history of shared intimacy. Love of the now dead person is love of him as he was when alive, not as he was for all the time that he was alive but as he was in our lives together.

A similar analysis can be given of honoring the dead (honoring is another mode of valuing). Honoring dead persons is not equivalent to honoring their memory or honoring postmortem persons.[23] There is a third possibility: when we honor the dead we engage in behaviors, actions, gestures, modes of address, that are, and are commonly understood to be, expressive of a particular way of valuing now dead persons as they were in their antemortem state. That *for* which or in virtue of which the person is loved are intrinsic or relational qualities of the living person (love of the dear departed is obviously not love of his remains) and that for which the person is honored are deeds performed during his or her lifetime. But on this analysis, our love and honor *concern* the dead person.

The love we express in remembering the dear departed is not, therefore, just the cherishing of an idea or an image held in memory but is directed toward the person him or herself as its object. Of course, those who continue to love the dear departed will normally cherish at least some of their memories of them. But that there is a distinction between cherishing the dead person and cherishing his memory is suggested by the fact that it is possible for one's memories to take on a life of their own, as it were, and for one to become so enamored of them that one loses sight of the deceased one him or herself. Somewhat like the sentimentalist who attaches value to a symbol and then absorbs herself in the sentiments evoked by the symbol at the expense of real interests, including the very interests the symbol represents,[24] one can sentimentally cherish one's memories of the deceased loved one without cherishing the deceased one him or herself.

The contention that we really can continue to love someone even after his or her death is bolstered by the following considerations. First, consider the following example. Suppose my beloved Lori travels to Peru to aid the local revolutionaries in their fight for social justice. For a time I hear nothing from her, and I do not know whether she is alive or dead. Would I – should I – say I love her only if she is alive? This seems to have no justification in the notion of love, and similar examples can be constructed for other evaluative attitudes.

Second, there are norms for expressing love of the deceased that overlap norms for expressing love of the living, and this enhances the plausibility of my argument. According to Elizabeth Anderson, each way of valuing something is governed by distinctive norms for that mode of valuation, and love in particular

> involves the performance of many actions which express that love, which show the beloved that he or she has a special importance to the lover. It entails particular ways of deliberating about questions concerning what is valued.... [it] includes distinctive emotional responses to the apprehension, achievement, and loss of things related to what is valued.[25]

Norms for the expression of love for the dead (as he or she was when alive) have much in common with norms for emotion, deliberation, and conduct that express love for the living. We show that we love the dead, in contrast to (say) honor the dead, by the particular way we remember them, that is, by the particular ways we are prone to feel, think, and act in relation to those now dead and whose loss we continue to experience. We thereby demonstrate not only that the person *had* special importance to us when alive, but that he or she continues to have the same sort of importance to us, though now dead. For example, romantic love involves despondency at the beloved's lack of reciprocation, and this despondency is felt both when the beloved *fails* to reciprocate because of indifference or callousness and when the beloved *can't* reciprocate because she has died. Love also involves grief at the loved one being harmed, and we are not only grieved by harmful actions that occur during his or her lifetime. We experience grief when our loved one's reputation is posthumously slandered and this, in conjunction with other ways of feeling, thinking, and acting in relation to him or her, testifies to our continuing love.

This overlap between norms concerning living persons and those concerning deceased persons is only partial, however, because the death of someone we care about both limits and creates new expressive possibilities.[26] There are many ways of expressing love for and devotion to the living, for example, that are not possible or appropriate with respect to the dead. Moreover, it is only with respect to the living that the various expressions of love can elicit, from the loved one, responses that modify the expression of love. Because many of the modes of expressing love for the living are not possible with the dead, survivors who continue to love develop repertoires of expressive acts that are adapted to the changed circumstances. Rituals of remembrance and symbolic acts of various sorts assume particular importance in this context.[27] But opportunities for further give-and-take with the loved one and mutual responsiveness are irrecoverably lost. Recognition of this incontrovertible fact, that *we have no future with the dear departed*, is sometimes accompanied by feelings of guilt over an imagined abandonment of the loved one, and it largely explains the grief, the pain, and sadness, that typically infuse these substitute expressions of love.

Love is but one mode of valuing persons. Honor, respect, and reverence – each governed by its own expressive norms and embodied in conventionally defined and accepted practices – are others, and sometimes the dead are appropriately valued in one or more of these ways. We cannot communicate to the dead that they are or remain important to us, of course. Nevertheless, we can express our continuing regard for them, and communicate that regard to the living, in the various ways we remember them. The dead are retained as internalized presences for us through memory in its various modes, but it is not the memories alone that we value and cherish.

If love is a way of valuing persons, the work of love in remembering the dead – to return to this notion – is also a work of valuing or, more precisely, continuing to value a loved one after his or her death, despite "the multiplicity of life's demands" that press on us and make this valuing a challenge and an achievement. This work of love, as well as other sorts of memorial work that express evaluative attitudes toward the dead, can be explained in the terms used by psychologists and grief counselors, as a natural psychological reaction to the death of a loved one or a form of emotional release. But in addition, each sort of work involves a mode of caring for and valuing another, and so, broadly speaking, they fall within the moral domain and are of moral significance, although, of course, instances of them can be morally flawed.

4. CONSEQUENTIALISM AND AN EXPRESSIVE ACCOUNT

Before presenting some arguments for a moral imperative[28] to remember the dear departed, I want to sketch in general terms the justificatory strategy that they employ. Its distinctive character will become clearer if it is set against and distinguished from another approach to justification, that of consequentialism.

(a) *Consequentialism*

With respect to remembering the dead in general, one standard type of explanation of the imperative takes the following form: we ought to remember the dead because of the good consequences that remembering them brings about or makes likely,[29] consequences that otherwise would not be realized or that would be less likely. Call views of this type *consequentialist* views. Consequentialist views about remembering the dead sometimes focus on the fact that the dead were innocent victims of wrongdoing and instruct us to remember them under this description. It is a common theme among those who regard themselves as bearing witness[30] to the forgotten, neglected, or untold suffering of history's victims that there is an intimate connection between remembering past horrors and opening up future possibilities where past horrors do not recur. For example, Primo Levi, a survivor of the Nazi death camps, writes: "the need to recount to 'others', to make the 'others' participate" in the horrors of Auschwitz "acquired in us before and after our liberation the vehemence of an immediate impulse." This impulse had for him a definite moral quality; his remembrances were motivated by his sense of a moral imperative: "people must never be allowed to forget lest it happen again."[31]

There are various explanations for why remembering is so important to the achievement of this goal. One explanation stresses the value of punishment: we should remember the victims (and the wrongs done to them) so that we don't forget the perpetrators, and we should remember the perpetrators because they should be punished for their wrongdoing. Punishing them will deter others from committing similar wrongs in the future. Another explanation emphasizes the value of forgiveness: remembering the victims (and the wrongs) keeps the memory of wrongdoing alive and this is required if genuine forgiveness of the perpetrators is to be possible. Memory is necessary here because forgiving wrongdoing is not the same as forgetting it. Moreover, there are sometimes good consequentialist reasons in favor of forgiving all or some of the perpetrators that outweigh whatever good may result from punishing them, for forgiveness may do more to curtail future wrongdoing than punishment in some circumstances.[32]

Memory is essential to the operations of punishment and forgiveness, which can make future wrongdoing less likely, but memory can help promote this goal in others ways as well. For example, another consequentialist justification looks to the relationship between remembering wrongdoing and establishing institutional safeguards against future wrongdoing. Remembering the victims of wrongdoing may be an essential part of a process of building and sustaining political structures that safeguard against a return to the wrongs of the past. Jürgen Habermas, in his contribution to the so-called historians' debate in Germany over how to respond to the legacy of National Socialism, speaks of an obligation inherited by present and future generations of Germans to remember, and to constantly renew the memory of, the victims of Nazi atrocities. He is not opposed to Germans distancing themselves from the Nazi past, only to its being done in such a way as to "cast off the burdens of a past happily no longer morally constraining." On the contrary, properly done, "the work of gaining distance and understanding liberates the power of reflective memory, thus enlarging our capacity to work out ambivalent legacies on our own."[33] Thus, the obligation of memory is not, for Habermas, an obligation of simple recall, or only an obligation to acknowledge and atone for the sufferings of the victims, but an obligation to employ memory in the service of social and political reconstruction. And memory is essential for this, he claims, for it is only by keeping alive the memory of those murdered by the Nazis and continually reminding itself of their fate that post-war Germany can avoid a return to traditional nationalism and militarism and fully enter the community of nations committed to liberal political values and the protection of human rights.

Also motivated by consequentialist considerations was Lincoln's invocation of the memory of the brave men who fought and died at Gettysburg. We, the living, he said, must dedicate ourselves to completing the "unfinished work they have thus far so nobly carried on": preserving the Union and ensuring survival of the principles of liberty and equality upon which our nation was founded. In so dedicating ourselves, we must not forget those who gave their lives. We must remember their sacrifices and take "from these honored dead . . . increased devotion to the cause for which they here gave the last full measure of devotion." Lincoln's address, partly meant to honor the war dead, also had a clear consequentialist purpose: it was intended to invoke their memory to spur the living to complete their work. Memory also played another role once the war ended, for the work was not completed, in Lincoln's view, simply with the victory of the North. What was needed to bring the war to a successful conclusion was a process of national healing and reconciliation, and this required forgiveness (rather than punishment) of those who sought to destroy the Union.

Remembering the dear departed, as a psychological phenomenon and as a moral imperative, differs in a number of ways from these and similar cases. When, as in the Levi, Habermas, and Lincoln examples, consequentialist considerations are invoked to justify a moral imperative to remember the dead, the dead whom we are admonished to remember are not particular individuals. They are *groups* of individuals: victims of political and religious persecution and racial genocide, soldiers who gave their lives in defense of country, and so on. Even if among those we remember are some who were personally known to us, perhaps even friends and loved ones, we are chiefly called on to remember them in these cases under a generic description, as one among many who suffered or sacrificed.[34] In cases of remembering the dear departed, by contrast, the fact that this was my friend or loved one does enter into how I remember them and should certainly have a bearing on how a moral imperative to remember them is interpreted. Memory of them differs, and should differ, from memory of persons qua members of certain groups or from memory of groups of persons. In addition, if remembering the dear departed is some kind of moral imperative, it would seem to be an imperative only for or especially for particular individuals, whereas those who are called on to remember in these examples are called on as persons with some general characteristic in common (e.g., descendants of the perpetrators or perhaps humanity at large[35]).

Let me expand on this. Remembering the victims of war and genocide *only* as generic victims of wrongdoing might be deeply regrettable; it might even be thought to do them a kind of injustice in the sense that there is much more to the story of their lives than their having been victims. So long as we remember them in this way – nameless, without an individual identity – the perpetrators may seem to have nearly accomplished their goal of totally eradicating their victims. For this reason, one might feel a kind of obligation to learn more about some of the victims in order to put a "human face" on their suffering.[36] With respect to the dear departed, however, the sense that we should not just remember them in terms of what was done to them by their victimizers is particularly strong, and properly so. Of course, because we already know a great deal about them, we *can* remember them in other ways as well, something which is not possible with most victims of large-scale wrongdoing. But it is not this ability alone that distinguishes the dear departed from the others. The distinction is arguably a moral one as well: because these are individuals with whom we had some sort of personal relationship and who occupied a particularly important place in our lives, we ought to remember them in ways that reflect how we knew them in life.

A final point of contrast: the type of consequentialist argument for remembering the dead that I have discussed so far concerns persons who died as a result of wrongdoing or who lost their lives in the fight against it. But as we will see, there are good and compelling reasons for remembering the dear departed that have nothing to do with their having been the victims of wrongdoing.

There are also consequentialist arguments for an imperative to remember the dear departed, and they appeal to valuable consequences of different sorts, including what certain ways of remembering do for the rememberer. For one thing, reflecting back on those who played a formative role in our lives and on our relationship to them may generate insights into how we became the sorts of persons we are and thus into our present identities.[37] With the passage of time, a certain critical detachment from our present selves may become possible so that we can better understand how our current values, beliefs, and dispositions have been influenced and shaped, for better or worse, by those we cared about and who cared about us. In this way, remembrance – which makes the dear departed available and accessible to us – facilitates self-understanding and self-development, which, in relation to matters of serious import, are essential ingredients of a human life that is well lived.

Remembering the dear departed (or, more precisely, the healthy remembering that is integral to mourning) is also beneficial from a therapeutic standpoint: it enables psychic healing so that the survivor can face the work of building a future, free of debilitating emotional disturbances. It is psychic healing in the sense that it involves the recovery of what Norman Care calls "the effectiveness of one's agency, that is, the effectiveness of one's capacity to control the content in one's life, including facing up to the next challenge that comes along in one's workplace or personal life."[38] Although we do not normally remember the dear departed *in order to* restore effective agency, recovery is facilitated by mourning and mourning is itself a way of remembering them.[39] C. S. Lewis movingly describes remembering his dead wife or, rather, a form of remembering that he achieved with difficulty, and notes its therapeutic effect:

> ... as I have discovered, passionate grief does not link us with the dead but cuts us off from them. This becomes clearer and clearer. It is just at those moments when I feel least sorrow – getting into my morning bath is one of them – that H [his wife] rushes upon my mind in her full reality, her otherness. Not, as in my worst moments, all foreshortened and patheticized and solemnized by miseries, but as she is in her own right. This is good and tonic.[40]

In the state of "passionate grief," the survivor clings desperately to the memories of his loved one as the main means of access to the person he has lost. However, if we persist in clinging to our memories with passionate grief, or if we repress our memories of the dear departed, we cannot properly work through our loss, and this will have a corrosive effect on our capacity to move on with our lives.[41]

In summary, when we reflect on why, if at all, we should remember the dead, the question is often thought to require an answer that appeals to the good that is promoted by remembering. The answer typically takes a consequentialist form, for consequentialism holds that the moral quality or value of actions (and not only of actions) is dependent on the good that is produced by them, in this case, by acts of remembrance. To determine this, we have to know *whose* good it is that one ought to promote, and consequentialist views differ on this. It may be one's own greatest good, or the greatest general good, or the greatest balance of good over bad for a certain group – one's nation, class, family, or race. But as I will now argue, consequentialism, in any event, provides only part of the answer to why we ought to remember the dead, and with respect to the dear departed, it misses something critical.

(b) *Expressivism*

A view is consequentialist if it has at least the following features: it specifies some intrinsically valuable states of affairs and assesses the value of actions, motives, practices, or dispositions in terms of how effectively they bring about or embody the best states of affairs (maximizing consequentialism) or states of affairs that, although not necessarily the best, are good enough by some measure (satisficing consequentialism). As applied to the case at hand, consequentialism tells us that we ought to remember the dead if and only if doing so can be expected to promote or embody a better state of affairs than available alternatives or at least a good enough state of affairs.

There is, however, another very different way of arguing for a moral imperative to remember: not in terms of the *good to be promoted* by remembering but rather the kinds of *attitudes that are called for* toward those who have died. In this alternative view, which I call an expressive account of remembering,[42] we ought to remember the dead not (or not only) because we ought to bring about certain consequences, and we do this *by* remembering, but because certain attitudes are called for toward the dead and we express them *in* how we remember.

Generally speaking, an expressive theory of morality rejects the conception of value held by consequentialists. For consequentialists, the fundamental object of value is the state of affairs and believing that the object is valuable involves believing that there is reason to bring it about. Even if consequentialists attend to the expressive dimension of action, it has, for them, only a derivative importance. However, the reasons involved in something being valuable do not only take an instrumental form, and there are numerous instances in which it is the attitudes our actions express, not the consequences they produce, that have paramount importance. For example, one who values the friendship he has with another person does not see his friendship as promoting some state of affairs that will make the world a better place, and he does not believe that he ought to do things for his friend because or insofar as it will do so.[43] Expressive theories need not deny the value of promoting good consequences, and some expressive views might even be hospitable to consequentialist thinking about value in certain cases. But they all reject, as impoverished, a purely teleological conception of value, and they focus their attention, instead, on an aspect of action neglected by consequentialists. With respect to remembering the dead, in particular, an expressive account concerns itself chiefly not with the consequences of remembering, but with whether the deceased are properly valued in the way we remember them and with how we should express our valuing in our memorial actions.

Because it is doubtful that we can properly ascribe the evaluative attitudes expressed in remembering the dead to someone who does not desire and make some effort to express this valuing by promoting certain ends – for example, by carrying on with or bringing to completion some of the deceased's cherished projects, by donating money to one of his favorite charities in his name, and so on – an expressive account of remembering is not indifferent to whether one aims to bring about certain states of affairs. However, in this sort of view, one does not try to bring about some state of affairs because one believes it is a good thing to do, independent of whatever value or importance the deceased has for oneself. Rather, one desires to do something and makes an effort to do it for the sake of or in recognition of the deceased person (i.e., it is with a view to the deceased person that one is motivated to act) and doing it *in remembrance* of one who has died is an essential part of what makes it a good thing to do. The goodness of doing something in remembrance of a beloved spouse, for example, is partly constituted by its being a way of expressing one's love for one's spouse. Thus, on an expressive account of remembering, in contrast to consequentialist accounts, the value of promoting states of affairs is usually derivative in this sense: it, intrinsically, depends on whether promoting them expresses an appropriate valuation of the person one cares about, that is, on whether, in so acting, we are properly valuing them.

Expressive theories appeal to norms of expressive appropriateness in evaluating action, and all such norms have the following imperative form, according to Elizabeth Anderson: "act so as to adequately express attitude B toward Z."[44] As I argued in Section 3, there are different ways of remembering the dead, that is, different attitudes toward the dead that remembering can express. On an expressive account, we specify a moral imperative to remember the dead by appealing to norms that tell us what attitudes to express toward the dead and that enable us to distinguish between inadequate and adequate ways of expressing these attitudes. The imperatives of an expressive account are imperatives of appropriate valuation or expressive appropriateness, and they can also be formulated using the language of moral duty or obligation, that is, as duties or obligations to express such-and-such attitudes in such-and-such ways. In this view, in order to determine, in each case, what a moral imperative to remember the dead requires us to do, we need to be sensitive to the variety of expressive norms and ways of adequately expressing attitudes.

As I have characterized them, an *expressive theory* and an *expressive account of remembering* specifically address both the appropriateness of the attitudes expressed and the adequacy of their expression. It is important to stress this because appropriateness and adequacy can come apart. We might adequately express attitude B based on our belief that it is the appropriate sort of attitude to have toward Z, but our belief might be mistaken. For example, the problem might not be that we don't know how to honor Z, but rather that we are wrong to think Z should be honored at all, either while he is alive or after his death. What we are doing, therefore, might be adequately expressing what would, under different circumstances, be an appropriate attitude to have toward the object of our attentions. There can also be inadequate expression of an appropriate attitude. It might be appropriate to honor Z, and we might recognize this, but we might not do enough or not do the right things to express it. An expressive account of the obligations of memory recognizes these different possibilities and directs us to ask questions both about whether certain attitudes are called for toward others and about the ways we should express them. The answers to these questions will very much depend on the details of individual cases.

This discussion of how an expressive theory differs from consequentialism in the way it understands and defends a moral imperative to remember the dead sets the stage for various nonconsequentialist arguments for an imperative to remember the dear departed that I take up in Section 5.

5. THE MORAL IMPERATIVE TO REMEMBER:
THREE ARGUMENTS

The attitudes expressed in remembering the dead and that constitute ways of valuing them are varied, reflective in part of the kind of relationship that we had with them. When we remember a revered teacher, and this inspires us to follow his teachings after his death, we thereby show the high esteem in which we continue to hold him. The valuing we seek to express in living our lives this way is not only a valuing of his teachings but a valuing of him, expressed in this particular reverential way. In the Jewish practice of *Yizkor*, recalling a deceased parent and contributing to charity in his or her name is an act of homage and profound respect that expresses not just my concern for those who may benefit from my good deeds but the value my parent had and continues to have to me. Remembering a deceased child involves thoughts, emotions, and actions that constitute the particular mode of valuation that is parental love. These are some of the expressive meanings of remembering the dear departed, some of the ways we continue to value them through remembering them after their deaths. Arguments for a moral imperative to remember the dead that look entirely to consequences, as these are understood by consequentialism, either miss or misplace the importance of expressing our concerns for other people in the ways we remember them. Expressing concerns in these ways is important and called for because these are fitting or appropriate ways of valuing other people and any argument for a moral imperative to remember the dead that involves such notions must contain clearly nonconsequentialist elements.

What I am trying to capture in these arguments is what I take to be a common and familiar experience – the sense of a certain *demand* in connection with remembering the dear departed – and each argument attempts to provide a theoretical foundation for this. The sense that we should not forget those dear to us who are dead, and that we are especially at fault if we do so, is powerful and widely shared, but its justifying grounds have not been adequately explored.

(a) *The rescue from insignificance view*

According to the first argument, remembrance is a chief means by which we overcome the finality of death and through which we affirm that death has not obliterated the significance of the one who has died. The key notion here is that of *significance*.

Thomas Nagel, in an early article on "The Absurd,"[45] claims that from a certain standpoint, "a nebula's-eye view" (p. 21), human life seems arbitrary and trivial. When I step back from the purposes of individual life and survey myself and the life to which I am committed *sub specie aeternitatis*, there seems to be no reason why I or anything that I do with my life matters. From this point of view, the history of human life, not to mention that of any individual human life, is supremely unimportant. But, he goes on, although human beings have the capacity to adopt this perspective, they do not as a matter of course live their lives from this standpoint.[46] The step into self-transcendence does not "give us an understanding of what is *really* important, so that we see by contrast that our lives are insignificant. We never, in the course of these reflections, abandon the ordinary standards that guide our lives" (17). For the most part, we take ourselves seriously and assiduously pursue our everyday projects and goals, despite the fact that there is a point of view from which we and all that matters to us seem not to matter at all. We do not ordinarily view ourselves as mere specks floating in an infinite, impersonal cosmos.

In confronting death (our own or someone else's), it is not unusual to entertain thoughts of the cosmic unimportance of any and all human life. The acknowledgment of our mortality seems to invite such deflationary reflections. But in living our lives, we generally put such thoughts out of our minds, and we do something similar in remembering the dead: the point of view they took toward their own lives is the one that is authoritative for us. That is, remembering the dead serves as a way of acknowledging the significance of their lives (and so of their having lived), not *sub specie aeternitatis*, not to the world or to society, but to *them* in a way that each of us can appreciate because it is natural for us to take ourselves seriously. In this way, we declare that it really does matter that *they* lived, and we affirm that their lives had point and meaning. Elie Wiesel suggests a similar thought in his answer to the question, "Why is memory important?" "To remember . . . is to say no to the sand of time covering the landscape of our being, it is to say no to forgetfulness, no to death."[47]

If it really matters that we exist and, therefore, that we existed, then it is imperative for the living to acknowledge this in some way, assuming there are no overriding reasons not to do so. (For example, we may not be able to bring ourselves to acknowledge the significance of someone's having existed because this conflicts with our self-respect, although there may be consequentialist reasons why we ought to remember.) Otherwise we concede that death robs our lives of meaning after all. Remembering is not our only avenue to the dead or the only means of acknowledging the significance of a person's having lived. But the injunction not to forget the dead derives its moral force, in part, from this important function of memory.

Affirming the significance of a person's *having lived* is not the same as affirming the value of *how he lived*. In some cases, a person's deeds and pursuits may have little or no value (or even negative value), so it would be inappropriate to give them positive recognition, either during his lifetime or after his death. If there is a moral imperative to remember such a person, it cannot be because remembering him is a way of acknowledging the worth of what he did with his life. But the present argument does not hold that we should only remember those persons whose actions and aspirations warrant the approval of reasonable or decent people. Even if there is little to admire about a person's life, and perhaps much to fault in his character, we can, and sometimes should, validate his significance as a human being in the minimal, existential sense of "significance" employed here. Hence, the moral imperative to remember the dead isn't canceled simply because there are moral or other grounds for criticizing the content of their lives.[48]

There are of course countless numbers of people who ought to be remembered for this reason, and no one person can be responsible for remembering them all. What the argument establishes so far is only that having significance is a basis for a moral imperative to remember the dead. Because this claim is indeterminate with respect to how the imperative is to be discharged and only demarcates a field of possible responsibility, we need to have some principled way of narrowing down that field, of determining who is responsible for remembering which specific people. In the case at hand, to whom should we assign the responsibility for rescuing these particular persons who are my loved ones (or my friends, or esteemed teachers, and so on) from insignificance by remembering them? A plausible principle is that if anyone deserves recognition from me for having existed, my loved ones do, and that if anyone ought to remember them, to rescue them from insignificance, I should. It is because of quite specific forms of connection that I have an obligation to remember those I loved, cherished, or esteemed and that *they*, in particular, should be rescued from oblivion by *me*. (Of course, those who never knew the deceased cannot remember him or her *as* the dear departed, but they can remember this person under another description.) These connections are found in the history of our relationship, in what we have come to mean to each other, and in the particular expectations, dependencies, and intimacies that give rise to special loyalties and ties.

In an expressivist analysis, we are not to focus on the consequences of remembering but on the evaluative attitudes remembering expresses, and we are to reflect on whether such attitudes are called for and on how they are adequately expressed in particular cases. What attitude(s) is (are) associated with the Rescue from Insignificance View? The following observation by James Hatley provides a clue: "The rites of mourning respond to the *dignity of one's having existed* [italics added] by giving a public and cultural expression to the fact that one's passing on belongs to other human beings as well."[49] The "dignity of one's having existed" is presumably closely connected with the dignity of an individual human life, and there are different accounts of its grounding. Most commonly, dignity is said to be based on the capacity to make rational or autonomous decisions, reflecting the influence of Kant, who held that the basis of dignity is the unconditional value that persons possess in virtue of being ends-in-themselves or free rational agents. Other accounts do not ground the possession of dignity in rationality or in autonomy, or in these alone, but in the irreplaceability of the individual or in the relationships of care that we have with one another.[50] Whatever the account, dignity is distinguished from other values in that it calls on persons to respond to it in ways that express a type of attitude that we call "respect." Different accounts of the basis of dignity will be associated with different ways of appropriately responding to it, but respect is the generic term that we normally use to refer to the mode of valuing human beings qua possessors of dignity. Hence, remembrance, insofar as it is a response to "the dignity of one's having existed," expresses respect for the deceased. Simply remembering others after their deaths, and not allowing them to pass into oblivion, can sometimes be an expression of this respect, and there are other ways to express it as well. Through respectful memory, we respond to the dignity of their having existed, thereby affirming that their lives had a point that not even death can reduce to insignificance. The evaluative attitude of respect is compatible with love and can be combined with it and others, but it is a distinctive mode of valuation.

(b) *The enduring duties view*

In the Rescue from Insignificance View, the obligation to remember the dead belongs in the first instance to those who were their friends or loved ones and can remember them under this description. Who, we might ask, is more appropriate than, or better situated than, a person's friend or loved one to remember him after his death and thereby rescue him from oblivion? In the argument to which I now turn, personal relationships play a different role. They do not serve as a basis for assigning obligations to rescue from insignificance to specific persons but are themselves a source of obligations.

The Enduring Duties View grounds duties to remember the dead on duties to the living and a backward-looking, nonconsequentialist analysis of posthumous duties. It holds that although duties are not owed to the dead, as such, they can persist beyond the death of the person to whom the duties are owed, and that their breach wrongs the person as he was when alive. The view holds further that in the case of the dear departed, duties of love and honor (among others) persist as duties to remember them in ways that are expressive of these attitudes. The Enduring Duties View, applied to the dear departed, thus makes the following series of claims: (1) we have special duties to persons with whom we have close personal relationships, including duties of love and honor; (2) death by itself does not cancel these duties; and (3) duties to remember in ways appropriate to the dear departed flow from or instantiate duties of love and honor, among others.

With respect to the first claim, it is often argued that we cannot summon up love and honor at will, and that because "ought implies can," we cannot have duties of love and honor. I believe that this conclusion is mistaken but not because I reject the claim that the feelings associated with love and honor are not subject to our immediate volitional control. For one thing, although they may not be voluntary in any straightforward way, this does not mean that the attitudes are beyond our control. For another, love and honor engage attitudes that are sensitive to reasons. Specifically, persons who love and honor another are prone to attend to and be moved by certain reasons for action and to downplay, or exclude from consideration both other reasons that support the same action as well as at least some countervailing reasons. For example, if x loves y, x will normally take y's being in distress to be a reason in favor of offering y emotional support and will downplay, or disregard, other reasons in favor of doing so (such as, y's father was always kind to x) and other reasons for not doing so (such as, it is inconvenient for x to do so). In other words, if x loves y, x will be motivated to offer support chiefly because y is in distress, and this reason will have a categorical quality for x because he grants it an importance in his deliberations that protects it against many (but not all) countervailing considerations.

Duties of love, duties of honor, and the like can be explained in terms of the reasons that structure a person's regard for the object of his love or honor. For example, offering support because y is in distress is a *duty of love*: it is an action that one necessarily treats as one's duty if one relates to another person the way a genuinely loving person does.[51] In general, duties of love and honor exist because there are distinctive patterns of privileged and protected reasons that persons who love and honor recognize and respond to.[52] Moreover, the principle "ought implies can" is satisfied, for although we cannot produce or retain such attitudes at will, agency is nevertheless expressed in the evaluative judgments we make concerning those we love and honor and our sensitivity to the reasons these judgments reflect.[53]

Let us now move on to the second claim. It is uncontroversial that we can be faulted for not fulfilling duties of love and honor, assuming there are such, even if the person to whom the duties are owed could, but never does, find out about our failures. Indeed, we can fail to do what we ought to do, namely, show the honor or concern that is called for, even if the person can never discover this because he is incapacitated. Taking this one step further, we can be faulted for not fulfilling duties of love and honor even if the person can never find out that we have failed to do so because this takes place after his death. This can be explained without having to suppose that there are such things as duties to the dead. Posthumous or surviving duties are duties that exist *now*, but the failure to fulfill them is a wrong to the person as he was *then*, when he was alive. The basis for the claim of surviving duties is the following: although the *bearer* of the correlative right has died, *moral reasons* for having a duty toward the deceased are implied by the reasons for attributing the corresponding right to the person when he was alive. These reasons survive, though the bearer of the right does not. In this analysis, although the death of a person may open up new possibilities for the expression of love and honor and close off others, a formerly grounded duty does not suddenly become null and void merely because the person, being dead, can no longer experience our concern.[54] The Enduring Duties View, it should be noted, does not claim that duties of love or honor *always* survive the death of the one to whom they were owed, so it allows that the circumstances of the person's death might be such as to relieve of us these duties. It maintains only that the death of a person does not, just by itself, relieve us of these duties.

According to the third claim, we fulfill duties of love and honor after a person has died by remembering him or her in ways that express our continuing love and honor. Memorial acts expressive of love and honor for the deceased cover a wide range, including engaging in various kinds of ritualized practice, contributing to charity in the deceased's name, taking up projects dear to the deceased and trying to bring them to fruition, and sharing memories of the deceased with one's family and intimates. Such acts have both a personal and a public side: they are invested with deep personal and emotional significance for the survivor, but many of them also have tangible form in objects, practices, speech acts, and so forth whose memorial significance can be recognized by others. At the same time, the very objectivity of these memorial tributes and their existence in the world apart from the meaning bestowed on them by the survivor may contain the seeds of a kind of forgetting: forgetting their point and the expressive meanings they once embodied. This, combined with the passage of time, can cause us to lose sight of those for whose sake we have done these things.

Remembering the dear departed, as an expression of caring, testifies to the depth and steadfastness of our emotional attachment to the person who has died. Those who treat remembrance as their duty, according to this account, are committed to sustain an attitude of valuing the loved or honored person as especially important in their lives, even after that person's death. Sometimes, as in the case of a child's relationship to his or her parents, or a student's relationship to his or her revered teacher, love and honor are intermingled with gratitude for benefits bestowed. In these cases, the recipient of the benefits is motivated to remember his or her benefactor partly out of gratitude, and the acts of remembrance involve expressions of gratitude. But even if we do not *feel* gratitude, we may still be bound by duties of gratitude to remember the dear departed in ways appropriate to this attitude.

In the Enduring Duties View, the duty to remember the deceased is dependent on the duties owed to that person when he or she was alive. I have a duty to remember my father derived from duties of love and honor, but a total stranger does not (although he may have a duty for some other reason). I have a duty to remember my deceased child as well as my deceased parent, each grounded in a duty of love and expressive of it, but I have duties of gratitude to my deceased parent that I do not have to my deceased child, and the mingling of gratitude and love partly explains the special character of the duty to remember my deceased parent. It is also possible for there to be a number of people, all of whom have a duty to remember the same individual according to the Enduring Duties View, but where the explanation and content of the duty is different in each case, depending on the particular relationships they had with this individual. The duties we owe those who are near and dear to us, such as duties of love and honor, embody norms for expressing modes of valuing persons we care about. These norms tell us who is an appropriate object of a certain sort of care, how we should structure our deliberations concerning those we care about, and how we are to act if we are to adequately express these attitudes. Because, in the Enduring Duties View, the duties owed the living persist in some manner after their deaths and are grounds for duties of remembrance in their survivors, the explanation of duties of remembrance and their manner of fulfillment will be as varied as the explanation and manner of fulfillment of duties owed the living.

(c) *The reciprocity view*

The Reciprocity View generates obligations of remembrance, but not in the same way as the Rescue from Insignificance and the Enduring Duties Views. Duties of remembrance, as the Insignificance and Enduring Duties Views explain them, are unconditional: we are duty-bound to remember, so doing so is not morally elective, and there is no obvious morally acceptable way of avoiding the duty if we do not accept it. In the Reciprocity View, by contrast, the duties of remembrance are in an important sense conditional. That is, as we shall see, it holds that we must recognize and accept obligations of remembrance *if* we are to legitimately impose obligations on our successors to remember us. To be sure, obligations of remembrance thus generated are also independent of whether or not we recognize or accept them, in that if we impose such obligations on our successors, we must be prepared (as a condition of moral legitimacy) to accept obligations of remembrance ourselves. But on the Reciprocity View, there is a way of avoiding obligations of remembrance altogether if one does not want to have them: one simply refrains from imposing similar obligations on one's successors. On the Insignificance and Enduring Duties Views, obligations of remembrance cannot be avoided in this way, for they do not rest on future-oriented considerations.

The Reciprocity View begins with some observations about *desires*, specifically desires that can only be fulfilled after the death of the one who has them. "A man's sense of his own experience," Thomas Nagel observes, "does not embody the idea of a natural limit. His existence defines for him an essentially open-ended possible future."[55] But a person's sense of an open-ended future runs up against the realization, particularly at times of personal crisis or with advanced age, of the imminence or inevitability of his own death. This realization is likely to be accompanied by what can be called posterity-directed desires, that is, desires about what others who will survive him or who are not even born yet should do for him or for the sake of what is important to him after he dies. One desire that generally individuals have about what others should do for them after they die – the one that the Reciprocity View focuses on – is the desire to be remembered by them. They care not only about how they will be remembered, but also that they will be remembered.[56] The narrator of Margaret Atwood's *The Blind Assassin* tries to explain the desire this way:

> Why is it we want so badly to memorialize ourselves? . . . What do we hope from it? Applause, envy, respect? Or simply attention, of any kind we can get? At the very least we want a witness. We can't stand the idea of our own voices falling silent finally, like a radio running down.[57]

We want a witness to our having existed, especially someone we cared about and who cared about us, because being remembered by him shows that he believes his relationship to us was important enough to be worth remembering. It is natural for us to want to be remembered, especially by them, and reasonable for us to think that, barring exceptional circumstances, this desire which is so important to us ought to be fulfilled.

It is not the desire to be remembered but the moral imperative to remember that concerns us here, however, and so we need to ask whether and under what conditions this posterity-directed desire can give rise to such an imperative. Here I follow the general outlines of Janna Thompson's account of the grounds of what she calls "inherited obligations."[58] The argument for the imperative to remember consists of two stages. First, we establish that the conditions obtain under which we are morally entitled to *demand* that our successors fulfill our desire to be remembered. Second, once this has been established, we show that our successors ought to *accept* this demand as binding on them and that it cannot legitimately be rejected by them. In order to establish what we can reasonably demand of our successors, posterity-directed desires must pass the following general "reciprocity test":

> We can regard our posterity-directed desires as morally legitimate demands on future people . . . if and only if we would be prepared to accept similar obligations in respect to the desires, deeds, projects, or goals of our predecessors.[59]

According to this test, "what is important for determining what moral demands we can legitimately make of our successors is how we would assess similar demands of our predecessors if they had been made."[60] Hence, we can legitimately demand that our successors remember us only if we would be prepared to acknowledge and fulfill a similar obligation to remember our predecessors. In this view, what is required is *consistency*: we cannot believe both that we have a legitimate claim against our successors that they remember us after we die and that we have no obligation to remember our own deceased predecessors, if the only difference between the two cases is that one involves future people and the other past people. If an individual does not care about being remembered after he dies or does not want to burden his successors with this responsibility or thinks himself unworthy of being remembered, so does not demand that they remember him, then the reciprocity test cannot establish that he has an obligation to remember those who came before him. The obligation would have to be established in some other way. But given that we do want to be remembered by our successors, and especially by those who were near and dear to us, and that there is nothing pathological or irrational about this desire as such, the reciprocity test tells us what we must be prepared to do in respect of our predecessors, as a condition of moral legitimacy.

Passing the reciprocity test is not a sufficient condition for our successors actually *having* a moral obligation to satisfy our posterity-directed desires, however, because we may have grounds for thinking that our successors have an obligation to fulfill a posterity-directed demand without it necessarily being the case that our successors are obliged to fulfill it. Our successors have a moral obligation to honor a posterity-directed demand only if they cannot reasonably reject the obligation we have imposed on them. Thus, if circumstances change such that fulfilling the obligation in a certain manner would cause our successors great hardship, then they would probably be justified in not doing so. But there are various modes of remembering, and while engaging in some of them may expose our successors to great hardship – for example, an oppressive or genocidal regime may outlaw forms of commemoration of the dead – other less risky ones will usually still be possible and will suffice to fulfill the obligation, at least until conditions improve.[61]

According to the Reciprocity View, the obligation to remember is founded on the importance to individuals of their posterity-directed desire to be remembered and on what they must be prepared to accept if they are to be entitled to impose a similar obligation on their successors. If our successors acknowledge the obligation and are prepared to act on it, then they in turn are morally entitled to impose an obligation to remember on *their* successors, and if the latter are prepared to accept it, then they in turn are entitled to impose an obligation on their successors, and so on. Whether one starts with acknowledging an obligation toward one's predecessors and subsequently imposes an obligation on one's successors, or vice versa, the two sorts of obligation are inextricably linked. For my purposes, the important part of the reciprocity test is this: the moral imperative to remember the dead depends on our reasonable concern that our posterity-directed desire to be remembered be honored. In this sense, the account is forward-looking, but it is not for this reason consequentialist: remembering the dead is obligatory because it is a requirement of reciprocity, not because it promotes desirable states of affairs.

What combination of attitudes toward our predecessors and toward us by our successors would satisfy the Reciprocity View? With respect to family members, it will often be the case that lovingly remembering our deceased parents, or honoring them, will be appropriately reciprocated by being lovingly remembered or honored by our children in turn. However, this is not invariably so. In addition, we may be morally entitled to expect our children to honor us after we die even if we are not prepared to accept an obligation to honor our own parents after they die, as long as we recognize some sort of reciprocal obligation. Reciprocity does not necessarily require that the attitudes expressed in remembering our predecessors be unvarying from one generation to the next, or that the attitudes expressed in how we remember our predecessors and those expressed how we are remembered by our successors exactly match. In general, the Reciprocity View requires that we be prepared to accept an obligation to remember as a condition of imposing an obligation on our successors, but it also allows that there are various ways of reciprocating that may satisfy this requirement, depending on the particularities of intergenerational relationships.

There is one attitude that is uniquely associated with the Reciprocity View, what I call *fidelity to a tradition of remembering*. Those who engage in acts of reciprocal remembering typically see themselves as part of, and as helping to maintain, a practice or tradition of fulfilling inherited obligations, a tradition that binds together many generations extending into the past and the future. They are motivated to remember the dead partly out of concern to perpetuate this tradition. This concern will also likely motivate them to try to set a good example for their successors by fulfilling the legitimate expectations of their predecessors, as well as to educate their children to appreciate and maintain this tradition. As Thompson notes, "maintaining a tradition of generational reciprocity is essentially a social responsibility that can only be carried out in a community that exists over generations,"[62] and the family plays a particularly important role in maintaining traditions of remembering the dear departed.

(d) *The three views in tandem*

The three nonconsequentialist accounts of the moral imperative to remember – the Rescue from Insignificance View, the Enduring Duties View, and the Reciprocity View – are not mutually exclusive. For instance, the Reciprocity View can obviously avail itself of the other two views. If the Enduring Duties View establishes that a person has memorial obligations, and if he accepts this and is willing to carry them out, then he is in a position to legitimately demand of his successors that they remember him, although not necessarily to demand that he be remembered in the very same way. If he demands of his successors that they remember him, then he must be prepared to accept a similar obligation with respect to his predecessors, and the Enduring Duties can provide further support for such an obligation. The Rescue from Insignificance View can similarly provide additional reasons for an imperative to remember the dead that supplement the Reciprocity View. Furthermore, the Rescue from Insignificance View assigns the responsibility to remember the dear departed in the first instance to those who had a personal relationship with them, and duties of love and honor arise out of the historical and emotional connections that constitute this relationship. The fulfillment of these duties, according to the Enduring Duties View, does not end merely because the person no longer exists. So here the Rescue from Insignificance View and the Enduring Duties View work in tandem to support memorial obligations.

Our motivations for remembering the dear departed are often complex, but there is also complexity of a different sort because there are multiple reasons why we ought to remember them. We ought to remember the dear departed because in doing so we declare that death has not eliminated what was distinctive and valuable about them; because we expect to be remembered after we die by those who are near and dear to us; and because we thereby give our predecessors the love and honor that we still owe, even after their deaths. These reasons correspond to the three views I have discussed, but they are not esoteric or exceptional. On the contrary, they are considerations that occur with some frequency in people's ordinary thinking about how to relate to their dear departed.

6. MOURNING AND THE DEATH OF PARENTS

The above arguments are relatively abstract and leave much unsaid. They only hint at the enormous diversity of memorial expression. They also do not give much of a sense of the personal meanings that remembering the dear departed can help us to retrieve from their deaths. There is obviously no set number of ways in which we remember the dear departed or formula for how we ought to do so, and no single or simple answer to the question of why it matters to us to remember them. How we remember, how we should remember, and why it is important to us to remember, vary in ways that reflect the character and significance of the personal relationships that we had with these individuals and the expectations and understandings that existed between us. Especially noteworthy in this regard is the emotional impact of the death of parents and its potential to trigger change both in one's adult identity and the extent to which one takes responsibility for one's life. This is what I turn to next. Before this, however, I want to make some general comments about remembrance and mourning. Later I will expand the discussion to include remembrance of parents after the period of mourning is over.

Mourning is a significant theme in the writings of Jacques Derrida,[63] where it is examined in relation to the death of close friends and colleagues. Mourning, he says, is characterized in part by internalization of the lost friend.[64] "Upon the death of the other we are given to memory, and thus to interiorization, since the other, outside us, is now nothing" [M, p. 34]. At the same time, however, we realize that our memories are *only* "traces" of the other who cannot be contained within our interiorizing memory, and this realization leaves us grief-stricken and inconsolable:

> The "within me" and the "within us" acquire their sense and their bearing only by carrying within themselves the death and the memory of the other; of an other who is greater than them, greater than what they or we can bear, carry, or comprehend, since we then lament being no more than "memory," "in memory." Which is another way of remaining inconsolable before the finitude of memory... death constitutes and makes manifest the limits of a *me* or an *us* who are obliged to harbor something that is greater and other than them; something *outside of them within them*. [M, pp. 33–34]

The phrase "outside of them within them" conveys the deeply problematic character of mourning, as Derrida characterizes it: we mourn the dead friend or parent, but our mourning is engaged in an impossible task, the task of interiorizing in memory what resists interiorization, of making a part of ourselves one who, in death, most emphatically and palpably stands apart in his or her otherness.

In addition to the impossible task of mourning, Derrida claims, perhaps with less plausibility, that mourning involves an impossible choice between two infidelities, what he calls at one point the "unbearable paradox of fidelity" [WM, p. 159]. In mourning, interiorizing the friend or loved one furthers self-interested purposes of our own. But apart from its doing so, interiorization is also an incorporation of the other into the self, as a consequence of which "the other no longer quite seems to be the other" [M, p. 35], and in Derrida's view, this fails to show "respect for the other as other" [ibid]. An aborted mourning may manifest such respect, but it is at the same time an infidelity. For mourning the passing of those we care about is what care demands, and if we do not mourn, we retrospectively cast doubt on the genuineness of that care. Moreover, there is a cost from the standpoint of fidelity to oneself: one's sense of self-worth is jeopardized and one's capacities to get on with life and meet other responsibilities are undermined if one does not go through the process of mourning. Derrida puts the dilemma this way:

> Is the most distressing, or even the most deadly infidelity that of a *possible mourning* which would interiorize within us the image, idol, or ideal of the other who is dead and lives only in us? Or is it that of the impossible mourning, which, leaving the other his alterity, respecting thus his infinite remove, either refuses to take or is incapable of taking the other within oneself, as in the tomb or the vault of some narcissism? [M, p. 6]

The impossibility and infidelity of mourning the other are enacted on the uncertain boundary between self and other, between the survivor and the friend or loved one for whom he mourns.[65]

As I have suggested, the impossibility that Derrida describes is a defining feature of mourning in general, but the emotional intensity, painfulness and personal meaning of the process varies, depending on the closeness and history of the relationship with the deceased and the particular characteristics of the individuals involved. When we turn to the bereavement literature for discussion of this subject, we find that it has typically focused on the experience of losing a spouse or a child, and especially the loss of a young child or adolescent. There is considerably less in the psychological literature about the impact of parental loss on the adult child,[66] a deficit that is regrettable as well as surprising, given that "growing life expectancies are making midlife parental loss so increasingly common that it is now largely considered a normative life-span transition."[67] There is also scant literature on the long-term effects of parental death on the lives and outlooks of adult children when the mourning period is over. Yet, the death of one's parents, particularly the death of both of one's parents, unlike the death of one's spouse or child, is unique in several ways because of the central role our parents played in the formation of our self-identity and the strong identification we have with them. Confronting and coming to terms with their death is a developmental milestone, a "rite of passage" for adult children, and how the survivors deal with it can have a deep and lasting effect on their basic life goals and the order of their priorities.

Parental death is profoundly significant for surviving children for a number of reasons.[68] First, there is the nature of the emotions that constitute our reaction to the death of parents. The fear of abandonment through the death of one's parents is one the most persistent and inconsolable fears of childhood, and this most primitive fear remains a source of apprehension, even if not acknowledged as such, well into adulthood. Martha Nussbaum remarks how the emotions triggered by the death of her mother have a complex narrative history going back to the beginnings of the parent–child relationship:

> It would not be possible to have an adequate understanding of my grief without grasping it as one strand in a history of deep love, of longing for protection and comfort, of anger at the separate and uncontrolled existence of the source of comfort, of fear of one's own aggression, of guilt and the desire to make reparations. The grief itself bears the traces of that entire history.[69]

Parents play a powerful role in creating a foundation from which the child experiences the world and develops other relationships, and when the parent dies, especially when both parents die, the foundation is shaken and the surviving child is often left feeling bereft. What is called into question by their deaths is the innocent sense of safety and security that, except in the most serious cases of parental neglect or abuse, we carry with us from earliest childhood. As Alexander Levy notes,

> Whatever our relationship with them and however well or poorly we get along, parents project an illusion of permanence, a constancy that suggests life to be a knowable, reliable, trustworthy, and therefore, feasible endeavor.[70]

The sense that we have a "home" to return to if we need to, or that we can always count on our parents to be there, if not as a source of emotional support then, at least, as a kind of anchoring presence in our lives, is no longer sustainable once we accept the reality of our parents' deaths, and our memories of them rekindle primitive fears of loss of comfort, stability, and love.[71] What's more, the illusion of parental permanence is linked to the illusion of our own, so that parental loss drives home to us, in a way few other experiences can, our own morality.

Second, parental death provides opportunities and incentives for the surviving children to recast self-conceptions and construct new adult identities. Because our sense of who we are is partly constituted by the unalterable fact that we are the child of these particular parents, when they die, most acutely when both die, there is commonly, for a period at least, an "identity crisis" of sorts, confusion or uncertainty about what is most important to oneself, about how one defines oneself, and about what self-image can guide one satisfyingly through major life decisions. But this confusion also lays the groundwork for new possibilities of self-knowledge, self-definition, and personal transformation. Parental death, connected as it is to the realization of one's own mortality, often leads to a sense of urgency to reconsider one's priorities and life plans. When the grief recedes, one may be able to attain sufficient psychic distance from one's parents to conduct a critical review of one's life in relation to them. Goals that one has made central to one's life might move to the periphery, and important goals or projects that one has neglected might take on new and compelling value. And there may also be an enhanced sense of responsibility and accountability for the choices one makes.

Remembering our deceased parents can make possible a kind of life review and self-scrutiny that are not available from other sources, and the work of remembering is not finished with the end of the mourn-ing period: "It is precisely because the ongoing relationship is recog-nized and maintained," Alan Pope notes, "that the surviving adult child is able to come away from this experience fundamentally changed in ways that extend beyond the restoration of pre-bereavement levels of functioning."[72] After our parents die, their life stories are complete and, perhaps for the first time, we can begin to understand the totality of their influence on us. Victoria Secunda remarks on this:

> In dying, the deceased become forever fixed, at least physically.... The dead do not themselves change; the *living*, and their memories of the dead, do. It is the very immutability of parental death that allows adult children to begin to take their own and their parents' measure in ways they could not before.[73]

Gaining perspective on their lives in a way that we could not while they were alive, we are able to more accurately assess both their strengths and weakness as parents and as human beings. We may begin to focus on the numerous ways in which their lives, decisions, and beliefs are relevant to our own. Reviewing their conduct and lives and comparing them to our own, we may discern certain qualities in ourselves whose similarity to theirs we could not fully appreciate while they were alive, and we may endorse those qualities or, if we disapprove of them, resolve to distin-guish ourselves from them in these respects. Through honest, unsparing recollections of our deceased parents, we can get a more accurate pic-ture of ourselves both in relationship to them and apart from them. In other words, in knowing and remembering our parents objectively, we can achieve a more realistic view of ourselves. And with a clearer sense of self, we may be able to take greater control of the direction and shape of our lives.[74] As Dr. Evan Imber-Black, a family therapist, remarks: "Unless you take the opportunity to ask yourself how you want to be like your parents and how you don't, you may not be able to experiment, to be open to new experiences, to find out who you are."[75]

Third, this brings us to another explanation of the special impor-tance that parental death has for surviving adult children which typically sets parents apart from others among the dear departed: their absence allows and encourages us to take greater responsibility for our lives and to uncover and realize capabilities that might have been obscured or repressed while our parents were alive. Their death compels us to recognize that we are no longer children, and it may trigger reflection on how their influence has controlled us, often without our being aware of it. Through this awareness, autonomy may be enhanced by the transition to a new role, that of being a parent to oneself rather than a child to another.[76]

These developments with respect to adult identity and personal autonomy and responsibility following the death of parents are not only psychologically noteworthy: they are also morally significant. Self-determination is a valuable aspect of autonomy, and it is facilitated by an understanding of the operation of our agency, in particular, by an understanding of the profound influence our parents have had on its exercise and direction, something that is often not fully recognized until they have died. As adult children come to take more responsibility for themselves, they may become less defensive about and less prone to make excuses for their past, and in this way more fully take responsibility for it. Furthermore, parental death can trigger change in our identities by creating conditions for self-reassessment. Our self-conceptions may emerge more sharply delineated; certain elements may be rejected and ultimately lose their power to shape our conduct; others may be endorsed and strengthened. Reflection on my parents, their qualities, and our relationship, can lead to greater clarity and certainty about who am I and what I stand for, and this can deepen my understanding of the responsibilities that I have and the things that I value; or it may point toward new responsibilities that I should undertake and things I should value that I have not in the past. As I attempt to understand myself in relation to my parents, my identity might not remain just as it was, and because identity is normatively significant as a source of both values and obligations,[77] so too is the work of mourning and its indefinite aftermath.

7. RITUALS OF REMEMBRANCE

To sum up this chapter so far: I have argued that sometimes it is morally imperative for us to remember the dead, in particular, those I have called the dear departed. I, therefore, reject the view that remembering the dead is always morally elective or supererogatory, perhaps a good or praiseworthy thing to do that reflects favorably on the rememberer's character but not something that is obligatory and whose omission might therefore be a wrong. Consequentialist views provide some of the grounding for this imperative, but they cannot account for the full moral significance of acts and practices of remembrance. In an expressivist view, which the cases discussed in this chapter require, remembering the dead is evaluated in terms of its expressive meanings, and the value of its consequences varies with the expressive meanings of the actions that bring them about. Certain attitudes ought to be expressed because they are ways of valuing the dear departed that are called for in view of the attributes they possessed, what they did, and their relationship to and history with the valuing agent. In general, acts can be judged by their expressive qualities even if the person toward whom they are directed does not perceive those qualities and, in fact, cannot possibly appreciate or respond to them. What we do by remembering the dear departed can be assessed by asking whether it reflects a proper appreciation of the value of this particular person, and this remains an open and morally significant question even though that person no longer exists. Indeed, although I have not explored this possibility here, we should expect an account of remembering that attaches moral weight to emotions and evaluative attitudes (i.e., an expressive account) to have something important to say about our obligations of remembrance in other cases as well, in particular, those involving collective remembrance.

My philosophical defense of intuitions about a moral imperative to remember the dear departed still needs to confront and take account of certain empirical truths about memory. Specifically, because "ought implies can," any account that proposes an obligation or responsibility to remember must acknowledge the limitations of the human faculty of memory and the obstacles that they and the erosive power of time present to the fulfillment of this obligation. I discussed this in Chapter 1[78] as a problem of the fragility and transience of memory, which affects both personal and collective memory. If we do have an obligation to remember the dear departed, then, in view of this problem, it is incumbent on us and those who care about us to consider ways of supporting memory and its activities so that the imperative to remember is less vulnerable than it would otherwise be to the shortcomings of individual memory. A parallel point can be made about supporting imperatives of collective memory through collective action. This is what the obligation entails in light of the attrition of memory, personal as well as collective, within individual lives and across generations.

It can and often does happen that persons, individually or collectively, are committed to remembering the dead (they are not looking for a way to evade their responsibility, for example), but because this commitment naturally and predictably weakens over time, they need help in order to sustain it. One sort of help is provided by *rituals of remembrance.* In the case of collective memory, commemorative rituals play a critical role in embodying and shaping the memory of a group and transmitting it to subsequent generations.[79] Rituals can play an analogous role with respect to personal memory, supporting its exercise and shoring up its weaknesses by embedding it in a network of social relations. Memories of the dear departed, like other memories, normally tend to lose their vividness the farther removed in time we are from actual contact with those we loved and honored. What's more, as we immerse ourselves in the onward flow of life and acquire new interests and responsibilities, even those we once loved may become increasingly peripheral to the lives we construct for ourselves and, as a consequence, their memory may fade. But rituals of remembrance provide a context and vehicle for memory and give instructions for its operations, and therefore rituals can help safeguard the memory of the deceased from the natural fluctuations of individual and collective memory. Edward Casey puts the point succinctly: "the commemorating that is accomplished by a memorializing ritual is an especially efficacious remedy against time's dispersive power."[80]

We can understand why rituals are particularly efficacious in this regard if we consider some of their defining characteristics. As Roy A. Rappaport observes, they "tend to be stylized, repetitive, stereotyped, often but not always decorous, and they also tend to occur at special places and at times fixed by the clock, calendar, or specified circumstances."[81] The very repetitiveness and relative invariance of ritual enactment work to counteract the tendency to forgetfulness. Occurring as they do at relatively fixed places and times, and structured by repetitive and conventionally prescribed ceremonial observances, rituals not only preserve the memory of the deceased but also give the living clear directions for how and when to remember. They supply a normative framework to guide people's understanding and fulfillment of their memorial responsibilities. Also, because rituals are repeated many times in the course of an individual life or in the life of a group, they reinforce earlier memories with later memories acquired in the iterated performance.

Rituals of remembrance are also essentially and importantly inter-personal. They are undertaken not only in relation *to* others or in the presence of others, but *with* others in a common action of communaliz-ing, and they join the individual in solidarity with others. The bonds of solidarity provide additional motivation to fulfill memorial responsibil-ities, and they thereby reinforce memorial observance that might oth-erwise lapse if individuals had to rely solely on their own limited and tenuous powers of memory. Furthermore, individuals may come to feel a certain sense of responsibility for the ritual's success, and this can foster identification with the ritual and further reinforce memorial obser-vance. In short, rituals can have a powerful influence on how individuals and groups remember and their ability to sustain that memory, and rit-uals can be effective weapons to combat the erosion of memory over time.[82]

Because of the way in which rituals preserve and regularize remem-brance of the deceased, they also facilitate the integration of remem-bering with other aspects of a person's life. Memorializing rituals are constituted by norms that specify appropriate times and places for re-membering the dead and, within this circumscribed context, the man-ner in which we are expected to remember them. Rituals thereby give us a way of structuring and conducting our lives so that we can continue to remember even as we attend to our other responsibilities and pursue the various activities, goals, and relationships that are important to us.[83] Remembering through ritualized activity thus helps indirectly to fortify the commitment to remember.

What these remarks about the role of rituals of remembrance sug-gest is that they have more than psychological or symbolic significance for those who engage in them. Memorializing rituals help us to remain faithful to our obligations of memory; they give definite prescriptions for remembering; and they make available ways of integrating the obligations of memory with other demands and occupations of life. Memorializing rituals therefore play an important role in securing for memory of the dear departed a more or less stable, well-defined, and harmonious place in the moral life of the individual.

There is no guarantee, of course, that rituals that help sustain per-sonal memory will continue to do so over time. As with rituals of collec-tive memory, rituals for personal remembrance might lose their original function as they become uncoupled from what initially gave them point and meaning.[84] If memory is associated with them at all, it will have a pro forma quality that reflects little emotional engagement with the deceased. This is a common enough occurrence, to be sure, but it is not a reason to neglect ritual's contribution to personal memory and the responsibilities associated with it. Indeed, without rituals of personal remembrance and the sustaining interpersonal dimension that they bring to the activity of remembrance, memory and the commitment to remember are considerably more vulnerable to deterioration than they are with them.

8. HOW LONG WE MUST REMEMBER

With commemorative rituals, individuals do not have to rely solely on their own psychological resources in order to fulfill their responsibilities of remembrance. Rituals act as a "remedy against time's dispersive power" and assist individuals in the fulfillment of their memorial responsibilities. But the efficacy of memorializing rituals themselves depends on the ongoing willingness and commitment of participating individuals to remember, and although rituals can help strengthen and sustain such commitment, the "remedy" is no cure. Individuals may lose interest in these rituals or, as I have said, the rituals will not retain their original meaning. It may also be that remembrance is not sustainable over the long run because such rituals are simply not available, either generally or to particular individuals.

The question I now want to pose has to do with the evaluation of this diminishing commitment, and I should say at the outset that nothing in my account so far implies that one would necessarily be morally blameworthy if one's resolve to remember weakens over time. The question, "How long must I keep on remembering?" may signify an attempt to evade moral responsibility, but it is not unusual for people to wonder about this, and there may be nothing discreditable about asking it. Given the increasing difficulty over time of holding on to the memory of the dear departed, it is reasonable to wonder how strenuously we should fight against the erosion of memory and if our responsibilities of remembrance do not eventually come to an end. Or so I would argue. In closing, I want to make three comments about this. First, there is a way of thinking about this question that conveys a mistaken and deeply flawed picture of the moral imperative to remember the dear departed. Second, because this way of thinking should be rejected, there is a sense in which the responsibilities of remembrance are open-ended and not time limited. And third, depending on how the question is asked, it may be a sign that one has stopped caring about the deceased, but one does not necessarily do anything wrong by ceasing to care.

With respect to the first point, it might be thought that the moral imperative to remember the dear departed must be of limited duration because, eventually, we have to get over our loss and get on with our lives. If this is what one has in mind, the question might just be an oblique way of asserting that the time has come for one to do this. However, recovering from the loss of a loved one and forgetting the person one has lost are not the same thing, as I noted in Section 4 where I discussed the process of mourning. Memories of the dear departed may be infused with grief, but unlike grief, remembering is not something to be gotten through, or to recover from, so that we can rebuild and renew our lives. The question might also reflect something else, namely, a view about remembering the dear departed as some kind of onerous task, of which we might properly say, "There, I have done all that I ought to do – for now or forever – so let me move on." However, the work of care in remembering the dead is not "work" in the familiar sense: necessary perhaps, but definitely to be kept to a minimum. Rather, it is more akin to a vocation, and, as such, is simply not the sort of responsibility of which it can be appropriate to say that it is something to get out of the way.

This leads to the second point. Because the duties of remembrance are not specific tasks whose performance relieves one of further obligation, there is no definitive end to them. They are not the sort of obligation that can be discharged once and for all and, in this sense, they are not time limited. Indeed, for all I have said so far, they might endure for as long as the survivor does. But even if we reject this flawed conception of the responsibilities of remembrance, there is a more credible reason why they do not necessarily last as long as we do. The reason is not that, at some point during our lives, we can say we have done enough to fulfill them, but rather that we have stopped caring.

Death itself, as I have argued throughout this chapter, does not cancel obligations of remembrance. But death has as one of its common sequelae the gradual diminishment of care about the one who has died. We know this because memory fades, and memory is partly constitutive of care. If I care about someone and then stop remembering that person, not just on a few occasions but more or less completely, then I have stopped caring about him. It is plausible, then, to regard duties to remember the dear departed as grounded at least in part in care, and this transforms the question about the duration of these duties into a question about whether and under what circumstances it is wrong to stop caring.

The short answer is that I cannot see any good reason why we must be blameworthy if we do not go on caring about – or do not make an effort to go on caring about – the dear departed for the rest of our lives, especially in view of the fact that the sorts of mutuality and reciprocity that are characteristic of intimate relationships and that sustain them over time are not possible between the living and the dead. To be sure, if we care about them, we will and ought to remember them for some indeterminate time after their death. We would be unfaithful to them and to our relationship, and we would retrospectively raise doubts about the quality of our relationship, if we did not do so. But the morality of remembrance should make allowances for the fragility of memory and for the limitations of the human capacity to sustain care for the deceased long after their deaths, and it should have an appropriately tempered view about how long a former relationship should continue to hold sway over the living. A realistically demanding morality, one that is constrained by these factors, should permit us to forget even those who were near and dear to us and who, for some time after their deaths, remained so.

NOTES

1. Daniel Mendelsohn, *The Lost: A Search for Six of Six Million* (New York: Harper-Collins, 2006), pp. 486–487.
2. Having acknowledged this, for the most part I do not draw the distinction between ethical obligations and moral obligations in this chapter. Generally, I use the latter terminology. See also, Chapter 4, Note 71.
3. See Michael Stocker, "Duty and Friendship: Toward a Synthesis of Gilligan's Contrastive Moral Concepts," in *Women and Moral Theory*, Eva Kittay and Diana Meyers (Eds.). (Totowa, NJ: Rowman and Littlefield, 1987), pp. 56–68.
4. This is what Joseph Raz argues in *The Practice of Value* (Oxford: Clarendon Press, 2003), pp. 30–33.

5. See the discussion of retrospective construction of meaning in Chapter 2, Section 3.

6. Soren Kierkegaard, *Works of Love* (New York: Harper and Row, 1962), pp. 317–329.

7. Compare the discussion in C. A. J. Coady of direct-object remembering and propositional-object remembering. Though most cases of "remembering x" are "no more than a sort of systematic remembering that," according to Coady, he acknowledges that "at least some cases of remembering things do not seem to yield easily to this treatment." See C. A. J. Coady, *Testimony: A Philosophical Study* (Oxford: Clarendon Press, 1992), pp. 139–141. Remembering the dear departed, as I am characterizing it, is one such case.

8. Martha Nussbaum, *Upheavals of Thought* (Cambridge, UK: Cambridge University Press, 2001), pp. 64–67.

9. Edward Casey, *Remembering: A Phenomenological Study* (Bloomington: Indiana University Press, 2000). I have learned much from this incredibly rich and insightful book.

10. The distinction between recognizing-in and recognizing-as, and between subtypes of recognizing-as, comes from Casey, ibid., pp. 132–135.

11. See the discussion of this in Chapter 1, Section 5.

12. For more, see Section 7 of this chapter.

13. I owe this point to Joseph Raz.

14. See Robert Brown, *Analyzing Love* (Cambridge, UK: Cambridge University Press, 1987), p. 21.

15. From David Velleman, "Love as Moral Emotion," *Ethics 109*, 2 (January 1999): 338–374, at 352–353.

16. Joan Callahan, "On Harming the Dead," *Ethics 97*, 2 (January 1987), 341–352, at 349, 347.

17. I thank Joseph Raz for helping me to clarify my argument here.

18. Velleman, op. cit., p. 360.

19. Ibid., p. 365.

20. Niko Kolodny, "Love as Valuing a Relationship," *Philosophical Review 112*, 2 (April 2003): 135–189, at 156.

21. One problem with Velleman's account, according to Christine Swanton, is that it "misses the essential feature of love as a bond and makes it difficult to distinguish love from a separate mode of moral response – appreciation" (*Virtue Ethics: A Pluralistic View* (New York: Oxford University Press, 2005), p. 117). A problem with Kolodny's view is that in its focus on the relationship, it is strikingly counterintuitive: loving a person, which involves valuing the person, seems very different from (although it is connected with) valuing a relationship with this person.

22. The distinction between antemortem persons and postmortem bodies is also briefly mentioned in the discussion of the duty of accurate and truthful remembrance, in Chapter 4, Section 6. However, the distinction plays a less critical role in that context than in the analysis of loving remembrance that I give in this chapter.

23. Thus, for example, honoring a revered teacher who is now deceased does not simply consist in not desecrating his body or keeping it from harm.

24. See Joel Feinberg, "Sentiment and Sentimentality in Practical Ethics," *Proceedings and Addresses of the American Philosophical Association 58*, 1 (September 1982): 19–46.

25. Elizabeth Anderson, *Value in Ethics and Economics* (Cambridge, MA: Harvard University Press, 1993), p. 11.

26. I thank Margaret Walker for urging me to think more about the overlap between these norms.

27. See Section 7 of this chapter.

28. I will from this point on refer only to a *moral* imperative, and I will not distinguish the moral from the ethical. It should be clear what normative domain my arguments belong to. See Note 2.

29. Or alternatively, tries to bring about. However, for the sake of simplicity, I will not include this possibility.

30. For more on bearing witness and its relationship to memory, see Chapter 6.

31. Quoted in Richard Kearney, "The Crisis of Narrative in Contemporary Culture," *Metaphilosophy 28*, 3 (July 1997): 183–194, at 191.

32. For a discussion of the comparative advantages and disadvantages of punishment and forgiveness as responses to former human rights abusers, see Pablo deGrieff, "Trial and punishment: Pardon and oblivion," *Philosophy and Social Criticism 22*, 3 (1996): 93–111; and Martha Minow, *Between Vengeance and Forgiveness* (Boston: Beacon Press, 1998).

33. Quoted in Charles S. Maier, *The Unmasterable Past* (Cambridge, MA: Harvard University Press, 1997), p. 47.

34. Every September 11th, New Yorkers commemorate the attack on the World Trade Center by reading the names of all of the nearly 3,000 victims. For the family members of these victims, the names are associated with flesh-and-blood individuals; for others who had no personal knowledge of or acquaintance with the victims, each name just increases by one the magnitude of the horror. Other times of the year, when New Yorkers pause to remember *all* of the victims of 9/11, they obviously are not remembering them one by one, but rather as a group.

35. See the discussion of moral (as distinguished from ethical) imperatives of collective memory in Chapter 4, Section 6, and Section 5 on Margalit.

36. *The Jewish Week* ("The Power of a Name," Sandee Brawarsky, April 29, 2005, p. 12) reports on an annual Yom HaShoah commemoration in which individuals at a number of New York City synagogues read the names of individual victims of the Holocaust, many of whom are unknown to the readers. The article notes that in Judaism, a person's *name* has special significance: it represents an individual's soul or essence. Similarly, Henry David Thoreau is quoted as having written that "a name pronounced is the recognition of the individual to whom it belongs." The *New York Times* ("At Holocaust Museum, Turning a Number Into a Name," Joseph Berger, November 21, 2004) reports on a project undertaken by Yad Vashem, the Holocaust museum and archive in Jerusalem, to assemble "the largest and most comprehensive

listing of Jewish victims' names – more than three million, or half of those who perished – along with biographical details, photograph and nutshell memoirs." I interpret these readings and listings as an effort to humanize the victims and to rescue their memory from the anonymity of victimhood.

37. For more on this as it relates specifically to parents, see Section 6.

38. Norman Care, "Forgiveness and Effective Agency," in S. Lamb and J. G. Murphy (Eds.), *Before Forgiving*, (New York: Oxford University Press, 2002), p. 217.

39. According to Casey, op. cit, pp. 240, 243: "mourning itself is to be construed as a way of establishing an internal memorial to (and of) the lost other. . . . the memory of others we once loved proves indestructible: in spite of every effort to forget them, we commemorate them within our psyche by means of intrapsychic memorialization."

40. C. S. Lewis, *A Grief Observed* (London: Faber and Faber, 1961), pp. 44–45.

41. For more, see the discussion of what I called "the going-on problem" in Chapter 1, Section 4.

42. See Elizabeth Anderson, op. cit., 30–38.

43. Cf. T. M. Scanlon's discussion of teleology and friendship in *What We Owe to Each Other* (Cambridge, MA: Harvard University Press, 1998), pp. 87–90.

44. Op. cit., p. 33.

45. Thomas Nagel, "The Absurd," in *Mortal Questions* (Cambridge, UK: Cambridge University Press, 1979), pp. 11–23.

46. Irene Nemirovsky describes one of the characters in her novel *Suite Française* in the following terms:

> In spite of the exhaustion, the hunger, the fear, Maurice Michaud was not really unhappy. He had a unique way of thinking: he didn't consider himself that important; in his own eyes, he was not that rare and irreplaceable creature most people imagine when they think about themselves. ((New York: Alfred A. Knopf, 2006), p. 49)

The belief in one's own individual significance that I take to be fundamental to how we lead our lives is not to be confused with the belief that one is rare or that one is irreplaceable in the sense that one's death would be a loss to the world.

47. Elie Wiesel, *Ethics and Memory* (Berlin: Walter de Gruyter, 1997), p. 15.

48. There may be limits to this. If the person was a "moral monster," there may be a consequentialist moral imperative to remember him because of what he did, but not an imperative to remember him because his having existed, in itself, has significance.

49. James Hatley, *Suffering Witness* (Albany: State University of New York Press, 2000), p. 24.

50. For discussions of dignity, see John Kleinig, *Valuing Life* (Princeton: University Press, 1991), pp. 20–22; Ronald Dworkin, *Life's Dominion* (New York: Alfred E. Knopf, 1991), pp. 166–167, 238–240; Eva Feder Kittay, "Equality, Dependency and Disability," in Marian Lyons and Fionnuala Waldron (Eds.), *Perspectives on Equality: The Second Seamus Heaney Lectures* (Dublin: The Liffey Press, Ltd., 2004).

51. To treat it as one's duty is to honor the rational force of the duty in one's reasons for acting. It does not mean that one provides support *because* it is one's duty.

52. The distinction between "privileged" and "protected" reasons, and the account of duties of love and honor in terms of them, follows John Gardner, "Evaluating Wrongdoing," presented at the Columbia University Legal Theory Workshop, October 8, 1998.

53. On how attitudes can express agency in a sense different from voluntary control, see Angela M. Smith, "Responsibility for Attitudes: Activity and Passivity in Mental Life," *Ethics 115*, 2 (January 2005): 236–271.

54. See the discussion of loving memory in Section 3.

55. Thomas Nagel, "Death," in *Mortal Questions*, op. cit., pp. 9–10.

56. Avishai Margalit claims that "the human project of memory, i.e., *commemoration*, is basically a religious project to secure some form of immortality" (*The Ethics of Memory* (Cambridge, MA: Harvard University Press, 2002), p. 25). I am *not* claiming here that the desire to be remembered after our death is the desire for a kind of immortality. I believe, however, that we (most) want to be remembered after our death by those who were near and dear to us, as a token of what we and our relationship meant to the one who remains behind.

57. Margaret Atwood, *The Blind Assassin* (New York: Nan A. Talese), p. 95.

58. Janna Thompson, "Inherited Obligations and Generational Continuity," *Canadian Journal of Philosophy 29*, 4 (December 1999): 493–515. See also her "Historical Obligations," *Australasian Journal of Philosophy 78*, 3 (September 2000): 334–345.

59. Ibid., "Inherited Obligations," p. 503.

60. Ibid.

61. Thompson elsewhere rejects family relationships as a basis for imposing posterity-directed obligations. "A father," she claims, "cannot reasonably demand that his children keep his promises or make reparation for the wrong he has done" because families are not the sort of collectivity that is "capable of making and keeping transgenerational obligations." See *Taking Responsibility for the Past* (Cambridge, UK: Polity, 2002), pp. 36–37.) It is not obvious to me that (or why) families do not have this capacity. To be sure, there are many things that parents cannot reasonably demand of their children, such as that they be willing to sacrifice their lives and well-being to avenge the family honor or that they bankrupt themselves to discharge a parental debt for which they are in no way responsible. But examples like this, which point to the need for some moral constraints on what parents may legitimately demand of their children, do not establish the stronger claim that Thompson makes.

62. Ibid., pp. 513–514.

63. See Jacques Derrida, *The Work of Mourning*, P.-A. Brault and M. Nass (Eds.). (Chicago: University of Chicago Press, 2001) [WM]; *Memoires for Paul de Man*, trans. C. Lindsay, J. Culler, and E. Cadava (Trans.). (New York: Columbia University Press, 1986) [M].

64. Here Derrida follows Freud's account of mourning in *Mourning and Melancholia.*

65. Remembering and mourning the dead friend are not, for Derrida, merely natural psychological responses to loss. They are, he repeatedly reminds us, the survivor's responsibilities. Implicit in friendship is a *promise*, he says, a promise that, though made to the living friend,

    from the first moment that it pledges . . . pledges beyond death. . . . When the friend is no longer *there*, the promise is still not tenable, it will not have been made, but as a trace of the future it can still be *renewed*. You could call this an act of memory or a given word, even an act of faith. (*Memoires for Paul de Man*, pp. 149–150)

    The promise leaves a trace that binds the future, even beyond the death of the friend, and it retains its moral force even then. Indeed, in words reminiscent of Kierkegaard's remarks on the test for the genuineness of love, Derrida claims that the promise is tested by the death: "A promise has meaning and gravity only on the condition of death, when the living person is one day all alone with his promise." [*ibid*] Remembering is one way of honoring this promise – "the memory of a friendship [is] the renewed fidelity of a promise" [ibid., p. 131] – and also one way of discharging the "debts" we owe to our friend, debts that are different from the garden variety sort in that they cannot be fully and finally discharged. However, because "the mere recognition of a debt already tends towards its cancellation in a denial," the special burden of our debts to our friends may make it seem unwise or "inadmissible" to talk about a debt-based duty to remember. See *The Work of Mourning*, pp. 223–224. The connections between memory and responsibility are the chief concerns of the *Memoires*, but mourning and remembering do not exhaust the responsibilities that Derrida believes the surviving friend has. "Like the Sound of the Sea Deep within a Shell: Paul de Man's War," *Critical Inquiry 14* (1988): 590–652, written in response to revelations about de Man's allegedly anti-Semitic journalism in Nazi occupied Belgium, explores other aspects of the responsibilities of friendship. Here Derrida speaks about fulfilling what he describes as his "responsibilities" to a friend who can no longer speak in his own name, and he associates "responsibility" with "responding," with an obligation to respond for de Man, not so as to clear him of blame, but to ensure that he gets a fair hearing. During de Man's lifetime, Derrida did not know and could not foresee that he would need to answer for his friend in this way. But for Derrida the terms of the "promise that pledges beyond death" are not prescribed in detail in advance. Rather, they have an open-ended quality that may obligate friends to respond for one another in ways that were not and even could not have been foreseen during the course of their friendship.

66. I have benefitted especially from the following small handful of sources: Alexander Levy, *The Orphaned Adult* (Cambridge, MA: Perseus, 1999); Alan Pope, "Personal Transformation in Midlife Orphanhood: An Empirical Phenomenological Study," *Omega 51* (2005): 107–123; Victoria Secunda, *Losing Your Parents: Finding Your Self* (New York: Hyperion, 2000); and Debra

Umberson, *Death of a Parent: Transition to a New Adult Identity* (Cambridge, UK: Cambridge University Press, 2003).

67. Pope, ibid., p. 108.
68. Something close to parental death can occur before biological death. For adult children of parents with advanced Alzheimer's disease or in permanent coma, their parents are already, in a manner of speaking, dead. The children may do much of their grieving while their parents are still alive, which explains their muted emotional reaction when their parents actually die.
69. Martha Nussbaum, *Upheavals of Thought* (Cambridge, UK: Cambridge University Press, 2001), p. 175.
70. Levy, op. cit., p. 15.
71. The classic work by the British psychiatrist and psychoanalyst John Bowlby on "attachment behavior" is relevant here. See his *A Secure Base: Parent-Child Attachment and Healthy Human Development* (New York: Basic Books, 1988); and *Attachment and Loss. Vol. III: Loss: Sadness and Depression* (New York: Basic Books, 1980).
72. Pope, op. cit., p. 117.
73. Secunda, op. cit., p. 61.
74. Adult children who write memoirs of their deceased parents, or who just revisit their parents' lives after their deaths, often learn at least as much about themselves as about their parents in the process. Often too it is in pursuit of greater self-knowledge that they engage in these memorial activities. Or they do so in order to acknowledge their parents as the source of traits in themselves that they value and do not want to change.
75. Quoted in Secunda, op. cit., p. 240.
76. See Pope, op. cit., pp. 117–118; Umberson, op. cit., pp. 94–97.
77. See Chapter 1, Section 7.
78. Section 5.
79. For discussion, see Paul Connerton, *How Societies Remember* (Cambridge, UK: Cambridge University Press, 1989), especially chapter 2.
80. Casey, op. cit., p. 229.
81. Roy A. Rappaport, "The Obvious Aspects of Ritual," in *Readings in Ritual Studies*. Ronald L. Grimes (Ed.). (Upper Saddle River, NJ: Prentice-Hall, 1996), pp. 427–440, at 426.
82. Geoffrey P. Miller, "The Legal Function of Ritual," *Chicago-Kent Law Review 80* (2005): 1181–1233, has a useful discussion of the nature of ritual, along with extensive citations to other sources.
83. Relevant here is Secunda's brief discussion of the value of maintaining family rituals after parental death in op. cit., pp. 269–272. The purpose of this sort of ritual, she says, quoting from Dr. Evan Imber-Black, *The Secret Life of Families* (New York: Bantam Books, 1998), is "to make and mark transitions for individuals and [the] family." Family rituals that memorialize the dear departed do this too: they secure a kind of continuity with the past and permit families and family members to transition to a new life without the dear departed even as they continue to remember them.

84. David Gross claims this has actually happened. He says that the "speeding up of modern life has led to a kind of deritualization of experience that has itself been destructive of memory . . . in the contemporary period there has been a noticeable drying up of public ritual, and with it the evaporation of public memory" See David Gross, *Lost Time* (Amherst, MA: University of Massachusetts Press, 2000), p. 109.

6

MEMORY AND BEARING WITNESS

Those who are alive receive a mandate from those who are silent forever. They can fulfill their duties only by trying to reconstruct precisely things as they were, and by wresting the past from fictions and legends.   – Czeslaw Milosz[1]

1. WITNESSING IN THE CONTEMPORARY WORLD

The previous chapters have explored a number of conceptual and normative issues related to individual and collective memory, including: the nature of and differences between these two types of memory; the reciprocal relationship between individual and collective memory, on the one hand, and individual and collective identity, on the other; the virtues associated with taking responsibility for one's personal past; the role of collective memory in repairing historical injustice; the relationship between history and collective memory; and the ethical and moral obligations of remembrance, collective remembrance as well as personal remembrance of the dear departed. Although collective memory is not reducible to the aggregate of individual memories, I have claimed that collective memory and individual memory do not exist in completely separate domains. On the contrary, each inevitably contributes to and is intertwined with the other. The collective memory of a group is incorporated, explicitly or implicitly, into the individual memories of its members, at the same time that they put the stamp of their personal memories on the memories they share. There are also analogies with respect to some of these issues between individual and collective memory, as was clear from my discussion of taking responsibility for one's personal past in Chapter 2 and collectively doing justice to the past in Chapter 3.

I now want to conclude with an account of a particular phenomenon that is importantly related to memory and that shows in yet other ways how collective and individual memory are interconnected, that of *bearing witness*. What I am concerned with is bearing witness as itself a kind of memorial act – that is, both a way that people give shape to their memories and the shape that they thereby give them – and as a means whereby the past is preserved for and passed on to future generations, so that they in turn can remember. Bearing witness can concern itself with the plight of intimates as well as strangers, individuals as well as communities, so it encompasses more than the discussion in Chapter 5. But bearing witness, when it is a way of remembering the dead, is still only one way of doing so.

Bearing witness has received much attention recently from various quarters, due in no small measure to the role it has played in drawing the world's attention to and maintaining its awareness of the atrocities collectively known as the Holocaust. It has acquired, in our age, a certain status as a fitting, morally serious, and compelling response to the twentieth century's episodes of mass cruelty and killing, as well as to more distant evils, such as the treatment of Africans under slavery. However, discussions of bearing witness in the popular culture and in scholarly writings have not been confined to instances of large scale wrongdoing or historical injustice. Frequently, bearing witness is associated with finding and registering one's "voice" (a connection I will explore in Section 5), that is, with telling one's own story and having it heard in the right way, and this is said to be critically important in situations that involve wrongdoing on a small scale as well as large scale or perhaps no wrongdoing at all. For example, it is a central theme of the psychological literature on the treatment of victims of psychic trauma, including childhood sexual abuse.[2] In many of these discussions, bearing witness is valued chiefly for its potential therapeutic and other consequences, for its ability to bring about healing of one sort or another as well as political change or punishment, so when there is claimed to be a moral imperative to bear witness, the justification for it is usually cast in consequentialist terms. Whether consequentialism can provide a complete account of the moral value of bearing witness or – as I will argue – bearing witness has other critical functions whose value cannot be explained in instrumental terms, is a question that I will take up in Sections 4 and 5. For now, I simply want to observe that bearing witness, largely because of its connection to personal and collective trauma, has come to occupy a prominent place in the contemporary world as a way of speaking about and preserving memory of the past. What's more, bearing witness is a mode of engagement with the past that has received considerable attention in the last several decades from several disciplines, including law, medicine, psychology, and literary studies. Arguably, it is the mode of engagement with the past that has dominated these discussions. For these reasons, it warrants special treatment in a philosophical investigation of memory. If we want to shed additional light on how memory addresses the past, why there are obligations of memory, and how these obligations get attached to particular people and communities, we should study it closely.

Obligations of remembrance – the overarching subject of this book – may include obligations to bear witness, but the former are not exhausted by the latter. Bearing witness is one, but only one, way to remember, and it is not always appropriate, let alone required. This is because bearing witness concerns itself with a fairly restricted range of considerations. As we commonly think of the situations that call for bearing witness, what one bears witness to is the suffering of others, or the circumstances of their deaths: to their having been murdered, persecuted or tortured, oppressed, dispossessed of their property, or in some other way grievously injured or harmed, all of which attest to their vulnerability. The salient characteristic of these individuals, for purposes of bearing witness, is their suffering or the unjust circumstances of their death. (Naturally, this does not preclude remembering the person in other ways as well.)

Now this might lead us to think that bearing witness must be a depersonalized sort of remembrance because we are remembering a person under a generic description such as "victim of persecution or torture." The individual person drops out and only the general feature of suffering remains, or his memory is invoked merely to make a larger point about the evils of the past or the moral arbitrariness of fate. But this is a misunderstanding that I want to clear up at the outset. Although bearing witness can function like this, remembering need not lose sight of, and indeed can still give a central place to, the individual who suffered, even as it directs its attention to her suffering or the wrong done to her. The *target* of bearing witness, that at which bearing witness is directed, can be a particular individual even as the *focus* of bearing witness, that in virtue of which one bears witness and that makes one's concern intelligible, is the suffering of this person.[3] Moreover, this suffering is a distinct bad from the suffering of another person precisely because it is that person's suffering and not another's, even if the bad-making property is in each case the same. I will assume, in what follows, that the depersonalization charge can be successfully met.

Bearing witness often concerns itself with the dead, in particular, the victims of wrongdoing and misfortune, but this does not exhaust the possibilities: one can bear witness to one's own past suffering as well as to the suffering of others who have survived, and suffering is not the only thing one can bear witness to. Moreover, the phenomena of bearing witness vary in other respects. In some instances, witnessing only speaks to a relatively small audience and is soon forgotten or perhaps remembered only by a few other individuals. In others, acts of bearing witness may have a larger public, even historical, significance. They may become part of the public record and perhaps also shape and be incorporated into the collective historical consciousness. And, as we will see, there are other distinctions to be drawn as well.

The concerns that link this chapter to the ones that went before are the relations between bearing witness and memory. But bearing witness as remembering also has a specific point that it shares with other instances of bearing witness that do not have a memorializing function: witnesses seek or are supposed to seek to uncover and/or relate "the truth" about what happened (or is still happening) or about what was (or is being) done. If this is not only what witnesses do but what they ought to do, then an obligation to bear witness to the past suffering of those who are now dead is not simply an obligation to remember them in the light of this suffering. More than this, it is an obligation to get at and tell the truth about this suffering, a truth that may be hidden or obscured or is one that others may, for various reasons, not want disclosed. Certainly, this formulation of the obligation accords with a common feature of the phenomenology of bearing witness, because it is in such terms that those who bear witness ordinarily understand what they are doing. They suppose themselves to have a responsibility to find out the truth, to tell it, and to hold fast to it.

The notion of an imperative to speak the truth in the context of bearing witness, however, raises numerous questions and requires considerable elucidation. Who is the audience to whom those who bear witness speak or should speak the truth? What is the point of their speaking it? Can some speak the truth with particular authority, and does the obligation to learn and speak the truth fall particularly heavily on some rather than others? Do those who experienced the suffering themselves or first-hand enjoy some epistemic or communicative advantage as compared with those who did not? How much of the truth must be told? Supposing that this depends on what is considered both relevant and critical to an understanding of what happened and may still be ongoing, what does this in turn depend on? And what sort of truth is at issue here? Is it the sort of truth that the historian (ideally) aims at? Or is there a quite intelligible sense in which the witness might be telling the truth even if she falls short of or does not aspire to factual accuracy or completeness? These questions about the imperative of truth-telling arise with respect to bearing witness as a memorial act, but they are pertinent to bearing witness in general.

I begin in Section 2 with an analysis of the general concept of bearing witness, which I construe as involving the provision of *testimony*. Although I allow that there are ways of bearing witness that are not inscribed on texts or even documentary evidence that is text-like, I find it useful to structure my account along the lines of C. A. J. Coady's definition of "natural testimony," which is modeled after his definition of "formal testimony." Briefly put, what emerges is that bearing witness is a type of address to an audience in need, crucially dependent on trust in the witness, who has the relevant authority or competence to serve as a witness. This account clarifies how bearing witness fulfills the functions of recording the past and preserving the memory of it for others, and it also serves to highlight those features that set bearing witness apart from other ways of remembering the dead. The analysis is then elaborated in Section 3 by a typology of witnessing that distinguishes between different objects of witnessing and different ways in which a witness may be related to them. The discussion here is intended to further refine the analysis of bearing witness and to add some complexity to the account of its memorial function.

I turn next, in Section 4, to the moral value of bearing witness. We can understand the value of bearing witness to some extent in consequentialist terms, but I hold that consequentialism cannot do complete justice to bearing witness any more than it can to remembering the dear departed. Part of the explanation, as Robert Merrihew Adams suggests, is that bearing witness has *symbolic meaning*, and its symbolic meaning is a source of nonconsequentialist value. I argue that this account, while plausible as far as it goes and essential to a proper appreciation of its value, is incomplete, and I try to supplement it in Section 5 with a discussion of bearing witness and voice. To anticipate, I will argue the following. In a range of important cases, the address of the one who bears witness is or partly consists in a claim or demand to be heard. Specifically, it is a claim or demand to be heard as a person in possession of the truth about what took place and the right to tell it, even if the audience does not, and perhaps especially if the audience does not, want to hear it. It is a demand to be heard because *she* is the one testifying, and the reason she addresses to the audience is accepted as valid only if the audience accords her the authority to make this demand. The moral importance of acceding to this demand, then, partly consists in this: we affirm the dignity of those whose personhood was denied by violations of their rights when we give respectful attention to their testimony about the wrongs they suffered.

I go on to explain, however, that we fail to realize the full moral power of bearing witness and its moral significance as a way of addressing injustice if we limit those who may bear witness to the immediate victims of injustice. To make this point, I introduce in Section 5 the concept of a "proxy witness," that is, someone who serves as another's voice and exercises the victim's right to speak the truth. Section 6 develops the account of proxy witnessing by examining the grounds for the *authority* to serve as a witness for another. I argue that individuals – as well as communities – can legitimately take responsibility to testify about wrongdoing done to persons who are dead or silenced if they have the authority to speak on behalf of the voiceless, and that under certain conditions, they do indeed have such authority. I end with some remarks on the problem of the false witness. Proxy witnesses who lack such authority, who know they lack the moral credentials to speak on behalf of the voiceless but claim them nevertheless, exploit the voicelessness of the victims, and manipulate the audience to whom they give testimony. What cases of false witnessing underscore is that bearing witness crucially depends on an assumption of trust in the one bearing witness, and this is something we are particularly well advised to keep in mind when important matters hinge on whether or not we accept the witness's testimony.

2. THE CONCEPT OF BEARING WITNESS

The relationship between bearing witness and witnessing is unidirectional: that is, those who bear witness are witnesses, but not every witness *bears* witness. This is in part because bearing witness is an exercise of agency and a kind of undertaking, whereas one can be a witness simply in the sense of being a passive observer or an observer who is not allowed to turn away. There is a familiar use of "witness" in which it has the same meaning as "directly observe." This is witness in the sense of *eyewitness*, as when we say, for example, "I only heard about the incident second hand, but John actually witnessed it." In this usage, witnessing is not conceptually connected to undertaking anything or to testifying, for one can directly observe some event without even mentioning it to someone else. In contrast to this, there is a well-accepted sense of witnessing in which it involves testifying, so is a social practice with some sort of interpersonal dimension. This is a defining feature of bearing witnessing as I understand it. To be sure, being an eyewitness may be thought to have some special importance as a source of authority about an event's occurrence, something which I will say more about later in this section. But bearing witness is not synonymous with directly observing, and one can bear witness to events at which one was not present.

Besides the fact that there must be an undertaking to communicate, there is another sort of undertaking that acts of bearing witness necessarily communicate, namely, standing by one's testimony. When one bears witness, one puts oneself in a particular moral position vis-à-vis others in that one holds oneself out as a reliable witness and is rightfully held accountable for the truthfulness of one's communication. In addition, the term "bearing" is frequently used, as in "bearing a burden," to suggest that the undertaking is in some way burdensome or difficult for the witness. This is how W. James Booth understands it:

> Witnessing, to borrow Elizabeth Spelman's phrase, is a kind of repair work, a restorative labor. Labor: "bearing witness" points to a weight being carried as a duty perhaps but by no means joyously, or even with the bittersweet pleasure of nostalgia.[4]

One way in which bearing witness might be difficult is if the witness puts himself, and those he cares about, at some risk by his act of witnessing. Perhaps, if he testifies, he or his loved ones will be tortured or murdered.

Bearing witness can also be difficult if there are no risks of this sort, but because of the emotional trauma that it causes the witness to relive. Moral courage, to say nothing of physical courage, and resoluteness of will may be needed to bear witness both to one's own pain and the pain of others: "There is something dutiful, even heroic, about the witness," Booth claims. "It is not just the trying circumstances and obstacles that stand in her way, but her determination, despite all, to shoulder and move forward with her burden."[5] However, although I do not deny that the notion of bearing witness often connotes risks for the witness or others personally connected to him and that it can be heroic to bear witness, neither is required by my account. Still, there will normally be some difficulty involved in bearing witness, even if only the difficulty of being heard.

Bearing witness, as I have said, is linked to giving testimony, and one way to begin thinking about this is to consider witnessing in the circumscribed and highly artificial context of a legal or quasilegal proceeding. Starting here, with an instance that is familiar and relatively well-understood, we might be able to get a better handle on features of witnessing that occur in nonformal settings and, because those who bear witness are witnesses, on features of bearing witness as well.

A witness in a legal proceeding provides testimony, that is, evidence for the truth of some proposition p that others are invited to accept as true on the basis of the witness' say so. The formal character of the testimony derives from the facts that the competence or authority to testify and the various circumstances under which testimony is properly provided and credited are specified by formal rules. What counts as valid or creditable testimony in the context of daily life is not so rigidly circumscribed, of course, but in other respects, there are a number of parallels between formal testimony and its lay cousin. C. A. J. Coady lists the following conditions of "natural" testimony" which are patterned after those of "formal" testimony:[6]

A speaker S testifies by making some statement p if and only if:

(a) His stating that p is evidence that p and is offered as evidence that p.
(b) S has the relevant competence, authority, or credentials to state truly that p.
(c) S's statement that p is relevant to some disputed or unresolved question (which may, or may not, be p?) and is directed to those who are in need of evidence on the matter.

As with other speech acts, such as asserting and arguing, the point of testifying is to inform an audience that something is the case: that is, they all have roughly the same illocutionary point. But testifying differs from these in its mode of achievement of this point. As Coady notes,

> in the case of testifying, of either the formal or informal variety, the way of achieving the point is through the speaker's status as one having a particular kind of authority to speak to the matter in question, a matter where evidence is required.[7]

Without authority in the relevant domain, the speaker does not merely fail to convince her audience or move others to action by her testimony. Failures of this sort are not uncommon occurrences, because witnesses are often disregarded, ridiculed, or silenced, even when they do possess the requisite authority to testify. The speaker also did not necessarily fail because she merely provided false testimony, that is, false information. Indeed, she may not have. Rather, the problem is of a different order. One way of putting it is this: her utterance does not count as testimony at all because she fails to meet the threshold condition for testifying, that is, having authority with respect to the matter about which one testifies.[8] If she deliberately presents herself as having the requisite authority to speak to the matter in question when she does not, she is only *pretending* to testify. Or, alternatively, she does really testify but the stance she adopts does not connect up in the right sort of way, or at all, with what she is testifying to or about. At any rate, whether or not she is only pretending to testify, she obviously cannot be a genuine witness but only a false (illegitimate) one, and this is independent of the truth-value of what she says.[9] I will say more about the authority to testify in this section and in Section 6 where I discuss the authority of proxy witnesses.

To testify that *p* is not merely to present evidence that *p*. To argue that *p*, for example, is also to present evidence, but in this case we are asked to accept *p* on the basis of its following from certain other propositions, and whether or not the argument is a good one is independent of the credentials of the person making the argument.[10] There is something about the *speaker* that makes witnessing different from other instances of presenting evidence that or informing an audience that *p*. The difference is that testifying and witnessing centrally concern not only what is said but who says it, and when we believe testimony we believe what the witness says partly because there is nothing obviously defective about the evidence, itself, *but also, importantly, because we trust the speaker or have no particular reason not to do so.*[11] Avishai Margalit refers to testimonial trust in the following:

> My attitude toward a potential witness often is prior to my attitude toward her testimony. My belief *in* (her) is prior to my belief *that* (what she says is true) and cannot be reduced to the latter.[12]

A speaker we have not trusted and never will trust, or whom we have ceased to trust, may utter truths, but she cannot or cannot continue to function for us as a witness to these truths.

Although testimony is most frequently discussed and most naturally understood as a speech act, I do not want to categorically exclude other modes of representation from my account. Thus, I want to allow that other media, such as rituals and forms of artistic expression, may also, in some circumstances, have a testimonial function and hence that their creation and repetition can serve as a way of bearing witness. (Consider, for example, the weekly vigil of the Mothers of the Plaza de Mayo held on behalf of the children who "disappeared" during Argentina's so-called dirty war; or the powerfully moving paintings by Jewish inmates of the brutalities of daily life in the Theresienstadt concentration camp.) But whether or not this is so depends on how closely the features of the particular medium and its context resemble those specified in the speech act analysis, including the intention that one's enactment serve as evidence that others need.

(a) *Testimonial authority*

Condition (b) in Coady's definition of testimony – the relevant authority or credentials to vouch for the truth of p – looms large in our thinking about witnessing, in formal settings where testimony is given in a court of law or before an official commission or the like, as well as in more run-of-the-mill situations where we rely on the testimony of others who have a particular expertise that we lack. Although, as I discuss at greater length in Section 3, one can bear witness to good as well as bad, praiseworthy as well as blameworthy conduct, bearing witness frequently concerns significant wrongdoing, perhaps wrongdoing on a massive scale. In these cases, the question that needs to be addressed is what the conditions of possessing authority are that put one in a position to serve as a witness to, to bear witness to, wrongdoing. Simply put, what gives a speaker (or a writer, because bearing witness may take the form of writing) the authority to bear witness to wrongdoing and the suffering it produces? What kind of authority is involved here?

One source of authority to bear witness to wrongdoing is first-hand experience of it. The notion of first-hand experience covers importantly different cases. There is the first-hand experience of the observer or bystander (an eyewitness), the person who is the target of wrongdoing (the direct or primary victim), and the family members, partners, or close friends of the victim (whom we can refer to as secondary victims, to distinguish them from the direct victim).[13] In legal contexts, testimony that is not first-hand is often dismissed as hearsay, but we are much more relaxed about this in everyday situations, often unhesitatingly accepting as true or relying on reports that are not first-hand. Indeed, on reflection there is nothing surprising or necessarily discreditable about this, for social intercourse depends on a general willingness to trust such reports. But in the case of bearing witness to wrongdoing, the fact of having had first-hand experience, especially as a victim, seems to give testimony special epistemic and moral weight.

First-hand testimony, it might be claimed, has a special status compared with testimony that is not first-hand because of the peculiar evidential value of the former and the sort of truth it possesses. Margalit seems to share this view when he discusses a particular sort of witness to wrongdoing who provides first-hand testimony, namely, one who is not merely an observer of wrongdoing but who tells us "what it is like" to suffer it. (Margalit calls this a "moral witness.) This is someone who has experienced "suffering first-hand – as a victim," and not merely "as a sympathetic bystander, observing the suffering without being a victim oneself,"[14] and the authority of such a witness to testify to wrongdoing, Margalit asserts, derives from his or her experience of actually being a victim, an authority that those who do not have this experience lack.[15] Of course, not everyone who suffered and survived is able or willing to bear witness to their suffering, but those who are speak from a vantage point to which someone who has not suffered, or suffered in the same way, does not have access.

The claim that the one who has suffered has special authority to bear witness to the wrong that caused it (and perhaps also to suffering more generally) can be defended in the following way. There is a knowledge of suffering, it may be argued, that can only be had by actually experiencing it, and this knowledge is something that even the most empathic bystander cannot possess. ("Knowledge-by-acquaintance of suffering," Margalit calls it.[16]) It is not unusual – indeed, it is all too common – for those who have not themselves suffered wrongdoing to downplay its seriousness. They may become impatient with what they perceive to be the constant self-pitying complaints of the victims. The perpetrators or beneficiaries of the wrongdoing, in particular, are likely to deny or minimize or explain away the wrongdoing that they have caused or benefited from, whereas the victim, precisely because he has experienced the wrong firsthand, is not likely to do so. If the ability to bear witness partly depends on the ability to render salient what was salient for the person whose experience is being related, then, as a general matter, the victims have an advantage over those who have not experienced the same or similar injustice. The victims are in this sense better at bearing witness to their suffering than the others are. Of course, we should not deny, and it would be quite implausible to hold, that those who have been victimized cannot be factually wrong about the events that they describe, or mischaracterize how they experienced these events in the past. Indeed, by the standards of scientific history, they are sometimes "flawed vector[s] of truth about the past."[17] But the fact that the victims are not immune to such errors, and maybe even often commit them, does not imply that they enjoy no epistemic advantage over those who have not had comparable experiences. On the contrary, we do not expect complete historical or factual accuracy from the bearers of memory, so should not judge their testimony by standards which are not appropriate to it.[18] Moreover, in view of this advantage, others who have not had comparable experiences ought to adopt a posture of epistemic humility in relation to the victims' testimony. Even with respect to the factual accuracy of the victims' accounts, arguably there should be a rebuttable presumption in their favor.[19]

In addition to the epistemic, the authority conferred by the actual experience of injustice is partly moral in nature. That is, it is not only a matter of having knowledge that others lack, but also of having, by virtue of one's status as a victim, a *moral title* to bear witness to suffering that others who have not been victims of the same or similar wrongdoing do not have, or do not have to the same degree. Laurence Thomas, in his article, "Moral Deference,"[20] makes some observations that are relevant here. Speaking of the experience of persons in "diminished social categories," he writes:

> ... [there is a] sense of *otherness* that inescapably comes with being a person belonging to a diminished social category.... This sense of otherness is not something that a person who does not belong to one's particular diminished social category can grasp simply by an act of ratiocination.[21]

Moreover, persons in diminished and nondiminished social categories "have different emotional category configurations,"[22] so they experience misfortune and pain in radically different ways. These points make sense of and underpin a requirement that Thomas calls "moral deference":

> Moral deference is owed to persons of good will when they speak in an informed way regarding experiences specific to their diminished social category from the standpoint of an emotional category configuration to which others do not have access.... Moral deference is meant to reflect the insight that it is wrong to discount the feelings and experiences of persons in diminished social category groups simply because their articulation of matters does not resonate with one's imaginative take on their experiences.[23]

For similar reasons, we can say that the victims of wrongdoing – many of whom are diminished social category persons – are owed moral deference, specifically because of their experiences as victims. That they are owed moral deference as victims is an acknowledgment of the *moral* authority they have to testify to the wrong they suffered – an authority that derives from the fact that they are speaking from a privileged vantage point. The requirement of moral deference does not preclude questioning aspects of the victim's account of his experience, for example, the accuracy of some of his reports of past events. But if this is done, it must not be with the intent or effect of dismissing and devaluing him as a testifier or undermining the overall credibility of his testimony.

Victims who do not survive to bear witness to their own suffering might still leave behind someone who can carry on their memory and testify for them, such as a family member or a close friend. Those who have suffered directly may or may not live to testify to what they have endured, but family and close friends may have suffered too as secondary victims, and this can entitle them to bear witness to the wrongdoing both on their own and on the direct victims' behalf. In each of these cases, the authority to bear witness is explained in terms of victimization. In addition to these two types of victim, Trudy Govier introduces the category of "tertiary victims": "In many cases serious harm to a person also harms the community or group of which he or she is a member."[24] This suggests that bearing witness can be a collective as well as an individual activity: a group of people, acting collectively or through its representatives, might bear witness to the harm inflicted on some of its members and, through this, to the harm inflicted on the group.[25]

Among those who bear witness as secondary victims are descendants of the original victims who may have been born long after the original injustice. And a tertiary victim can bear witness on behalf of the victims who belonged to it, all of whom, direct and indirect, may be dead. (It can do this because a group can survive changes in its membership.) The authority of descendants of the original victims to bear witness to the harm they suffered, and of tertiary victims to bear witness to the harm suffered by group members in the past, is partly epistemic and partly (or largely) moral in nature and, as we will see in Section 6, that authority can be derived from the particular significance that family history and membership in a community possess.

(b) *Address and audience*

The second part of condition (c) of Coady's definition of testimony states that witnesses direct their testimony to those in need of evidence. In other words, witnessing is an activity of *communication* directed to an *audience*, an audience with some particular need for evidence that the testimony of the witness might provide. I will say more later in this section about why an audience may need this testimony and what of value it may gain from it, but here I want to focus on the communicative function of witnessing and the audience the witness addresses. I take, as my point of departure, the feature of witnessing stressed by psychiatrist Dori Laub: "Testimonies are not monologues; they cannot take place in solitude. The witnesses are talking *to somebody*."[26]

The communicative function of witnessing is obvious when testimony is provided in a court of law or a commission of inquiry. The victims of apartheid in South Africa, for example, testified before the Truth and Reconciliation Commission to an audience that included the commission members and many others as well. In fact, their testimony was directed, in part, to South African society as a whole. There was, we might say, a difference between the audience *to* whom they bore witness and the audience *before* whom they bore witness. Often the audience to whom testimony is directed is much larger than the audience before whom testimony is given, and the smaller forum is seen as providing an opportunity to reach the larger audience.

One can communicate a truth without even knowing that one is doing so, but on the conception of witnessing that structures my analysis of bearing witness, testifying is an intentional act. This is not to deny that sense can be made of the notion of unwitting or even unconscious testimony.[27] Indeed, if Shoshana Felman is right, unconscious testimony, which communicates truths by indirection, is the key to understanding the operation of Freudian psychoanalysis:

> Psychoanalysis . . . profoundly rethinks and radically renews the very concept of the testimony, by submitting and by recognizing for the first time in the history of culture, that one does not have to *possess* or *own* the truth, in order to effectively *bear witness* to it; that speech as such is unwittingly testimonial; and that the speaking subject constantly bears witness to a truth that nonetheless continues to escape him, a truth that is, essentially, *not available* to its own speaker.[28]

According to Felman, psychoanalysis uncouples "bearing witness" to the truth from "owning" it, and this has radical implications for the concept of testimony. That one can bear witness to a truth that one can only dimly if at all grasp or articulate is, in her view, Freud's revolutionary insight, an insight that illuminates and is further illuminated by historical and literary dimensions of testimony. However, it is doubtful that we can square the notion of unconscious testimony with the claim that the authority to bear witness must be at least partly epistemic, for it seems that the patient-cum-witness does not have this authority if the truth is "not available" to him and "continues to escape him." To make the point another way, if "S has epistemic authority with respect to x" is to be unpacked, roughly, as "S's statements about x give others reason to accept what he says as true," then there is a problem with the analysand's testimony precisely because, as analysand, he lacks insight into and understanding of his emotional problems. To avoid these complications, I will suppose that the analysand does not, strictly speaking, bear witness to a truth that is inaccessible to him. He may take himself to be in possession of, or represent himself to others as being in possession of, the truth. He may also provide indispensable material that can help the analyst uncover the truth. But lacking insight and self-understanding, the patient lacks the competence or authority that testifiers must possess.

Along with other types of intentional communication, witnessing is subject to certain ethical requirements. For one thing, communication that is not shaped, as far as possible, by a concern to be intelligible and comprehensible to its intended audience or that is obfuscatory is not only inadequate as communication, but also objectionable on moral grounds. In addition, there is a requirement of nondeception. Onora O'Neill, speaking in a different context, makes the following relevant observation:

> Those who aim to communicate are obliged to attend to the characteristics and capacities of their intended audiences, and to take account of what is needed to address them in ways that eschew deception.[29]

A witness may possess the authority to testify, so she may not be a false witness strictly speaking, but she may misuse that authority by misinforming or presenting only part of the truth or engaging in some other abuse of testimony. In formal settings, and even sometimes in informal ones, solemn assurances may be sought to increase our confidence in the witness' reliability. But of course this provides no guarantee that we are not being deceived and in some circumstances it can be morally insensitive to challenge the credibility of particular witnesses.[30]

The notion of an audience also figures in many discussions of shame, and we can clarify the role that audience plays in witnessing by distinguishing it from the role it plays in explaining the emotion of shame. Accounts of shame that speak of an audience link this to the idea of being observed, a notion that is used metaphorically to make a point about the particular self-consciousness involved in the experience of shame. Gabriele Taylor remarks:

> .... it is of course not necessary for feeling shame that the agent believe or imagine there to be some observer who views him under some description. The actual or imagined observer may merely be the means of making the agent look at himself, he is in no way essential. What is essential is the shift in the agent's viewpoint *vis-a-vis* himself.[31]

It is a contingent matter, then, whether one who experiences shame actually believes or imagines there to be an audience observing his state or action. The role of the audience in witnessing differs from this in three respects. First, the audience chiefly occupies the position of addressee, not observer, although it is also possible that an audience (not necessarily the same one) observes the witness' state or action; second, it is essential that the witness believes there is or might be an audience to whom he is communicating; and, therefore, third, to refer to an audience for witnessing is not merely to speak metaphorically. Witnesses may be addressing an audience that does not yet and perhaps never will exist; or they may think an audience is receptive to their testimony when in fact it is indifferent; or a receptive audience may be beyond their reach; or they may be addressing multiple audiences at once, without clearly differentiating between them; and so on. But in all these cases, witnesses aim to reach an audience.[32] Indeed, witnessing and bearing witness lose their essential point if there is no audience addressed by the witness, or at least if he does not believe that there is or will or might be one.

The fact that testimony is addressed to an audience with a need for evidence on some matter also explains how bearing witness to something that happened in the past differs from reminiscing about it. As I discussed in Chapter 5,[33] reminiscing can arise involuntarily or it can be undertaken for the sheer pleasure of reliving the past. Typically, it is not an introspective affair carried out in private; rather, it occurs in and is drawn out by social settings. As Edward Casey observes, "reminiscers naturally seek partners in a common enterprise of reliving the past wistfully."[34] The communal or interpersonal character of reminiscing is not explained merely by the fact that we wistfully relive the past in the company of others. Rather, "as an engagement *with* other rememberers, whether undertaken with others in person or only with them in mind, reminiscences are addressed . . . *to* others,"[35] to others either as listeners or as active coreminiscers.[36] Reminiscing has this much in common with witnessing. Still, crucial differences remain. For one thing, unlike witnessing, reminiscing can arise unintentionally: that is, one can just find oneself falling into reminiscing. For another, reminiscing is rarely undertaken for the sake of some goal external to the process of remembering, whereas witnessing often is. What is most significant is that what a witness provides is *evidence*, and he provides it to an audience because that audience, for some reason, needs it. When someone reminisces, by contrast, he is simply sharing his memories, and the others with whom he shares these memories may simply take pleasure in them and in sharing their own memories in turn. Reminiscing and witnessing may both be modes of address, but the point of the address differs in the two cases, as does the nature of the relationship between the individual in question and his listeners.

I suggested in the paragraph before last that there are complications in the notion of addressing an audience because there are different sorts of audiences and different sorts of relationship between them and those who bear witness. The witness may be mistaken that there is a receptive audience for his testimony; or even if it exists, he may not be able to communicate with it, perhaps because he is forcibly prevented from reaching it with his message; or the audience that will listen to his testimony may not yet exist but be a real possibility, and he is addressing it, this possible future audience. Perhaps the audience will come into being partly as a consequence of the power of that very testimony. These different scenarios suggest some of the communicative challenges facing those who bear witness. In cases of impeded or unrealized communication with an audience, what sustains the act of bearing witness is perhaps not something as strong as the *expectation* that eventually one's testimony will be heard by a receptive or sympathetic audience. Indeed, one may assess the chance of this happening as rather low. However, when there is little expectation of this, bearing witness may yet be sustainable by *hope*, which consists in part in a desire for something that one believes is both desirable and possible, though not certain, along with the readiness to act on that desire.[37] Witnesses often persevere out of what Margalit calls a "sober hope:"

> Moral witnesses can – and often do – act like survivors of a shipwreck who find themselves on a desert island and figure that they have nothing to lose and perhaps something to gain by sending a bottle with a message

into the ocean.... There is nothing irrational in sending the written message with little expectation but with great hope that it will reach helpful eyes. This, I maintain, is the kind of hope the moral witness can assume.[38]

In general, witnesses give testimony that they have some hope will be understood, as they intend it to be understood. Being heard as one intends to be heard is often psychologically beneficial for the witness as well as a morally weighty matter, apart from whatever action is taken by the audience upon hearing the testimony. At the same time, there is a possibility of failure in this regard, as with any communicative act. The audience that is likely to respond appropriately may be inaccessible. Or the one who bears witness may misjudge his audience in various ways, by mistakenly believing, for example, that it will not be indifferent to his testimony or that it will believe in the veracity of his testimony. Failures of communication may be due to some feature of the audience, or some failure on the witness' part to properly gauge how his testimony will be received by it. And sometimes communication may be unsuccessful because of some flaw in the testimony itself.

Thus, for witnessing to accomplish its purpose, the audience must be of the right sort and be in the right relationship to the witness, and must possess attributes to properly receive and respond to the testimony. What these attributes are will vary, depending on the nature and point of the testimony that is given. With respect to testimony in a court of law, the audience (i.e., jury) must, among other things, be capable of keeping an open mind about the guilt or innocence of the accused and of impartially assessing the relevance of the testimony to the issue at hand. With respect to testimony about moral wrongdoing, other capacities, including the capacity for compassionate concern for and response to the sufferings of others and the capacity for moral outrage, will often be necessary in the audience, if the testimony is to be taken up by it in the right way. And in cases of testimony that is provided in circumstances that do not involve matters of legal or moral import, the particular need being addressed by the testifier likewise determines what condition the audience should be in to respond to it appropriately. In addition to these various attributes, it is necessary for successful witnessing that trust be placed in the witness, specifically, trust that the witness has respect for the truth and that she is saying what she actually believes. For an audience that distrusts a witness in these respects will usually dismiss her testimony from the outset, however trustworthy the witness may actually be.

Bearing witness, I said in Section 2, can be a way of remembering and of memorializing, and what is distinctive about it in this mode is that it is always *in relation to an audience*. When remembering the dead takes the form of bearing witness to the wrongs they endured or the circumstances of their death, it is inseparable from, or takes the form of, testimony to an audience. It has this peculiar quality of directedness that is not shared by all ways of remembering. Moreover, remembering by witnessing may also have effects that other ways of remembering lack or are not as closely associated with, such as psychic healing for the witness-rememberer and reparative action taken by the audience in response to her testimony. Another difference that is occasionally found between bearing witness and other ways of remembering is that bearing witness may require courage and perseverance and so be a demanding form of remembrance. Having said that, it may still be required of us in fulfillment of our obligations of remembrance, unless, that is, other weighty moral considerations indicate otherwise.

(c) *The need for testimony*

Following condition (c) in Coady's definition of testimony, a witness offers evidence that is directed to an audience in need of evidence relating to some question or matter. In the most common case, a witness is necessary or useful because the audience is in real doubt about or ignorant of some matter for which the witness' testimony provides evidence. This is the function of testimony that Hobbes has in mind: "For no man is a witness to him that already believeth, and therefore needs no witness; but to them that deny or doubt, or have not heard it."[39] But as Coady points out,[40] there are other circumstances in which witness testimony may be valuable to an audience that Hobbes seems to have overlooked. For one thing, an audience may legitimately be more confident of the truth of some proposition than a witness is, yet the witness' testimony, when combined with other reports, may increase the audience's level of confidence in that proposition. This sort of consideration is important when a high level of confidence is needed for a particular purpose, as in criminal trials. For another, even though an audience is, with good reason, certain about some matter, it may have its confidence shaken if it is presented with telling counterevidence. Here a witness' testimony does not remove doubt, but may, on the contrary, cause an audience to reconsider some matter of which it was previously convinced. Broadly speaking, testimonial evidence – the only kind of evidence that I am speaking about here – is evidence that is relevant to a matter with respect to which the intended audience needs clarification, education, corroboration, direction, admonition, and so forth.[41]

As this indicates, there are many reasons why an audience might need evidence of the sort that a witness, and perhaps only a witness, can provide. Testimony might have an archival function, that is, it may supply the audience with information about past events that are not adequately known. However, the mere fact that testimony provides knowledge is plainly not sufficient to establish a *need* for testimony. We also have to show that the past events are significant enough, from a moral or social or historical standpoint, that they ought to be known or that knowledge of them is required for some morally or socially significant purpose.

For example, because wrongdoing may be, and often is, hidden from public view, witness testimony can bring the truth to light and provide evidence sufficient to justify punishment. If the witness is himself a perpetrator – a possibility I will discuss in Section 4 – his testifying to his own responsibility for wrongdoing may pave the way for reconciliation with his former victims. In addition, testimony about wrongdoing may be needed in order to spur others to assist victims of injustice or violence and to work to eliminate its causes. Especially in cases of large-scale wrongdoing, the extent of wrongdoing may be so extreme that those who merely read about it or hear about it distantly either cannot believe or refuse to believe that it actually happened. Witnesses to horrific crimes can provide testimony that shocks others out of their denial or complacency and that galvanizes humanitarian intervention and reparative response. And finally, the testimony of victims expresses the experience of wrongdoing and, if appropriately preserved, is a means of transmission of that experience to others, including future generations. Here, the need met by testimony is linked to the moral imperatives of memory.

I want to underscore this last point. Those who bear witness might address their testimony to multiple audiences, in particular, to future as well as present generations. Often the primary audience is the former, perhaps because currently existing people do not need to be reminded of some recent particularly serious wrongdoing or because they are unwilling to acknowledge and come to terms with it. At any rate, with the passage of time, and as the victims of the original injustice die out, it may become increasingly likely that individuals and groups will not remember what happened in the past or might even question whether it occurred at all. Aware of this, witnesses may provide testimony that is directed as much if not more to future generations than to contemporaries, precisely to prevent this from happening. The need here, we might say, is the need to remember, and it is this need that the one who seeks to preserve the memory of past injustice by bearing witness addresses. Thus an audience may need evidence with respect to some matter not only because it is in dispute or unresolved, but also because it is in danger of being expunged from the collective memory.[42]

3. SOME TYPOLOGICAL REMARKS

Persons who bear witness are witnesses, witnesses provide testimony, and testimony, in accordance with Coady's analysis, offers evidence by one who has testimonial authority to an audience in need of evidence. This is the general conception of witnessing that I assume in the rest of this chapter, and now I want to consider it in more detail. Specifically, I focus on two of its aspects: the nature of what is witnessed and the witness' relationship to it. I do this ultimately to help us better understand the memorial function of bearing witness, both *what* can be remembered in this way and *who* can play this particular memorial role. This section ends with a brief comment about an extended sense of testimony and witnessing.[43]

(a) *Bearing witness to right and wrong, good and bad*

I have mostly been discussing bearing witness in the context of situations involving misfortune or wrongdoing of various kinds. It will of course often not be possible in practice to draw a sharp distinction here because misfortune and wrongdoing can intertwine and conspire with one another to cause serious hardship for their victims. But the distinction can be drawn in the following way: misfortunes to which one bears witness are serious setbacks to persons' interests[44] – for example, disease, disability, injury, death – that are due to the vicissitudes of nature or other occurrences for which no human agent (or agents) can be held morally responsible;[45] and wrongdoings to which one bears witness are violations of rights or other moral norms resulting from the unjustifiable and inexcusable conduct of others.

There are some noteworthy differences between testimony about wrongdoing and testimony about misfortune. Witnesses who testify to wrongdoing may be dismissed or discredited by the audience they address if that audience contains individuals who are responsible for the wrongdoing or if the audience itself is implicated in it. Because misfortunes are the result of the workings of impersonal nature or plain bad luck, and no blame is assigned for them, witnesses who testify to them may be less likely to encounter these problems.[46] Furthermore, supposing the testimony of witnesses is heard and judged creditable, witnesses to wrongdoing may provide evidence that supports a finding of guilt, which in turn justifies punishment or a demand for restitution or compensation. The testimony of witnesses to misfortune, by contrast, may call on the sympathy of others to provide aid and give comfort, which they may be obligated to do, but there is no one to blame, hence no one to punish or to secure compensation from, for the misfortune itself.

Harms due to moral wrongdoing also have a particular expressive meaning that harms due to misfortune do not, and this gives witnessing harms due to moral wrongdoing a significance and a point that witnessing harms due to misfortune lacks. Serious moral wrongdoing does not just violate the rights of the victim to noninterference. It is also a communicative act that expresses this: you (the victim) are of no account, morally speaking, or do not count as much as I do, and you may be used in whatever way I see fit. This implicit claim, conveyed to the victim, itself wrongs him, apart from whatever other harm results from the other's conduct.[47] The focus of bearing witness to (serious) moral wrongdoing, therefore, is not only the violation of the victim's rights, but also the powerful message of moral inferiority conveyed by it, itself a moral violation. No such message is conveyed by harms due to misfortune, however, and if a message of any sort is conveyed, it is that we are all ultimately at the mercy of nature and luck.

Terrence Des Pres claims that "survival is a collective act, and so is bearing witness. Both are rooted in compassion and care, and both expose the illusion of separateness."[48] Although I would not go so far as to say that bearing witness is necessarily a collective act or is always rooted in care and compassion, it is the case that those who bear witness to wrongdoing or misfortune are often motivated at least in part by compassion for those who have been harmed or have suffered. When one is so motivated to bear witness, the witness sees the suffering of others as the sort of thing that could happen to anyone, himself included. And because the other is seen as a fellow human being, witnessing motivated by compassion involves a sense of shared humanity and acknowledges a fundamental human equality with respect to susceptibility to pain, misery, hardship, suffering, affliction, and the like.[49] Moreover, compassion imparts its moral value to witnessing that is reflective of compassionate concern. As Lawrence Blum argues, "part of the moral force of compassion" consists in its promoting "the shared experience of equality in common humanity,"[50] and this is true as well for the moral force of compassionate witnessing. Compassion is not the only morally significant attitude that bearing witness to wrongdoing or misfortune can express, however. Acts of bearing witness can also express and be motivated by *solidarity* with the victims of misfortune or wrongdoing, by a sense that one shares common interests with them and is united with them in the pursuit of common objectives.

Although I have begun by discussing bearing witness in relation to these negative categories, which is how it is most commonly thought of, it seems arbitrary to limit it to these. We may plausibly speak not only of bearing witness to misfortune but to good fortune as well, and of bearing witness to morally praiseworthy as well as morally blameworthy conduct. The positive cases have the same generic features as their negative counterparts, that is, they involve testimony provided by one with the relevant authority to an audience that has some need (which can cover a wide range) for evidence. Just as with misfortune and wrongdoing, an audience may need the testimony of a witness to good deeds and morally praiseworthy actions, for otherwise these might go unrecognized or be forgotten. Consider, for example, the testimony of Jewish survivors concerning the heroism of the non-Jews who hid them from the Nazis and thereby risked their own lives and the lives of their loved ones. Witnessing can also testify to good fortune, to make a point about the extent

of our dependence on God's loving kindness, or to deflate the preten-
sions of those who claim special merit for themselves, or for some other
reason.

However, although the notion of bearing witness has wide application,
a moral imperative to bear witness might not have the same moral force in
all these cases. It seems that a duty to bear witness to good fortune, if such
duty exists, is in general weaker than a moral imperative to bear witness to
serious wrongdoing and misfortune. Whether there is a similar asymmetry
between bearing witness to serious wrongdoing and bearing witness to
exemplary moral behavior, that is, whether bearing witness to the former
is in general a more compelling duty than bearing witness to the latter,
is less clear. Indeed, I am inclined to think that such a claim about the
relative strengths of these duties cannot withstand careful examination
of cases.

(b) *The witness' relationship to wrongdoing*

I now want to say more about the witness' relationship to the focus of
witnessing, in particular to wrongdoing. I have already said that a witness
to wrongdoing can either be one who is directly affected by it or one who
is affected as a relative, friend, and so on (i.e., a secondary victim), or
one not affected in either of these ways (the witness may simply be an
observer or reporter of them). Another important distinction is between
the witness who testifies to wrongdoing as a perpetrator of it and the
witness who testifies as its innocent victim. Although the line between
culpable wrongdoer and innocent victim cannot always be sharply drawn,
we need to keep the distinction in mind if we want to understand the
different sorts of burdens associated with bearing witness.

Confession, on some occasions, can be thought of as an act of bearing
witness in which one testifies to wrongdoing (or in its religious version,
sin) as its perpetrator.[51] In this case, the witness openly admits that he
has committed wrongs or participated in wrongdoing, typically although
not always in the hope that those he has wronged will forgive him or be
lenient with him. The wrongs that he has committed or participated in
are ones that he takes responsibility for, and he asserts and gives evidence
of believing that what he did was wrong, not that it was permissible or justified. Confession can be faulted in various ways. For example, a witness

may testify against himself to something that he did not do (a false confession), or for which he is not as responsible as he maintains, or he may claim a role for himself in the commission of the wrong that is different from the one he actually played. Finally, not only individuals but groups of individuals can confess to wrongdoing. Groups of people can collectively take responsibility for past wrongdoing without confessing to it, of course, but commonly what we might call "collective confession" goes hand-in-hand with the former.

Confession was integral to the process adopted by the South African Truth and Reconciliation Commission for granting amnesty to individuals who committed wrongs under the former apartheid regime. Immunity from civil suit and criminal prosecution was available, but only on a conditional basis: it was only granted to those individuals who personally applied for it, who testified fully before the TRC about their politically motivated crimes and misconduct, and who accepted responsibility for what they had done.[52] The TRC recognized that there are gray areas where the line between perpetrator and victim cannot be clearly drawn and that perpetrators may also be seen in part as victims, but it refused to regard this fact as absolving the perpetrators of their individual responsibility for wrongdoing. Further, although some perpetrators who testified before the TRC offered apologies and asked for forgiveness, this was not a requirement of granting amnesty. What was required was confession, not sorrow or contrition.[53]

One of the reasons given by the commission for requiring full acknowledgment by the perpetrators of their deeds as a condition for granting amnesty was that this was necessary to uncover the full extent of the crimes and atrocities committed under apartheid. Here, confession was enlisted in the service of truth-finding and memory: the collected information from amnesty applicants would help provide a fuller picture of the past, and its widespread dissemination would overcome ignorance or denial of the past among the general community and government officials. As this example illustrates, confession can be a particularly telling way of bearing witness to past wrongdoing and shaping a community's collective memory of historical injustice. Confession not only corroborates the victims' memories and claims but validates them in an especially conspicuous way, and it establishes a public record of past transgressions that is particularly convincing because it is based on the testimony of the perpetrators themselves. Apology is not required for these tasks, and confession, which is a necessary but not sufficient condition of apology, can achieve these results without apology.

We can combine the various classifications in this and the last subsection to yield the following variations on the basic structure set out in Section 2. A person can relate to acts or practices or states of affairs as: (1) a victim only, whether of misfortune or wrongdoing (an innocent victim); (2) a perpetrator only (one who confesses); (3) as neither a perpetrator, nor a victim (a bystander, journalist, etc.); and (4) as both a perpetrator and a victim of wrongdoing (a guilty victim). There are also positive counterparts to some of these in which a "victim" is replaced by a "beneficiary" (of good fortune, for example, or good deeds) and a "perpetrator" is replaced by a "benefactor." Whatever the particular conjunction of variables, the witness in all of these cases testifies and so addresses an audience, actual or hoped for. The testimony may be about something in the past and so be the form that remembrance takes. Or it may concern something that recently transpired, but that the witness believes is in danger of being forgotten if it is not witnessed. Bearing witness can therefore be both a way of remembering and of recording events for others, so that they in turn can remember and transmit that memory to those who follow after them.

(c) *Bearing witness to one's convictions*

There are some other uses of the term "bearing witness" that might be mentioned, although they depart somewhat from the examples I have presented so far. Consider, for example, the religious martyr who is said to testify or bear witness to his faith by his death. Another example from the religious domain, similar to but less extreme than that of the martyr, is the born-again Christian who stands up at prayer meetings and bears witness to being saved by Jesus and the presence of God in his life. Individuals can also testify to nonreligious convictions by dedicating their lives to certain ideals or causes and being willing to suffer hardship, possibly even death, to achieve them. Cases like these are relevant to the concerns of this chapter because bearing witness to one's convictions can leave a legacy that becomes an integral part of the collective memory of a community and helps shape its collective self-identity.[54] In addition, testifying to one's beliefs before an audience brings one's private convictions into the public domain, and one's convictions can sometimes be reinforced by the memory of one's having affirmed them to others. But if these and like examples are to be assimilated to the account of bearing witness that I have presented, we need to explain how the notion of evidence works in them. What is being offered as evidence for what?

One suggestion is that their deeds constitute evidence that they *have certain deep-seated beliefs* or convictions. This, however, is a rather detached way of describing what their actions express. A slightly better description would be that their deeds constitute evidence for the *sincerity* of their beliefs. Yet, even this fails to fully convey the import of their actions. What is left out is that their respective actions give evidence of the *importance* that their beliefs have for them, or the importance to them of believing in what they believe, an importance that, as they see things, justifies sacrifice, suffering, perhaps even death. This sort of evidence – of the importance to oneself of what one believes – is different from evidence that something happened or that terrible wrongs were committed, which is what many cases of bearing witness provide. But it is not such an idiosyncratic use of the notion of evidence to warrant excluding such cases altogether from the purview of this chapter. Moreover, as we will shortly see, what is true of the martyr, the born-again believer, and the idealist is also true of many others who bear witness, especially to serious wrongdoing. Like them, the testimony of those who bear witness to wrongdoing not only expresses what they believe but also what they believe *in*, something they care about deeply and that affects their lives in significant ways.

4. THE SYMBOLIC VALUE OF BEARING WITNESS

Moving on from the conceptual and typological preliminaries of Sections 2 and 3, I now want to address the normative question: What is the moral value of bearing witness?[55] There is the consequentialist answer which says: bearing witness promotes or may reasonably be expected to promote desirable outcomes of various sorts, and its moral value is entirely accounted for by the good consequences that do or are expected to flow from it. Among these consequences are the following: bearing witness, because of its testimonial character, is often crucial to restoring the mental health of survivors[56]; it may be a necessary part of a process of reconstructing societies devastated by violence and internal divisions; it can focus attention on the needs of those who are in peril and generate support for humanitarian assistance[57]; it can bring crimes or evidence for them to light and help bring the guilty to justice; it can inspire others with examples of exemplary loyalty and heroism; and so forth. Of course, outcomes may be uncertain and may not actually result; and bearing witness may have multiple and unintended consequences, good as well as bad. But these possibilities can be accommodated within some type of consequentialist outlook.

More troubling for such a view is that ordinary moral thinking suggests there is a point to and value in bearing witness quite apart from whether it is likely to or is believed likely to achieve desirable outcomes. I do not mean, or just mean, the *psychological* value of "getting things off one's chest," of giving vent to one's repressed emotions, and the like. Rather, I mean *moral* value, in the sense that one is a good or better person for having witnessed, though in vain. Bearing witness, in other words, can express character and conviction, and its relationship to character and conviction is an important part of the explanation of its moral value. Even when there are some good consequences, there remains a kind of *impotence* at the heart of bearing witness to suffering, a kind of moral distress at one's helplessness that may be fully warranted, even if one has done all one could have in the circumstances and there is nothing to regret from a consequentialist standpoint. The victimization and misfortune of others cannot be undone or compensated for by bearing witness to it, and this is something that witnesses are often acutely and painfully aware of. Given this, we can ask the following question:

> What goodness can be expressed in a witness that must continually affirm its inability to affirm, that must continually find itself in quandary, and whose most articulate response to the victimization of the other must simply leave the other victimized?[58]

Of course, one might be able to point to some good consequences that bearing witness, impotent though it might be to fully redeem the dead, has brought about. But the witness finds himself in a "quandary," and the quandary and the distress that attends it contain an ingredient that does not seem amenable to consequentialist treatment. What consequentialism cannot acknowledge is that his distress may be a function of, and evidence for, his having commitments the value of which cannot adequately be accounted for exclusively in consequentialist terms.

Consequentialists who look to the desirable consequences that bearing witness can be expected to have have no account to give of the moral value of witnessing apart from these. The "goodness [that] can be expressed in a witness" is only what is derived from good consequences. And this is problematic because, intuitively, it seems that an appeal to consequences does not give us a complete answer to the question about value. The answer, it seems, should not just be that without good consequences there is no goodness expressed in bearing witness; nor should it be that the sense of impotence that is such a common feature of bearing witness to the suffering of others signifies nothing of moral significance apart from the consequences it can be expected to yield. Rather, it seems that there is something intrinsically valuable about the affirmation itself, some goodness that is expressed thereby in the one who bears witness, even if the response to the other's victimization leaves the other victimized and even, as it is sometimes put, one bears witness "in vain." Indeed, one's continuing to affirm *despite* this may both show the depth of one's conviction and contribute to its intrinsic value. And as for the distress mentioned above, this arises from the realization of the impossibility of undoing the harm to the victim and it might be warranted even if one cannot be faulted on consequentialist grounds. For arguably the distress is an expression of where the witness stands vis-à-vis fundamental values of good and bad, right and wrong, and his being committed to these values is itself morally valuable and important, apart from whatever good he is or, more to the point, is not able to promote by bearing witness. What we need is an account that makes plausible and justifies these intuitions.

Robert Merrihew Adams would agree with these intuitions and, in Chapter 9 of *Finite and Infinite Goods*,[59] he presents an explanation of the moral (or as he sometimes calls it the "ethical") value of witness or testimony that eschews appeal to consequences. His explanation is deeply intertwined with a theistic theory of ethics in which God, identified with the Transcendent Good, provides the metaphysical foundation for all value. There is much, however, that is plausible in that explanation independent of any commitment to the existence of a supernatural being. In Adams's view, the moral value of witnessing is not solely conditional on the consequences it produces or is likely to produce. Rather, it is also intrinsic to the activity as a particular type of symbolic expression, and it is possible to give an account of its value from this standpoint, and to appreciate its importance for the ethical life, without having to invoke supernatural explanations.

Adams opens Chapter 9 with an incident from the life of the theologian Dietrich Bonhoeffer, a leader of resistance to Hitler in the Protestant Church in Germany. His friend and biographer, Eberhard Bethge, relates how shocked he was when Bonhoeffer, along with others at an outdoor café at a German seaside resort, gave the Hitler salute in response to a loudspeaker announcement of France's surrender to Germany. How was Bonhoeffer's salute to be understood? As later events bore out, his salute certainly did not signify that he had given up his opposition to Nazism or that he had lost his nerve. He was, rather, in the early stages of a change of strategy, from public protest to subversion of the German government from within. With the growing power of the Nazi regime, Bonhoeffer had come to realize that acts of public protest, for example, refusing to give the Hitler salute, were both personally risky and probably ineffective.

Adams's response to this incident sets the stage for his account of the moral value of witnessing. He says he would not presume to fault Bonhoeffer for giving the salute. Nevertheless, he thinks, and he supposes others agree, that there would have been something admirable about his refusing to do so, at least if the expected consequences of his refusal to salute would not have jeopardized the struggle against Nazism: "I would *like* his life story better if it did not contain that Hitler salute" (216), Adams admits. To be sure, if Bonhoeffer had refused to salute, his act of protest would have been, for all he could tell at the time, a symbolic gesture. It would not have done any good in terms of advancing the resistance. But it would still have had enormous moral value *as* symbolic expression. Adams describes his evaluative orientation as follows:

> The content of one's testimony matters, as well as its truthfulness. Being truthful about one's name and address does not matter in the same way as expressing what one believes about a great moral or religious issue. And I think that is because in the latter case one is testifying, not just *about* something, but *for* or *against* something. (217)

Testimony, as a type of communication, is subject to certain ethical requirements, including truthfulness. But there is much more than the truthfulness of testimony to consider if we are assessing witnessing from an ethical point of view. Centrally important for Adams is what the witnessing and the testimony express or reveal about "what one is for and against." Specifically, they may express one's "love of the good and opposition to the bad," perhaps in a largely symbolic manner, and this, he argues, can be morally good quite apart from any desirable consequences that might be thought to flow from them; in other words, intrinsically good.

Love of the good and opposition to the bad also play a central role in Adams's conception of the good or virtuous life. To love the good is to be *for* it, to be disposed to favor it in action, desire, and feeling, or at least not to go against it in its various forms, and what is good for a person is a life characterized by this love or, as Adams puts it, "by *enjoyment of the excellent*" (93).[60] The value of this love is not just the value of the consequences it produces, and although witnessing may only have a symbolic relationship to the good, "the value of what we stand for symbolically is . . . important to the moral quality of our lives" (219). To be sure, one way of expressing one's love of the good and opposition to the bad is by striving to produce good consequences and to prevent bad ones. But we can also be for the good and against the bad even if there is little or nothing that we can do to promote or defend the goods that we rightly care about. Here, in Adams's view, is where symbolic expression is particularly important, for *symbolically* expressing love for a good or hatred of an evil may be the best available way of *being* for or against it when circumstances are such that our ability to bring about or attempt to bring about good consequences or to prevent harm is severely limited. From the point of view of what the act reveals about the agent, specifically about the agent's loves and hates, symbolic action is not necessarily any less important to the moral quality of our lives than bringing about good consequences of some type or other.

This account, I suggest, gives us part of the answer to the question about the moral value of bearing witness: bearing witness to the suffering of victims of wrongdoing may be understood (in part) as a symbolic act whose moral value consists in its expressing one's intrinsically valuable allegiance to the good and/or repudiation of the bad, where "bad" is not confined to wrongdoing but includes misfortune as well.[61] Bearing witness to the suffering of those who were wronged, like punishing those who wronged them, and bearing witness to the suffering of those who endured misfortune, cannot restore the victims to their former state, of course. But bearing witness to the suffering of those who were wronged can symbolize one's commitment to the moral order that was upset by, or the moral norms that were breached by wrongdoing and undeserved suffering, and it can symbolize this long after there are no perpetrators left to punish. In this way, bearing witness symbolically allies us with morality. Robert Nozick makes a similar point about ethical conduct in general:

> Ethical principles codify how to behave toward others in a way that is appropriate to their value and to our fellow-feelings with them. Holding and following ethical principles, in addition to the particular purposes this serves, also have a symbolic meaning for us. Treating people (and value in general) with respect and responsiveness puts us "on the side of" that value, perhaps allying us with everything else on its side, and symbolizes our intertwining with this.[62]

Witnessing the suffering of the victims of wrongdoing likewise "puts us on the side of" the values embodied in ethical principles, values that we uphold in the very act of bearing witness to the violation of these principles. Indeed, one measure of the importance that we give to morality in our lives is that we deem it appropriate, perhaps even obligatory, not to forget the suffering of those who fell victim to wrongdoing but to bear witness to it. Bearing witness to the good that others have done or tried to do also intertwines us with values expressed in ethical principles, but in this case, their values and the values expressed in the principles agree. As for bearing witness to misfortune, it too can symbolize one's refusal to acquiesce in undeserved suffering, only now this is suffering brought about the operation of chance rather than the actions of morally responsible human agents. The testimony of the witness may or may not contribute to relief of the sufferers' condition, but the act of bearing witness to their plight can itself be a way of taking a stand against the arbitrariness of human suffering.

Bearing witness to the suffering of the victims of wrongdoing is an important way of being for morality, but this should not be taken to mean being for morality *instead* of being for the particular victims who suffered from its violation. What then does being for the victims involve? What, in addition to revealing something about *us* as persons, does bearing witness do for *them*? Here, I recall a point made earlier about the particular expressive meaning of harms due to wrongdoing. Serious and deliberate wrongdoing tells the victim and bystanders that the victim's interests are either inconsiderable or not as morally weighty as those of the wrongdoer. If the victims had a chance to protest their treatment at all, the protests probably fell on deaf ears or may have only provided a pretext for further acts of cruelty. Bearing witness to past suffering sends a countermessage to this:[63] it symbolically asserts the moral status of the victims, their coequal membership in the moral community, by giving them and their suffering a voice. And when we heed that voice, we affirm that status, however belatedly. Their voice may have been silenced or discredited in the past, but now there is someone who speaks for them and of what they endured and who has or claims to have the moral authority to do so. I will discuss this aspect of witnessing at greater length in Section 5.

Adams's account of the moral value of symbolism helps to explain the moral value of bearing witness because this can be an important form of symbolic expression. But there are various ways of expressing allegiance to the good – witness is one, sacrifice and thanksgiving are mentioned by Adams as others – and an account in these terms must tell us specifically *how* we are for the good, and what aspect(s) or instance(s) of the good we are for, in each case. With regard to the first point, for example, standing for something is sometimes considered an act of *integrity*. A few remarks about the relationship between this and bearing witness will help to further clarify the latter and where its value lies.

The notion of standing for something is central to the meaning of integrity. In one familiar sense, integrity is principled action, or more broadly speaking, action that expresses one's deeply held or cherished values, principles, and projects. There are two components to this: one must have certain cherished values or projects and one must be committed to them, where being committed means not only acting in accordance with them but *sticking* by them when it is costly to do so (within limits). Some persons have little in the way of principles or values that determine what they stand for. Others are not unprincipled but lack the courage of their convictions; that is, their actions deviate from their principles in the face of pressures or constraints that they ought to be able to resist. And there are other possibilities as well.[64] Commonly, if somewhat obscurely, the person of integrity is described as someone who "'keeps his inmost self intact,' whose life is 'of a piece,' whose self is whole and integrated."[65] In the case of moral integrity, to stand for something the way a person of integrity stands for something is to take responsibility for one's conduct in a particular way, by acting in accordance with and being faithful in word and deed to deeply held moral values and principles.

The value of integrity is both personal and social. We admire persons of integrity who stand for the good because they have a strong sense of self-identity, because they know who they are and what they stand for, and because what they stand for is worthy of their allegiance. Under these conditions, integrity contributes to the good life. And from the social standpoint, integrity provides the basis for reliance, trust, and personal relationship. Although it is specifically about the importance of symbolic expression rather than integrity, Adams's observation applies to integrity as well:

> .... [we] have interests in the intrinsic quality of each other's lives. In particular, it matters to us what other people are for and against, as that profoundly affects the possibilities of alliance and social union with them. A morally good person, from this point of view, is not just a useful person but an ally of the good and of those who love the good. (220)

Relations among persons who lack integrity are unstable and filled with mutual suspicion. Short term collaboration may be possible, but over the long term there will not be sufficient trust in one another's intentions to make cooperation possible.

There are different ways of being an ally of the good, symbolic as well as nonsymbolic, and both, as the discussion of Bonhoeffer illustrates, may entail risks. Symbolically expressing one's allegiance to the good, like nonsymbolically pursuing the good, can be dangerous, but one who acts despite the danger may be displaying integrity in doing so. Indeed, one cannot truly be an *ally* of the good, however one expresses that allegiance, if one is not willing to stick by one's commitment to it and to incur some cost or make some sacrifice in doing so, should that be necessary. To the extent that symbolically allying oneself with the good requires or exhibits integrity, in other words, to the extent that the two overlap, we can explain the value of the former in terms of the value of integrity (or more specifically, moral integrity). And the value of bearing witness, as a kind of symbolic expression, can be explained in the same way.

However, there are different conceptions of integrity and this complicates the comparison with bearing witness. The conceptions that have gained currency in the philosophical literature basically conceive of integrity as a relationship that the agent has to him or herself and hence as a personal virtue.[66] In contrast to this, the type of symbolic expression that I am interested in here, that is, bearing witness, is essentially interpersonal. (To be sure, integrity has social implications in that it provides the basis for reliance and trust, but this is compatible with a fundamentally self-regarding or self-protective conception of integrity.) With witnessing, one provides *testimony* – as Adams himself notes in discussing the witnessing of the religious martyr[67] – and in testifying one addresses another, even if that other is remote. Understood in this way, an essentially self-regarding conception of witnessing is incoherent. The *content* of the testimony can be about what the witness herself has experienced, but the *stance* of the witness is other-directed.

Again, however, there are other conceptions of integrity. Cheshire Calhoun, for example, proposes a different view, according to which integrity is enacted in relationship with others and is "the social virtue of acting on one's own judgment because doing so matters to deliberators' common interest in determining what is worth doing."[68] Integrity so conceived is "tightly connected to viewing oneself as a member of an evaluating community and to caring about what that community endorses."[69] I think this understanding of integrity directs us to something important about bearing witness as well.

The symbolic value of bearing witness is value that is *realized in and through the activity of addressing* an audience, of standing before an audience and bringing good or bad to its attention, and thereby declaring one's allegiance to the good. It is not to be understood exclusively in consequentialist terms, for there can be moral value in address apart from whatever good may come of it,[70] even if no good comes about as a result – if, say, the audience turns out to be indifferent, or in denial, or unsympathetic – and even if good outcomes are not expected. Witnessing does not lose its point or value simply because our ability to effect change in the world is extremely limited, at least for the foreseeable future. At the same time, the witness is typically not indifferent to whether or not an audience exists, or will exist, that will listen attentively and sympathetically to the testimony and respond to it in the way she intends. She has some hope, perhaps only very slight, that it will have this sort of impact and she gauges the effectiveness of her testimony by whether it receives the hoped for response. Unless she is engaged in a sort of moral self-aggrandizement – which of course is possible – the witness wants, hopes, and intends her testimony to do more than express *her* commitment or loyalty to the good.

Calhoun's understanding of integrity is relevant here. For the audience to respond to the witness' testimony in the way she typically intends and hopes, it is necessary for it to share or come to share her values to some extent. Either the audience already agrees with her sense of right and wrong or it undergoes some sort of moral transformation because of the testimony itself. This presupposes that the person who bears witness, like the person of integrity, views herself as a member of an evaluating community, even if it is has not yet materialized. She doesn't only want to fill in the historical record so that her audience will have a better understanding of what happened in the past. She cares about what this community endorses and wants it to share her moral responses to the past, her repugnance or outrage or compassion or, in the case of the positive counterparts mentioned earlier, her admiration or gratitude or vicarious pleasure in the good fortune of others.

5. WITNESSING, SELF-REPRESENTATION, AND MORAL AGENCY

We often contrast acts that have symbolic value with acts that "really make a difference in the world," usually to the former's disadvantage. I want to resist this moral devaluation of symbolic expression. However, the account inspired by Adams has gone only part way to explain the moral value of bearing witness. Bearing witness has moral value because it reveals or expresses our allegiance to the good and the right, our repudiation of the bad and the wrong. This much I hope to have established. But it also has moral value because of what it does for or with respect to those who, because they are dead or have been traumatized by injustice or misfortune or intimidated or some other reason, have been silenced. And this, as we will see, helps to explain the particular importance that *address* – and not just public declaration, which was discussed in the last section – has in my account of bearing witness. To pursue this, I now want to consider how bearing witness is related to the notion of voice, and how voice – or having a voice and its being attended to – connects up with the moral standing of the victim. I approach this topic by first looking at

some of the more prominent uses of the notion of voice, not limiting this
survey to explicitly moral uses of the notion. All of these uses, however,
have a moral dimension and because of this there is a close relationship
between the understanding of voice and its importance in these discussions and what I want to claim about voice in this section. I begin with
trauma and its treatment.

People who have undergone brutal, humiliating, or degrading treatment are often traumatized by it and find it difficult to speak about what
they have suffered. They may be afraid to cause pain to loved ones by
recounting the event; they may fear being devalued or thought less worthy
of respect for having gone through such an experience; or (as is common
among victims of childhood sexual abuse) they may believe themselves
to be somehow partially or chiefly responsible for the wrong inflicted
on them and be tortured by guilt. The mere idea of remembering the
experience often produces fear and anxiety and, as Margalit notes with
respect to humiliating experiences, remembering them carries particular
risks that remembering painful experiences may not:

> We do in fact remember the facts of physical pains to a remarkable
> degree, but we can hardly relive them. On the other hand, we can hardly
> remember insults without reliving them.[71]

To remember one's past humiliation is to risk experiencing the humiliation all over again, and when the price of speaking is reliving, speaking
risks retraumatizing the victim.

If, despite the emotional risks and psychological distress, the survivor
of trauma is able to bear witness to what she has undergone, and her
testimony receives acknowledgment and validation from others, the survivor may find relief from painful and humiliating memories.[72] If the
testimony is not taken up in this manner, this may be experienced by
the survivor as a kind of repetition of the earlier traumatic event, and
fear or anticipation of this response may deter her from testifying. "The
absence of an empathic listener," says Dori Laub, "or more radically, the
absence of an *addressable other*, an other who can hear the anguish of one's
memories and thus affirm and recognize their realness, annihilates the
story."[73] Here the distinction between an actual and a hoped for audience becomes important, for it may be difficult to hold firm to the belief
in an addressable other when one is only testifying to an audience that

might exist. Facing a hostile or indifferent world, one may despair of one's testimony ever finding a receptive and sympathetic audience.

The victims of trauma are harmed twice over: first, by the violent acts and, second, by their remaining silent about them. If they are to recover psychologically and emotionally from the trauma, they must be able to tell their stories of what was done to them and these stories must be heard by caring others who are able to listen sympathetically to them. The stories must be *theirs* not only in the sense that they must speak them out of their own mouths, but also in the sense that they must be told from *their* point of view. And the listener must validate the victim's story as an authentic expression of the victim's own understanding of what she has undergone, even if there are reasons to question the accuracy of that understanding as a descriptive report of what happened.

The literature on trauma and traumatic memory is a rich source of material on the psychological significance of testimony and bearing witness.[74] Here, the metaphor of "voice" – as in gaining one's voice – is often employed to indicate what is needed if victims are to be liberated from, as Laub puts it, "enslavement to the fate of their victimization."[75] The metaphor has other uses as well, not in relation to trauma. One occurs in discussions of the meaning and value of constructing personal illness narratives. Arthur Frank, for example, argues for the importance of allowing and encouraging those who suffer from illness to speak for themselves, to find their own voice, rather than submit to the reductionistic and objectifying categories of modern medicine.[76] The case study, written from the professional's standpoint, objectifies the experience and sufferings of the ill and subjects the ill person to the norms and projects of health care providers. By contrast, he argues, encouraging patients to write their own illness narratives helps liberate them from the hegemony of medicine and gives them the space to develop their story in different directions in order to facilitate a process of self-discovery through the trial of illness. Similarly, and with an explicitly political purpose, disability rights advocates insist that justice for persons with disabilities is only achievable if they can successfully (re)claim the authority to tell their own stories in their own way, so that the depiction of their lives is not left to those who lack first-hand experience of stigmatization.[77] The metaphor of voice in the literature about first-person illness narratives and disability, as in the trauma literature, calls for persons to find their own ways of articulating their life experiences and for others to take them seriously as authoritative tellers of the truth about those experiences.

The metaphor of voice (and the correlative metaphor of silence) also plays a central role in feminist writing where it is used to illuminate various aspects of women's experience and moral and psychological development. Carol Gilligan in *In a Different Voice*[78] and Mary Field Belenky et al. in *Women's Ways of Knowing*,[79] for example, adopt the metaphor as the unifying theme of their work and see themselves as champions of a voice that is typically neglected, marginalized, or devalued. Belenky, et al. describe what they learned from extensive interviews with ordinary women:

> In describing their lives, women commonly talked about voice and silence...in an endless variety of connotations all having to do with sense of mind, self-worth, and feelings of isolation from or connection to others. We found that women repeatedly used the metaphor of voice to depict their intellectual and ethical development; and that the development of a sense of voice, mind, and self were intricately intertwined.[80]

Here, as in the illness narrative and disability examples, being silent, or being *silenced*, is associated with powerlessness and specifically with a power relation that obtains when a dominant group's experiences, achievements, and values are established as the norm for all.[81] Accordingly, to gain a voice is to become empowered to challenge entrenched hierarchies and stereotypes that mark one as deficient or defective.

Common to the various uses of the voice metaphor is an emphasis on the validity and authority of subjective experience. The point of the metaphor, in other words, is that each person has her own way of seeing herself and her world, that she must therefore be allowed to speak for herself (especially about matters of vital importance in her life), to define and articulate her own interests and values and to say how she understands the circumstances in which she finds herself. The authority one possesses to speak for oneself does not amount to incorrigibility, of course: one can make mistakes, be self-deceived, and so forth.[82] But although the authority can be challenged, on a more fundamental level it continues to demand our respectful attention. Denying someone her voice by, for example, systematically not permitting her to speak for herself, or by allowing her to speak but only about trivial matters, involves a kind of *usurpation*: because she lacks her own voice, another's characterization of her interests and experiences and of their importance to her inevitably supplants her own. She is not responded to as someone with special authority to tell the truth about her life and experience, but rather in terms of categories and modes of understanding that effectively deny her that authority.

This naturally has significant adverse psychological consequences. But the recognition by others that one possesses this authority, and the permission to speak from one's own experience, also have enormous *moral* import, and the denial of this authority is a moral offense, even if it is unwitting. Margaret Walker puts the point this way:

> ... rights to truth – to its being told, but also to telling it – are not only instrumental but are fundamental rights for women and men, for they secure the moral, civil, and political dignity of those, including most women, who have been systemically silenced and epistemically discredited. In these ways, they have been denied not only opportunity, equality, or well-being, but denied effective moral agency itself.[83]

This connection between the right to *tell* the truth and securing the dignity of those who have been silenced is also frequently mentioned as one of the chief reasons for creating truth commissions, rather than or in addition to trials, to deal with atrocities and other large-scale wrongdoing. Providing a platform for victims is not merely a means to obtaining information or bringing about individual and collective healing, but is itself doing justice to the victims. As Elizabeth Kiss describes one of the core functions of truth commissions,

> those who lives were shattered are entitled to have their suffering acknowledged and their dignity affirmed. . . . More important, we have an obligation to listen. . . . Justice requires that we treat people as ends in themselves. We affirm the dignity and agency of those who have been brutalized by attending to their voices and making their stories a part of the historical record.[84]

Bearing witness to one's own suffering and victimization, testifying to and about them, is, in this view, a right of the victim. That is, it is a right of the victim to tell the truth, as far as and in whatever way she is able, about what she has undergone and the harmful impact it has had on herself and on what and on those she cares about. The witness must rely on memory to do this, and of course, as I have said on more than one occasion,[85] there is always an interpretive and selective dimension to memory. Some past events are omitted in the recounting or recede into the background; some take on particular prominence because of their relation to the narrator or to the community to which he belongs;[86] some are given a largely symbolic meaning in the telling; and so forth. Were we to use the very same criteria to assess the veracity of the witness' testimony as we use to assess the claims of professional historians, such variability would be extremely problematic. However, we do not or at any rate should not. Error and distortion are possible, which is something both the audience and the witness should be aware of. Sometimes there might even be deliberate fabrication.[87] But it would be a mistake to conclude from these possibilities that there can be no truth – or only the so-called subjective truth of what the testimony conveys about the witness's emotions and motivations – in the testimony of those who bear witness.

We can understand what it is for someone to be qualified, perhaps uniquely well qualified, to speak on a matter while at the same time leaving room for her to get some of the facts about it wrong. As we saw before, arguably a witness is owed moral deference in recognition of her special moral authority to testify to wrongs she herself has suffered, but the obligation of moral deference is not premised on the assumption that the witness is a reporter par excellence of the events she has lived through. The question I am addressing now, however, is what *truth* the testimony of the one who bears witness can possess, not the basis of her *authority* to testify, although these are obviously not entirely separable issues.

The one who bears witness to something she has experienced is relating it from *her* point of view; therefore, what she is testifying to has an uneliminably subjective character. This is manifested in what she selects to emphasize and de-emphasize, in the meanings, symbolic and otherwise, that she attaches to it, and in the fact that witnesses may relate their experiences of the same events in very different ways. Further, the point of introducing the metaphor of voice, as I have said, is to emphasize the authority of this subjective experience. Deference to this authority is in turn linked to affirming and securing the dignity of the teller, and this has a bearing on how we characterize the truth of the witness's testimony. That is, arguably the connection between deference and dignity would be significantly weakened if all we can say about the testimony of the witness is that it is "its own truth" and that its correspondence to what actually happened or was experienced should be of no concern to the audience. But then this suggests that the testimony of the witness can possess more than a "subjective truth."[88] Naturally, her testimony does not literally mirror past events: memory does not operate this way. Nevertheless, there are constraints on what can count as a truthful recounting of the past, no matter how it is remembered and told,[89] and witness testimony sometimes satisfies these.

Corroboration from credible sources of central aspects of the testimony – from other victims, letters, diaries, and so forth – may be possible and would enhance confidence in its veracity. When corroboration by others is not available, as is often the case, we have to consider what other basis there might be for trusting the witness and relying on what she is telling us. One concern that may arise at this point is whether the testimony expresses what the witness actually believes about the past. Another concern is about a very different matter, namely, the accuracy of the testimony. The question here is whether – as might or might not be the case – her testimony is true of the past and also whether it accurately conveys how she experienced it. To some extent, we may be able to draw on evidence of past performance to justify our reliance on the witness's testimony. However, such evidence may be lacking or inconclusive. In these circumstances, an audience might simply be dismissive of the witness or, if this seems inadvisable, exercise extreme caution in relying on her testimony.

The connection between shaping and telling the truth, on the one hand, and dignity and moral agency, on the other, not only helps to explain the moral value of bearing witness to one's own suffering, but also bearing witness to the suffering of others, both as a memorial act and as testimony on behalf of those still suffering. There are those who were victims of wrongdoing who were only later able to tell of it, to find a voice to express it. There are also victims who have not lived to tell about what they suffered, and those who, though alive, are unable to speak the truth about their victimization because they have been incapacitated by it. In these cases, the testimony of others can become, as it were, the voice of the silenced.

If one is unable to exercise the right to speak one's own truth, then another may be warranted in serving as one's *proxy* with respect to telling the truth, to speak in one's stead, by proxy. What gives another standing or authorizes another to serve in this capacity is a matter which I will turn to in Section 5, but here I want to say something about the function and significance of this proxy relationship. The proxy may be an individual – a family member perhaps or a friend or colleague – or the proxy may be a community to which the victim belonged, such as a religious or ethnic community. Whoever serves as a proxy speaks a truth on behalf of one who is not able or willing to tell it – truth about what the victim was subjected to and how it affected him. Without a proxy to tell the truth on his behalf, the wrongdoing (and the victim) may be forgotten by those who ought to remember it (and him), or if remembered at all, the wrongdoing may be denied or trivialized or excused. There is, of course, no assurance that the proxy's testimony will be taken up by a receptive and responsive audience. This is one of the perils of bearing witness generally. But by giving voice to the voiceless victim, the proxy may be able to help create such an audience for his testimony.

A proxy's testimony may be instrumentally valuable insofar as it leads to an end of the victim's oppression, restoration to him or his heirs of possessions that were stolen from him, compensation when restitution is not possible, and so forth. Telling the truth on his behalf can bring about other changes as well, such as reviving worthwhile projects that the victim pursued but that have languished since his death or motivating others to find ways of preserving his memory. But the right to tell the truth about oneself and the value of doing so are not only to be explained in instrumental terms, and the same holds for giving a voice to the voiceless.

The capacity and standing to speak for oneself about one's experiences, interests, and values, and about one's relationships with others – what we can call the capacity for self-representation – is intimately connected to, indeed partly constitutive of, one's having the status of a moral agent.[90] It is particularly important, moreover, that one be able to, and have the standing to, speak for oneself about the wrongdoing to which one is or was subjected, for wrongdoing is a denial or at least a discounting of that status. The function of second- and third-person testimony can be explained similarly: bearing witness to the suffering of those who, now dead or otherwise silenced, cannot bear witness to their own suffering – giving victims who have been silenced by wrongdoing and death a voice– is not simply *reporting* or recording the truth of their plight. Rather, it *gives voice to* their plight, *insists* that their plight be heard, and so is a way of affirming their dignity and moral agency. The victim speaks through the proxy, as it were, and in so doing the proxy exercises on the victim's behalf his right to tell the truth about his life and experience, a right which is of fundamental importance for moral agency.

This affirmation of the victim's status as a moral being and agent may "only" be a symbolic act, but it is not for this reason to be discounted as a poor substitute for bringing about good consequences. For Adams, as we saw in Section 4, the moral value of symbolic expression consists in what it says about us, about the goods that we love and the evils that we hate. In the context of the current discussion, the moral value of symbolic expression is chiefly restorative: giving a voice to the voiceless by bearing witness to their plight, insisting on and being heard, symbolically restores the standing that was denied them, not as a consequence of the testimony but as a feature internal to the relationship between testimony and audience. It also says something about us, of course: not just that we hate evil, but that we hate it because of what it did to individuals, because it not only denied them their rights but took away the voice with which they could express their moral outrage at their victimization.

Giving a voice to those who are voiceless because of misfortune cannot be explained in quite the same way, nor does it have the very same significance, as giving voice to those rendered voiceless by wrongdoing. Misfortune does not have wrongdoing's expressive meaning: it does not convey a message of moral inferiority, of lack of moral standing. Yet, here too bearing witness can have enormous symbolic value, both as a kind of protest against the arbitrariness of their suffering and as a way of affirming the inherent worth of their lives.

6. PROXIES AND THE AUTHORITY TO BEAR WITNESS

The victims of injustice may not have survived to bear witness to it. Even if they did bear witness, and this was recorded and preserved in some fashion for future generations in order to keep the memory of that injustice alive, the passage of time often blunts the impact of their testimony. As for the original perpetrators, they are likely to be reluctant to take responsibility for their participation in the wrongdoing and to confess to it. These are some of the reasons why others, whom I have called proxy witnesses, may need to bear witness to that injustice themselves. Among these are persons who were not born at the time of the original injustice but who nonetheless carry on the memory of the original events and the plight of the victims by taking up the task of bearing witness. Sometimes proxy witnesses are called secondary witnesses,[91] but I will reserve the term "secondary witnesses" for a narrower category: namely, individuals or groups who did not themselves experience or participate in the original injustice but who bear witness to the wrongs that others experienced or participated in *and* that they or their successors have already borne witness to. Because secondary witnesses bear witness to what has already been witnessed, they form a link in a chain of witnessing initiated in the past and carried forward into the future; they might also participate in an intergenerational transmission of witnessing because they feel an obligation to do so. Not all proxy witnesses are secondary witnesses in this sense, for as we have seen, the original victim or perpetrator, for one reason or another, might have been silenced or might have remained silent, and no one might yet have come forward to testify for them.

Because proxy witnessing is done by persons who have not themselves experienced or participated in the original wrongdoing the way the victims or perpetrators did, questions may be raised about the authority and standing (as well as responsibility) of proxy witnesses to do this. An extreme view, suggested by poet Paul Celan's line, "No one bears witness for the witness,"[92] is that only those who have direct experience of a particular evil or wrongdoing have the moral standing to bear witness to it.[93] Testimony loses its function or authority as testimony when it is provided by those who did not personally experience the original events. This view is worth stating, but chiefly because it challenges us to find other explanations for the authority to bear witness.

We can think of authority in this context in something like the following way: W has authority to bear witness to x just in case W's testifying about x gives an audience A reason – not necessarily overriding – to pay heed to what W says. (Whether there is a prima facie reason to pay heed to W's testifying depends on facts about W, his testimony, and the particular need the audience has for witness testimony.) A critical moral question about proxy witnessing is what gives proxies the moral authority – the moral credentials, so to speak – to bear witness to the plight of their predecessors. Bearing witness to the suffering of one who cannot bear witness to it himself may give him a voice and symbolically assert his moral standing, as argued in Section 5. This is part of the explanation of the symbolic value of proxy witnessing. But the question I postponed there has to do with moral warrant. Not just anyone, it would seem, has the moral right to play this proxy role. Indeed, in some cases, it would be the height of presumptuousness (or worse) for one to claim that he may speak in this way on behalf of another. What we need to ask, then, is who is morally entitled to be a proxy witness and on what grounds.

One way to acquire the authority to bear witness for another is to have been the victim of the same or the same sort of injustice (although perhaps not in quite the same way) as the one on whose behalf one is testifying. Primo Levi, speaking as one of the survivors of Auschwitz, testifies for "the drowned," for those who did not survive and who "weeks and months before being snuffed out, had already lost the ability to observe, to remember, to compare and express themselves." He appears to believe that the shared experience of the concentration camp gives him some sort of moral standing, some limited moral and epistemic authority, to tell "the story of things seen close at hand, though not experienced personally."[94]

A second way, in general, to acquire authority, so the authority to be a proxy witness in particular, is through an explicit process of transference. For example, someone who has not been able to bear witness to his own suffering might on his death bed choose someone else who has knowledge of his situation to bear witness on his behalf. However, although victims may sometimes be represented by others for this purpose, because they have clearly transferred their rights to testify on their own behalf to them, this has only marginal significance in explaining the source of this authority. With respect to large scale wrongdoing that sweeps up entire populations, there is usually no one to transfer rights to, even if this is something the victim wanted to do. And even in less serious cases, it will often not be possible to trace an individual's (legitimate) claim to bear witness on behalf of another to an earlier explicit transfer or series of such transfers. According to a modification of this explanation, although the victim may not have explicitly delegated authority, he may have given his consent in some other manner, for example, tacitly or hypothetically, and this is sufficient to support an authorization to bear witness on behalf of another. There are serious difficulties, however, which I cannot go into here, concerning the conditions of these alternative kinds of consent and the moral force that they are supposed to possess.

A third way to acquire authority preserves the link that exists in the case of the original victims between the right to bear witness and suffering harm or wrong. The focus here is those who suffer in a different way as a result of the original wrongdoing, as the "representatives of family lines," to use Janna Thompson's term.[95] Thompson introduces this term in the course of mounting a defense of claims to reparation for historical injustice. My interest here is different. However, what she says about the relation between the descendants of the victims of wrongdoing and those to whom the wrong was done also provides the basis for an argument on behalf of the moral authority of (some) proxy witnesses.

In the case of certain kinds of injustice, Thompson claims, it is not only individuals who are wronged but families as well. When the perpetrators "seek to wipe out family lines, keep them in perpetual slavery or submission, or attempt to prevent individuals of certain kinds from maintaining family relations, carrying out family obligations, or receiving entitlements as members of a family" (133), injustice has been done against the family as an association that persists over time, as an intergenerational network of relationships. From the standpoint of the so-called representative of a family line, the injustice done to his or her forebears is a constitutive element of a particular family history and historical legacy, one that is likely to engender in the descendant "feelings of anger, regret, sadness, or insecurity" (134). It is not likely that the suffering experienced by the descendants can be traced through any readily discernible causal connection to the original wrong.[96] The intervening causes and effects are too numerous and complicated. But this is no matter, Thompson maintains, because "it is the meaning of the injustice to descendants, not the immediacy of the causal relationship, which is crucial. . . . Descendants suffer because what happened to their family is important to their identity as individuals" (134).

If Thompson is right about the suffering of the representatives of family lines whose history contains serious wrongdoing, then we ought also to recognize the authority of those representatives to bear witness to the suffering of their forebears, even if there has been no explicit transfer of rights or some other effective kind of consent. These descendants are custodians of their family history, and their own identities are bound up with that history. If direct victims have the moral authority and right to tell the truth about their own suffering, as I have claimed that they do, then there is this sort of proxy witness who has the moral authority to bear witness to that suffering as well: namely, the representative of a family line whose history contains serious injustice against that family line. For this class of injustices, the wrong done to the original victim is also a wrong done to the descendants qua members of a particular family, and in testifying to that wrong, they also testify to their present suffering (a different kind of suffering than the suffering of the original victims, to be sure), which is a natural and fitting response to it.

Merely being part of a family whose history contains serious wrongdoing does not confer the authority to serve as a proxy witness. For the thought that this wrong was done to my forebear, to my family, may not engender "feelings of anger, regret, sadness, or insecurity" in the descendant; and even if it does, he may be disqualified from being able to serve as a proxy witness because of his prior behavior. He may experience occasional distress at the fate of his ancestors, but he forfeits any right to bear witness to it – as a representative of a family line – if he abandons his family.

With respect to the first point, susceptibility to these sorts of negative feelings is an indication that a person regards himself as a representative of a family line, and he may not view himself this way. To regard oneself as a *representative* of a family line is, among other things, to value one's belonging to this particular family and to be disposed to certain feelings, including moral feelings, which reflect one's sense of connectedness to and identification with other members of the family, such as pride and shame. As a representative of a family *line*, one is disposed to such feelings not only with respect to the well-being, successes and failures of individual living members of the family, but also with respect to how well members who lived in the past fared. Naturally, there are psychological limits to how far back in time one's concern for one's family line and the well-being of one's forebears extends because this concern depends on the strength and character of one's identification with them, and these dimensions of identification are affected by how far in time one is removed from their object. In fact, at some distance, the feelings that register what one's forebears experienced may be little different from the ways one feels about what completely unrelated persons experienced. But one cannot be a representative of a family line of any duration if one considers one's family background to be merely an accidental feature of oneself and has no special regard for the members who make up one's family or concern for how well one's family fares over time. The present argument for the authority to bear witness does not apply to these individuals because they do not particularly care about what their family history contains. But then these individuals may not be interested in bearing witness anyway.

It may be objected that even if one is a representative of a family line against which injustices have been committed, one does not thereby have personal grounds for bearing witness similar to those possessed by the original victim. For this requires that the representative speak for those who have been harmed (including himself), and to be harmed, it may be said, is to be made worse off than one otherwise would have been. But if one wouldn't have been born at all if one's family history had not contained injustice, then the injustice done to one's forebears has not harmed one, because one is not made worse off than one would otherwise have been if the injustice had not been committed. We encountered this argument before [97] and here I will simply note that there are at least two ways of responding. First, one could accept this account of harm, draw a distinction between harming and wronging, and formulate the argument in terms of family members who have been wronged (not harmed) by the injustices done to their forebears.[98] Second, one could hold that family members can be harmed, even though they are not made worse off than they otherwise would have been, by adopting an identity-independent notion of harm.[99] The harm, although not dependent on fixed identity over time, would still affect particular family members in unique ways. Each approach has much to recommend it, but I will not argue for either of them here.

An additional fourth argument for the authority to bear witness on behalf of others draws upon the notion of a *tertiary* victim, here understood in the sense of a group (larger than the family) to which the original victims belong and by which they are embraced. Examples of such groups include religious, ethnic, political, and national communities. A tertiary victim is a group or community that has itself been harmed – or wronged – because of the nature of wrongs done to its members. The previous argument in terms of representatives of family lines can serve here as a model. Thus, if descendants within a family suffer because what happened to their family, what is contained in their family history, informs and shapes their identity as individuals, then for analogous reasons, a community of individuals can suffer because of the ways its members were treated in the past. In this view, the authority of the members of a community to bear witness to the earlier wrongs stems from the meaning that their particular collective history has for them. Injustices can be transmitted through family lines as well as larger communities: in both cases the history of those injustices is part of the injurious legacy that is passed from one generation to another and that contributes to their self-definition. Those in succeeding generations who inherit this legacy thereby acquire the authority to bear witness as proxies for the original victims.

There are various ways in which groups can be harmed or wronged.[100] One explanation refers to the threatening atmosphere engendered by wrongdoing. Individuals who belong to a particular group some of whose members are victims or survivors of mistreatment but who are not yet victims or survivors themselves, may nonetheless feel threatened and vulnerable to similar mistreatment because, like those who have been harmed, their membership in this group is seen by others as a salient fact about them. Because they experience anxiety and insecurity, these individual members can be said to be harmed as well, although not in the same way as the victims and survivors; and because these feelings are diffused through the group, we can say that the group suffers harm. The extent to which individual harms will be magnified by virtue of the operation of generalized insecurity and fear depends on a number of factors. Groups may be geographically dispersed, so that some of the members in one area will be comfortably insulated from the mistreatment suffered by those in another. Groups also have a history, a history that may contain serious wrongdoing done to its members but perhaps only in the relatively distant past with little or no likelihood of recurrence. However, group harm does not depend solely on the persistence of the original injustice. Even if there is no present danger to current members of a group because they are no longer subject to persecution or other forms of wrongdoing as their predecessors were, their history contains injustice and – I am supposing – it is a matter of deep concern, and deeply distressing, to them that it does so. This legacy is part of their collective identity, and the damage to their identity caused by this history of injustice gives them a right to be proxy witnesses.

As a tertiary victim, a community has the moral authority to bear witness to the wrongs that it and its members suffered in the past and that they continue to suffer from because of the meaning that this history has for them. How a community feels about a past injustice done to it, and similarly for how people feel about a past injustice done to their family, depends to some degree on what has transpired since the original injustice. The sense of injury is likely to be strongest if there has been an entire history of injustice that continues up to the present time, or if there has been a resurgence of the same sort of wrongs that were committed earlier (consider, for example, the troubling reappearance of anti-Semitism in France and elsewhere in Europe in the past few years).

Furthermore, when a community, as tertiary victim, bears witness to the plight of past members, it focuses on the wrongs done to them qua members of the group. They are remembered as persons who suffered as, for example, Jews or Tutsis or Armenians, in other words, because they belonged to one of these groups. If they belonged to families that have survived, their representatives also have authority to bear witness on their behalf, but this authority derives from a different source, namely, the harm that is passed on to them as persons with a particular family history. Because there are these different sources of authority to bear witness, there are characteristically different ways in which authorized agents remember the victims of past injustice. The victims of wrongdoing on whose behalf representatives of family lines bear witness are individuals about whom their descendants have varying degrees of personally identifying information, and they will be remembered in ways that reflect this fact. The injustice done to them counts as injustice against a family line in virtue of their possessing certain relational properties, such as "father of" or "grandmother of," and these terms typically refer to relationships that are characterized by more or less intimate knowledge of that individual's personal qualities. When communities, or representatives of them, bear witness on behalf of those among their members who were the victims of wrongdoing in the past, it may do this in addition to or in lieu of the witnessing done by family members. However, the community itself may know little or little of a personal nature about these victims, especially if no representatives of their family line have survived.

Despite these differences, proxy witnessing by family as well as community is vulnerable to a sort of deterioration relating to the amount of time that has elapsed between the original injustice and subsequent witnessing. As witnessing is passed on from one generation to another, distortions are introduced by collective and familial memory, so that what may have started off as more or less accurate testimony about suffering and its circumstances comes over time to have little resemblance to what actually occurred. In time, collective and familial memory may come to more closely resemble something like myth. However, the moral authority to bear witness that derives from the harm suffered by families and communities does not necessarily diminish simply because memory becomes less reliable as an accurate record of the past.

The two arguments, one grounded in the meaning of family membership, the other in that of community membership, share a common logic. In each case, the past injustices did not merely harm or wrong individuals, but also a group – a family (considered as a network of relationships that extends over time) or a larger community – to which they belonged. The family or community has a history, a history that contains injustice, and this history helps forge and constitute the identities, individual and collective, of the victims' descendants and successors. And bearing witness in the two cases – by representatives of family lines as well as communities and those who speak for them – has the same point and moral significance: each aims to restore the moral standing and affirm the dignity of those who can no longer speak for themselves.[101]

Although I believe these arguments provide grounds for the authority to bear witness, I do not want to claim that they are the only plausible ones that can do so. For example, I am inclined to think that for extremely serious moral wrongs like genocide and other horrific crimes, familial or communal ties are not necessary to ground this authority. Everyone, it may be said, has a right (if not an obligation) to bear witness to this sort of evil, simply by virtue of our common humanity with its victims. In cases where this is so, the arguments discussed here confer *additional* authority on certain parties and provide them with additional reasons to bear witness. In other cases, it may be that *only* these parties can properly claim the authority to bear witness because of the particular relationship they have with the victims.

I want to end by saying something about the general problem of false witnessing and, particularly, about the problem as it relates to proxy witnessing. A false witness, as defined in Section 2, is not a party who utters falsehoods, at least not necessarily; nor is a false witness necessarily a party who deliberately deceives. Rather, the term refers to a party who *lacks the authority* to testify in some domain but who nevertheless holds himself out as possessing it. A false witness does not merit the trust of his (or its, in the case of a community) audience and will likely forfeit any further reliance on his testimony if he is discovered. If his abuse of trust is intentional, it is normally to derive some benefit for himself, such as fame, notoriety, compensation for past injustices, and the indulgence of a sympathetic audience. Proxy witnesses, of course, are not the only ones who can be false witnesses in this sense. Persons who "testify" to what they themselves suffered may also lack the authority to do so and yet claim to have it. However, false witnessing may be a more serious problem in regard to proxy witnesses than those who testify on their own behalf, because it can be more difficult to ascertain whether the former have the requisite authority to testify and should be trusted, so there are more opportunities for being misled. When the authority to speak about the suffering of others is dependent on historical connections to the original victims, new possibilities of false witnessing and abuse of trust arise.

A proxy's lack of authority can be explained in various ways by referring to the different grounds of authority to bear witness I have discussed in this chapter. An individual may claim to have suffered from the same injustice as the one on whose behalf he is testifying, when he did not. He may claim to be a representative of a family line when he is not because he doesn't really care about this family and because what happened to his family is not important to his identity as an individual. Or a community and those who speak on its behalf may lack the authority to testify on behalf of what they claim are former members, because the latter never affiliated with the community or because the community ostracized or excommunicated them. These are all possibilities, and, depending on the context, they should be considered when deciding whether to trust a proxy should this question arise. Part of the problem, of course, is knowing just when to raise the question, that is, when to have suspicions about the legitimacy of the proxy. And once the question of whether to trust the proxy has been posed, consideration must also be given to what sort of further investigative work should be done and how exhaustively to pursue it. These are matters of some importance, because relying on the testimony of a false witness can have negative consequences of various sorts, including generating unwarranted skepticism about all proxy testimony and giving those who want to deny the reality of what the witness testified about a pretext for doing so. Similarly, discounting the testimony of a legitimate proxy witness can have other negative consequences because, among other things, an audience may need this testimony if past injustice is to be repaired and ongoing injustice alleviated. And then there is the morally significant symbolic damage that wrongly discounting the testimony of a proxy does by leaving the original victims as they were when their rights were violated, without anyone to give them a voice.

7. FINAL THOUGHTS

The discussion of bearing witness provides a fitting close to this book by bringing together its concerns with both the individual and the social aspects of memory. For one thing, although witnessing is often thought of as something individuals do individually, I have claimed that it can also be done by communities. For another, although in either case it is individuals who (ultimately) do the witnessing, bearing witness always points beyond itself and cannot be adequately explained or appreciated without reference to its larger social and communal connections. Frequently, those who bear witness regard themselves as part of a community – familial, religious, or political – and by bearing witness confirm their membership in this community. They testify, as persons who share a community with others, to the wrong that has been done to them and the loss that has been suffered by it. And then, of course, it is conceptual of bearing witness that it cannot be done in isolation, and, in the cases that interest me, it is essentially a social practice that requires a moral community as its audience.

NOTES

1. Czeslaw Milosz, *Nobel Lecture*, December 8, 1980, available online at http://nobelprize.org/literature/laureates/1980/milosz-lecture-en.html.
2. See, for example, the collection of essays edited by Cathy Caruth, *Trauma: Explorations in Memory* (Baltimore: Johns Hopkins, 1995); especially, Dori Laub, "Truth and Testimony: The Process and the Struggle," pp. 61–75; Bessel A. Van Der Kolk and Onno van der Hart, "The Intrusive Past: The Flexibility of Memory and the Engraving of Trauma," pp. 158–182.
3. A similar distinction between target and focus is made by Bennett W. Helm, "Love, Identification, and the Emotions," available at http://server1. fandm.edu/Departments/Philosophy/staticpages/Helm/Helm-Love_Identification.pdf

4. W. James Booth, *Communities of Memory: On Witness, Identity, and Justice* (Ithaca: Cornell University Press, 2006), p. 86.
5. Ibid.
6. This is one of two lists of defining features that Coady gives, one for formal testimony, the other for natural testimony. The one quoted here pertains to natural testimony, and it largely parallels the elements of formal testimony. See C. A. J. Coady, *Testimony: A Philosophical Study* (Oxford: Clarendon Press, 1992), p. 42.
7. Ibid., p. 43
8. See Rae Langton, "Speech Acts and Unspeakable Acts," *Philosophy and Public Affairs* 22, 4, (fall 1993): 293–330, especially 315–316. Langton claims that the ability to perform certain acts depends on the speaker's authority. For example, it is "the umpire, and not the bystander, [who] can call a fault" (311). With respect to witnessing, we might say that one cannot testify if one lacks authority in the relevant domain. Whatever else it is, one's speech act just does not count as testifying.
9. The case of Benjamin Wilkomirski is a particularly interesting example of a false witness. In 1995, Wilkomirski published what he claimed was a memoir of his experiences as a young boy in the Nazi death camps, when he was too young to understand what was happening to him. At the end of the book, titled *Fragments: Memories of a Wartime Childhood*, there is a sort of afterword in which he explains that he grew up in a world in which children were not supposed to have a memory of the Holocaust and in which nobody listened to what he had to say. But then he had a number of encounters, with psychoanalysts and others, that, he claims, jarred his memory and compelled him to write his memoir. The book received numerous prizes and enormous critical acclaim. But in 1998, Daniel Ganzfried, himself the child of a Holocaust survivor, published a series of articles challenging the authenticity of Wilkomirski's account. Ganzfried claimed, and this is now beyond dispute, that the author of the book was not Benjamin Wilkomirski, born in Riga in 1939 and the child survivor of death camps, but Bruno Doessekker, who was born Bruno Grosjean in 1941 to an unwed mother who abandoned him. Grosjean was raised in an orphanage and finally adopted by the Doessekker family in 1957.

  The book, at first hailed as a major contribution to Holocaust literature, was now discredited as a fraud. But when confronted with this accusation, Wilkomirski did not admit to having fabricated his account. On the contrary, he claimed to have always recalled the horrors of the camps and stood by his "memories." There is dispute about whether Wilkomirski was attempting to perpetrate a hoax, but a number of commentators on the affair suspect that he actually came to believe his recovered "memories." He even explained and rebutted the charges of fraud by comparing them to the reception he received as a child from adults who refused to believe his stories about the camps. For a fascinating discussion of the Wilkomirski affair, see Philip Gourevitch, "The Memory Thief," *The New Yorker* 75, 15 (June 14, 1999): 48–68.

10. Of course, we often lack sufficient knowledge of the grounds for believing p. That's why we have to rely on the testimony of others, including experts. Indeed, our knowledge would be severely limited if we eliminated from it the part that originated in testimony. For more, see Note 11.

11. Jonathan Adler argues that though testimony relies on trust, this does not undermine the reliability of testimony as a source of knowledge, in *Belief's Own Ethics* (Cambridge, MA: MIT Press, 2002), pp. 135–161.

12. *The Ethics of Memory* (Cambridge, MA: Harvard University Press, 2002), pp. 180–181.

13. See Chapter 3, section 4 where I also draw a distinction between direct or primary victims and secondary victims.

14. Margalit, op. cit., p. 150.

15. It is not clear whether Margalit believes that the special authority of the moral witness is partly moral in nature. Perhaps he means to deny this when he says, confusingly: "The adjective *moral* [in the expression *moral witness*] has to do with the content of the testimony, not with the epistemological status of what the moral witness witnessed" (pp. 163–164). At any rate, it is pretty clearly epistemic authority that he has in mind when he claims that "the authority of the moral witness comes, among other things, from the ability to "describe *this*" (168). The moral witness knows things that others who have not had his experiences cannot know.

16. Ibid., p. 149.

17. Booth, op. cit., p. 92.

18. In some circumstances, the testimony of those who bear witness provides a valuable historical record of actual events, a record that might otherwise be unavailable. This is the function that Annette Wieviorka attributes to the clandestine writings that were buried in the Warsaw Ghetto by some of its Jewish inhabitants during World War II. She relates this to the function of testimony about the Holocaust in the postwar years:

> In the years following the war, the primary aim of testimony was knowledge – knowledge of the modalities of genocide and of the deportation. Testimony had the status of an archival document. . . . Today . . . the purpose of testimony is no longer to obtain knowledge. . . . The mission that has devolved to testimony is no longer to bear witness to inadequately known events, but rather to keep them before our eyes. ("On Testimony," in Geoffrey Hartman (Ed.), *Holocaust Remembrance: The Shapes of Memory*, (Oxford: Blackwell, 1994), pp. 23–32).

Those witnesses left testimony that was indispensable for the construction of an accurate historical account of life in the Ghetto, and they did it expressly for that reason. However, the one who bears witness as a memorial act does not have the conveying of knowledge as his primary aim and is not first and foremost a repository of facts about the past.

19. For a discussion of a related set of issues, see Bat-Ami Bar On, "Marginality and Epistemic Privilege," in Linda Alcoff and Elizabeth Potter (Eds.), *Feminist Epistemologies* (New York: Routledge, 1993), pp. 83–100.

20. Laurence Thomas, "Moral Deference," *The Philosophical Forum*, 24, 1–3, (Fall-Spring 1992–1993): 233–250.

21. Ibid., p. 240.
22. Ibid., p. 241.
23. Ibid., pp. 243–244.
24. Trudy Govier, "Forgiveness and the Unforgivable," *American Philosophical Quarterly 36*, 1, January 1999: 59–75, at 60.
25. As discussed in Chapter 3, a group is harmed when people suffer various sorts of latent and indirect harms stemming from membership in the group. For an account of wronging groups, see Chapter 3, Section 4.
26. Dori Laub, "Bearing Witness or the Vicissitudes of Listening," in Shoshana Felman and Dori Laub, *Testimony: Crises of Witnessing in Literature, Psychoanalysis, and History* (New York: Routledge, 1992), pp. 57–74, at 70–71. See also Roger I. Simon, *The Touch of the Past* (New York: Palgrave Macmillan, 2005), pp. 91–92:

> Testimony consists of representations either by those who have lived through specific events or, alternatively, by those who have been told of such lived realities, either directly or indirectly, and have been moved to convey to others that which has been impressed upon them.... Thus, whether across generations or cultures, testimony is always directed toward another, attempting to place the one who receives it under the obligation of response to an embodied singular experience not recognizable as one's own.

The notions of placing another under an "obligation of response" and of an "embodied singular experience," or something like them, are explored in Section 5.
27. Whether the unconscious states in question should be classed as testimony at all is controversial. But I don't need to resolve this issue here.
28. "Education and Crisis, Or the Vicissitudes of Teaching," in Felman and Laub, op. cit., pp. 1–56, at 15.
29. *Autonomy and Trust in Bioethics*, (Cambridge, UK: Cambridge University Press, 2002), p. 185.
30. As an example, consider the question of whether survivors of genocide should be subjected to cross-examination in criminal trials of the perpetrators.
31. *Pride, Shame and Guilt* (Oxford: Clarendon Press, 1985), pp. 65–66.
32. Victor Klemperer, writing in his diary of life as a Jew in Dresden under the Nazis, said: "I will continue to write. That is my heroism. I will leave a testimony, an exact testimony." See Victor Klemperer, *Ich will Zeugnis ablegen bis zum letzten* [*I Will Bear Witness to the End*], Walter Nowojski and Hardwig Klemperer (Eds.) (Berlin: Aubau-Verlag, 1995), p. 99. He, like many other witnesses in similar circumstances, was writing for anyone who would listen, but especially for future generations. See also Note 18.
33. See Chapter 5, Section 2.
34. Edward Casey, *Remembering: A Phenomenological Study* (2nded.) (Bloomington: Indiana University Press, 2000), p. 115.
35. Ibid., p. 116.
36. Casey allows for what he calls "auto-reminiscing," but he explains this as a situation in which I address myself as my partner in reminiscence.

37. But in extreme situations, even hope may be elusive and difficult to sustain. Cf. this remark by Iwona Irwin-Zarecka:

> The commandment "to record" was itself a sacred one, rooted in the Jewish tradition. Fraught with dangers, it was also a direct response to the Nazis' concerted effort to erase all possible traces of their crimes, and to erase the memory of the whole people. There was then a real sense (and as the future has shown, a justifiable fear) that unless a record be made, the experience of camps and ghettos would move into oblivion. At the time, many a report was indeed not believed, only strengthening the conviction that witness be given. Those reports that were destined for the outside world were, of course, also a desperate cry for help. But a great deal more of the bearing of witness was done without such hope for immediate results, indeed, with often only a slight hope that the record would itself survive. The duty to memory – to universal memory – prevailed. (Iwona Irwin-Zarecka, *Frames of Remembrance* (New Brunswick, NJ: Transaction Publishers, 1994), pp. 163–164).

> According to Irwin-Zarecka, the conviction that one has a duty to memory, even in the direst circumstances, functions for some as a powerful moral motivator. The duty to memory – or to remember – is of course a major theme of this book, but whether the conviction can be powerful enough to overcome hopelessness is an open question.

38. Margalit, op. cit., p. 156
39. From *Leviathan*, quoted in Coady, op. cit., p. 30.
40. Ibid., p. 32.
41. A question that I will not try to settle here is whether it is a condition on evidence, in general, that someone needs it. According to one view, whether or not some proposition is evidence for some other is simply determined on the basis of relevance and the logical relationships that obtain between them. X might therefore be evidence for y even though no one needs evidence for y, perhaps because y is not something that anyone believes. However, because I am only discussing testimonial evidence, I will not pursue this issue.
42. This is an appropriate place to say something about a particular kind of testimonial narrative aimed at preserving and transmitting a record of the past, which is discussed in John Beverly's book *Testimonio* (Minneapolis: University of Minnesota Press, 2004). Here are the key features of Beverly's characterization of testimonio, which is similar to my account of bearing witness in several respects:

> First, "the situation of narration in testimonio has to involve an urgency to communicate, a problem of repression, poverty, subalternity, imprisonment, struggle for survival" (32). The narrator testifies chiefly to ongoing wrongdoing and injustice.
> Second, the narrator in testimonio "speaks for, or in the name of, a community or group" (33). My account does not require this but certainly does not preclude this possibility.
> Third, the one who testifies is "someone who has lived in his or her person, or indirectly through the experiences of friends, family, neighbors, or significant others, the events and experiences that he or she narrates" (3). In my terms, the narrator is either a primary or secondary victim.
> Fourth, "the truth claims for [testimonio] ... depend on conferring on the form a certain kind of epistemological authority," of a different order from "the authority of the fact-gathering procedures of anthropology and journalism" (86). The authority of

the narrator is also moral, and both sorts of authority derive from the fact that the narrator has either directly or indirectly lived through the events he or she narrates. Narrators, therefore, have "the power to create their own narrative authority and negotiate its conditions of truth and representativity" (73). See Note 15, and Section 2(a).

Fifth, there is in testimonio "a pledge of honesty on the part of the narrator that the listener/reader is bound to respect" (33). This pledge grounds the audience's trust in the narrator and, therefore, in what he is narrating. As in all cases when we are asked to accept testimony, be it testimonio or not, we need to trust our informant.

Sixth, "the trope that usually accompanies testimonio [is] the voice of the voiceless" (19). Testimonio challenges the authority of the more powerful, gives voice to the neglected, oppressed, and marginalized members of society. I discuss the notion of "voice" in Section 5.

Seventh, "there are moments in testimonio when we hear something that does not fit with our sense of political or ethical correctness. These moments summon us to a new kind of relationship with others, a new kind of politics" (2). The narrator in testimonio addresses an audience that *needs* to hear the story because the plight of the oppressed and poor is easily neglected by those who benefit from the status quo. The audience needs to be roused out of its complacency to recognize injustice and work to create a more just political order.

And eighth, "testimonio is both an art and a strategy of subaltern memory" (73). Testimonio not only records the past. It also represents an effort by the oppressed and marginalized members of society to wrest control from the more powerful over who writes the history of the oppressed and how it is written.

43. I want to thank Chris Jordens at the Centre for Values, Ethics and the Law in Medicine, Sydney, Australia, whose writings on witnessing (much of it unpublished) were helpful to me in writing this section.

44. The term is Joel Feinberg's – see *Harm to Others* (New York: Oxford University Press, 1984), p. 33.

45. Or where the connection between the setback and human agency is so remote or the causal factors so complex that no human agents can reasonably be held responsible for the setback.

46. Although other problems may arise. Misfortune places others under an obligation to assist, and blame may be appropriate if the response to the misfortune is inept, discriminatory, uncaring, and so forth.

47. See, for example, John Kleinig, "Punishment and Moral Seriousness," *Israel Law Review* 25, 3–4, (Summer-Autumn 1991): 401–421. Also, Jeffrie Murphy:

> My own . . . view involves the claim that victims may be harmed symbolically as well as physically by those who wrong them. Wrongdoing is in part a communicative act, an act that gives out a degrading or insulting message to the victim – the message "I count and you do not, and I may thus use you as a mere thing." (Jeffrie Murphy, "Forgiveness in Counseling: A Philosophical Perspective," in S. Lamb and J. G. Murphy (Eds.) *Before Forgiving: Cautionary Views of Forgiveness in Psychotherapy* (New York: Oxford University Press, 2002), pp. 41–53, at 44)

This view is shared by many other philosophers.

48. T. Des Pres, *The Survivor: Anatomy of Life in the Death Camps* (Oxford: Oxford University Press, 1980), p. 39.

49. Of course, when one bears witness to the suffering of a loved one, that person is not seen only as a fellow human being, but as someone who is

different from other fellow human beings because he or she is loved. Still, I would not want to claim that compassion. in this sense, plays no role in these cases.

50. Lawrence Blum, "Compassion," in Robert Kruschwitz and Robert Roberts (Eds.), *The Virtues: Contemporary Essays on Moral Character* (Belmont CA: Wadsworth Publishing Co., 1987), pp. 229–236.

51. Although confession is generally associated with wrongdoing, there are other standard uses as well. In religious discourse, for example, a confessor can be "someone whose holy life serves as a demonstration of his or her religious faith, but who does not suffer martyrdom" (*Chambers 21st Century Dictionary*).

52. See the discussion of TRC in P. E. Digeser, *Political Forgiveness* (Ithaca: Cornell University Press, 2001), pp. 139–145; Trudy Govier, *Forgiveness and Revenge* (New York: Routledge, 2002); and Martha Minow, *Between Vengeance and Forgiveness* (Boston: Beacon Press, 1998), pp. 55–57.

53. See Minow, op. cit., p. 77.

54. For a discussion of the martyr and idealist, see Coady, op. cit., pp. 52–53. For how early Christian communities constituted their identity through the memory of martyrdom, see Elizabeth A. Castelli, *Martyrdom and Memory: Early Christian Culture Making* (New York: Columbia University Press, 2004). Castelli's account draws on Halbwachs's theory of social memory.

55. The discussion in this section answers this question for bearing witness in general: that is, for bearing witness to what is ongoing, to what is likely to or may occur, and to what has occurred in the recent or more remote past.

56. See Martha Minow, "The Hope for Healing: What Can Truth Commissions Do?" in *Truth v. Justice*, Robert Rotberg and Dennis Thompson (Eds.).(Princeton: Princeton University Press, 2000), pp. 235–260; Ana Julia Cienfuegos and Cirstina Monelli, "The Testimony of Political Repression as a Therapeutic Instrument," *American Journal of Orthopsychiatry 53*, 1, (January 1983): 43–51.

57. See David Robertson, Richard Bedell, James V. Lavery, and Ross Upshur, "What kind of evidence do we need to justify humanitarian medical aid?" *Lancet 360* (July 27, 2002): 330–333.

58. James Hatley, *Suffering Witness: The Quandary of Responsibility after the Irreparable* (Albany: State University of New York, 2000), p. 41.

59. (Oxford, Oxford University Press, 1999).

60. Of course, love of the good will consist for most of us primarily in the enjoyment of some particular goods (people or things or causes). But a healthy and proper enjoyment, Adams maintains, will recognize these are instances or manifestations of a pluralistic, open-ended, only partly understood realm of goodness. This part of Adams's account resurrects a sort of Platonism about values, and one can accept that love of the good is constitutive of the good life without embracing it. See next Note.

61. There are elements of Adams's account that I do not follow and that are not needed for my purposes here. I have already mentioned the theistic basis of Adams's ethics, and I include as well his view that the individual goods it is proper to love are to be understood as instances or aspects of *The Good*.

62. *The Nature of Rationality* (Princeton: Princeton University Press, 1993), p. 29.
63. It may, of course, do more. As I said earlier, it may also have a variety of desirable outcomes.
64. For more, see Jeffrey Blustein, *Care and Commitment: Taking the Personal Point of View* (New York: Oxford University Press, 1991), chapter 9. See also Damian Cox, Marguerite La Caze, and Michael P. Levine, *Integrity and the Fragile Self* (Burlington, VT: Ashgate, 2003).
65. Gabriele Taylor,"Integrity," *Proceedings of the Aristotelian Society* (Suppl.) 55 (1981): 143–159, at 143.
66. The relationship, according to Cheshire Calhoun, is either "to her desires (they are wholeheartedly endorsed or else outlawed)," or "to her character (she cultivates and protects its depth)," or "to her agency (she takes special responsibility for what gets done through it and governs herself by at least some deontological principles)." See Cheshire Calhoun, "Standing for Something," *Journal of Philosophy* 92, 5, (May 1995): 235–250, at 253.
67. Adams, op. cit., p. 216.
68. Calhoun, op. cit., pp. 258–259.
69. Ibid., p. 254.
70. To be more precise, the aspect of address that I have been discussing, and whose intrinsic moral value I have been defending, is publicly taking a stand on the side of the good and the right or against the bad and the immoral. But this is only part of what address involves and therefore only partly explains its moral value. For the rest of the explanation, see Section 5.
71. *Ethics of Memory*, op. cit., pp. 119–120.
72. See Note 56.
73. Laub, "Bearing Witness," op. cit., p. 68.
74. See Note 2.
75. Op. cit., p. 70.
76. *The Wounded Storyteller: Body, Illness, and Ethics* (Chicago: University of Chicago Press, 1997).
77. See, for example, James Charlton, *Nothing About Us Without Us: Disability, Oppression and Empowerment* (Berkeley: University of California Press, 1998).
78. *In a Different Voice: Psychological Theory and Women's Development* (Cambridge, MA: Harvard University Press, 1982).
79. Mary Field Belenky, Blythe McVicker Clinchy, Nancy Rue Goldberger, and Jill Mattuck Tarule, *Women's Ways of Knowing: The Development of Self, Voice, and Mind* (New York: Basic Books, 1986).
80. Ibid., p. 18.
81. This resembles Iris Marion Young's definition of "cultural imperialism," in *Justice and the Politics of Difference* (Princeton: Princeton University Press, 1990), p. 59.
82. On this, see John Hardwig, "Autobiography, Biography, and Narrative Ethics," in H. L. Nelson (Ed.), *Stories and Their Limits* (New York: Routledge, 1997), pp. 50–64.

83. Margaret Walker, "Truth and Voice in Women's Rights," in *Recognition, Responsibility, and Rights: Feminist Ethics and Social Theory*, Hilde Nelson and Robin Fiore (Eds.). (Lanham, MD: Rowman and Littlefield, 2003).
84. "Moral Ambition Within and Beyond Political Constraints: Reflections on Restorative Justice," in *Truth v. Justice*, op. cit., pp. 68–98, at 73.
85. See Chapter 2, Section 3.
86. Beverly discusses the importance of community in this connection. See op. cit., pp. 40–41.
87. The recent flap over James Frey's memoir, *A Million Little Pieces* (New York: Random House, first published 2005), raises some interesting questions about the role of truth in memoir, the boundary between fact and fiction, and the responsibility of a writer of memoir to his audience. In 2005, "The Smoking Gun," a Web site that specializes in investigative journalism, published a lengthy report that challenged some of the basic claims in Frey's memoir of his battle with drug and alcohol addiction. Responding to these charges, Frey wrote the following self-serving defense in a special "Note to the Reader" in the most recent 2006 edition of the book:

    There is much debate now about the respective natures of works of memoir, non-fiction, and fiction. That debate will likely continue for some time. I believe, and I understand others strongly disagree, that memoir allows the writer to work from memory instead of from a strict journalistic or historical standard. It is about impression and feeling, about individual recollection. This memoir is a combination of facts about my life and certain embellishments. It is a subjective truth, altered by the mind of a recovering drug addict and alcoholic.

    It is not clear what "subjective truth" is supposed to mean here. Of course, we should not expect "strict journalistic" accuracy in a memoir: events are filtered through the author's memory and then are shaped by his literary intentions and sensibility. If by "subjective truth" Frey is only alluding to these truisms about the writing of memoirs, then there is little to fault him for. However, the inevitable effects of memory and literary production must be kept separate from the willful deceptions ("embellishments") that Frey is accused of and that he subsequently confessed to.
88. A number of terms have been used to describe the sort of truth that the testimony of witnesses possesses, including subjective and emotional truth. These are contrasted with so-called objective truth, the sort of truth that, for example, the testimony of an impartial and disinterested eyewitness can possess. However, these distinctions are misleading and deeply confused. For one thing, emotional truth, although subjective in an obvious sense, is arguably a species of objective truth, although this must be understood differently from propositional truth. See Ronald de Sousa, "Emotional Truth," *Proceedings of the Aristotelian Society*, (Suppl.) 76 (July 2002): 247–263. For another, the very notion of a purely subjective truth with no objective validity is incoherent. There is only truth – or, if you will, objective truth – and different species of it.
89. See Note 9 for the cautionary tale of Benjamin Wilkomirski.

90. See Walker, op. cit., note 83.

91. Thus, for example, Dora Apel discusses the role of artists as secondary witnesses in the following way:

    Artists as secondary witnesses, then, are those who confront the horror of the Nazi genocide and the suffering of its victims, and who continue to bear witness through reconfigured forms of contemporary testimony to events they have never seen or experienced. (Dora Apel, *Memory Effects: The Holocaust and the Art of Secondary Witnessing* (New Brunswick, NJ: Rutgers University Press, 2002), p. 21)

    Dori Laub says of the survivors and interviewers of the survivors of the Holocaust that they jointly engage in an act of bearing witness, and that the interviewer-listener "takes on the responsibility for bearing witness that previously the narrator felt he bore alone." The interviewer-listener resembles a secondary witness. He is not what we would ordinarily think of as a proxy witness, although perhaps he comes close. See "An Event Without a Witness: Truth, Testimony and Survival," in *Testimony*, op. cit., Note 26, pp. 75–92, at 85. Here bearing witness becomes a collaborative activity in which the listener helps elicit testimony from the survivor that might not otherwise be forthcoming.

92. Quoted and discussed in Felman, op. cit. endnote 21, p. 3.

93. There is, of course, a sense in which no one can bear witness for the witness, that is, no one can experience what he experienced in just the way he experienced it. Perhaps this is what Celan means. But I take him to be saying more, namely, that there is something morally transgressive in attempting to bear witness for a witness.

94. Primo Levi, *The Drowned and the Saved* (New York: Vintage, 1988), p. 84.

95. "Historical Injustice and Reparation: Justifying Claims of Descendants," *Ethics 112*, 1 (October 2001): 114–135, at 132–135.

96. See Chapter 3, Section 8.

97. See Chapter 3, Section 3. This is an illustration of what Derek Parfit calls the "non-identity problem." See Derek Parfit, *Reasons and Persons* (Oxford: Oxford University Press, 1984), pp. 351–79.

98. For the distinction between *harming* and *wronging*, see Rahul Kumar, "Who can be wronged?" *Philosophy and Public Affairs 31*, 2 (spring 2003): 99–118.

99. See Lukas Meyer, "Past and Future: The Case for an Identity-Independent Notion of Harm," in *Rights, Culture, and the Law: Themes from the Legal and Political Philosophy of Joseph Raz* (Oxford: Oxford University Press, 2003), pp. 143–159

100. See Chapter 3, Section 4.

101. I argued in Chapter 5 that remembering the dear departed can express a variety of emotions and attitudes – respect is only one of them. Here, I am speaking specifically about bearing witness to the wrongs suffered by members of one's family in the past. Bearing witness, as I noted earlier in this chapter, does not exhaust all the ways of remembering.

SELECT BIBLIOGRAPHY

The following is a selective list of works that were particularly helpful to me in writing this book. Only books are included.

Anderson, Elizabeth. *Value in Ethics and Economics.* Cambridge, MA: Harvard University Press, 1993.

Appiah, Kwame Anthony. *The Ethics of Identity.* Princeton: Princeton University Press, 2005.

Beverly, John. *Testimonio.* Minneapolis: University of Minnesota Press, 2004.

Booth, W. James. *Communities of Memory: On Witness, Identity, and Justice.* Ithaca. NY: Cornell University Press, 2006.

Campbell, Sue. *Relational Remembering: Rethinking the Memory Wars.* Lanham, MD: Rowman and Littlefield, 2003.

Care, Norman. *Living With One's Past.* Lanham, MD: Rowman and Littlefield, 1996.

Casey, Edward S. *Remembering: A Phenomenological Study* (2nd ed.). Bloomington: Indiana University Press, 2000.

Coady, C. A. J. *Testimony: A Philosophical Study.* Oxford: Clarendon Press, 1992.

Connerton, Frank. *How Societies Remember.* Cambridge, UK: Cambridge University Press, 2004.

Derrida, Jacques. *The Work of Mourning.* Pascale-Anne Brault (Ed. and Trans.), Michael Naas (Ed.). Chicago: Chicago University Press, 2003.

Digeser, P. E. *Political Forgiveness.* Ithaca, NY: Cornell University Press, 2001.

Evans, M., and Lunn, K. (Eds.). *War and Memory in the Twentieth Century.* Oxford: Oxford University Press, 1997.

Feldman, Shoshana, and Laub, Dori. *Testimony: Crises of Witnessing in Literature, Psychoanalysis, and History.* New York: Routledge, 1991.

Freud, Sigmund. *Standard Edition of the Complete Works of Sigmund Freud* (Vol. 12). J. Stachey (Trans.). Hogart: London, 1914.

Gilbert, Margaret. *Sociality and Responsibility: New Essays in Plural Subject Theory.* Lanham, MD: Rowman and Littlefield, 2000.

Gillis, John R. (Ed.) *Commemorations.* Princeton: Princeton University Press, 1996.

Gross, David. *Lost Time: On Remembering and Forgetting in Late Modern Culture.* Amherst, MA: University of Massachusetts Press, 2000.

Halbwachs, Maurice. *On Collective Memory,* Lewis A. Coser (Ed. and Trans.). Chicago and London: Chicago University Press, 1992.

Hatley, James. *Suffering Witness: The Quandary of Responsibility After the Irreparable.* Albany: State University of New York, 2000.

Irwin-Zarecka, Iwona. *Frames of Remembrance: The Dynamics of Collective Memory.* New Brunswick, NJ: Transaction Publishers, 1994.

LeGoff, Jacques. *History and Memory.* Steven Rendall and Elizabeth Claman (Trans.). New York: Columbia University Press, 1992.

Maier, C. S. *The Unmasterable Past: History, Holocaust, and German National Identity.* Cambridge, MA: Harvard University Press, 1997.

Margalit, Avisha. *The Ethics of Memory.* Cambridge, MA: Harvard University Press, 2002.

May, Larry, and Hoffman, Stacey (Eds.). *Collective Responsibility.* Lanham, MD: Rowman and Littlefield, 1991.

Middleton, D. and Edwards, Derek (Eds.). *Collective Remembering.* London: Sage Publications, 1990.

Minow, Martha. *Breaking the Cycles of Hatred: Memory, Law, and Repair.* Princeton: Princeton University Press, 2002.

Neisser, Ulric, and Fivush, Robyn. *The Remembering Self: Construction and Accuracy in Self-Narrative.* New York: Cambridge University Press, 1994.

Nietzsche, Friedrich. *Untimely Meditations.* D. Breazeale (Ed.), R. J. Hollingdale (Trans.). Cambridge, UK: Cambridge University Press, 1997.

Poole, Ross. *Nation and Identity.* London: Routledge, 1999.

Plumb, J. H. *The Death of the Past.* New York: Palgrave Macmillan, 2004.

Rotberg, Robert and Dennis Thompson (Eds.). *Truth v. Justice.* Princeton: Princeton University Press, 2000.

Thompson, Janna. *Taking Responsibility for the Past: Reparation and Historical Justice.* Cambridge, UK: Polity Press, 2002.

Williams, Bernard. *Truth and Truthfulness: An Essay in Genealogy.* Princeton: Princeton University Press, 2002.

Yerushalmi, Yosef Hayim. *Zakhor: Jewish History and Jewish Memory.* Seattle: University of Washington Press, 1996.

INDEX

Adams, Robert Merrihew, 330–332
Améry, Jean, *At the Mind's Limits*, 137–138
Anderson, Elizabeth, 35, 246, 259
Ankersmit, F.R., 17, 177, 230n9
Apel, Dora, 196
apology, 143–144
appropriation, 69–74, 76–77. *See also*
    rationalist account of responsibility;
    taking responsibility for one's past;
    volitional accounts of responsibility
Appiah, Kwame Anthony, 172n46
Atwood, Margaret, *The Blind Assassin*, 277

bearing witness. *See also* symbolic value;
    testimony; voice
  concept of, 307–308
  consequentialist account of, 328–330
  and hope, 318–319, 338–339
  importance in contemporary world,
    302–303
  as mode of remembrance, 302, 303, 320,
    321–322
  moral value of, 328–337, 337–345
  to right and good, 324–325
  truth of testimony in, 304–305, 342–343
  to wrongdoing and misfortune, 322–324
Beverly, John, *Testimonio*, 359n42
Bittker, Boris, 159
Blum, Lawrence, 324
Bonhoeffer, Dietrich, 331
Booth, W. James, 33, 55n68, 105n33, 139,
    174n78, 233n57, 237n75, 307

Calhoun, Cheshire, 336, 337
Callahan, Joan, 255
Campbell, Sue, 185

Card, Claudia, 95, 149
Care, Norman, 25, 85, 96, 265
Casey, Edward, *Remembering*, 249–251,
    296n39, 289, 317–318
Celan, Paul, 346
Coady, C.A.J., 294n7, 308–309, 320. *See also*
    testimony
Cockburn, David, 213, 220
collective guilt, 148–149, 170n23
collective identity. *See also* personal identity
  analogous to personal identity, 43
  and collective memory, 43–44, 144–145,
    162–163
  and collective shame, 155–156
  distinguished from group identity of
    individual, 43, 121–122, 173n73
  and myths, 194–195, 198
  and obligation, 47–48, 49, 144, 146,
    228
collectively taking responsibility for the
    past. *See also* collective memory; taking
    responsibility for one's past
  and change of significance of past,
    142–143
  distinguished from accepting
    responsibility, 112–113
  for wrongs done to a group, 115
  and relation to collective identity, 144,
    146–147. *See also* collective identity
  and settling the historical record,
    114–115, 140–142
collective memory. *See also* collectively
    taking responsibility for past;
    collective identity
  as answerable to discipline of history,
    179, 203